Professional Photoshop

The Classic Guide to Color Correction

DAN MARGULIS

John Wiley & Sons, Inc.

New York • Chichester • Weinheim • Brisbane • Singapore • Toronto

Publisher: Robert Ipsen
Editor: Cary Sullivan
Managing Editor: Frank Grazioli

Library of Congress Cataloging-in-Publication Data:

Margulis, Dan 1951–
Professional Photoshop 5 : the classic guide to color correction / Dan Margulis
p. cm.
"Wiley computer publishing."
Includes index.
ISBN 0-471-32308-X (pbk. : alk. paper)
1. Color computer graphics. 2. Adobe Photoshop. I. Title.
T385.M3636 1998   98-39148
006.6'869--dc21   CIP

Printed in the United States of America
10 9 8 7 6 5 4 3 2

CONTENTS

Preflight: What Shall We Do with This Image?

Should we match the original photo or what a viewer who was in the camera's position would have seen?

Today's Calibrationist, Today's Color Manager

We all want the monitor to look like the print. Without a dose of common sense, most "solutions" will fail.

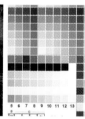

Color Correction By the Numbers

Highlights, shadows, neutrals, fleshtones: get these numbers right, and the rest will fall into place.

The Steeper the Curve, The More the Contrast

Give the most important areas of the image an extra dose of detail by careful control of curve shape.

Plate Blending as Poetry

In bright objects, contrast depends not on the dominant inks but on the weakest—the unwanted color. If you don't have a good one, *make* one.

Sharpening with a Stiletto

Unsharp masking can bring images into focus—or destroy them with haloes and graininess. Those who aim well can sharpen more.

In Color Correction, The Key Is the K

GCR and other black generation decisions and their effect on printing, color correction, and retouching.

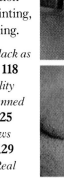
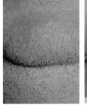

Managing Photoshop's Separation Settings

Photoshop 5's color changes are confusing. Here's how to restore the status quo—or go in a new direction.

RGB Is CMY

Once you realize that the two are basically the same, you're in a position to exploit their differences.

HSB Is LAB

These two separate color from contrast. That philosophy can be the start (and heart) of effective corrections—of certain kinds of pictures.

All Colorspaces Are One

Each colorspace has its own strength, and each can handle easy corrections. As the assignments get tougher, the smart operator switches often.

12

The Resolution Issue, Resolved

The abbreviation *dpi* is used for too many things. This chapter sorts it all out and suggests better terminology.

13

Keeping the Color In Black and White

The big secret here is a paradox: if you want the black and white to look good, you have to correct the color.

14

Math, Moiré, and the Artist: A New Angle on Descreening

Prescreened originals need not be a problem if you keep two words in mind during the entire process.

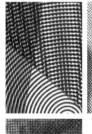

Multitones and Extra Plates: The Fifth Color Follies

Duotones are easy to make even if there isn't an extra ink available. If there is, think hi-fi color.

There Are No Bad Originals

Restorations of older photos are thought to be difficult, but many of the techniques one would use on their modern equivalents work well.

Consider a millionaire, and consider a pauper. Which one improves his lifestyle more by being smarter about how he spends money?

The pauper, obviously. And for exactly the same reason, we who are involved in publishing need to be smarter about the way we handle color images.

Our industry has been democratized, but at a price. Both input and output aren't as reliable as they've been in the past. The input—scans, captures from a digital camera, computer-generated art—can be very good indeed, but it can also be very bad, and it is more likely to be bad than it was four years ago.

In the old days, our work generally was going to some kind of offset press. There are many more targets now: desktop printers that use several different technologies, hybrid presses, large-format printers, high-speed copiers, devices that only accept RGB input, you name it. Not only that, the targets are moving: quality doesn't stink, like it did four years ago, but these products aren't mature, either. They are improving month by month, meaning that our ways of handling them have to change frequently. Although some of these devices are excellent, more often than not, they don't have the range of capabilities of a traditional press, making us color paupers rather than millionaires.

Some people say, the fancy tricks may be all well and good if the product is an annual report printed on a sheetfed press with expensive coated paper, but for something printed on one of the above-mentioned "junk" devices, why bother?

This gets it exactly backwards. The worse the printing conditions are, the more important it is to milk the most out of the image. A skilled technician can make an enormous difference to the quality of color laser output, for example.

A picture is worth a thousand words, but a good-looking picture, an appealing picture, is worth much more. *Everybody* wants their pictures to look good in print.

The Two Worlds of Photoshop

The first edition of *Professional Photoshop* was written as Photoshop 3 was being brought to market, in early 1994. It sold out in weeks. It has been kept in print ever since, even though there was no new edition for Photoshop 4: there was no need, since the color engine of Photoshop didn't change and neither did any of the techniques.

It's true that the flashiest part of Photoshop is its special effects, its creative potential. It's also true that many people make an excellent living employing them, in high-end advertising and multimedia work.

On the other hand, for every person who makes money in this way, many more do so in the second, less glamorous, world of Photoshop: the world of vivid and lifelike reproduction of real photographs, without any special effects. And, given that poorly prepared images stand out on the printed page like a fireworks display on a moonless night, the people who do so tend to be fairly concerned about maximizing quality, for reasons of pride if nothing else.

There have been great changes in the industry in the more than four years since the first edition, changes that dwarf the impact of Photoshop 5. I've tried to make some compensating changes here.

Around 80 percent of the content and images are new, so basically it's an entirely different book. This is so even though five chapters are completely analogous to their counterparts in the first edition. My hope in doing this that it may reinforce some of the lessons for those who have read them with different images.

This book is about color correction, particularly about preparation of images for print. All pretense to the contrary has been dropped. All chapters that don't relate to this topic have been mercilessly excised to make room for more of the good stuff— expanded sections on unsharp masking, channel blending to beef up the unwanted color, the Photoshop separation method, the handling of prescreened originals, the impact of fifth colors, and restoration of elderly photographs.

As those who are familiar with my books and columns will know, the method of presenting this is, shall we say, different from what is found elsewhere. Though it is a how-to book, there are few step-by-step recipes, and no Extremely Hot Tip boxes with an orange gradient in the background on every other page. There is no CD of exercises. Instead, the presumption is that you bought the book because you wanted to read it and think about it.

My objective is to present complicated issues in simple language. Many readers will be Photoshop experts, but there is no need for you to be one, since most professional color correction is done with just a few tools. Many readers will be professional photographers or retouchers or otherwise have a strong background in imaging, but this is not necessary either. The major question in color correction always is, do you like Image A better than Image B, or not? With great respect to the afore-mentioned experienced folk, you don't need a lifetime in the trade to be qualified to answer that question.

The opening of Chapter 7, where I lam-pooned a color scientist spouting content-free jargon, was written in 1991. It was the start of the first piece I ever wrote on color correction, a study of GCR and the role of the black plate generally. This was, and remains, a complex topic, and one that is not understood even by some very experi-enced professionals. And yet, its basics can be grasped by any layperson—provided they are not obscured by the meaningless professorspeak I was making fun of in those paragraphs.

Consequently, that piece got an over-whelmingly favorable response, and I've tried to emulate that approach ever since. I've found that people get into a lot of trou-ble by being afraid to admit what they don't know, and that a lot of what professionals *assume* everybody knows, they don't. I wrote the column that is the basis of Chap-ter 12 here as sort of a throwaway. So many people were confusing the concept of printer and scanner resolution that I felt I had to write a quickie to explain it, even though I thought it would be of interest only to rank beginners.

As I drafted the column, however, it became clear to me how wrong I was.

The sheer number of types of resolution that can be referred to by the deceptive abbreviation *dpi* has, I now realize, baffled experts, as well as beginners. It therefore came as no surprise that this, too, got a large and sympathetic response.

Who Are You, the Reader?

The first edition of this book was, I thought, aimed primarily at professional retouchers. It did not occur to me in 1994, although it should have, that it would be of interest to professional photographers, who were beginning to realize that the workflow of the late 90s would call for them to be CMYK-capable.

Also, people who are not full-time image handlers, yet sometimes have to prepare a color photograph for printing, face obvious disadvantages. Such people—and there are many more of them than there were four years ago—need plain and down-to-earth explanations of the basic principles.

And yet there is a group, and a fairly vocal one, for which the first edition, though the most advanced text then available, was too easy. In response, the second half of this book has some examples that are more difficult than any in the first edition. And many of the general concepts introduced in the later chapters are also a little tricky.

In short, the water gets deep in certain places. I've made it a priority, therefore, to use everyday language even when discussing the most complicated topics. If you are a total beginner, please don't feel as if you should be able to follow every facet of some of the tougher examples in Chapters 10 and 11. However, I think you'll be able to fathom the objectives pretty easily. I do run these writings by laypeople before I print them, and they all say they grasp in a general way what's going on even if they don't understand the specific commands.

No mercy, however, is shown to those interested in crutches. All commands that come under the description of kid stuff will be avoided. There is no need for Levels because we use curves. There is no need for any of the sharpen filters other than Unsharp Mask. And we sort of breeze by silhouetting and masking. If you're an advanced user, you already know how to do this; I prefer to concentrate on talking about when it's necessary, because most users who consider themselves advanced resort to masks far too frequently.

By the same token, I refuse to offer panaceas for problems that can't be solved, or to which nobody knows the answer. For example, I do not hide the fact that the phenomenon of dot gain is not well understood. And, as is my custom, special scorn is reserved for those who have offered foolproof solutions without understanding what the problem is they are purporting to solve, or even whether it is a problem in the first place.

Such persons frequently try to make color correction some kind of mystical procedure. They attempt to baffle us with pseudo-scientific babble, with color-management panaceas, with assurances that everybody is shortly going to adopt revolutionary new technologies.

We are not, however, launching a space-craft. We are trying to make an image look lifelike and convincing so as to get an approving emotional response from those who look at it. Photoshop offers some powerful techniques to do this, but most of these techniques have been around for years.

A Three-Part Structure

This is neither a Macintosh nor a Windows book. Although I use a Mac, there's nothing Mac-specific here. In a way, it's not even a Photoshop book: most of the recommended maneuvers translate easily to any scanner program or image processing application you may be using.

The structure is divided into three parts. First, the basics. It makes no sense to jump in and correct things without knowing why we are doing it, so there is a chapter on what the objectives are. Because calibration and color management have been brought to the fore by various changes in Photoshop 5, Chapter 2 discusses the why of these things, without getting into the specifics of how Photoshop has implemented them. These two chapters, I think, should be easily understandable to laypeople— although some of the ideas in them seem to bewilder certain color scientists.

There follow four chapters on the most important tools in color correction: setting a full range; using curves to target the interest area and bring out contrast in it; insuring that the weak color, which is critical in retaining detail, is robust; and maintaining precise control of unsharp masking.

For the sake of simplicity, these chapters use CMYK techniques only, ignoring the fact that many originals start out in different colorspaces.

The second part of the book, which starts with Chapter 7, brings the other colorspaces into the picture, enumerating the strengths and weaknesses of each one. We begin with a full discussion of the role of the black plate in CMYK, when to vary black generation, and what it means for both color correction and presswork. This leads naturally to a discussion of the technical difficulties of making a color-space conversion, Photoshop's default ideas on how to do it, and how to improve on them. Chapter 8 also covers the specific color handling changes in Photoshop 5, and how to reconcile the differences with earlier versions of the program.

We then proceed to a comparison of two closely related colorspaces, RGB and CMY, followed by a similar comparison of two radical alternatives, HSB and, especially, LAB. In both chapters, we consider the types of images that are ideal for correction by each method. And we wind up with a chapter suggesting that, for the confident operator, all colorspaces are actually one.

The third part of the book concentrates on special cases. There are chapters on the various types of resolution; on how to convert color images successfully to black and white; on how to avoid moiré when dealing with prescreened images; on the ramifications of having a fifth ink available, including methods of duotoning; and we close with a chapter that deals primarily with the restoration of old, damaged prints.

This is not a book about scanning, although those who master the principles of this book will automatically be expert scanner operators as soon as they learn to mount originals; the skill set is the same. Nor is it about digital photography as such, although most photographers who adopt these methods find that they shoot somewhat differently afterwards.

And it is not about general retouching, although the topic does come up. Those who understand curves do not resort to selections or masks nearly as often as less skilled Photoshoppers. Everybody has to use masks when a picture is damaged or where the client is looking for some major move that is simply not in the original art-work at all. But global correction is usually not only faster, but gives better quality.

Even so, we have to talk about where local retouching is useful and when it is mandatory. This may change your philosophy about when to do it, just as your philosophy on monitor calibration may change even though this is not a book about monitor calibration.

The Assumptions

We start with a digital file. It can come from a scanner, a digital camera, or from parts unknown; it doesn't matter whether it has a profile associated with it; it doesn't matter what colorspace it's in. The goal will be to make it print as well as possible. The destination is therefore almost always a CMYK file. The assumption is that printing conditions are roughly those of magazines, although we discuss how to cope with different ones, such as those of newspapers. And the assumption is that we don't have forever to work on the images.

The color management novelties of Photoshop 5.0 offered so many snares—mostly undocumented—for the unwary user, that the program blew up in Adobe's face when it was released in May 1998. In a notorious magazine review, I said that, "on the whole, Photoshop 5 is a major disservice to the industry." Other users said even less agreeable things. Many trashed the upgrade and went back to Photoshop 4, which is not what I advocate doing.

For this reason, although the book uses Photoshop 5 terminology throughout, where there is a major difference from preceding versions, this is noted. Particularly, Chapter 2 gives quick instructions on how to turn off most of the new color features so

that the program will behave like past versions. Chapter 8 shows how to set dot gain in Photoshop 5, which requires a lower number than was formerly the case.

A corrective version, 5.0.2, introduced a color "wizard" whose goal was to steer users away from stupid color settings, such as the ones that were the defaults in 5.0. The methodology, however, didn't change. If you have settings that work well in 5.0, they will work identically in 5.0.2 and 5.5.

If you believe in wizards, color should probably not be your field. Learn what the settings mean. No upgrade changes the basic principles of color correction. Master curves, and you'll be able to cope with any version of Photoshop, now or in the future.

None of the original images in this book were sabotaged in any way to make the "correction" more impressive. Also, if we are talking about curves, the corrected version will not have more unsharp masking, say, than the original. If we are talking about a single plate and its impact, the other plates will be unchanged from original to correction.

In response to requests for specific values, in most sets of corrections I have added a circular swatch of an important color in the image. It is identified by its CMYK values. In the corrected version a similar circle appears, based on the values taken from the same point in the image.

Also, a number of readers found the sections on plate blending the most challenging part of the first edition. In response, there are many more blend examples here. And because many people couldn't keep all the acronyms of the graphic arts straight, I've added an index of them at the end.

As I pointed out in the last paragraphs of the first edition, improvement in skills is never-ending. My own technique, as you will see from some side-by-side examples, is better today than it was then. There have also been some changes in my attitude.

First, I'm much more prone to correct in LAB, or to use hybrid moves that involve more than one colorspace, than I was previously. Chapters 9–11 are the result.

Second, I've become interested in personal preferences and have done research in that area. When confronted by two versions of the same image, I now state more confidently whether one is absolutely better and would be recognized as such by almost every viewer, or whether it would be preferred by the majority but not by everyone.

Third, I was too quick in the past to say that certain files were too poor to be corrected. I would never have thought, for example, of taking a video grab and making a full page ad of it, trying to do serious color work with an indexed-color document, or preparing a file for printing when the scan resolution is a quarter of the screen ruling. Having had to do these things, I now realize that, while difficult, they are by no means out of the question.

For the past several years, I've been teaching three-day intensive courses in color correction to small groups of masochists. To the extent that this book is better than the first one, it's largely due to these people, who were in fact teaching me by their comments and experiments.

I also owe thanks to my editors, the late Tom McMillan of *Electronic Publishing* magazine and Cary Sullivan of John Wiley, and to Michael Kieran, who gave this manuscript a careful read when he was supposed to be on vacation in France.

Readers of my columns have shaped the direction of this book by a number of very perceptive questions and comments. Particularly, I tip my hat to those from economically disadvantaged countries, who often work with antiquated computers and press equipment but who have a burning desire to improve the look of what they produce, and who often have had to jump through hoops to find a local Internet service provider to send me e-mail.

As I remarked earlier, those who work with high-quality sheetfed presses and fine papers can be likened to millionaires, and those who print on newsprint and suffer with poor equipment to paupers. The biggest gain from good technique will accrue to the paupers—but those who take the time to share their knowledge (and those who are on the receiving end of it) are wealthier than they know.

* * *

It's customary at this point to state that the persons named above have no responsibility for any errors that remain and to express deep remorse if any do. Given a topic so personal and subjective as this one, such a stance isn't appropriate. So, I reiterate what I said in the first edition: if you find something here you consider to be an error, I am *not* sorry, but rather delighted that you have enough confidence in your own grasp of the subject to think so.

In the good old days, certain swashbuckling scanner operators were rather dismissive of the role of photographers. There are no bad originals, they would say, there are only bad scanner operators. Updated, that is the theme of this book: there are only bad Photoshop operators. There are no bad originals.

Professional
Photoshop

CHAPTER 1

Preflight: What Shall We Do with This Image?

Before tackling color correction, a fundamental question needs to be answered: is the idea to reproduce a photograph as accurately as possible, or to reproduce what a human viewer who was in the position of the camera would have seen?

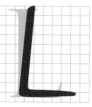 et there be light, the Lord said, and since then it's been nothing but headaches for those of us interested in quality color printing.

The big problem is not so much that the Lord created such a large visible spectrum, but that He also endowed us with an acutely sensitive and highly adjustable visual apparatus. The combination of these two factors makes it quite impossible to create digital images that have even remotely the clarity of real life.

Can a camera capture the majesty of the Grand Canyon? Anyone who has ever been there knows that it cannot. To generalize further: Photographs can never rival reality. Their tonal range is too small. More important, when the human eye is confronted with a preponderance of similar colors it adjusts unconsciously, gaining sensitivity to those colors at the expense of others. A camera lacks this flexibility. It faithfully records what it sees, even if the human eye would see something different.

Figure 1.1 A scene from Grand Canyon National Park. It's a fine image, but it isn't prepared for print as well as it should be. To see what one touch of curves and another of unsharp masking can do, turn ahead to Figure 1.2.

When we look closely at the Grand Canyon, with its rich redness, our eyes compensate to let us pick up a greater variety of reds. The camera sticks to its original settings. Even if it could magically make itself more sensitive to reds, though, it could not record nearly the range of colors that the eye can see.

Defining "Quality"

We can probably agree that a color photograph is "worse" than the image would appear in real life. Similarly, an amateur photographer using a $12.50 disposable camera will surely produce a "worse" image of the Grand Canyon than a professional with a first-quality instrument.

If we convert the image recorded by either photographer to digital information, we will get a "worse" image still. Just as between real life and a photograph, between a photograph and a scanned photograph there is a decrease in the range of colors that can be portrayed, and a loss of some detail.

Next in line of deteriorating quality comes the printed piece. Again, image quality and color space is lost, all to the detriment of realism.

There is yet another quality leap between color printing on reasonably good paper, such as is used in this book, and printing on poor stock, such as newsprint. A final indignity that can be imposed on an unfortunate photograph is to lose its color altogether, on those occasions when we must print it in black and white.

Now that I've trashed the entire printing process, it should be pointed out that the news is not all bad. If we can't achieve real-life or even film-like on the printed page, well, neither can anyone else. The viewer,

consciously or not, understands this and cuts us a break. The viewer judges the quality of a printed picture in comparison to other printed pictures, not against original transparencies and certainly not against what the viewer might perceive in person.

The *really* good news (or, for the lazy, the really *bad* news) is that, even in our relatively low-quality world, skill means a lot. Just as there is a huge gap between the work of a professional photographer and someone who just points a camera and clicks the shutter, the difference between the work of a color technician and that of a dilettante will be obvious even to the most inattentive observer.

That analogy can be carried further. In photography, a number of crutches have emerged that enable the less skilled to improve their pictures. Things like auto-focus and automatic exposure are a big help to people who don't know how to set these things manually, but the camera's judgment cannot ever be as good as a professional's. In our own field, there are similar crutches, such as Photoshop's Auto Levels command.

The similarity with photography breaks down in one important area, however. The objects that the photographer takes pictures of, whether outdoors or in the studio, are generally just as easy or as difficult to shoot as they were five years, or 50 years, ago. That is not true for us: technology has reduced the price of capturing the base product, the digital file, that we work with, but it has also reduced its quality from the days when drum scanners reigned.

Plus, now we have much more of a range of printing conditions to plan for. Back then, it was pretty much output to film, print on an offset press. Now, we have a bewildering variety of desktop printers, digital proofers, large-format printers, high-speed color copiers, and platesetters, not to mention devices that don't accept CMYK input at all.

Our job, therefore, *is* harder than it was five years ago. Of course, that means that we will have to be *better.*

The Goals in Color Manipulation

Before charging into color correction with both guns blazing, we'd best have some idea of what we're aiming at. This is a ticklish topic, and one that many people ignore.

Leaving aside the cases where we want the printed piece to be at odds with the original photograph (as when the sky is overcast in the original but we want happier-looking weather) the standard instruction in the industry is "match the art." By this, we are supposed to understand that we are to produce something that reminds the viewer as much as possible of the original photograph, granted that we are smashing it into a grotesquely smaller range of colors.

Plainly, we can't be too literal about this. If the original photograph has a scratch or dust on it, nobody would question that "match the art" means take it out.

Next, there is general agreement that if the photograph is flat, it is the job of the computer artist to fix it. By "flat" we mean lacking contrast, which means lacking a good range, which means that either the whites are too dark or the blacks too light, or both.

In printing, our color range is so limited to begin with that we can't afford such flat images, even when the original photograph itself is slightly flat. So, to most professionals, "match the art" means, set the lightest white in the original to the value of the lightest white that we can print and still show detail, and set the darkest black in the original to the darkest combination of inks that we can conveniently accommodate. The results of this approach cause no end of astonishment to the uninitiated. Nobody thinks that a snapshot will reproduce as well as a high-quality transparency, but that is because the transparency has so much more of a dynamic range. Once we scan and correct the two, they'll each have the same range, and as long as the snapshot was as detailed as the transparency, it will print just about as well.

Should We Match the Art?

Another major issue, particularly in dealing with photos taken outdoors, where lighting conditions are unpredictable, is that when we compress the colors of the original into our colorspace, we sometimes exaggerate an existing color cast.

Color casts are—well, Figure 1.1, that's a color cast, albeit a mild one. If you compare it to Figure 1.2, it looks like there's a yellow piece of Saran Wrap lying over it. Every color is affected.

Casts are usually caused by suboptimal lighting conditions, but they can also be introduced or aggravated by lousy scanning. Casts come in every conceivable color strength, and some affect only certain lightness ranges. Even a relatively mild one can damage an image, because casts play havoc with neutral colors. By neutral colors, we mean whites and grays. Neutral colors, as will be repeated over and over in these pages, are one of our chief torments. They must be carefully balanced, or they won't stay neutral. The lighter the gray, the easier it is to mess up.

Annoyingly, many things in life are of a neutral color, and if our image shows them otherwise people will think we don't know what we are doing. Paper, asphalt roads, elephants, shadows, packaging materials, porcelain; the list is endless. In Chapter 3 you will encounter a picture of a horse that your logic will tell you must be white, yet is distinctly pink on the page.

The question is, should we correct this, assuming that the horse is actually pink in the original?

The argument against correcting is simple. If we horse around with the color balance, we may change a lot of things besides the horse. Although a pink horse does prove that a color cast infects the original, perhaps the photographer or the final client *likes* the way it is affecting the other areas.

As against that, if we were looking at the horse ourselves, rather than at a photograph, we would see a white horse, not a pink one. Human eyes are highly efficient at rejecting color casts in ambient light. Cameras are not so good at it. Probably the lighting conditions at the time *were* slightly pink. Our eyes would have compensated. The camera didn't.

I find this to be a convincing argument. So do most other color professionals.

For the purposes of this book, war is hereby declared on color casts. When we identify them, we will reduce or eliminate them. If you agree that this is the right approach, read the next section carefully. It's not obvious, yet it follows logically.

Matching the Meaning

Success in color correction depends very much on the imagination. We need to visualize the kinds of changes that are possible and the effects they may have.

Instead of showing you a picture of what I am starting to talk about, I would like you to *imagine* a couple of pictures. As we go along, there will be quite a few more of these hypothetical situations.

First, please imagine a picture of your own yard, taken at 15 minutes before sunset on a day with pleasant weather.

Ready?

The first question is, did you imagine what your yard looks like at that time of day, or how it would look in a *photograph?* There's a big difference. At that time of day, it is much darker than at, say, noon. Once again, though, our eyes would have compensated by becoming more sensitive to dark colors. Once again, the camera would not. Even if the lightest and darkest areas of the photograph are correct, overall the image will be darker than you remember.

This is exactly what occurs when we are in a relatively dark room with the lights out. We adjust to the environment and after a while it seems normal to us. If the lights get turned on suddenly, we are dazzled; we rub our eyes, and it takes time for us to start to discern obvious visual details.

When our vision adjusts to changed surroundings, it's not as if we can see more colors. We just evaluate them differently. If we increase the range of dark colors we see we have to decrease how many light colors we can perceive. If we are staring intently at the incredible reds of the Grand Canyon, we lose the ability to see the normal range of greens.

As it happens, color correction by computer can work in exactly the same way. The question is, should we do it?

Figure 1.2 *A quick correction of Figure 1.1, using techniques discussed in Chapters 3 and 6.*

In other words, Photoshop lets us do exactly what our eyes do at 15 minutes before sunset: lose discrimination in lighter colors so as to be able to make finer distinctions among darker ones. Thus, we will see moderately dark tones as lighter than they are in the original photograph.

It seems to me that if we are going to correct a pink horse to agree with what our eyes would have seen, it must follow, as the night the day, that we must correct this sunset as well.

As you can see, the simple decision that color casts should be corrected leads to some unexpected logical consequences. Let us extend the concept further, with one final, more agreeable imaginary picture. Imagine, please, an attractive individual of whatever sex you prefer. This person is clothed in a bathing suit, drinking a piña colada, standing amid tropical foliage at a resort hotel somewhere in the Caribbean.

Relaxing, isn't it?

In deciding what to do with this image, as color technicians we need to know a little bit more. Imagine further, then, four different possibilities. Suppose that this is:

a. a picture of a family member, for personal use and enjoyment;

b. a posed picture to be used to sell bathing suits in a clothing catalog;

c. intended as a promotional piece for the hotel;

d. a shot for a horticultural magazine article discussing the flora of the island.

I put it to you that these four scenarios require four different corrections, even though the basic picture is the same. Part of the reason is just a matter of commercial priorities: in cases a, c, or d we do not care particularly whether the color of the person's bathing suit exactly matches the original, but in case b we care very much indeed. Mostly, though, it is just a matter of placing ourselves in the position of an actual observer. We would be concentrating on whatever most interested us. If that happened to be the person, or the bathing suit, or the palm trees, that particular area would gain definition at the expense of things that were not as important to us. Furthermore, those unimportant areas would lose color: they would seem to us to be more gray.

What the camera saw was accurate. But it was not real. That, in short, is the case for aggressive color correction.

You Be the Judge

We now embark on three hundred pages of image evaluation and enhancement. A few words on procedure first.

Most of the images in this book come from commercial CDs of stock photography. None have been sabotaged so as to create something easier to correct. For those interested in acquiring these images or knowing where they came from, each one's source is identified in the Notes and Credits section of this book, as are some of the quotations and more oblique references made in the text. When there are before-and-after versions of such an image, the "before" version is, colorwise, exactly as it appears on the disk. When necessary, I have resampled down to a more appropriate resolution and/or sharpened the image. When the image was not in CMYK mode to begin with, I converted it using the default Photoshop separation settings suggested in Chapter 8. Unless otherwise indicated, all of the "before" pictures have had the same overall sharpening applied as their "after" counterparts.

A book about color manipulation is not like other instructional books. There is much more room for the reader's opinion. The basic question, after any color move, must be, *does the picture look better now?* You do not need fifty years of experience and twelve advanced degrees to answer this. If you disagree with my assessment in certain cases, you shouldn't be surprised.

Color means different things to different people. Varying interpretations of what is important in a picture are possible, as we saw in our imaginary trip to the Caribbean. And possibly more important, individuals do see color differently.

There is a widespread belief, quite untrue, that except for color-blind people, we all see more or less the same thing. This is disproven by the industry-standard color perception test, the Munsell test, in which one is asked to arrange in proper order a series of pegs that vary only slightly from one another in hue.

I have administered this test to more than a thousand people, and can categorically confirm something that will not surprise you, that people in their twenties on the whole have much better color perception than older folk. Furthermore, in my experience, young women do best of all.

It is not just a matter of deterioration: people develop patterns, and each individual sees different things. To get personal for a moment, now that I am in my forties, I don't see green as well as I used to. I know this for a fact, because I have periodically taken the Munsell test over the last 25 years. One is supposed to take the test at close range in a light booth, but in 1975, I could get a perfect score on it from a distance of ten feet away. Nowadays, I can still do this with the red segment of the

test, but with greens I can't get a perfect score no matter how close I get. I don't know what you expect; I don't fit into the same pants I wore in 1975 either, among many other problems.

A person who sees color the way I did when I was 25 will not just be able to see detail in greens that I can't. If we are both looking at a red, for example, I may see it as a rosier color, less of a fire-engine sort of red. Or maybe I react to red differently anyway as a result of some childhood experience. It has also been seriously suggested that blond individuals see color differently than do persons with darker hair. The point is that no two people will ever totally agree on what color represents. If you like the way a picture looks, then its color is right for you regardless of what I think.

To see an example of disagreement in action, have a look at Figure 1.3. Which image do you like better overall?

My own answer is, no preference. I doubt that this is *your* answer. If it is, chances are you are, like me, a male over the age of 40.

I make this assertion with some confidence, because I have run these two images in a magazine article as well as the first edition of this book. In both cases, I was using it to argue in favor of the approach addressed in Chapter 5, that when two inks dominate (as cyan and yellow do here) the weak color, magenta here, becomes extremely important. The bottom image is a correction in magenta only. The top one corrects both cyan and yellow.

I said then that, if anything, the bottom image is better than the top one, proving my point. Overwhelmingly negative reader feedback convinced me to run some preference tests. After asking a couple of hundred people their opinion, I now know that about 90 percent prefer the top one.

Because of my history with the Munsell test, I can guess why the rest of the world disagrees with me. My ability to perceive modest variations in reds and magentas hasn't deteriorated over time. Bring on Superman, and let's see which of us can call out the positioning of the red pegs from a greater distance. Chances are, I'm much more sensitive to this variation than you are, and that's the kind of variation that exists in the bottom version.

On the other hand, I regret to say that my perception of green variations is now only about that of the population at large. Given that by purchasing this book you identify yourself as someone with an interest in the graphic arts, you probably have better than average color perception. In the top image, which is entirely green variation, you may well see more of it than I do.

In short, we are likely to have different opinions about this picture because it is likely that we physically are not seeing the same things. You can't blame me for liking the bottom one; if I am your client you can't get upset by my decision to reject the top one in favor of it.

Confronted with such seeming irrationality on the part of clients, many of us have given up and decided that everything is subjective.

It isn't. Turn the page and have a look at Figure 1.4. Which do you prefer this time?

I vote for the bottom one. So do you. Of hundreds of people who have seen these two images side by side, not one has ever preferred the top one. Every race, every nationality, every gender, every age of viewer says the bottom one is better. And so, of course, it is.

To *correct* means to make better. Given the unanimity of opinion, it is certainly fair to say that the bottom image is a *corrected* version of the top one: not just different, but *better*. Your clients know that the bottom one is better just as well as we do, and if you persist in giving them images that look like the top one when the bottom one is possible, you will pay a price, sooner or later.

Note, in addition to the extra detail in the leaves, that the insect has become browner in the corrected version. That happens to be what the human visual system does when confronted by a surplus of one color. This hopper would seem brown to us when sitting on a bright green leaf, but green in a different environment.

This interesting phenomenon of human vision, that we perceive colors differently depending on what surrounds them, is called *simultaneous contrast*.

Cameras do not have this capability. Imagine, please, three executives sitting next to one another. They are wearing business suits. One of the suits is charcoal, one is black, and one a navy blue. A human observer sees considerable difference between the three. A camera does not, at least not as much as it should when they are so close together.

Should we therefore take action? It seems to me that if you feel you should correct for a color cast, you logically must feel we should correct for the suits as well.

The CMYK Standard

People involved with color printing for a living tend not to be very tolerant of those who preach other standards than the one we all use, which is CMYK. Within about a hundred pages, I think, you will be a believer, if you are not already. For the time being I ask you merely to accept that CMYK is the system that all printers and virtually all prepress professionals employ, and the one that will be used throughout the first part of this book.

CMYK is the abbreviation for the four inks—cyan, magenta, yellow, and black—that are used in normal printing. These four are sometimes referred to as the *process colors.* *K* is the abbreviation for black because at one time it was customary to refer to cyan as *blue* and to magenta as *red,* so the letter *B* is ambiguous. In the pressroom, *blue* and *red* are still synonyms for cyan and magenta, which can lead to confusion. In this book, *blue* and *red* mean what they do in everyday English.

Every color that the press can reproduce with these inks is expressed in terms of percentages. $70^C0^M100^Y$ means 70 percent of the maximum cyan plus the absolute maximum yellow, with no magenta. If the black value is zero, we omit it.

The numbers just given describe a color known as Kelly green. If you are to become a color corrector you will have to understand this intuitively: you must know approximately what will result from any mixture of colors. Similarly, you must know the general impact of changing any of these numbers slightly. Suppose, for example, that we increase cyan. This will

Figure 1.3 *Which of these two images do you prefer? Do you consider it a close call?*

move us toward a color we might call forest green. If we remove cyan, on the other hand, we will tend toward chartreuse, and eventually, if enough cyan comes out, toward yellow.

Yellow cannot go higher, since it is already maxed out, but if we reduce it we will start to see a purer, yet less intense,

Figure 1.4 Once again, which do you prefer? Hint: several hundred people have voted on this one, and the verdict is unanimous.

we want it a whole lot, because we can do more to add punch to the image by manipulating it than we can with the dominant plates.

The unwanted color controls how "clean" or "dirty" the dominating color appears. When working with green, the addition of magenta moves it toward gray. Magenta has such a powerful impact on green that if we can engineer detail into the magenta we are certain to see it in the green, even if the cyan and yellow plates have poor contrast. The unwanted-color channel is so surpassingly important that, if need be, we will construct one out of fragments of other channels. We will spend all of Chapter 5 discussing this.

To get an idea of how the four color plates interplay, have a look at Figure 1.5. This is a quiz. These are the four plates of an image. Please decide which is which, without the benefit of seeing the entire image in color. If you like, write down your answers now, before turning the page.

green. Magenta cannot go lower, since it is at zero now, but if we increase it, interesting things will happen, and happen fast.

In a situation like this, where two of the three colors predominate, the odd man out (the magenta here) is called the *unwanted color.* This is somewhat of a misnomer. It is not unwanted at all by the intelligent artist:

Four Plates, One Objective

This test is not that easy, except for identifying the black. The purpose of black is to strengthen dark areas. Consequently the black plate is invariably the lightest of the four. That means it is Plate 2 here.

Untangling the other three is more difficult. It was a pretty crummy day in Prague when this picture was taken. We know this, even without benefit of seeing the image in color, because the sky is not blue. If it were, the cyan plate (whichever the cyan plate is) would be much darker than the other two, and the yellow much lighter. The magenta would be in the middle, and this would be too easy of a quiz. Instead, as the devil would have it, the three CMY plates, 1, 3, and 4, are about equal. So the sky is gray.

Just as the black plate is always the lightest, the yellow is commonly the darkest. Here, Plate 4 is darkest—is it the yellow?

If it is, the large spire in the background is a yellow tower. The arched window at the bottom of the church will also be yellow, as will the lower windows of the two right-hand buildings. Muddy yellows, to be sure, since there are traces of all three other inks in each of these, but yellows just the same.

Furthermore, the circular gilded scupture in the triangular gable at center is strong only in Plate 3. If Plate 4 is yellow, that sculpture is perforce either magenta or cyan.

Faced with a choice of windows that are reflecting basically cyan, magenta, or yellow, I am inclined to think cyan. That also gives us steel-gray spires in the background rather than yellowish-gray ones.

If Plate 4 is the cyan and Plate 2 is the black, Plates 1 and 3, which are very similar, are magenta and yellow. Which is which?

I'd refer again to the circular sculpture—it appears to be the purest color in the entire image, since it's about the only part dominated almost completely by one ink. Would you rather have it be yellow or magenta? Also, the building at right and the small structure at lower left are strongest in Plate 3. Do these buildings have a yellowish tinge, or are they pink?

Figure 1.5 *These are, in random order, the cyan, magenta, yellow, and black plates from a certain image. Can you tell which one is which?*

You take it from there. Once you have yourself convinced, check Figure 1.6, which shows all six possible permutations of these colors, and see whether your choice appears to be the winner.

You should at this point be very clear on the circle of colors, especially in terms of the complementary colors that they damage so effectively. Magenta falls between red and blue. It kills green. Cyan falls be-tween blue and green. It kills red. Yellow falls between green and red. It kills blue. And black kills everything.

You should also adopt professional terminology regarding color ranges. We call the lightest significant white area of the image the *highlight*. In Figure 1.5, we can surmise from studying the four plates that the windowsills of the small building at center answer this description.

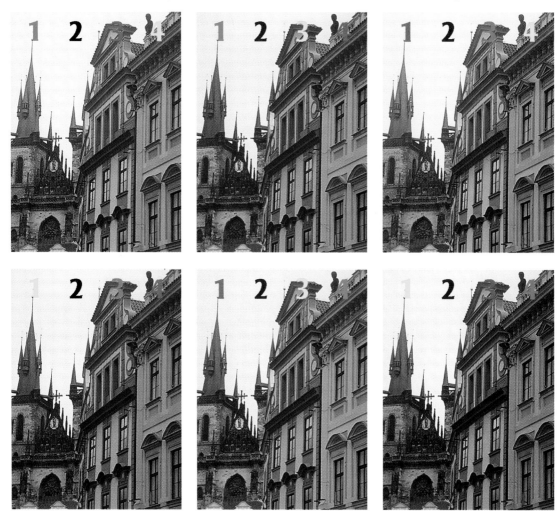

Figure 1.6 *Six color permutations of the image of Figure 1.5, showing what happens when the cyan, magenta, and yellow plates are shuffled around. The numbers at the top of each image show which of the plates of Figure 1.5 are being used for what color. Was your guess about which plate was which correct?*

The darkest significant neutral area of the image is called the *shadow*. This can be confusing, since we often deal with literal shadows. But for graphic arts purposes, the *shadow* of this particular image is at the top of the large arched window in the church.

Quartertone, midtone, and *three-quartertone* are the intermediate ranges of the picture. There is no set demarcation between these areas. A value of 25 percent is plainly quartertone and 50 percent is midtone, but what about 35 percent?

This seeming ambiguity is not as bad as it sounds. Since nobody can guess color values with single-digit precision, we need more inclusive words. If you look at what you perceive to be Kelly green somewhere in an image, you can't possibly (I don't think) tell whether it is $65^C2^M97^Y$ or $71^C4^M93^Y$. You can, and should, think to yourself, cyan three-quartertone, magenta highlight, yellow shadow. That way, if you are planning some other correction in the image that would affect the cyan three-quartertone, you will realize that it may also have an impact on the Kelly green.

Though the exact numbers were unimportant there, here is one that you *do* have to wear next to your heart. $5^C2^M2^Y$, approximately, is the magic number that defines the minimum highlight that most presses can carry and still show detail. Upwards of 75 percent of images have bright white areas somewhere. Our eyes are acutely sensitive to variation in light colors. Consequently, highlight value is crucial to the success of the overall image.

The darkest shadow area is not nearly as important a number, because we lose a lot of color perception in dark areas. Also, this value varies a lot depending upon what kind of paper and press the job is being printed on. If preparing the image for magazine work, assume $80^C70^M70^Y70^K$ is the darkest shadow that can be held if we expect to see any detail. An image with no area that can legitimately be made into a shadow is unusual, although some do exist, as Figure 3.3 will demonstrate.

Obviously, we can get much higher and lower than these two endpoints. There is nothing in Photoshop to stop us from making areas $0^C0^M0^Y$, or for that matter $100^C100^M100^Y100^K$, although employing that kind of a shadow is a good way to make a lifetime enemy of one's printer.

Our biggest disadvantage is that we don't have access to as big a range of colors as a photograph, but we still can't push the envelope that far. Not all presses can reproduce a one percent dot. On the shadow side, every press reaches a point where detail can't be held, and this point is usually in the 80s or, if we are lucky, low 90s.

Not that we can't cheat in certain cases. Figure 1.7, which is about as simple a correction as can be imagined, demonstrates the perils of dogmatic adherence to numbers. It is not so much a color correction as a range correction. All it takes to recognize its effectiveness is a little common sense.

The sun is the lightest area of the image. Orthodoxy suggests setting that value at $5^C2^M2^Y$. But what is the point? Do you see any detail there? The sun's defining characteristic is its brilliance. We have nothing to lose by zeroing it out, and by doing so we open up valuable real estate.

In just the same way, the danger of an excessively dark shadow is that it will lose detail and seem to be nothing but an area of solid black. In the camels, the drivers, and the ground, that's exactly what we have already. So how can we hurt things by going beyond the usual limits? By increasing the range of the image, we get more contrast. Do you see it in the clouds?

If you agree that the second version of this image is palpably better than the first, it seems that you must also agree that before doing anything to a picture, a careful analysis of its strengths and weaknesses is key to success.

And, in the process, we will make the image look more vivid, more lifelike, by making it look more like what a human observer would see and less like camerawork. At the risk of being repetitive, we need not match the art, but match the art's meaning.

The major areas for consideration are:
• In dark environments, the human visual system adjusts and sees everything as lighter, but the camera does not.
• If ambient lighting conditions favor one color, humans won't notice, but the camera will.
• If similar colors are in close proximity, human beings will see more difference in the colors than is actually there, but the camera will lump everything together.
• The human visual apparatus sharply reduces the perceived intensity of reflected flashes of light, but the camera puts in catchlights wherever it sees them.
• When humans concentrate on a single object, that object gains contrast and everything else loses it, but the camera is egalitarian.

The Power of Curves

Photoshop is one of the most terrifying applications around in terms of the number of capabilities, tools, and commands thrown at the user. Luckily, the profes-

sional can ignore most of them when correcting color.

In the arsenal we will bring to bear against inadequate color in the coming chapters, the most useful weapon is also the most frightening.

Input-output curves (found under Image: Adjust>Curves) are by far the most important correction tool in Photoshop or any other color manipulation program. They operate in close conjunction with the density readout provided in the Info palette (if it isn't visible on the monitor, go to Window: Show Info).

Curves can remap the entire image or affect only a limited range of one color, or anything in between. If we leave a particular color's curve alone, we will get a straight line at a 45° angle. If we start adding points, we may get sections of the curve that are steeper or flatter than others. In the areas that are steeper, the image will show more contrast, and in flatter areas there will be less. When the curve is higher than the original 45° line, the image will be darker than it was at first, and in areas where the curve is lower, the image will be lighter.

With Photoshop 5, we can enter curve points directly from the keyboard, or we can move the points up and down with the mouse as with all previous versions. We can check Preview in the Curves dialog box to get an interactive feel as we manipulate. However we decide to do these things, the density readout in the Info palette will show both the present value and what will happen if the new curve is implemented.

The power of curves is immense. We will come back to them over and over. If you understand how to apply curves you will get great color even if you never use any other feature or tool in Photoshop.

Obviously these other things have their uses. I will list the principal ones in a moment. First, however, now that we have defined the most underrated feature of the program, a word about the most overrated, the one that most often snags nonprofessionals into needless or even counterproductive correction cycles.

Photoshop makes it seductively easy to "select" areas of an image to be worked on in isolation, so that any changes will affect only the selected region and not the rest of the image. Human nature makes us want to fix things that are obviously broken. So, upon encountering a pink horse, the natural, understandable reaction of most Photoshoppers is to select it and make it white.

This is not the best approach. If there is a pink horse in our image it may be our most blatant problem, but it is not our only one. Whatever caused the horse to appear pink will also have an impact on the rest of the picture. It will be subtler, probably because we are seldom as sure about what colors are impossible as we are about pink horses. An overall correction of the picture is likely to make everything look better, not just the horse.

There are certainly times when we have to select. Clearly, if we are silhouetting part of an image or extending a background, there is no way around making a selection first. When one important area of an image is horrendously defective and the rest is more or less OK, we also need to select. If we are trying to enhance some small area with one of our retouching tools, it makes sense to isolate it from any surrounding areas that are much different in color or

texture. And when we have made some sort of electronic intervention to cover up some problem and we wish now to cover up the fact that we did it, the selection tools can help hide our tracks.

To think like a professional, when the idea of selecting crosses your mind, take your hands off the mouse and sit on them. Make a selection only when you are sure there is no other sensible way to handle the problem you are trying to fix.

Figure 1.7 *Cost-free color correction. There is almost no detail in either the brightest or darkest areas of this image. This means that we can go beyond normal limits in portraying them (bottom), giving ourselves more contrast without losing anything of value.*

All the Tools You'll Ever Need

Although we will be covering a wide variety of color problems, the fraction of Photoshop's tools that we will use is rather small. All the rest are unnecessary unless we get involved in heavy special effects, and sometimes not even then.

So, without further ado, and from left to right on the monitor, here are the tools of our trade. There will be a brief explanation of some of these when they are first introduced, but if you are not familiar with them ahead of time and are a coward by nature, recourse to the manual may be an option.

Starting with the toolbox, at the top we will need (although not as much as you probably think) the selection tools: the lasso, the magnetic lasso, marquees, and the magic wand. In conjunction with these, the various simple commands located under the Select heading in the menu bar.

Next, the *practical tools:* there is nothing elegant about cropping off part of a picture or rotating it, but in the real world we frequently have to do it for efficiency's sake. So we will need the crop tool, and the Image: Rotate command. We also have to be familiar with the Quick Mask feature in the toolbox, and the Foreground/Background color change box.

The retouching tools for our purposes consist of the rubber stamp tool, the airbrush, the blur/sharpen/smudge tool, and the dodge/burn/sponge tool.

On to the menu bar. We will frequently change File: Color Settings>CMYK Setup, normally to change the method of black generation, as discussed in Chapter 7,

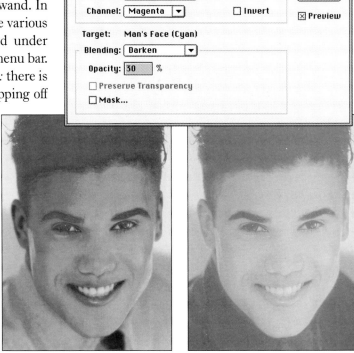

Figure 1.8 Mathematical blends of two plates are a recurring theme in color correction. The cyan plate of this image (left) is weak and lacking in facial detail. The magenta plate (center) is more desirable. To create a cyan that is more detailed yet still lighter than the magenta, Photoshop lets us average the two: the image at right is a 70–30 blend, but only in areas where the magenta was originally darker, to protect the color of the shirt.

THE PREFLIGHT ANALYSIS

✓ Despite the maturity of the prepress process, there is no general agreement on a very fundamental question. Should the color technician try to match the original photograph, or what human observers would have seen had they been in the position of the camera?

✓ Humans and cameras do not see things the same way. If you have decided to make your images match the meaning of the art rather than the art itself, several sorts of correction will become very familiar.

✓ Our color perception changes so that colors we know to be white or gray appear that way to us, regardless of the ambient lighting. The camera, however, will see a color cast if there is one, and will incorporate it into the photograph.

✓ When we focus on a certain object we will see more detail in it and less in surrounding objects. The camera will treat them all equally. This means that some pictures must be corrected differently in different contexts.

✓ When looking at an image with an obvious color defect, do not go charging in to fix it. Corrections are generally best made to the image as a whole. The horrible defect you see may be your biggest problem, but it won't be your only one.

✓ Since printing has a smaller color range to begin with than does an original photograph, it's imperative not to waste any of it. This means that special attention must be paid to the lightest and darkest points of the image, to make sure that they are close to the limit of what the press can reproduce.

✓ Individuals often disagree on which of two variations of an image is better. However, there is a certain category that virtually every viewer prefers, namely, images with more detail. The things people disagree on usually concern color.

✓ Photoshop has a dazzlingly complete suite of commands and tools, but there is no need to be intimidated. High-level image enhancement and color correction require only a fraction of them. The overwhelming majority of professional color correction work is done through manipulation of input-output curves.

✓ Color casts that are nearly invisible on the monitor can be quite offensive in print. The only way to ensure that the image doesn't retain such a cast is to examine color values in the Info palette and correct if necessary.

occasionally to adjust for different dot gains and/or ink limits, as discussed in Chapter 8, and occasionally for really weird purposes, such as to create false separations from which we can steal channels for later blends or masks.

Mode eventually has to be CMYK, and that is our bread-and-butter correction colorspace. In the second part of the book, we'll get heavily into the attractions of other options: RGB, HSB, and especially LAB. And in the third part, we'll consider grayscale, five-color printing, and duotones.

Photoshop's mathematical Filter options give creative artists lots of exciting choices. Here is where one can find twirls, mosaics, and motion blurs, and here is where we will leave them. In our world, the only filters we need are Unsharp Mask and its complement, Gaussian Blur, for which Dust & Scratches is sometimes a good substitute.

The awesome capabilities of Image: Adjust>Curves overshadow other important options under the same menu bar item. With Image: Image Size we control resolution, and with Image: Canvas Size we can arrange to have two files at the same exact size, a prerequisite for compositing.

Image: Adjust>Selective Color lets us get at particular colors wherever they occur, without affecting the rest of the image. It is more accurate but less flexible than Image: Adjust>Hue/Saturation, which has received a nice upgrade in Photoshop 5. Both of these commands should be used *after* basic curve corrections, because the presumption is that a global curve change will make all colors fall into place.

Image: Duplicate lets us make a second version of an existing document, very important in correction. As shown in Figure 1.8, Image: Apply Image allows us to cross-breed plates or files, as does a Photoshop 5 innovation, Image: Adjust>Channel Mixer.

The options under Layer have great significance in retouching. They are only slightly off-topic here, even though we are mainly discussing global correction. Layers make certain techniques much easier.

Select: Feather is an important command that lets us achieve soft edges when we are silhouetting or are forced to make a locally selected correction. Used to an extreme degree, it can also be an effective fadeout tool. Select: Color Ranges is a useful way to isolate individual colors.

Of the palettes accessible under the Window command, the ones we will be visiting constantly are the density monitor (a.k.a. the Info palette), especially now that Photoshop 5 allows us to have four fixed measuring points in every image, and the toolbox. There will also be frequent side jaunts to the Layers, Channels, and Brushes palettes.

There you have it. With this small group of tools, the whole gamut of professional color is accessible. Provided, of course, that we bring along the most important tools of all: our eyes and good judgment.

CHAPTER 2

Today's Calibrationist, Today's Color Manager

Everyone needs to calibrate, everyone needs to manage color. By analyzing what things in the process can vary and deciding whether we care if they do, we can get the great results that elude those who use calibration as a substitute for thinking.

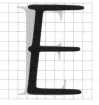

xamples similar to Figure 2.1 are popular in all kinds of color books. The reader is invited to state whether the two patches of green are actually the same, or their dissimilar appearance a mere optical illusion.

Here's an even tougher question. Suppose that you and I disagree as to whether these two greens are the same, and suppose that the digital file that produced them is not available for inspection. Now, how do we determine which one of us is right?

These may seem like baby questions. They are in fact quite deep. Grasping their ramifications is a major step on the way to understanding the whole concept of color management. And, because Photoshop 5 has implemented a particularly opaque brand of it, full of traps and snares for the unwary user, it's more important than ever to get a handle on what's going on.

The topic of this chapter is, how do we know what our images are going to look like when they are printed? Knowing how to correct color in Photoshop won't do us a lick of good if we can't predict this.

As you might expect, this is a complicated topic. It is made immensely more difficult by those in the industry who try to make it

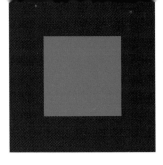

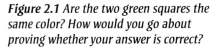

Figure 2.1 Are the two green squares the same color? How would you go about proving whether your answer is correct?

seem simpler than it actually is, who peddle magic bullets wrapped in pseudo-science.

Not that these are wicked people. Quite the contrary. An extreme earnestness is often their distinguishing feature. An overweening belief in mathematical verities can, in these people, produce an almost Zen-like state. Enraptured by their mathematics, they overlook the most obvious points of common sense—and of color science. In the first edition of this book, I coined the term "calibrationist" to describe such a deluded person. In response, I have myself been called a "perceptualist."

Those parts of the first edition, though still accurate, have become obsolete because the ideas I was attacking have since fallen by the wayside, as they deserved. They've been replaced by more sophisticated variants, of which the color changes in Photoshop 5 are a representative.

I don't propose to talk about these specific changes until Chapter 8, because I believe too many people are terrorized by them. The purpose of this chapter is to inoculate you against such psychological difficulties with a prophylactic dose of basic principles.

How can one be against calibration? It helps, first of all, to know what it is. There is a big difference between "calibration" and "repeatability." Nobody would deny that if we print from a certain file today, and then try again next week, we want the result to be exactly the same.

Yet, certain steps in the production process are inherently unpredictable. If we

understand where these breakdowns can occur, we can insure repeatability without falling victim to calibrationism's siren call.

An image manipulated in Photoshop can be intended for one or many purposes. Most likely, we are planning to print it on a press, but there are several kinds of presses and each one has different color characteristics. All papers print differently. Worse, the same press model will behave differently depending upon age, materials being used, speed of the press run, and even the weather, among many other variables.

Perhaps we are going to video, which can produce many colors that are beyond the capabilities of a press but which cannot match the press's detailing, or possibly to a desktop composite printer. But, again, there are many species of color printers and each one has different capabilities, or, as a calibrationist might say, a differing gamut. We will concentrate on printing presses here, not just because that is where most of you will be going with your images, but because prepress is the most difficult case. If you master it you should breeze right through any other color problem.

By now you may be thinking, though, how can this system possibly work? If there are many different types of presses, and printing conditions vary from plant to plant and day to day, how can we get the repeatability that we want?

This quandary scares a lot of people, but there is nothing new about it. Printing was unpredictable long before color got to the desktop. So it is not surprising that a system evolved to take care of most of the problems. The system still works.

This is the basic reason that third-party color management has flopped. For the large majority of users, it is an SSP—a solution in search of a problem. It also tends to be more expensive, less efficient, lower quality, and more prone to error. The market has given color management the treatment it usually accords to products with these attributes.

In spite of this history, Photoshop 5 has implemented, as a default, certain color management technology. If misapplied, or if one doesn't realize where the settings have changed, disaster can result. Many experienced users of Photoshop 4 have panicked, and concluded there is something seriously wrong with Photoshop 5.

I would say there is something seriously wrong with Adobe's development process for Photoshop 5, that it would inflict such a set of defaults on users who don't need them and have no idea how they work, but that's another story. Photoshop 5 has many improvements, and one can certainly make the new color model work.

While how to configure Photoshop 5 is obviously a topic of overriding importance, discussing specifics at this point would be mind-numbing—and counterproductive, in my opinion.

As Santayana remarked, those who cannot remember the past are condemned to repeat it. If you find Photoshop 5's color changes incomprehensible, and look only for a quick fix, you are condemned to relive this experience at some point in your career. More likely, at several points. Photoshop 5 is not the last challenge. The principles are much more important than the implementation. Many calibrationists don't understand them, which is why their nostrums don't work. If you *do* understand them you will have little difficulty adjusting to the changes of Photoshop 5, Photoshop 6, a new type of large-format printer, or any other obstacle fortune places in your way.

That said, if you must have a quick fix and are more interested in the how than the why, I provide one in the box on Page 27. Do these things, and Photoshop 5 will behave pretty much like previous versions, if that's what you're trying to achieve.

And with that, I set aside the specifics of how Photoshop manages color until Chapter 8. The intervening chapters, which discuss the basic concepts of color correction, will be just as valid no matter what your Photoshop color settings are and no matter what your printing conditions.

Printing Basics

Printing presses come in many shapes, sizes, configurations, and prices. However, there is one unifying thread among all commercial presses, and this feature solves many of the calibration problems.

This happy feature is that the pressman has a great deal of control over how the colors will appear. Granted, he does not have the monstrous range of color correction abilities that we do in Photoshop. Most adjustments on press are relatively minor, though, and the pressman has a good set of tools to make them, either in localized areas or on the job as a whole.

If we make final film for a job and present it, saying, print this to your normal house standards, to Printer A who uses Press X and also to Printer B who uses Press Y, it is hereby guaranteed that the two will produce different-looking results, even if they use the same paper.

If, instead, we have Printer A run the job first, and then show the result to Printer B, Printer B will have little difficulty in coming up with something that looks identical, all by twiddling little dials that control the ink flow on the press. Although B's press conditions and normal ink settings vary from A's, one offset press still behaves basically like another, and it is easy enough to juggle things to match what the client wants. All the printer needs is to have something to look at to match.

Plainly, the best thing to try to match is a sample that has been printed elsewhere from the same film. This is called a *press proof,* and if this were a perfect world we would have one for every job we print. However, an initial press proof costs hundreds of dollars.

The less expensive substitute that we need, however, has to have the characteristics (and the limitations) of a printed piece. Imagine, for instance, telling a pressman to try to match the color of a sample of the picture pulled from a color copier, or from a cheap dye-sublimation printer.

That would never work, because these three devices don't behave in the same way. The color copier can probably print brighter oranges than either of the others. The dye-sublimation printer probably has the best blues of the three. The press, for its part, will have much better-looking pastel colors.

Contract Proofs

Nobody can match the unmatchable, so printing companies quite rightly refuse to accept work under these circumstances. They insist on a proof that is designed to emulate the conditions on press. Historically this has been a combined, laminated color proof that has been generated from the final film, using a process that tries to compensate for dot gain. These proofs are frequently referred to offhandedly as matchprints, but were I to use this term so generically my publisher would shortly be hearing from lawyers for Imation Corp., whose trademark it is. Matchprint, then, is the leading brand of such "contract proofs," which take around half an hour apiece to make and cost around $100 for a standard page, more for larger sizes.

Such film-based contract proofs are universally accepted as a substitute for press proofs, although they are far from infallible. The two images in Figure 2.2 look identical on the contract proof. I am betting that neither the printer of this book nor any other printer on this planet can make the two match, given the layout of the page.

The two images are made with different quantities of black in relation to the CMY inks. For reasons amplified in the discussion of GCR in Chapter 7, the colors are theoretically identical—provided that the ink balances on the press are normal. My prediction is that the presence of so much black ink surrounding the pictures will make it impossible for the press crew to control color balance and that the image on the bottom will seem heavier. Was I right?

Most commercial printers will also accept digital contract proofs, in which fields the names of Iris, Kodak, DuPont, and Imation are the most prominent. These are professional devices and carry professional prices, but in recent years desktop inkjet printers have gotten so much better that a few can print something that can serve as a contract proof. Provided, of course, that you know how to calibrate; that you know how to manage color.

To summarize the typical production scenario: we start by creating attractive color pictures using Photoshop. If we are professionals, we do not trust the colors on the monitor as much as the numbers reported by the Info palette. If the numbers say $52^C45^M45^Y15^K$ that is a gray even if the monitor displays it as chartreuse.

We then, in all probability, import our Photoshop result into a page makeup file, likely into QuarkXPress or Adobe PageMaker. To make sure all of our positionings and croppings are correct, we send a copy to a laser printer or a composite color printer. Once satisfied, we go to our imagesetter (or to a service bureau, if we don't have the resources to buy an imagesetter) and get film, from which a Matchprint or equivalent contract proof can be made. Alternatively, if we are using a direct-to-plate process, some kind of digital proof will be made. If we like it, we sign off, and if not, it's back to Photoshop.

That was a pretty hasty summary. Now let's take the scenic route through the whole process, paying special attention to what are profitable targets for calibration or other color management techniques.

Black and White Printing

Black and white is the simplest form of printing, and to start the tour, we'll simplify it further by limiting the discussion to pages containing type only, no pictures.

In the old days of hot-metal typesetting and letterpress printing, proofreaders were paid a great deal of money because they had a unique skill. They had to be able to read type *backwards*. Since the type set in the Linotype machines of those days was actually mounted on press, and this type was what made direct contact with the

Figure 2.2 These two images appear identical on the contract proof, but probably not here. They have different balances of black ink to CMY. The heavy inking in the background presumably throws the normal numbers off enough to make the two look different.

printed sheet, it had to be the mirror image of what the desired final product was. As we say in the graphic arts, it had to be *wrong-reading*.

Nowadays, proofreaders read type the way the rest of us do, if a bit more carefully, but the concept of right-reading and wrong-reading still is important. At virtually every stage of the process, the orientation of the job flips. Why is it that proofreaders now have an easy job compared to their predecessors?

In the letterpress days, the type became part of the printing plate. Today, the plate is either imaged directly from a digital file or made by photographic contact with the final film of the job. This final film may or may not be made by contact from some type of preliminary film. This, in turn, may or may not be a successor to a lot of smaller pieces of film that were stripped together by hand. The type that is responsible for the whole mess may have been output either on film or on paper, in which case it was photographed or scanned onto film.

You may now do some mental gymnastics and reach the conclusion that since the final page must be right-reading, the plate has to be wrong-reading. That means that the film that makes the plate has to be right-reading, and the preliminary film that makes the film that makes the plate must be wrong-reading, and so on down the pecking order.

That analysis is clever, but faulty. In offset printing, the plate never hits the paper. Instead, the plate, which is made of anodized aluminum, is wrapped around a press cylinder that spins at high speeds. It is continuously drenched with a combination of black ink from one direction and water from another. The dark areas of the plate, which represent the type, attract the ink more than the water and the light areas do the opposite. As it rotates, the plate cylinder makes contact with another cylinder of the same size. The second cylinder is covered by a layer of rubber known as a *blanket*. It is the second cylinder, the blanket cylinder, that contacts the paper.

Naturally, as the plate cylinder turns, a mirror copy of its contents is deposited (or *offset*, get it?) onto the rubber blanket. The blanket must be wrong-reading because it is the final thing that contacts the paper, so the plate, contrary to our previous analysis, must be right-reading, so the final film must be wrong-reading, so the intermediate film must be right-reading.

Generally, therefore, printers ask for film to be wrong-reading, except for those printers who use some intermediate process between film and plate (for example, making several copies of the film for simultaneous printing), and need it right-reading.

This terminology gets iffy when dealing with film, which unlike paper, metal type, an aluminum plate, or a rubber blanket, can be read when it is upside down. A wrong-reading piece of film becomes right-reading by the simple expedient of turning it over. When a professional calls a negative *wrong-reading,* other professionals assume that this means with the business side of the film facing the viewer. The business side, or emulsion, is where the imagesetter does its work; the other side is called the base. The emulsion side gives better results for duplication, so when we make one set of film from another by photographic contacting, their emulsions should face one another (we call this *E to E* contacting) and the orientation reverses.

If, in handling a negative, you have any doubts as to which is the emulsion side, it is normally the side that looks duller, but the infallible way of telling is to take a razor blade and scratch the film in a nonprinting area. On the emulsion side, the scratch will remove the black coating, but on the base side, it will not.

Professionals indulge in a lot of technically loose talk among themselves, such as calling cyan *blue* and magenta *red,* and using the ambiguous term *wrong-reading* to describe the type of negative most printers want. A better term is *down negative* (meaning, it reads correctly with the emulsion down, as opposed to an *up* negative). Best of all is the unambiguous (if somewhat lengthy) RRED, for Right-Reading with Emulsion Down. I strongly suggest you use the terms RRED and RREU.

The Screening Pattern

Type is usually easy for the printer, since it prints in solid black. Photographs, which need a larger range of tones, are a complication. We want grays, but have no gray ink to work with: only black ink and white paper.

This problem has been around for a long time, and the solution always has taken pretty much the same form. If you examine George Washington on a dollar bill, you can see an old but workable technique. We sense depth and realism in Washington's face because we perceive several levels of gray in it. Upon closer inspection, this perception is provoked by black lines of variable thickness, small enough that we do not notice without looking for them.

Nowadays we tend to use a predefined pattern of dots of various sizes rather than lines. We could use something else, randomly spaced tiny black frogs if we wanted, but the principle is always the same. If the black objects are small enough, viewers can be fooled into thinking they are seeing gray.

For the time being, assume that we use a conventional *screening* method: a pattern of black dots that vary in size but are a uniform distance apart. The logical way of describing this would be in terms of the number of dots per inch, but for obscure reasons, people say *lines* per inch. The values traditionally used in printing are 65, 85, 100, 120, 133, 150, and 175. Since screening is done digitally today, there is nothing to stop us from using some other number, but there are good practical reasons not to.

Turning Off the Problem

Most users will have better luck with the Photoshop 5 upgrade if they turn color management off altogether. This is a several-step operation. If you would like to have Photoshop 5 behave more or less like Photoshop 4, first open Photoshop 4. Go to File: Color Settings>Monitor Setup>Save (you pick a name). Now quit, open Photoshop 5, and make the following changes in File: Color Settings, which has four suboptions.

Under RGB Setup
- Load the file you saved from the Photoshop 4 Monitor Setup. If no such settings are available, choose "Monitor RGB."

Under CMYK Setup
- Under Ink Options>Dot Gain, enter .65 times the number you are accustomed to working with in Photoshop 4, or use the following more accurate formula: Photoshop 5 dot gain = $PS4dg - 3 - (.3 \times (40 - PS4dg))$.
- Change Separation Options to match their Photoshop 4 equivalents, or use the settings suggested in Chapter 8: Light GCR, 85% black ink limit.

Under Grayscale Setup
- Change Grayscale Behavior from "RGB" to "Black Ink" if your destination is print; leave it at "RGB" if it's the Web, a film recorder, or other RGB device.

Under Profile Setup
- Uncheck "Embed Profiles" for all four options.
- Change all Assumed Profiles to "None."
- Under Profile Mismatch Handling, change all to "Ask When Opening."

Suppose that we are using 150. This means that each dot would be a maximum size of .0066 by .0066 inches, and in an area where the dots were actually this large, the ink would be solid, with no differentiation between dots. The opposite of this condition would be no dot at all, so that only the blank paper is visible. At these extremes, there will be no detail whatsoever, just pure white or black. Therefore, we almost never have any use for either of them.

The size of the dots we use is defined as a percentage of the largest possible. An Info palette reading of 50 percent indicates that the final dot will fill half of the space that it would if we were printing solid black.

Photoshop does not know, however, what that space is going to be, as the screening value is determined in the next step.

From Photoshop or, more commonly, from some other application, we now arrange to have an imagesetter or platesetter set our dots. It is at this point that we specify screen ruling, and it is now that serious calibration must begin.

The Info palette told us that our dot was 50 percent. The 50 percent will carry through as an instruction to the imagesetter. Digital files don't deteriorate, so this one will also say 50 percent tomorrow.

Imagesetters, however, are fractious beasts. The laser beams with which they write are subject to voltage fluctuations and change over time. The processors that develop their film must be maintained carefully. Variations in age and temperature of chemicals and in processing speed affect the density of the image.

Similarly, if film stripping or duplication is involved, a lot of things can go wrong. The duplication takes place in a vacuum frame, where final film is exposed through a high-intensity light source shining through the intermediate film. Once again, changes in light intensity, vacuum, length of exposure, and processing conditions will annihilate any hope of getting the same result the next day.

For these reasons, image-setting and stripping companies go to great lengths to keep tabs on these factors. By

Why Not an RGB Press?

One of the more puzzling questions for the graphic arts student is, given the apparent superiority of the RGB colorspace, and given that the human eye is believed to perceive red, green, and blue as the primary colors, why don't printers use RGB (or even RGBK) inks rather than CMYK?

Well, mainly, if you only have red, green, and blue inks on your press, how are you going to print a yellow? An orange?

Red, green, and blue light is what our eyes react to. The ink on paper is merely used to manipulate it. We use magenta, for example, because it governs the amount of green light that reflects from the page. The more magenta, the less green light. Meanwhile, magenta has little to no impact on red or blue light, reflecting substantially all of it back to our eyes.

Thus, each process color is used to control one primary. The problem with using red as an ink is that it controls *two*. Red ink would block out both blue and green light. Using such inks would make it impossible to reproduce colors that are formed when only one flavor of light is absent. One perceives yellow when red and green light reflects from the printed page. If all of our inks blocked two of the three colors, we'd be out of business.

In short, we use CMY inks because they can be used to form R, G, or B, whereas R, G, and B would not be able to form C, M, or Y.

and large they succeed in making their product repeatable and predictable.

From here on, however, chaos reigns. Even though we are still talking about black and white, we have reached the point where there is going to be enormous variation no matter what.

Paper and Dot Gain

Next to the question of whether the pressman is in a surly mood that day or is feeling mellow, the biggest variable is the paper that the image will be printed on. To get an idea of how big a deal this is, consider printing an image on newsprint, which is the worst paper in common use, versus printing it on the coated stock of this book.

There is a much smaller range of colors to work with. Newsprint is yellowish-gray, so whites cannot be as crisp as we would like. Nor, perhaps surprisingly, can blacks be as black: newsprint is porous, and the ink seeps into it. The book paper's coating resists this intrusion. We see more ink, and thus a richer black.

Much the same thing happens every morning when I go through my normal routine of spilling part of my cup of coffee on a copy of the *New York Times.* Most of the coffee gets absorbed by the newsprint. If I spilled the same amount of coffee on a page of this book, less would be absorbed. More important, the stained area would look smaller: as the newspaper absorbs coffee, the stain appears to spread.

It works the same way with ink. In the case of the *Times,* 65 little cups of coffee per inch are being spilled wherever a picture appears. Coffee spreads. So does ink. When coffee spreads, we just see an ugly stain. When ink spreads, we see a darker gray than we ought to.

This phenomenon, *dot gain,* happens on every press and every paper. Obviously, though, it happens to a greater extent in poorer-quality papers. It is also influenced by the speed of the press, the brand and color of ink, how tightly the blankets are mounted on the cylinder, the type of imagesetter that produced the final film, how heavily the pressman is running the ink, when the press was last washed, and how humid a day it is, among other things.

If you are thinking that it is impossible to predict with any precision how much dot gain there is going to be, you are exactly right. Certainly, images prepared for use on book paper would be unacceptable if we tried to print them in a newspaper, but there are huge differences even among newspapers. *USA Today* has greater dot gain than the *Times,* which in turn has more than the *Wall Street Journal.* Your local paper is probably drastically different from any of the three.

Color Printing

Thanks largely to Photoshop, newspapers as well as the rest of the printed world are moving rapidly toward more color. Of course, adding color compounds the difficulties of predictability.

Just as black and white printing takes place without any gray ink, color printing does not employ a tutti-frutti technology that magically produces any hue. Instead, images are reproduced using four separate hits of ink on four different units of the press. There is complete agreement throughout the graphic arts industry that the four basic colors should be cyan, magenta, yellow, and black, although some devices are starting to use additional colorants. There is no agreement as to what order to print the inks in, and, as you might expect, the order makes a considerable difference. Some printers think black should go down first, because there is less of it, so the sheet will not be as wet when it goes into the second unit. Others feel that the first, second, and third inks will inevitably work their way into the subsequent units, contaminating those inks. They therefore favor yellow first, because it is the lightest ink and the contamination would be less noticeable, and black last.

Last, but certainly not least, of the many reasons that it is not possible to make generalized calibrations at the printing stage, *it is entirely normal, appropriate and correct for different units of the same press to have slightly different dot gains.* Generally, black ink has the highest dot gain and yellow the lowest, but press conditions can skew these even more.

Now that it has been established that presswork is very much a give-'em-what-we've-got-and-hope-for-the-best kind of process, the question becomes one of getting the printer something that can be matched. That does not mean an exact prediction of press conditions. As we have seen, that is impossible. What it does mean is that contract proofs have to be somewhere in the neighborhood of what the press can print.

To start with, if the contract proof is on a paper that is much whiter than the stock that will actually be used, forget about a match. A match is also impossible if there is a radical difference in dot gain from the contract proof to the press.

Accordingly, the manufacturers of contract proofs generally have six or more different methods: they can produce proofs that emulate low, medium, or heavy dot

gain, and they can be made on white stock for commercial work or slightly off-white to predict publication results.

If all this seems horribly confusing, it is. I've had more requests to write about dot gain than any other topic. We'll revisit it in Chapters 7 and 8.

Three Types of Calibration

It's fairly obvious that the pressroom situation is one of these things that is not particularly desirable but that we have to live with. To start the discussion, I invite you to say *why* the situation is bad. We are going to have to cover many different devices, including human beings. And the word *calibration* to mean the process of making things look alike is much too loose. We need some sub-definitions, to find out when this nebulous thing is really necessary. Let me offer the following.

Standardization, for present purposes, means bringing the device, whatever it is, up to commonly accepted professional norms, so that it behaves more or less like other devices of its class.

Repeatability means the capability of the device to behave exactly the same way tomorrow that it does today.

Color management is the process of passing files between different devices but cleverly altering them in such a way that the colors match as closely on both as circumstances permit.

Not all these things are achievable, which is no surprise. Not all are desirable, which may be. Let's consider how these concepts relate to four very different devices: a press, an imagesetter, a monitor—and a photographer.

First, standardization. Four different devices, and four different answers. Believe it or not, the press is the one that needs the least standardization. As long as we don't do things like put red ink in the magenta printing unit, it doesn't really matter if the particular press performs exactly like others. If it doesn't, we take care of that through color management.

There is a lot more of a case to be made for standardizing a photographer. An eccentric style of photography is much more apt to be a *bad* style than eccentric press settings are.

It's fairly important to have a standardized monitor, and it's extremely important to have a standardized imagesetter.

Is that the way you would have scored these four? Let's turn to repeatability. Is it important that a job turn out exactly the same if we do it a month from now as today? It would seem so, but again there is an exception. Why is it necessary for a *photographer* to be repeatable? Similar shots taken in similar scenes under similar lighting don't have to be identical. There is much less reason for repeatability in photography than in the other three devices.

How about color management? It's convenient to have it between monitor and press, even though with experience one can get by correcting color on a black and white screen. As a practical matter, we *don't* need it between monitor and imagesetter. Photoshop does let us color-manage this part of the process through transfer curves embedded in EPS files, but why bother? All these concepts interrelate. Imagesetters are easy to standardize and easy to keep repeatable. If properly maintained, there's no reason for us to pay attention to them.

The dangers of unthinking calibrationism are largely two: failure to understand where calibration is necessary, and insistence on implementing it where it is not. I would like to discuss now some of the more notable failures of calibrationist concepts in recent years, and offer some explanations of why the conventional wisdom of the day turned out to be incorrect.

Applied Calibrationism

Although presses are not capable of the same repeatability as an imagesetter, printers realize that they have to try to do the best they can. This is why every reputable commercial print shop includes color control bars somewhere on each press form. The idea is to measure them to verify that ink densities don't vary too much from the house standard.

Similarly, most applications capable of printing in color will automatically generate such control patches, and some service bureaus actually look at them to make sure that the film is imaged to the proper density. This is a sensible step, not so much because the imagesetter's voltages vary from hour to hour, but because the efficacy of the developing chemistry does.

How strange it is, then, that some of the people who are most vociferous about the necessity of spending hours and hours calibrating—er, standardizing—their monitors, often with hardware extras costing over a thousand dollars, fail to see the necessity for *repeatability*. Monitor performance, like that of an imagesetter, varies from day to day. Plus, monitors are susceptible to accidental twirling of dials, changes in lighting conditions, and/or changing of software setups.

Sensible people, therefore, check their monitors frequently. In production environments, once a shift isn't excessive. This doesn't have to be a hugely time-consuming procedure. All you need is a printed sample of a file that you know the monitor is supposed to match, more or less. Every shift, you open that file, compare it to the print, and if it no longer matches, find out why, and fix as necessary.

I cannot tell you the number of establishments I have visited where some guru has purportedly calibrated the monitors—and then left them unchecked for six months or more.

This is stupidity, more than calibrationism. The more responsible calibrationists wouldn't tolerate this. But it does hold a lesson about how far people can be gulled into trusting what they perceive to be technology.

A better example is an extension of what we were discussing earlier. Treating a photographer as a piece of equipment, I suggested we need to standardize him to some extent but that repeatability was not a big issue. Now, how about color management?

I certainly say there is no need to color-manage a photographer, but there are those who never saw a device they didn't want to calibrate. And so, in the early nineties, the idea was broached that something needed to be done to compensate for the specific film used in the photograph. Fuji products, for example, tend to have a cooler appearance than their Kodak counterparts. By color management, we can correct for this. If we know the kind of film, we can alter the file so that it would resemble something shot with exactly the same exposure conditions but with a different brand of film.

Several vendors, sold on this logic, began to incorporate methods of compensating for the film. You can see a relic of it in Photoshop, when you open a Kodak Photo CD image. Several input profiles specify a particular kind of film.

To say that this idea flopped would be an understatement. The images actually looked *worse* than before, and the better the photographer, the worse the results.

How can this be? Can you give the technical explanation that eluded, and thus befuddled, the calibrationists?

I can, and I need not resort to jargon to do so. You can't pile one color management system on top of another. Those who advocated this system did not realize that color management was *already going on.*

Color management does not become something else just because no fancy hardware or algorithms are involved. Consider the following.

Most of my work appears in magazines and books. Printing conditions in the two are similar. Suppose that, beginning with an RGB file, I have to prepare an image for use in a newspaper instead. Images darken up in a newspaper. I therefore must compensate by providing a lighter original than I normally would. I can do so in at least three different ways:

• I can handle the work exactly as if it were for a magazine, except applying curves to make it somewhat lighter, relying on my experience to tell me how far to go.

• Before converting to CMYK, I can enter a higher dot gain number in Photoshop 5's Edit: Color Settings > CMYK Setup box. Photoshop responds by giving a lighter separation, and by changing the monitor preview so that a CMYK image *looks* darker than before.

• I can do everything as though it were for a magazine, and rely on something outside of Photoshop to lighten the file to make it more suitable for newsprint. Today, it's virtually certain that that something else would be a pair of *ICC profiles.*

ICC stands for International Color Consortium, a group set up to formulate such standards. A *profile* is a description of how we expect a given device to behave. Most people don't realize that this highfalutin word can apply just as well to non-ICC compliant color management.

In the second approach above, nobody calls it a profile, but that's in fact what it is. It's a change in Photoshop's profile of the CMYK colorspace. And in the first example, the presence of the profile may not be obvious, but it's there nevertheless: the profile was in my head, and I altered the file to accord with it.

Can you magine the disaster that would result if, due to some kind of confusion, two, or even all three, of these methods were applied all at once? If the newspaper decided to lighten my files on the supposition that people don't realize that newspaper printing is too dark, little thinking that I had lightened my file already?

The same thing that happened when people tried to color-manage photographers, that's what. The result looked absurd, because nobody realized that color management was already going on. Many professional photographers, to the shock of the calibrationists, have some vague awareness of the characteristics of the film in their camera—they have a mental profile of it, in other words—and they alter their shooting technique to compensate for it.

This same problem derailed the most cherished tenet of calibrationist theory: the notion that one can color-correct successfully based on the appearance of a monitor, rather than the traditional method of going by the numbers.

The Two Measuring Devices

Back to the puzzler of Figure 2.1. Are those two greens the same, or not? If you and I have different opinions, how are we to decide which one of us is right?

In disputes like this, it's helpful to have a referee, some agreed-upon party who can render an impartial decision.

There are a number of artificial color-measuring devices—densitometers, spectrophotometers, colorimeters—that could be of assistance. These powerful machines have been around for about 50 years. They cost $1,000 and up and, if well maintained, last a decade or so.

The problem is, every such device that I have ever tested in similar situations has shown an alarming defect. They all report incorrectly that the two greens are the same color.

I know for a fact that the greens are not the same, because I have referred the matter to some more sophisticated color measuring devices. These devices work under a much broader range of viewing conditions, are considerably more expensive, have a longer mean time between failures, have been conditioned by about ten million years of evolution, and have the unique ability of evaluating colors in context. These devices uniformly report that the two greens are different, which, for me, makes it so.

The superior measurement device is, obviously, the human visual system. Many of the failures of calibrationism are due to an inability to understand how superior it is—so perhaps we should analyze how it stacks up next to the competition, in terms of our three definitions.

A standardized human being is a vastly superior color measuring device to anything artificial and, for that matter, to any other animal. There is somewhat more variation in the ability of specific models of the human device than one would like, but the best representatives of the species outperform the best machines in every significant way.

Repeatability, however, is a different story. There, the machines have us beat. They may make flawed decisions, but the decisions will be flawed in exactly the same way tomorrow as today.

Translation: the machines are very good at making sure our processes *stay* standardized, once we reach that happy point.

But in helping us get there, they are hopelessly bad—which does not stop calibrationists from advocating their use in this illogical fashion.

In trying to reconcile two disparate devices, there are a couple of ways to go, at least. One is to ask each device to image something along the lines of Figure 2.3. Then, reserve a few hours to measure each individual patch of color with a densitometer, run it through some kind of software that compares the two and splits the difference, and generate a couple of profiles.

This type of calibrationism has spawned several software packages that create

Figure 2.3 *A typical image of color patches used to create device profiles with the aid of densitometry.*

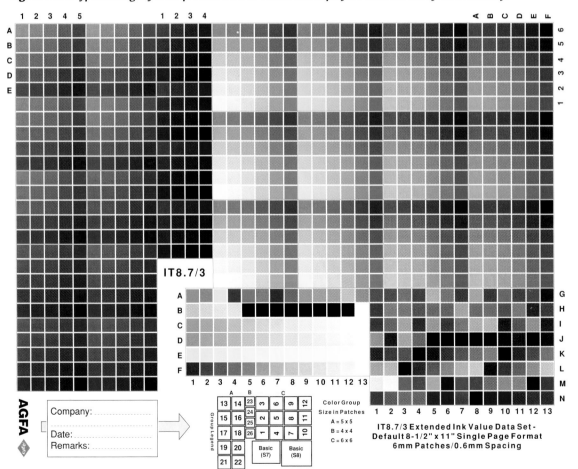

profiles based on a series of such measurements. A couple of magazines have run comparisons of images created using the resulting profiles. Although some of the results were reasonable others were very bad—so bad that some of my friends who happen to be color-blind could identify the objectionable colors.

The other method is to pull a few pictures from each device and see whether they look alike. If not, adjust.

The second method is much faster. As it happens, it also yields higher quality. When the two devices are fairly close in terms of what colors they can produce—as are, for example, positive film and a high-quality monitor—almost any calibration method will work. When they are very different, as printing conditions are from a monitor, the human measuring device has a decided advantage because of its peculiar ability to evaluate colors in context and thus, decide whether two things look alike.

In Figure 2.4, we have two color swatches. To a densitometer, that's all they would be, two different colors, match 'em if you can. To Photoshop's Info palette, one is $10^C40^M10^Y$ and the other $10^C40^M50^Y$. Again, two colors.

$10^C40^M10^Y$, as it happens, is the color of bubble gum, but of very little else. $10^C40^M50^Y$, as it happens, is a typical flesh-tone value for Caucasians.

These two colors are not of equal importance, folks. In deciding whether two devices match one another, one is vastly more significant. A human color manager grasps this without too much difficulty.

An even more important argument for human intervention in the profiling process is suggested by Figure 2.5. In color correction, as we will see in the next chapter, the biggest gain comes from using a full range of tones. In principle, that would mean everything from zero to 100% of every ink, but in practice that isn't possible, particularly in the shadows. No, the question is, at what point does our press (or whatever) fail to hold detail? Every device has such a fail point, where the image simply gets too dark to be decipherable. Knowing where it is is critical to effective reproduction. This is an example of a determination a densitometer can't make. And yet, you and I can easily decide which of the four versions of Figure 2.5 are acceptable and which can't be handled effectively by the production process of this book.

That Extra Color Management

In analyzing the difference between a human and an artificial device, we forgot to mention the third factor. A human brings to bear one of the most sophisticated color management schemes imaginable.

That scheme accounts for our perception that the two greens of Figure 2.1 are different, as well as for our rejection of color casts in the ambient lighting. Much of what we discussed in Chapter 1 pertained to how to make our printed images look as if the color management of the human device had been applied to them.

We can turn off many of Photoshop's color management capabilities if we like. Those of the human visual system are another story. This is why we frequently see mistakes like the top half of Figure 2.6 in print.

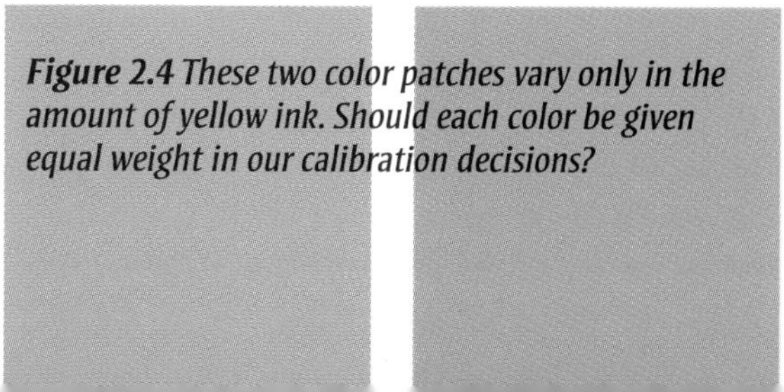

Figure 2.4 *These two color patches vary only in the amount of yellow ink. Should each color be given equal weight in our calibration decisions?*

Figure 2.5 An important calibration question: how heavy can ink coverage be before the press fails to hold detail? Which of these images do you think are too dark for the press conditions of this book?

The obvious defects are a failure to hold detail in the highlight, plus a green cast pervading the bridal gown. When professionals see this type of image, they immediately suspect that the person who produced it trusted the monitor.

Not that we couldn't compare these two images side by side on a screen and see the difference. But if we are looking at the top one alone (which is much more likely) it becomes much harder to distinguish what's wrong with it, thanks to our built-in color management system.

In print, we see the cast because the printed image reflects the light that hits it. Our vision has already adjusted, or calibrated, itself to this ambient light, which we have corrected to neutral. By comparison, the green cast becomes obvious.

If, on the other hand, we are staring at the image on a monitor, the light is coming from the image itself, and we calibrate to *that.* The more we look at it, the more neutral the color seems to become, and the more apt we are to say the color is OK.

Scientists do not know exactly why and how this effect takes place. Either the eyes physically adjust to the lighting conditions, or the brain filters the data to satisfy its preconceived notion of what is gray. Or perhaps the two work in tandem. One way

or another, the phenomenon is known as *chromatic adaptation.* It is well documented. The first scientific papers on it date back to the 1850s.

Similarly, we adjust to bright lights by narrowing our pupils, making ourselves more sensitive to dark colors, and less to variation in brights. And so we don't see on screen the loss of highlight detail that is so evident on the printed page.

Hardened calibrationists react to these problems by saying the monitor must not have been good enough, that its color management must have somehow fallen short. But really the problem is merely another case of how piling one color management system on top of another can't work. Rather than blaming the monitor, they should blame God, for His irritating design of a self-calibrating human visual system.

The Profile Approach

Michael Kieran, a color expert, caused a little stir during a lecture tour in mid-1998. He passed out CDs of stock photos and invited the audience to select an image at random. He then proceeded to color correct it with great success—after first "calibrating" his monitor by turning the color off altogether, and only restoring the color when he was done applying his curves.

Indeed, one *should* be able to correct in this way, without too much difficulty. In fact, one who corrects by the numbers on a black and white monitor will easily do better than one who relies only on the screen.

Although certain prepress establishments have been known to intentionally keep monitors out of calibration to prevent retouchers from doing this, there isn't a need for such a doctrinaire approach. By all means, calibrate the screen—just don't rely on it for highlights, shadows, or neutral colors. That is why we have an Info palette.

But there is more to life than neutral colors. Once you have verified that what you perceive to be a neutral color is also perceived that way by the Info palette, you can then trust the monitor to be reasonably accurate with respect to other, non-neutral, colors. Here's what I said in the first edition of this book:

> Today's monitors do quite a good job in emulating most colors, and if you are reasonably careful you can trust your screen about the greens of plants, the reds of autumn, and so forth. The technology falls flat, however, in light or dark areas, where it is impossible to tell whether the value is acceptable for printing. It falls even flatter, along the lines of a pancake that has been run over by a steamroller, in portraying neutral grays.

> This last problem is not going to go away. As previously discussed, our visual systems tend to reject color casts and to see what we expect to be gray *as* gray, regardless of ambient lighting conditions. What this means is, before laying out a small fortune on some system that purports to make your monitor a precise predictor of what will

happen on press, ask yourself whether all that expensive subtlety is really necessary, considering it is incontrovertible that when you stare at a monitor, your color perception changes. If you stare at a screen that is showing approximately gray, it will become *absolutely* gray for you very shortly.

I quote this at length because it is a stolidly mainstream view today, whereas four years ago calibrationists considered it sacrilege. The idea of a total reliance on screen appearance without referring to any numbers is now, as far as I can tell, dead, victim of an assumption that a perfect monitor could be built, victim of a reality that the monitor itself was not the problem.

I still think that it's basically a waste to spend thousands of dollars on hardware calibrators and the like. It *does* make sense to spend a certain amount of time to get the monitor approximately correct. There is no room here for a chapter on how to do so, but here are three quick tips:

• The most important, and most underrated, factor in color correction is setting the dark point. The same goes for a screen. Users commonly have their monitors set wide open, so that a black on the monitor appears much richer and darker than it would on the printed page. When this is so, the images on the screen will have a lot more bite, and the printed equivalent will seem disappointingly flat.

• As Figure 2.1 reminds us, our perception of color is changed radically by the character of neighboring colors. Yet many users set the backgrounds of their monitor to some loud color or pattern, rather than the sensible gray. Anyone who professes a belief in calibrated monitors and yet keeps the background in such a

state is like the doctor who smokes three packs of cigarettes a day.

• To reiterate a point made earlier, monitors change from day to day, and it is imperative to check them frequently.

Each and every one of the above common-sense practices is vastly more important than the use of expensive calibration hardware. Yet a number of people who preach calibration ignore them.

The Dustbin of History

In retrospect, it's easy to say that those who advocated total reliance on the monitor should have known better. And yet, virtually every trade magazine was hyping it five years ago, along with many experts.

Even though it wasn't a solution in search of a problem (it would surely be nice if we didn't have to take the trouble to learn the by-the-numbers approach), the idea never had a chance, because as a matter of pure science it could not be made to work. And so, it failed. That is not the reason that all calibrationist ideas fail; before leaving the topic, let's consider a few other notable casualties:

• Calibrating scanning to a photographer's film. Like total reliance on the monitor, it didn't and couldn't work, because of perfectly obvious common-sense considerations. Unlike it, a complete SSP—the character of the film has never been perceived as posing difficulties in scanning.

• Stochastic screening. The idea was, instead of having the regular dot pattern of screen ruling that has been standard for nearly a century, we should print with much

Figure 2.6 Because of the self-adjusting nature of human vision, it's difficult to see the problems in the top version of this image on any monitor, however well calibrated.

smaller dots, arranged in a seemingly random pattern. Thus, printed images would give the illusion of continuous tone, just like an original photograph.

This is an SSP—few people can easily tell the difference between a 175-line screen and stochastic. Unlike the other examples, this one actually could work—provided that the printer took a lot more care with it than with the typical job. For a lot of technical reasons, especially dot gain, stochastic screens are difficult to print with. And so, despite all the attention, stochastic screening failed, just as anyone with common sense could have predicted. The only place it hangs on is in certain coarse-screen applications, such as newspapers, where it is *not* an SSP.

• The idea of scanning all images to exactly the same settings, forcefully advocated by Kodak in the early 1990s, the idea being to capture all possible detail and to match the photographer's intent. This naïve approach flopped because Kodak did not realize that in real life, nobody wants to match the art, and in real life, nobody cares whether the scanner is theoretically capable of capturing data that the photographer did not happen to supply.

• The idea that persons who need to have files prepared for more than one purpose, for, say, a newspaper ad, an annual report, and the Web, should use a single master file which would be magically massaged by computer in such a way that the three properly configured files would emerge from it, phoenix-like. Each output has different sharpening requirements, and different balances between color and contrast. So, a rough equality of all three images is possible, but it would always be the equality of mediocrity. The calibra-tionists seemed to be making the argu-ment that it's better to have equal quality on all devices than satisfactory quality on any of them. The market did not buy into this.

• The "RGB workflow," the calibrationist idea that all other colorspaces would disappear, that corrections would all be done in RGB, that CMYK was poison, and that separations would be done on the fly by software in the output device. Didn't work, couldn't work, because as we will see at some length in Chapter 8, it's simply impossible to design software that separates well enough. Without the capability to do *some* correcting in CMYK after the conversion, the color is not going to be as good as it can be. For some users, that's a fair price to pay for slightly increased efficiency, but for the vast majority it is not. And so, as nearly as I can tell, in spite of all the assertions that CMYK is for cave men and that I am a dinosaur, many more people correct in CMYK now than when the first edition of this book appeared.

Déjà Vu All Over Again

The theory of the new color handling capabilities of Photoshop 5—that is, the incorporation of ICC profiles as a default—is not as silly as most of those past revolutions. It's a relic of the one-file-for-all-purposes approach discussed above, but there is no particular need for it to be used in such a questionable fashion. For certain users, it offers certain benefits.

The basic idea is that each file is tagged with a profile that gives information about the conditions the operators had in mind when they prepared it. Then, if conditions unexpectedly change down the line, that profile can be compared to a profile of the new use, and the file altered to compensate.

Thus, an image intended to be used for commercial printing could automatically be repurposed for a newspaper if need be.

An attractive thought, no? Let's give its advocates a few moments to defend it.

Different devices handle color differently. And that explains why, without ICC profiles, the image on your monitor bears little resemblance to your original, which looks nothing like your printed proof, let alone a few thousand offset copies.

ICC profiles fix this problem by understanding the way a device sees color and recording that understanding. Profiles are then used to transform the image, ensuring high-quality, matching output. All of which means, you're able to judge color earlier and more reliably, reducing the need for expensive prints and proofs.

Best of all, profiles provide better color automatically. All you need is an ICC profile for each of your color output devices and an application that supports ICC profiles....

I will confess to having altered the above slightly. I substituted the acronym *ICC* for every appearance of the word *EfiColor.* Other than that, it's word for word, exactly as it originally appeared in 1990.

Will this implementation catch on where EfiColor did not? I doubt it. There's too little to gain, too much to lose. It's great for certain users, chiefly those who have to process large numbers of images and need good but not great quality. For almost everyone else, it's an SSP.

In comparison to the failed ideas of the past, this one most closely resembles stochastic screening. Both, unlike most of the others, theoretically work. Both are,

however, very difficult to work *with,* and open up the possibility of jobs looking worse than if they had been prepared by total amateurs. In stochastic screening, this happens if somebody doesn't appreciate the necessity of assuming a greater dot gain; in profiling, it happens if at some point in the process an incorrect profile is applied.

As for this, time will tell. For me, I've turned it all off just for safety's sake and because I'd like Photoshop 5 to work the same way past versions have.

There's no reason for *you* to do this, unless you agree with this rationale. If you work in the manner suggested in the following chapters, you can even use Photoshop's default profiles, although you have to take care that nobody else uses them on your files in a counterproductive way.

But if nobody else screws up your file, profiling won't do it of its own volition. The default on CMYK files has changed (details are in Chapter 8) but it does not involve ICC profiles. A particularly foolish default profile is used for RGB files, but unless you are planning to do serious color work in RGB this will make little difference, and anyway, it's easy to change.

If It Won't Work, It Won't Sell

If it seems like there is a lot of inertia in the industry, there is. But there are good reasons in this case. If the old-fashioned methods of correcting by the numbers are more widely accepted now than a few years ago, it's because they happen to work—which is exactly what you might expect.

They work because they date from a time when computers were inconceivably slower and more expensive than they are today. Think back to a time—just over ten years ago, actually—when hard drives cost

COLOR MANAGEMENT AND CALIBRATIONISM

✓Calibration and repeatability are laudable goals, but one has to examine the entire process to see where they are appropriate. Certain parts can and should be made repeatable, certain other parts should, but cannot be, and certain others can be, but should not.

✓There is great variation between print characteristics of different presses or even different units of the same press. Print quality is also influenced by tens of other factors that can change rapidly. Therefore, presswork is by far the most unpredictable part of the entire process.

✓Printers adjust their presses on each job to try to match a client-supplied high-quality proof. There is no such thing as just running a file. They will generally not accept a job without such a contract proof, which needs to be approximately correct for dot gain and for whiteness of stock.

✓Contract proofs aren't infallible. The layout of a certain page may make it impossible for the printer to match the proof.

✓The human visual system has its own powerful system of color management. A color changes appearance if there is a change in neighboring colors. This ability to see colors in context is not shared by artificial devices. Humans are, consequently, much better than machines at deciding whether two images look alike.

✓Human vision is self-calibrating in that it neutralizes any color imbalance in the ambient lighting. Unfortunately, this neutralization effect also occurs when staring at a monitor. Because of this, some color casts that would be obvious in print can't be detected on the screen—or at least, people can't detect them.

✓The word *profile* is used to denote the assumptions we work with as to the characteristics of our output device. The profile can be very formal, as in the ICC-compatible profiling that is an option in Photoshop 5, semi-formal, as in Photoshop's built-in separation, or completely informal, as in the case of a photographer who varies shooting technique depending on the type of film in her camera.

✓If you are panicked by color management, relax. Many expert opinions have been proven wrong in the past. If you understand the basic principles, it won't matter what version of Photoshop you use or how you choose to manage color.

almost a thousand times as much as they do now, and when a workstation as powerful as, say, a 486 or a pre-PowerPC Macintosh cost half a million dollars. You can understand that an RGB workflow would have been *extremely* attractive in that age, because RGB files are only three-quarters as large as their CMYK counterparts, and all mathematical operations take three-quarters as long.

The RGB workflow therefore would certainly have been adopted—if only it had worked! It didn't, so it wasn't.

As I hope this chapter has indicated, I *do* believe fairly strongly in calibration. But I do not make a religion of it; I insist that science and mathematics be my servants and not my master; when I see an image that looks lousy I say so even if a machine says it looks good. And so, I am not a calibrationist, but I am a color manager.

Who *is* a calibrationist, then? It used to be easy to spot them. They were the ones who thought that the idea was to make as close of a literal match to the original as possible. But those Neanderthals are gone. Today's calibrationist is much tougher to identify. A couple of years ago, I tried to clarify the matter with the following:

Data, data everywhere, and not a thought to think!...Calibrationists tend to have just enough of an academic background to convince themselves that their theories are valid and should be implemented by the world at large, yet not enough to realize what constitutes building on scientific quicksand... In the most extreme incarnations, calibrationists would rather have predictable scans than good ones; rather

have a good-looking histogram than a good-looking image; rather have how something looks aesthetically be decided by densitometer than by human observer; and, where there are several output devices, rather have equal color on all of them than acceptable color on any.

Admittedly, this isn't that precise a definition either. Perhaps I will just have to echo Justice Stewart, and say that I know the calibrationism when I see it.

With that, we leave the topic in favor of a survey of the proven techniques of color correction. Master those, and this diatribe will almost be irrelevant. You'll be able to work with or without ICC profiles, in any colorspace you like, on a black and white monitor if you wish, without proofing if need be.

Some of the concepts are difficult (as indeed are some of those in this chapter). But even as your eyes begin to glaze over, make sure your mind doesn't go into neutral. Fuzzy thinking, you will remember, is the hallmark of the calibrationist, not the successful color manager.

And so, if someone offers you what seems like a plausible scientific argument, like, say, offering to trot out a densitometer to measure whether the two greens of Figure 2.1 are the same, take a deep breath and think it over. If you allow yourself to be buffaloed by technology into believing things that your own eyes and intelligence can tell you are false, if you believe those two greens to be the same even though you and every other human perceive them as different—well, then, beware. Tomorrow's calibrationist could be *you*.

CHAPTER 3

Color Correction
By the Numbers

When looking at an image for the first time, we often see what we perceive to be many small problems. Normally, they are all part of a bigger problem, which can be solved all at once with a single application of Photoshop's most powerful tool, curves.

Monkeying around with the color balance of photographic images is not a sport for the timid, or so goes the conventional wisdom. Believing this, people go through the most simian sorts of shenanigans trying to make their color look believable. They select this area, sharpen that one, call up histograms of the image, apply strange filters, and generally try to demonstrate that if an infinite number of art directors employ an infinite number of digital tweaks somebody somewhere may throw them a banana.

And yet, ninety percent of color correction could be handled by monkeys. That ninety percent, using a strict numerical approach with little room for artistic judgment, is what this chapter is all about. To console the creative, in the next chapter we will pick up the nine percent gained by intelligent image analysis. The final one percent comes only from practice and is beyond the purview of this book.

The rules for this ninety percent of color are so simple that they can be stated in one sentence.

Use the full range of available tones every time, and don't give the viewers any colors that they will know better than to believe.

To see how this deceptively simple concept works in practice, here is an imaginary problem that may at first seem ridiculous. Figure 3.1 is the black and white image of me that used to grace my magazine column. The question is, supposing the unsupposable, that it were in color, how would the rules apply? What would be our objectives in correcting it?

At this point you may say, how can we possibly know what a black and white image should look like in color, any more than we know how colors would look to us if we were Martians?

That attitude assumes that we know nothing about the colors of this image. Actually, we know quite a bit. True, we have no idea what color my tie should be, but what about my hair? As you can see, I don't use Grecian Formula. What color hair do you think I have, green?

Similarly, we have no clue as to what color my jacket is, but men in business attire usually wear shirts that are either white or some distinct other color, not some muddy combination. Here, it appears to be a *white* shirt.

And, though my skin is dark, there are limits to the range of normal skin tones.

These considerations are very typical. The giveaways of problems in color reproduction are almost always fleshtones and neutral colors—grays and whites.

A General Approach to Correction

If we are to use the full range of available tones, we must find the whitest and darkest areas of the image, and make them as light and as dark as we can, given our paper and printing process. Many pictures are complex enough that we must mosey around quite a bit to find these endpoints. Here,

though, the lightest point is evidently somewhere in my collar, and the darkest is in the stripes of my tie.

At this juncture, we make a decision about how strictly we will adhere to our general guidelines on highlight and shadow. This decision depends on how significant we believe the particular endpoints are to the overall picture. In the case at hand, I would say that preserving detail in the white shirt is important, so we should try to stick with a conservative highlight, but I am not particularly enamored of holding detail in the stripes of the tie, so I would not go to excruciating lengths to stay within normal shadow range.

All that remains is to enforce our numerical decisions by means of curves. Since there are both neutral colors in this picture (the hair and the shirt) and

Figure 3.1 *This image is in black and white, but we can make generalizations about how we would treat it if it were in color.*

fleshtones, we must check, before applying the curves, that these colors stick to certain standards, which I am about to discuss.

Throughout the next two chapters, I will be assuming that the images begin in CMYK and that this is the colorspace we will correct in. This is for simplicity's sake. If, for the time being, you absolutely must use RGB, you can, by clicking on the eyedropper icon in the right side of the Info palette, display RGB and CMYK equivalents simultaneously. But if you do this, you are a sissy. Sooner or later you *will* correct in CMYK—why not now?

The standards change depending upon printing conditions. This isn't as tricky as it sounds. The production of this book is a typical example. As I put it together, I don't know who the printer will be, although I know it will be printed on coated paper on a web press. There are good and bad printers in this world. If we know we are going to be favored with one of the former variety, we can cheat a little. We can go with a darker shadow, suspecting that the superior printer will be able to hold detail in an area that his low-quality counterpart would not.

In my current situation, God knows whether the printer will be competent, but I, regrettably, do not. I must take a least-common-denominator approach and expect the worst while hoping for the best. I will, therefore, now and for the remainder of the book, assume magazine printing conditions. The numbers used throughout will reflect this.

The Magic Numbers

As a first step, we must force the image to meet four numerical requirements. Three of these cater to the most illogical feature of CMYK: the weakness of cyan ink.

In RGB, a neutral gray, regardless of how dark it is, has equal values of red, green, and blue. One might suppose that the same would be true in CMY, but it isn't. Magenta and yellow must be equal, true, but cyan has to be higher. If not, the gray will actually print somewhat reddish, because the cyan ink is supposed to absorb red light, and it does a lousy job of it.

Correction by the numbers is the foundation on which all quality rests. The fact that further improvement is possible beyond merely setting numbers is why this book has more than 300 pages. Be that as it may, those whose basic numbers aren't correct condemn themselves to third-rate color, regardless of their Photoshop skills. A numbers-conscious monkey could do better; a color-blind person could do better.

In the first edition of this book, I backed this provocative statement up by actually training a color-blind person to color-correct. His work was impressive, better than that of many students with perfect color vision but the wrong mentality.

The point having been made, I see no reason to repeat those images here, but Figure 3.2, which didn't appear because it was one of his failures, is a fitting way to start the discussion. Although it is a failure, it is also a success in a way, due to his adherence to the following numerical rules.

• The **shadow** is the darkest significant neutral area of an image. Well over 99 percent of images have *something* we can use for a shadow. Figure 3.3 is the exception.

In principle, the shadow should be set to the heaviest value we believe that the press can hold with detail. Thus, for high-quality commercial printing, the shadow value should be higher than for this book, which in turn should be higher than for a

Figure 3.2 *The bottom version is a "correction" of the original, top. It was executed by a color-blind person, and it looks it. But this was a skilled person, who works by the numbers. Can you figure out how he went astray?*

newspaper. If unsure, use what I'm using here: $80^C70^M70^Y70^K$. One or more of these numbers can be higher in a deep color. Navy blue, for instance, might be $95^C65^M15^Y50^K$.

Many printing applications put a set limit on the sum of all four inks, the better to allow ink to dry. The better the printing condition, the higher the allowable number. SWOP, the industry-standard Specifications for Web Offset Publications, mandates a maximum of 300, which most magazines tweak down to 280. My suggestion, $80^C70^M70^Y70^K$, sums to 290, close enough.

290 is not close enough, however, when preparing images for a newspaper, which is apt to ask for 240, or even for some desktop dye-sublimation printers. If a lower number is necessary, we reduce the CMY colors and increase black in roughly equal amounts. $70^C60^M60^Y80^K$ would therefore also be an acceptable shadow.

People don't have good color perception in areas this dark, so, if need be, we can take liberties with one or two of the ink values. Don't do this without a good reason, though. An unbalanced shadow often is a symptom of a color cast that may be subtly hurting other parts of the image.

• The **highlight** is the lightest significant part of the image, with two qualifications. First, it cannot be a reflection or a light source. These things are called *speculars,* or *catchlights,* and we ignore them. Second, it must be something that we are willing to represent to the viewer as being *white.* Assuming that all these requirements are met, use a value of $5^C2^M2^Y$.

Other experts suggest different things. They may tell you $4^C2^M2^Y$, $3^C1^M1^Y$, $5^C3^M3^Y$, or $6^C3^M3^Y$. But everyone agrees that magenta and yellow should be equal, and cyan a couple of points higher. There is such universal agreement because this highlight value is critical. Humans are quite sensitive to light colors, so a variation of two points in any ink could result in an unacceptable color cast.

Doubt the impact of an incorrect highlight? Then return to Figure 3.2. The "correction" by Ralph Viola, the color-blind person, has a lot to be said for it, as by-the-numbers corrections always do. There seems to be more depth, more snap, than in the top version. But the color is wrong.

That problem developed when Ralph was setting his highlight. He knew enough not to use the top of the wine glass: that's a reflection. He was looking for something very light, yet nonreflective, and *white*. And he thought that the label of the wine bottle *was* white, because he can't see yellow. So he arranged to set a highlight in the label, *making* it white. This created a blue cast throughout the lighter half of the image. Darker objects are not affected as much. The wine bottle isn't that bad. But the wood is now gray.

Those with normal color vision have no trouble detecting that the label shouldn't be white. A lot of people, though, fall into the same kind of trap when the off-color isn't quite as obvious.

Figure 3.2 really doesn't have a highlight, or at least not a highlight in all three CMY inks. You might say that there is two-thirds of a highlight in the label. We know it's yellow. We don't know *how* yellow. But we do know that cyan and magenta should be at a minimum. So, you might say that in this image we can set a highlight of $5^C2^M?^Y$.

Figure 3.3 certainly has a full highlight. Either the lightest area of the clouds or of the statue will do. Either one is definitely

Figure 3.3 *This image has no shadow at all, no point that can be considered to be a dark gray or black. Such images are rare—try to locate another one!*

white. But how about Figure 3.4? The obvious light area is the letters on the sign. No doubt these were white when they were freshly painted, but are they really white today? I don't think so, at least not in the sense that a marble statue or a cloud is white. I think we use the phrase *yellowed with age* for a reason. Force these letters to become a pure white, and you'll create the same blue cast Ralph did in Figure 3.2.

• For an area that is supposed to appear **neutral,** that is, white, black, or any shade

Figure 3.4 *The classic highlight settings assume a highlight that is not only light but white. In Figure 3.3, it's reasonable to assume that the statue and the brightest area of the clouds are, in fact, white. Here, the lettering of the sign is light—but can we guarantee whiteness?*

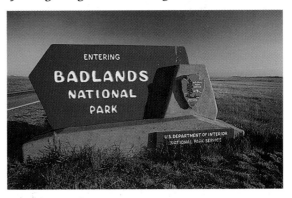

of gray, the magenta and yellow values should be equal and the cyan higher. How *much* higher is an open question; two or three points ought to do it in the highlights, six or seven in the midtones, nine or ten in the shadows.

If there is a problem meeting this requirement, it is better to be too heavy in the cyan than either of the other colors, since bluish grays are less obtrusive than greenish or reddish ones.

Figure 3.3 offers some interesting reminders about neutrality. It tempts some people to set a highlight in the statue and then forget the rest of it. The statue has to be neutral not just in its lightest point, but throughout. The dark folds also need to be measured, and neutralized if need be. Compare that with the clouds. Those should be white at their lightest point, agreed, but they're in the middle of a very blue sky, and I don't know that they need to stay neutral as they get darker.

- **Fleshtones** should have at least as much yellow as magenta, and up to 50 percent more in extreme cases. Where the yellow is equal to or only slightly higher than the magenta, this implies a very light-skinned person, such as a small child or a blonde. For Caucasians, the cyan value should be a fifth to a third as heavy as the magenta, depending upon how bronzed a person is. For a dark-skinned person like myself, $15^C50^M70^Y$ will do; lighter-skinned people can go $8^C35^M40^Y$ or even lower.

Finding a typical fleshtone value is easy enough with experience, but if you haven't tried it before, there are some snares to avoid. Measure only areas that are in normal lighting, not a shadow or a semi-reflection. Also, avoid any area where an individual might be wearing makeup,

especially the cheeks of a woman. You may wish to make a small selection of what seems like an appropriate area, use Filter: Blur>Gaussian Blur at a high value to make the selection take on a uniform color, and then measure that before cancelling the blur.

Except in persons of African descent, it is not customary to have any black ink in a normal fleshtone, but it sometimes happens, particularly if we are using nonstandard GCR settings (see Chapter 7 for more on this). If there *is* black in the fleshtone, count it as additional cyan, because it does the same thing: it pushes the fleshtone away from red and toward gray.

Writing Curves: A First Step

To start, we open up the image and check the ink values, using the Info palette, in the highlight and shadow areas, plus the areas of known colors—in this case, the shirt, the face, and the hair. Before doing this, click on the Photoshop eyedropper tool, and set the sampling to 3×3 rather than the default single pixel, which can give a false view of what is going on.

In simple pictures, we can keep these numbers straight in our heads, but as they get more complex, writing down the density values and what we propose to do with them can be helpful. To the extent the image does not meet our target numbers, we apply curves to force it closer to them.

To do so, open Image: Modify>Curves. Ignore the default curve. We never use it because it affects all four channels in the same way, and it is impossible that this could be right in CMYK. Go directly into the individual colors. To agree with professional practice and with the examples in this book, please set shadows to the right and highlights to the left. This is done, if necessary, by clicking on the light-to-dark bar at the bottom of the curves panel.

The horizontal axis of the curve represents the original values of the image. The vertical axis is the values the curve will cause the image to take, when we click OK.

The default curve is not a curve at all, but a straight line at a 45° angle. If we decide that we are going to change it (and we may well decide to leave it alone) we can keep it a straight line by changing one or both of the endpoints. Normally, though, we insert one or more intermediate points and adjust them up and down. If we do so, the straight line will become a curve.

If the entire new curve falls below the original 45°, the corrected image will be lighter than the original. If it falls above the default, the new image will be darker. Most of the time, we will want to write curves that fit neither description, but that make some parts of the image darker and others lighter.

Parts of such a curve will wind up being steeper than 45°, and, to compensate, other parts will have to become flatter. When the curve is applied, areas that fall in its steeper parts will gain contrast, and objects located in the flatter parts will, sad to say, lose out.

To locate highlight and shadow, I personally prefer to run the cursor over several likely areas and watch the Info palette. This lets me choose the second-lightest area as a highlight, if I decide that the real lightest area isn't important to the image.

If you are uncomfortable with this, you can open Image: Adjust>Threshold and, with the Preview option checked, move its slider until it becomes obvious where the light and dark points are.

In the imaginary color image of me, suppose that we measure the lightest area of the white shirt and discover that it is $12^C 10^M 18^Y$. Measurements of the stripes of the tie find $70^C 65^M 85^Y 50^K$.

We start by adding two points to each curve. In the case of cyan, we want what is now 12^C to become 5^C, since we are shooting for a highlight of $5^C 2^M 2^Y$. We will also insert a point that brings 70^C up to 80^C. Similarly, we adjust each of the other colors so that we hit the targets for highlight and shadow.

Before clicking OK in the Curves dialog box, we run our selection tool across the neutral areas of the picture. The Info palette will now tell us both what the values are currently and what they will become after the curve is applied. Ideally, the neutral areas will be truly neutral (i.e., equal magenta and yellow and slightly more cyan); if not, we will have to make further adjustments to the curves.

If a major amount of work went into these curves, we should take advantage of the Save option in the Curves dialog box before doing anything else. If we do this and then decide that a slight modification is necessary (or, heaven forfend, if we make some big mistake and are forced to File: Revert to the last saved version of the image) we can cancel the changes we made, then reopen the Curves dialog box and choose the Load option to reinstate the curves. Or, we can save the curves within an Adjustment Layer, which will allow us to change the curves later even if there are other intermediate changes, such as airbrushing and/or cloning.

That is really all there is to color correction, and if you truly understand curves, you know how they can eliminate color casts, increase contrast, and make the image more lifelike, all at once, without any local correction, without using any esoteric program functions.

So much for theory. Let's roll up our sleeves and correct some color.

Many Birds with One Curve

As we have seen, it can be awkward if there is no obvious highlight or shadow. Figure 3.5 has no such problem: the original has plenty of choices for each.

There are four reasonable guesses for highlight: the top of the small truck in the foreground, the street signs, the jacket worn by the woman in the lower left, and the trailer at the extreme left. The unreasonable guesses would be the reflections on the cars, which are catchlights, and the sky, which we can't guarantee is white.

Measuring all four of these likely suspects, the street signs turn out to be much darker than the other three, so they're out. The truck is typically $3^C3^M7^Y$, the jacket

Figure 3.5 Concrete buildings are normally neither pink nor blue. By forcing them to become neutral with curves, and by proper adjustment of highlight and shadow, the original, top, gets transformed into the image at bottom.

$5^C4^M4^Y$, and the trailer $6^C8^M8^Y$. So much for the trailer, which is slightly darker in all three colors. Our choices are to set a white highlight either in the truck (in which case the jacket is slightly blue) or in the jacket (in which case the truck is slightly yellow). The second alternative seems more logical.

This shows how sensitive we are to variations in light colors. There's very little difference in the two values—but doesn't that truck look yellower than the jacket?

At $5^C4^M4^Y$, the highlight is pretty good to start with. The shadow is another story.

The choices appear to be the tires of various cars, the windows in the darkest area of the building under construction, and the body of the black car at lower right.

You may well ask how I know that the car is *black* and not navy blue. If I set a navy blue car as a neutral shadow, the picture will turn yellow, just as the picture turned blue when Ralph thought a yellow label was neutral.

The answer is, I *don't* know just by looking at it. But I do know that tires are black, not navy blue. So, whether this car is darker or lighter than the tires, if it is a black car there will be the same relation of the CMY colors as there is in the tires. If it's a blue car, the yellow value will be much lower.

Figure 3.6 *The basic tools of curvewriting. Background, below: using the Threshold command to identify the shadow of the image. Top left: establishing sample points in highlight, shadow, and the two buildings at the sides of the image. Top right, the final curves used in Figure 3.5.*

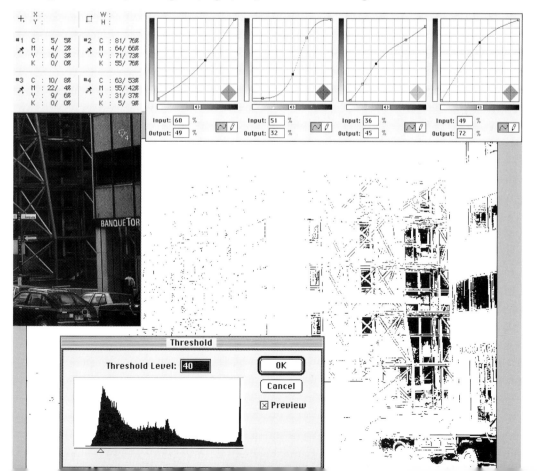

Upon investigation, this car turns out to be black. It's also darker than the tires or the windows, which makes it the shadow. But its values aren't good shadow numbers at all: $89^C69^M55^Y47^K$. That is, in fact, about halfway to navy blue. As the tires are halfway to navy blue as well, we know this is a cast, and not a real color. There is too much cyan, not enough yellow: this is a blue shadow.

There are still two more things to find out about this image before we start writing curves. One of them, fleshtones, we don't have to worry about, because there aren't any. But how about neutral colors? It's true that there's nothing that has to be a pure gray in the sense that my hair, or the statue of Figure 3.3, have to be. But there are things in this picture that should be *close* to gray: the street itself, and the buildings at left and right. Are they?

Not hardly. The street is $51^C45^M11^Y$—very blue. The light building at left is $21^C30^M8^Y$, midway between blue and magenta. And the right-hand building is $62^C53^M29^Y5^K$, blue, but not quite as blue as the street.

If this were the old days, now would be a good time to look for the scanner operator, with the objective of shoving this image down his throat. Regrettably, such remedial action is no longer possible. Fortunately, we can compensate for this inadequate art. Photoshop 5 adds a feature that makes doing so by the numbers a lot easier.

Figure 3.7 *In Figure 3.5, the cast was obviously undesirable. That isn't always the case. Is the blue cast above an aesthetic choice, or should we balance the image as at bottom?*

By clicking on the eyedropper tool in the toolbox and changing it to the sampling tool, we can expand the Info palette so that it shows the color values from each of up to four fixed spots in the image, as shown in Figure 3.6. With something as complex as this street scene, this is a big help. I'd plant a point in the highlight, one in the shadow, and the other two in the buildings at the sides of the image.

Incidentally, at this point, one can turn the monitor to grayscale. It is all monkey work from here on in. Now that we have a general read of the picture, we can color-correct in black and white just as easily—and the screen display refreshes ever so much faster.

Whether you are willing to take that particular plunge or not, it's pretty clear what has to happen here.

The cyan is a point or two too low in the highlight. In the light building, it's maybe OK, but in the street and the dark building, it's too heavy, and in the shadow it's seven points too high.

The magenta is the major headache. It's one point too high in the highlight, way too high throughout the quarter- to midtone range, but three points too *low* in the shadow.

The yellow needs a big boost, especially in its quartertone, so as to neutralize the street and the buildings. A bigger boost there, in fact, than in the shadow, where it's 13 points too low.

And the black is simplest of all. It's too weak. We need to bring 47ᴷ up to 70ᴷ.

The curves that do these things are shown in Figure 3.6. The improvement speaks for itself, but I'd like to make two points.

First, notice how much better the color of the scaffolding, and of the reddish building itself, are. And yet, no attention was paid to these objects, or even to other objects of approximately that color. This is very characteristic of this method of correction. If the basic colors are right the others fall into place, as if by magic.

Second, try doing this with Levels.

The Intent of the Photographer

At this point, you may throw up your hands in disgust and ask why photographers never get it right. Actually, they do. The incredible human optical system is what causes problems.

Everybody knows that when we are in a darkened room, our eyes adjust to the environment and become more sensitive. When somebody turns the light on suddenly, it dazzles us.

Not everybody realizes that the same thing takes place in color perception. Our brains want to reference everything to a neutral environment, so when we are flooded with light of one color we compensate by making our eyes less sensitive to it—all unconsciously.

The quick summary of what just happened is that we corrected the image to

Figure 3.8 The curves used to create the bottom version of Figure 3.7.

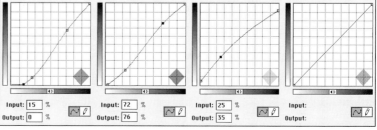

| Input: 15 % | Input: 72 % | Input: 25 % | Input: |
| Output: 0 % | Output: 76 % | Output: 35 % | Output: |

Figure 3.9 This type of the image has no neutral colors other than the highlight and the shadow. This allows more flexibility in correction than was the case, say, in Figure 3.5.

be what human observers would have seen had they been where the camera was. Humans ignore color casts. Cameras don't. We found a cast, so we deep-sixed it. Obviously, that is not "matching the art."

Perhaps you can think of a reason why the photographer might have wanted, for artistic reasons, the look of the original of Figure 3.5. I surely can't. Figure 3.7 might be something else again. The blue cast sets mood. I would like to think that the photographer did it on purpose.

But suppose that the decision is made that the cast is incorrect, that we are to do exactly what we did with Figure 3.5.

The analysis works the same way. Highlight? There isn't one. The pants are the lightest nonreflective thing in the image, and they aren't white.

Shadow? Pretty clearly in the black door

to the left. Currently $81^C66^M68^Y68^K$, which isn't bad.

Fleshtones? For sure. A typical value in the woman's arm is $29^C45^M44^Y1^K$. By the standards I set out earlier, this is an illegal value, cyan being twice as high as it should be, and yellow being slightly low.

Neutrals? Yup, virtually everything that's made of stone. The front part of the first step reads in its lightest area $24^C9^M1^Y$, a heavy cyan cast, as if we didn't know.

What to do? That's easy. We have to blow away the cyan that contaminates the highlight. The yellow has to come up sharply in the lighter part of the image, and the magenta come down slightly, so as to get neutral stone. Note that this will also correct the balance between magenta and yellow in the fleshtone. And the black plate appears to be OK as is.

Figure 3.10 *In the correction curve, below, note the dips in the magenta and black plates. This is to reduce the contaminating colors in the trees above.*

So, we now have an interesting blue cast version, and a nice-looking normally lit one. You can take your pick, but there's no need to limit yourself to these two choices. Photoshop allows us to split the

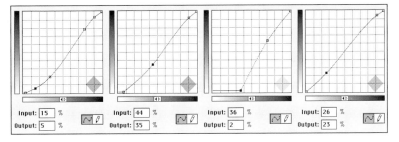

difference any way we like: 90-10, 50–50, whatever.

I am not a professional photographer myself, but I am given to understand by some of my friends who are that this business of shooting something with an intentional subtle cast is not as easy as a simian might think. If I were a photographer, and if I wanted the image to look more like the top half of Figure 3.7, I think I'd deliberately shoot the image too blue. Color-correcting a copy of it by the numbers as in Figure 3.8,

and then blending the two versions together, is a useful safety net to have.

And there is a flip side for the curve-savvy photographer: certain difficult lighting conditions can now be ignored. For example, suppose you are shooting a hockey game. Odds are, you have to shoot through glass, which will donate a slight green cast to the resulting image. For my money, it's a lot easier to apply curves in Photoshop later than to experiment with magenta filters. The results will look better, too, trust me.

You Oughta Be in Pictures

In these first two images, the presence of so many neutral colors and fleshtones compels the use of curves very similar to the ones I've shown. That is to say, the pictures are complicated enough that we are basically handcuffed, forced to use a certain shape of curve and no other.

In the next chapter, we'll talk about what to do when there *is* a choice of shape. Figure 3.9 gives us more room to maneuver

Figure 3.11 *The pink horses below are clearly wrong, but are merely the most obvious of many problems.*

because it has no fleshtones and really nothing neutral either. (In the western United States, roads are not as gray as they are in the east, for reasons I can't explain).

Therefore, there's not much to do here except pick a highlight and a shadow. The highlight might be in the marquee, the sign, or the second large poster. Not in the first poster: even though a large area seems white, it may not be in real life.

In fact, the marquee, at $11^C4^M29^Y$, is the lightest, but all three are ridiculously yellow. The shadow, on the left side of the marquee, verifies the yellow cast that pervades the image, reading $75^C66^M77^Y67^K$.

With only two points to correct, we enjoy unexpected freedom to shape the curves. Therefore, we can start catering to other items on the agenda.

In this case, it seems to me that the trees are not green enough. It's not that they are missing the yellow and cyan that are the dominant colors in any green. Instead, there is too much of the contaminating inks, magenta and black. This is a purely subjective decision, of course. Some of us can read the green values and know immediately that they are too gray, but if you aren't that familiar with the numbers, by all means rely on the screen—if reasonably calibrated—to advise you. The danger of relying on monitor display, as pointed out in Chapter 2, is in neutral colors, and trees aren't neutral.

Assuming you agree that something should be done to liven up the greens, putting dips into the center of the magenta and black curves, as I have done here, seems like the way to go. Such a move would not be possible in the first two exercises, which were full of neutral colors in which the three CMY inks had to interact precisely. But here, all we *have* to do is get the highlights and shadows right. We can do that whether or not we indulge in monkeyshines in the midtone areas of any or all curves. Figure 3.10 is one of many possible solutions.

| Input: 13 % | Input: 24 % | Input: 12 % | Input: 26 % |
| Output: 23 % | Output: 15 % | Output: 21 % | Output: 68 % |

Figure 3.12 *Since magenta starts out too high in the light areas and too light in the darks, the shape of the correction curve is eccentric. Cyan and yellow have to increase in the quartertone to eliminate the pink cast in the horses, while the magenta drops. And the black plate increases drastically throughout.*

Behold a Paler Horse

If you have never seen a purple cow, nor ever hope to see one, you should probably find another field of endeavor. For a final variation on the same old theme, we'll do battle with a purple horse.

In Figure 3.11, we begin by rounding up the usual suspects. Highlight: the forehead of the near horse, $2^C2^M2^Y$. Shadow: blinder of the far horse, $71^C57^M71^Y30^K$. Known colors: the horses obviously should be white, but the readings are $7^C26^M7^Y$, $10^C31^M16^Y$, and $15^C32^M18^Y$. Also, in the background is a Canadian flag that reads $10^C70^M75^Y2^K$, although I happen to know it should have more magenta than yellow. And several of the flags should have neutral white areas as well.

Fixing the color balance here is straightforward. We need to set highlight and shadow and then twist the curves somewhat to make sure that the horses become neutral.

The cyan is slightly too low throughout. We know this because in three nicely neutral areas—the highlight, the shadow, and the horses—the cyan is roughly equal to the yellow, whereas it is

supposed to be a few points higher. Since there is no specular highlight in this image, we can start our correction curve by making 0^C move to 3^C and keeping all other values correspondingly higher.

Rather than increase the cyan shadow directly, we place a point at 13^C and raise *that*. The horses need a bigger boost in cyan than the shadow does, so this should work well.

The yellow's highlight and shadow are OK as is. But we still need to reshape it in the quartertone, because in the horse, it needs to be equal to the magenta, which starts out around 15 points higher.

The magenta behaves peculiarly. It is correct in the highlight, too heavy in the quartertone, and too light thereafter. That sounds more difficult to fix than it actually is. We construct a curve that gives a minimum value of 2^M and is completely flat for a while, meaning that anything that was 9^M or lower will now stabilize at 2^M. It starts its climb slowly, so that 30^M becomes 15^M, and then skyrockets so that the midtones will in fact increase.

And the black plate gets very steep very fast. So, now we have correct highlights and shadows, and neutral horses. That's what Figure 3.12's numbers say, and good numbers usually mean a good picture.

Of Values and Judgments

In the corrections to these four images, we made almost no "artistic" judgments. It was all numbers, numbers, numbers. There was no need even to use a color monitor. And every single change was made to the image as a whole.

In short, once he got the hang of curves, there is absolutely no reason that an orangutan could not get these results. Years of retouching experience, artistic talent, and mathematical aptitude wouldn't hurt him, but they are not really needed.

Notice how these numerical adjustments have the habit of helping areas of the image that we never even thought about. Things like the red scaffolding on the brick building, the cars on the Hollywood road, and the flags behind the horse.

Artists who worry their images to death tend to see such shortcomings immediately and plunge happily and vigorously into a morass of individual moves. They isolate the horses and work on them; they fix up the flags one by one; they tediously darken the harnesses, and after eight hours or so of work they have 12 layers, 18 alpha channels, an 800-megabyte file, and an image that's not nearly as good as what the curvewriting orangutan would have gotten in 35 seconds.

Neutralizing our artistic judgment along with the color casts gave us images that came out much better than the originals—yet not as good as they might have been.

Determining that the horses are more important than the building, or that the statue is more important than the sky, are the kinds of logical decisions that are too difficult for either apes or calibrationists. In the next chapter, we will exploit our superior intellect, and with a combination of good numbers and curves that improve contrast in the critical areas of the image, we'll get the color correction monkey off our backs forever.

COLOR CORRECTION BY THE NUMBERS

✓ For 90 percent of the correction work we face, the rules can be stated in one sentence: Use the full range of available tones every time, and don't give the viewers any colors that they will know better than to believe.

✓ In each uncorrected image, we must find the highlight—the lightest white with detail—if there is one. Also, we must find the darkest area, or shadow. We will use curves to move these areas to the minimum and maximum values we expect to be able to hold detail with on press. Absent specific information to use different numbers, use $5^C2^M2^Y$ for highlight and $80^C70^M70^Y70^K$ for shadow.

✓ In choosing a highlight, speculars, meaning areas that are reflecting light or portraying a light source, should be ignored. Values of zero are acceptable for them. Similarly, dark areas without important detail can be allowed to print heavier than the recommended shadow values.

✓ Most pictures have some colors that are known to the viewer. The known colors are generally either fleshtones or areas that must logically be neutral.

✓ Neutral colors, of which there are plenty in nature, should have equal amounts of magenta and yellow, and slightly more cyan. The amount of black, if any, is irrelevant. As a bluish gray is less offensive than a reddish or greenish one, if you must depart from this, use more cyan.

✓ Photoshop 5's improved curve interface permits placement of up to four fixed measuring points in an image. Using this, we can see how a proposed curve will change values in all the significant areas: highlight, shadow, fleshtone, neutrals.

✓ Except in small children and other very light-skinned persons, yellow is always higher than magenta in fleshtones. Cyan is always at least a fifth of the magenta value. As skin tone gets darker, these imbalances increase. A dark-skinned individual may have a third more yellow than magenta, and cyan a third the strength of the magenta.

✓ Do not be seduced into a local selection of an area where the color is obviously wrong. Whatever is causing the undesirable color is also doing it in the rest of the picture, but it may not be apparent. Applying correction globally will cause overall improvements that you might not anticipate.

Figure 4.1 Below, each row shows the result of a single curve applied to each of the three originals, above. Can you guess the shapes of the three curves that created the three rows?

CHAPTER 4

The Steeper the Curve,
The More the Contrast

Color correction is a give-and-take operation. Once an image uses the entire available colorspace, there can be no gain in one area without sacrifices in another. Every improvement thus has a price. Fortunately, there are some real bargains out there.

C olor correction is like life. We are forever having to make decisions involving allocation of scarce resources. I have eight hours free during which I would like to improve my skills; should I spend it making sure I understand every feature of a program I already know pretty well, or should I learn a new one? I have a couple thousand dollars available to spend on hardware: should I buy a disk drive, more RAM, a portable viewing booth, or a new CPU?

Tough calls like this are what put the fun in color correction and distinguish the successful artist from the calibrationist.

As we saw in the last chapter, there *are* some free lunches available. There, we avoided being shortchanged by making sure we used the full available tonal space, every time. And we adjusted curves so that colors that were supposed to be neutral got that way.

Those moves were unconditionally positive. They improved things at no cost to any aspect of the image. Best of all, very little judgment was called for.

Once there is a full range in an image, however, we pay a price for any further moves. Sometimes the price is too high, but it is sometimes astonishingly cheap. To be an adequate color technician one need only grasp numbers. To be good at it one must be a bargain hunter.

To illustrate, we will use the same rules as last time. In correcting, local selection is not permitted. Neither is the use of any retouching tool. All moves must affect the image as a whole. The colorspace will be exclusively CMYK, and all corrections will be accomplished by means of curves.

As Long As It Catches Mice

In Spanish, there is a saying that goes, in the nighttime every cat is a gray one. Entirely too many computer artists amend this to say that all cats are gray as long as the highlight and shadow are correct. If that was your impression after reading Chapter 3, consider Figure 4.1.

The top row is the original version of each of three felines. I have preadjusted each to have a good highlight and shadow,

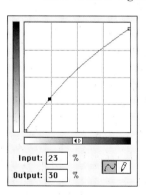

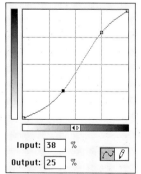

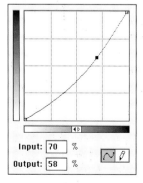

Figure 4.2 The three curves that created the alternate rows of Figure 4.1. Left, second row; Bottom left; third row; Bottom right, bottom row.

which for black and white work on this kind of paper is 2^K and 90^K, respectively. (If you are wondering why this shadow sounds a bit higher than its color equivalent of $80^C 70^M 70^Y 70^K$, it's because with four inks in play it's harder to see detail in such areas, and in CMYK there is often an arbitrary limit of 300 or less on the sum of the values of all four.)

Each of the other three rows shows what happens when a certain curve is applied to each of the three images. As you can see, the original was not the best possible reproduction of any of the three cats, because in each one of the lower three rows, there is one cat that's better—and two that are worse. I'll show you the three curves that made these rows in a minute. Meanwhile, can you figure out what they must look like?

The images in which we set highlight and shadow in Chapter 3 were all fairly busy, by which I mean they contained several important objects or colors. Many images are like this, but many more are not. Product shots, fashion shots, images of animals, food shots: all generally have just two or three color ranges that are important. The rest is just background.

So it is with Figure 4.1. Each image is about a *cat,* not a background. If the price for improving the cat is making the background lose some detail, so be it. Just as I only have a certain amount of money to spend on computer hardware, I only have a certain amount of contrast to spend on this image. And, in these pictures, I propose to spend it on cats, not backgrounds.

I'm starting the discussion with black and white images because they are simpler: there's no need to worry about how the plates interrelate. Now, let's talk about why setting highlight and shadow works, and how we can extend the principle to bring out more detail in the important areas.

Consider a black and white image in which the highlight value is correct, but the darkest value is only 60ᴷ.

Correcting this invariably creates a staggering improvement. A simple curve that leaves the zero point alone and moves 60ᴷ up to 90ᴷ will not just darken the picture: it will profoundly hike contrast throughout. Every detail will become more pronounced because there are now around a third more tones available. Any two locations in the picture will have more variation between them than before the correction. This variation is what gives an image snap.

This by-the-numbers method is a great start, but it is somewhat wooden. As we saw, it can even be mastered by a color-blind individual. Without such a handicap, the intelligent artist can do better.

Curvewriting boils down to this: the steeper the curve, the more the contrast.

The default curve is a straight line at an angle of 45°. If we change the default in any way, certain areas will become steeper than 45°, and certain others will become flatter. Any objects that fall in the steeper areas will improve. Unfortunately, anything that falls in the flatter areas will get worse.

In our hypothetical example the curve was steeper between 0ᴷ and 60ᴷ—and much flatter between 60ᴷ and 100ᴷ. We don't think about that part, because nothing in the image falls in that range. The correction therefore has nothing to lose. The curve damages an area of the picture that does not exist.

If you accept that, it is only logical to damage areas that *do* exist, but are not important. It is thus possible to trade quality in unimportant parts of the picture for extra mustard in the parts we care about.

A white cat lives in the light end of a curve. A black cat, in the dark end. A gray cat, somewhere in the middle. That's enough information for present purposes, but normally one would like to narrow it down a little and find the exact range. This can be done by running the cursor over the lightest and darkest area of each cat and recording the resulting Info palette numbers. Alternatively, with the curve of a single channel open, we can move across the image while holding down the mouse key. This will generate a circle on the curve that will indicate the value of whatever is currently beneath the cursor.

Granted that the highlight and shadow start out correct, it still is possible to write curves, as Figure 4.2 shows, that are steep where a specific cat is found. Provided, that is, that we agree with what any of these cats would say, which is, anyplace a cat is not is a place unworthy of our attention.

Now, one last question before we look at the curves. Each of these three curves is intended to make a single cat purr, at the expense of the other two. The first part of the question is, which row hosts the two *worst* cats? I assume you agree that it's the second row from the bottom. The gray cat there is great, but the other two are much the worse for wear.

Why are the black and white cats so poor in the row that favors the gray one, even compared to what happened to the white and gray one in the row that favored the black one? (Hint: if you know, you are a long ways toward also knowing why the best retouchers work in CMYK rather than

RGB—but we won't get into that for another few chapters.)

There is a big difference between a single image of three cats, and three images of one cat. If all three cats were in the same picture, we'd be stuck with the original, if its highlight and shadow were correct.

But if even one cat is missing, this opens up space to maneuver. This kind of retouching is much like shopping: it's one thing to know what you'd like to buy, and another to find the money to pay for it. Or, to use a better analogy, it's like horse-trading. To get what you want, you need to find something you're willing to part with.

The curves of Figure 4.2 each get steeper in the region occupied by one particular cat. To pay for it, they get flatter in the tonal ranges of the other two cats, squashing contrast. It would also be possible to write a curve that helped *two* cats at once, paying for it by damaging the third.

And why are the black and white cats hurt so disproportionately badly by the curve that is aimed at improving the gray cat? It's all a matter of range. The gray cat originally had the most variation in its color of any of the three (the white one, by a narrow margin, has the least). Therefore, the area it occupies on the curve is longer, more expensive to correct, requiring more of a sacrifice elsewhere.

High Key and Low Key Images

Discussing black and white at such length in a book about color is not a waste of time. To be successful in CMYK, we have to realize that we are working not with a single color image but with four black and whites. Each one can be treated individually, and yet the four together constitute a family whose relationships must be respected.

Consider an image where the highlight is correct, but the shadow is $70^C 70^M 70^Y 70^K$. This shadow value indicates that there is a red cast, because there isn't enough cyan ink. The cyan value should be 80, not 70. So, we have to fix it.

The obvious way to do so is to grab the 70^C point of the curve and drag it up 10 points. A second way would be to grab the top right point of the curve and move it to the left, preserving the straight line, but making it steeper. And there are many other ways of making 70^C become 80^C, as illustrated in Figure 4.3. Which one should we use?

Figure 4.3 If the objective is to make values that were 70 percent increase to 80 percent, any of these curves will do the job—but they will have very different effects on the image as a whole.

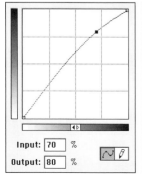
Input: 70 %
Output: 80 %

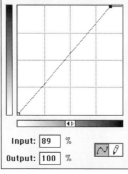
Input: 89 %
Output: 100 %

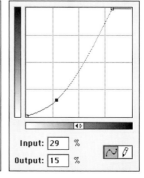
Input: 29 %
Output: 15 %

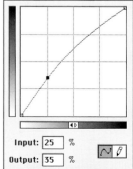
Input: 25 %
Output: 35 %

In real life, it would be unusual to have all of these choices, because we still have to meet the four basic requirements set out in Chapter 3. Namely, we need not only a good highlight and good shadow, but neutral colors where appropriate, and valid fleshtones. If the image has no neutral colors or fleshtones in it, we may be able to use any one of these four curves. But most images are not like that, so the chances are we can forget about two or three of these shapes.

Which may still leave us with a choice.

When a choice exists, we resolve it in favor of the option that makes the important areas of the image fall in steeper areas of the curve. A professional might use the term *keyness* here. The picture of the white cat is a *high key* image, meaning that the important areas are light. The black cat is a *low key* image. As far as I know, there isn't a specific term for the image of the gray cat.

Figure 4.4 is a rare specimen, an image that is high key and low key simultaneously. Everything of importance here is either light or dark—there is nothing in the middle. The correction is obvious: steepen the ends of the curves, flatten the middle in all three CMY colors. In the black, there is no need to bother about steepening the light end. As the circles of color value indicate,

Figure 4.4 *The term* high key *means an image where most important detail is in light areas;* low key *means important darks. This unusual image can be said to be high key and low key simultaneously. The corrected version, below, closes up some of the unused space in the middle in favor of more detail in both highlights and shadows.*

the ice is so light that there's no black in it at all.

Most color images are simultaneously high and low key, but in a far different way.

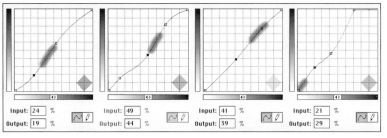

Figure 4.5 *By making the tiger (brown patches on curves) fall in steep areas of at least the CMK curves, detail is enhanced. It also emulates the phenomenon of simultaneous contrast, breaking the animal away from the background.*

| Input: 24 % | Input: 49 % | Input: 41 % | Input: 21 % |
| Output: 19 % | Output: 44 % | Output: 39 % | Output: 29 % |

Consider a picture of a lawn. The lawn is green. CMYK greens are mixes of yellow and cyan. And in the greens of nature, yellow always predominates. In a lawn we would see heavy yellow, semi-heavy cyan, and light magenta.

In other words, the yellow, if it were a black and white image, would be a low key image, whereas the magenta would be high key.

Or, to put it another way, the yellow is a black cat, the magenta is a white cat, and the cyan is a gray cat. The three curves we would use to correct such an image are in principle those of Figure 4.2.

Three different curves for three different cats. That is why we use the individual channels rather than the master curve, because we have already seen what happens when we try to correct all three cats with the same curve.

And while we are discussing why we do things one way and not another, let me bring up why we use curves rather than the Image: Adjust > Levels command.

Levels is nothing more than a curve with only three points: the two endpoints and a point in the exact center. Like curves, it can be applied to each channel individually. Effective moves are possible with it. High key and low key images can be handled well with Levels by moving the midpoint up or down. This isn't quite as accurate as locating the exact point at which the main object of interest ends, and raising or lowering that. In other words, light objects don't just end at 50 percent for our convenience; they are just as likely to pick 42, 37, or the square root of 1,500.

Besides, in certain images *all* of the channels resemble the gray cat.

On to Bigger Game

As color can be seen as a bigger, more complex, and more dangerous relative of black and white, so does Figure 4.5 relate to the kitties of Figure 4.1.

Correcting this image doesn't stop with setting a highlight and a shadow. Here, unlike the images of Chapter 3, we have one obvious object of interest, one object that defines the whole picture. We would like to bring out detail and definition in the tiger, and if that should happen to harm detail elsewhere that is just too bad.

This is done in exactly the same way we handled the cats, except that here we have to do it four different ways, one for each channel. The black channel resembles the white cat. The cyan and magenta channels resemble the gray cat, and the yellow resembles the black cat. Knowing this, if we were sloppy we could actually take the appropriate curves directly out of Figure 4.2, apply them to this image, and see a substantial improvement.

It's much better, however, to measure the exact range of the tiger and be surgical with the curve. The more accurately the curve targets the tiger, the more precise the correction, and the less the undesired impact on the background.

Too many people think that the way to do something like this is to select the tiger and correct it without touching the background. This invariably looks unnatural, regardless of how careful the selection. The curves method is the method of the eye.

This particular exercise is useful in understanding not only color correction, but also human evolution. Figure 2.1 showed how we perceive colors differently depending on what is next to them. Figure 4.5 shows why. Tigers like to prowl in areas

Figure 4.6 The bobcat in the original, top, is obviously the focus of the image. But is the snow important as well? If it is, the middle version preserves it, while extending range of the cat into the shadows. The bottom version sacrifices the snow in favor of an even more detailed animal.

just like this, where their color blends into the background. It was obviously rather useful for our prehistoric ancestors to know whether a certain stream had a tiger in it before going in for a swim.

After all, we don't run as fast as most other animals. We can't smell tigers as well as other animals can. And we certainly don't match up well *mano a mano* with a tiger. Our biggest advantage (other than our hands and our intelligence) is, we see color better than other animals do. And, per Darwin, evolution will enhance the advantages that animals already have. Hence, our unique sense of simultaneous contrast, which enables us to detect such slight variations as a tiger in a yellow stream when there is a yellow bank in the background.

Notice how, in addition to enhancing the tiger, the correction actually changed the color of the water, making it greener. This effect makes the true calibrationist howl as if several tigers were after him: sacrilege! This is not in the original art!! The water didn't change color just because a tiger happened to be in it!!!

But yes. Yes. Read *Origin of Species.* The way the human visual system works, water *does* change color when a tiger wades in. This is the natural equivalent of what I discussed artificially in Figure 2.1. It is also why the bottom half of Figure 4.5 looks so convincing.

Do We Suppress the Snow?

Figure 4.6, yet another feline, is a further variation on the theme of give and take in color correction. In Figure 4.5, most people would agree that the tiger is of such paramount importance that we would be willing to let all lighter and darker objects lose contrast. This time, it's not so clear.

The bobcat's range can be enhanced in exactly the same way the tiger's was. This time, the animal being more neutral than the tiger was, all three CMY channels resemble the gray cat of Figure 4.2. If we apply that shape of curve to the three channels, the bobcat will gain detail—but the snow will lose out. And the delicate detailing of the snow is one of the more interesting features of the image.

So there you have it. The more you are willing to suppress the detailing of the snow, the better the bobcat you can have in return. The more you want to concentrate on the bobcat, the lower you

make the lower point of the bobcat's range on the curve in each color. The more you do this, the flatter the snow will become. Your priorities on how far to go may be different than mine. Almost everyone would think that the middle version of Figure 4.6 is better than the top one. The vote might well split on whether the bottom one is better than the middle. The curves that produced both corrected versions are shown in Figure 4.7.

The successful retoucher is always on the lookout for something to suppress, some means of financing the improvement in the important areas. This means a continual hunt for ranges that are not in use.

As images get more complex, seat-of-the-pants responses have to give way to more careful analysis. Often, horrors, we actually have to take out a piece of paper and start writing down some readings, but the extra time is worth it, because usually we can find some unused color ranges, and when we do, we will mercilessly compress them.

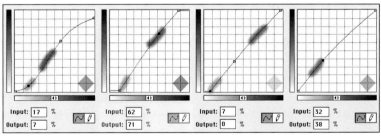
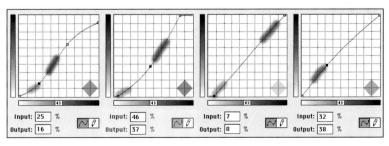

Figure 4.7 The curves that produced the bottom two versions of Figure 4.6. The bobcat's range is highlighted in brown and the snow in gray. Note, in the bottom curve, how much flatter the snow ranges of the magenta and, to a lesser extent, the cyan are. This accounts for a better bobcat—and much poorer snow. Was it worth it?

Figure 4.8 *The original, top, has little happening in the quartertone. The second version horns into this unused space. The third adds a Selective Color move to darken the windows.*

Figure 4.8 is the most difficult correction in this chapter. Because it's a busy picture it resembles more the images of Chapter 3 than the cats we have been working with so far.

If this were a black and white image, the strategy would be fairly clear. The lightest significant areas are the lights themselves, and they don't carry a lot of detail. The second lightest significant area seems to be either the rugs or the column in front of the desk. Whichever, it is much darker than the lights, and therefore, the range we can compress is everything between. Probably, we would treat the lights as specular highlights and blow them out to zero. We could then find the value of the lightest portion of the column, and lower that to about 5 percent. That would certainly steepen the curve.

Unfortunately, this is *not* a black and white image, so this approach won't work. Do you see why?

Figure 4.9 shows the magenta and cyan channels of the color image. In the magenta, the plan works just as outlined above. The lights are still the lightest object, and the columns are the second lightest. So we compress the range between them, not caring even if we take a sledgehammer to detail in the lightest areas.

But in the cyan plate, the second lightest object is not the column, but the red floor. And there, detail is critical because it establishes the grain of the wood. We definitely can't afford to crush the highlight the way we did in the magenta. And the black channel will have a similar problem.

Some quick measurements: the lightest spot in the original image is in the chandelier to the rear. It starts out at $7^C4^M4^Y$, a little high. The darkest point, $66^C77^M73^Y66^K$, is in the shadow beneath the farthest chair. A typical value for the red floor is $17^C94^M100^Y4^K$, and for the column is $30^C33^M53^Y1^K$.

There is no guarantee that the lights themselves should be white. Therefore, there is no particular need to have a balanced highlight. And, as the lights carry no detail to speak of, there should, contrary to usual practice, be no objection to having a zero value in any or all channels.

The shadow value appears to have a red cast, but further investigation is necessary. It *looks* like it should be neutral, but it's in the middle of a red floor, and that could contaminate the readings. It's a good idea to check the chair itself, which should definitely be black, although it's slightly lighter than the shadow itself. And the chair measures $68^C78^M66^Y61^K$—still red. (Reminder: a balanced shadow has roughly equal magenta and yellow, and about 10 points more cyan, with the black being irrelevant.)

For all this picture's complexity, that shadow value is our only restriction, the only one that *has* to be fixed. After all, the other areas that normally concern us don't exist here. There is no highlight, there are no neutral colors, and there is no fleshtone.

Therefore, there is considerable flexibility on how to write the curves. Naturally, we make them steeper in the areas that matter. Here's my approach:

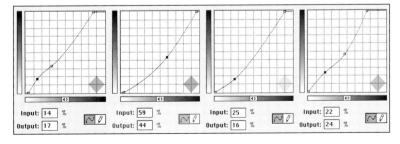

Figure 4.9 Above, the cyan, left, and magenta, right, plates of the original of Figure 4.8. Below, the correction curves that produced the middle version.

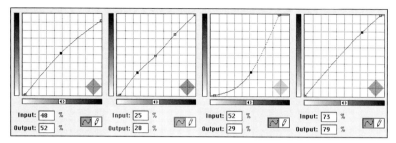

Input:	48	%	Input:	25	%	Input:	52	%	Input:	73	%
Output:	52	%	Output:	28	%	Output:	29	%	Output:	79	%

Figure 4.10 The original image, top right, has a yellowish cast. The porcelain should be more neutral. In correcting it, one tries for steepness in the lighter parts of the curve to enhance detail in the cake. Left, the final curves.

• **Cyan** needs to be strengthened in the shadow, but that doesn't mean just a wooden raise of the curve. Instead, let's emphasize the contrast in the floor, and between the walls and the darker areas of the image. So, since I don't care whether the lights have a dot or not, I make the curve start at the lightest point of the red floor, and raise the light part of the curve to make it steeper. Next comes a relatively flat area, reaching the range of the walls. This helps keep the second half of the cyan curve steep, adding definition in the shadows and breaking the windows away from the interior.

• **Magenta** is more straightforward. With no important detail in the highlights, I wipe them out. The shadow point needs to come down, but that is accomplished by finding the lightest point of the columns, and dragging *it* down until the shadow becomes reasonable. This, of course, makes the entire second half of the curve steeper.

• **Yellow** is such a weak ink that curve-steepening doesn't add much contrast to the image as a whole. Here, there is a modest gain by lightening the center part of the curve, representing the interior of the room, while holding the shadow point constant by moving the top right endpoint of the curve to the left. This last move will cause large parts of the floor to print solid yellow. We can get away with this in the

yellow plate, but it would be a bad idea with any other ink.

• **Black** is handled similarly to the cyan, with a couple of differences. First, there is no need to reduce the highlight, since we don't start with any black in the lights. Second, we really want to have a very steep top half of the curve, because there's detail in the darkest part of the foreground chair that a steep black can help bring out.

The second version definitely beats the first, but you might wish, on artistic grounds, to darken the sky to make the interior seem lighter by comparison. So, using Image: Adjust>Selective Color, I added cyan, magenta, and black to cyan. There is no pretense that this reflects what is in the original image. Omit it if you like.

Time for Some Dessert

Not every image is a candidate for this contrast-building treatment. As we will see in Chapter 6, faces are an example. Build contrast there, and you ruin complexions rapidly. Food shots are a different story, so we'll end with one. Extra color range puts life into a picture and translates, not surprisingly, to more appetizing-looking foods.

In comparison to what we've been working on so far, Figure 4.10 is, er, a piece of cake. Looking at the original for answers to the usual questions, we find as follows:

Highlight: several areas in both teapot and cup are $7^C4^M8^Y$. Certain parts of the

white flower behind it are somewhat lighter, but the highlight should be the lightest *significant* part of the image. In my opinion, retaining detail in the flowers is not important. Do you agree?

Shadow: In the black plate at foreground, $77^C66^M73^Y68^K$. The background is slightly darker than this, but again, the background isn't significant, at least not for me. The plate is.

Neutral colors: Yes. The silver pie server in the foreground should obviously be a shade of gray. However, at the moment it is, in the darkest area, $63^C48^M69^Y10^K$, a greenish yellow.

Fleshtones: none.

Areas we would like to beef up contrast: the cake. Currently it exists in a very short range, which explains why it looks so flat. I measure one of the lighter areas at $18^C20^M55^Y$ and a darker area at $22^C23^M67^Y$.

The things we *have* to do are to reduce and balance the highlight, increase and balance the shadow, and balance the pie server. In every case, these numbers are currently too yellow, but they are especially yellow in the midtone. So much so, that we probably have to raise magenta and cyan at the same time as we lower yellow there.

There is no black in the cake at all, so this doesn't present a problem with the shape of the black curve. As this image doesn't have as much subtle detailing in the shadows as Figure 4.8, we can afford a heavy hand in the black shadow, letting it reach 75^K.

As yellow doesn't add much contrast to an image, the simplest way to correct it is to grab the point at which the yellow cast is the worst, which is right in the middle, and drag it down until both the server and the shadow reach neutral values.

And magenta and cyan are similar. Each has to come up in the midtone and shadow and down in the highlight. Note that I have lightened highlight by moving the lower left endpoint to the right, rather than by choosing a point higher on the curve and bringing it down. This is to preserve steepness in the lightest part of the curve, which is where the saucer, cup, and teapot reside.

When you saw the original image, would you have considered selecting the cake to correct its color?

That problem went away by itself. We paid no attention to it at all. We just set the numbers to what we knew to be correct and everything fell neatly into place. It often does—when we consider the image as a whole and not as a bunch of pieces.

Of Contrast and the Paycheck

In early 1997, I did a lengthy review of various scanner-control packages that try to color-correct without human intervention. On certain images they get striking results. Novices think that this is magic, and in a way they are right. Set highlight and shadow properly, and the image magically looks a lot better. These programs try to identify the highlight and shadow point. If they are successful in doing so, bingo. Some are able to analyze color casts to some extent as well.

The big problem with such packages is that they don't think. They do just about as well as you or I would on images where the overall color balance is reasonable and where the highlight and shadow are easily identifiable. Figure 3.11, on the other hand, was part of my suite of test images, and every program messed it up pretty badly. Most of them made the horses even pinker than they were in the original.

COLOR CORRECTION AS HORSETRADING

✓ If the full range of colors is in use, there will be a price for any further improvement of the image as a whole. We should therefore always be awake to the possibility of a favorable tradeoff, where detail in an unimportant area can be exchanged for contrast in a more vital one.

✓ Any change in the default curve will make some areas steeper than they were before, and others flatter. Objects that fall in the steeper areas of the curve gain contrast; objects that fall in the flatter areas lose contrast.

✓ Applying contrast-intensifying curves globally is easier and faster than selecting parts of the image and working on them locally. Most of the time, the result is also more believable.

✓ Two separate images of two objects would, in this method, be treated entirely differently from a single image in which both objects appeared. Furthermore, the separate images each would look better than the composite.

✓ When we look closely at a certain object, it gains detail, while everything else in our field of vision loses out. The camera, on the other hand, is egalitarian. We are fully justified, therefore, in emphasizing the details that we would like the viewer to focus on, at the expense of those we consider less important.

✓ Before beginning, take an inventory. List all the ranges in each color that fall in important areas. Use it as a guide not only to the areas that deserve extra contrast but to those that can be sacrificed.

✓ Writing curves to increase contrast does not excuse us from the obligation to keep neutral colors neutral and to keep appropriate highlight and shadow values. Before applying the curves, check the Info palette to make sure that none of these requirements is being violated.

✓ The conventional wisdom in color correction is that everything depends on the quality of the original. That can become a self-fulfilling prophecy. With proper attention, decidedly mediocre originals can yield professional results.

✓ Yellow ink adds color balance but is too weak to help detail. Therefore, curve-steepening maneuvers are much more effective in cyan, magenta, and black.

Similarly, images like Figure 4.9, where there's a range of choices of highlight and shadow and finding the right one is critical, are quite difficult for nonhumans. Results like those obtained by the color-blind person in Figure 3.2 are not uncommon.

And in the cake image we just did, an automated program would do a decent, but not excellent job. It would choose the highlight to be the flower and the shadow to be the background. Reasonable enough, and technically accurate, but not as good as picking the lightest and darkest *significant* points, the white and black plates.

This two-chapter series of color corrections demonstrates that there really is a place for the thinking artist. No calibrationist system can hope to equal the work of someone who can make intelligent judgments about which areas of an image need emphasis and which can be sacrificed.

Yet the conventional wisdom still is that the changes we have just seen are impossible. Here is a quotation from a book on halftone reproduction that was published in 1993.

> It cannot be emphasized too strongly that the quality of all photographs reproduced by the halftone process depends entirely on the quality of the original. No printing process, however refined, can compensate for a sloppy original. While a good process technician might well be able to enhance part of an image, it is usually at the expense of a tone elsewhere. For example, if lighter tones are heightened, the blacks could at the same time lose some of their density.

* * *

Right.

Such sanctimonious piffle gets disproven every day. Anybody would prefer to start with the best image possible, but life isn't like that. As we have seen, a lot can be salvaged from second-rate originals.

No question, when we make an improvement, "it is usually at the expense of a tone elsewhere." But the author of these remarks did not grasp that this expense can be quite reasonable, in the hands of a thinking artist. It is quite true that every change suggested in this chapter had a cost. Fortunately, a lot of the time, the price was right.

When we go to the bank to cash our paychecks, the bank does not give us an extra percentage because we happen to be graphic artists. We are given a fixed amount of money, which we then have to allocate to best advantage.

Your spending decision can be entirely different from mine. It all depends on our priorities. If you wish to take a Caribbean vacation this winter, this may mean no meals in fancy restaurants for a while. If you are saving for a child's college education, you may have to skimp on the type of car you drive.

Few people seem to have trouble with this concept, and yet everybody says that color correction is difficult. Go figure.

CHAPTER 5

Plate Blending As Poetry

In strongly colored areas, detail in the weakest ink—the unwanted color—is critical. If you don't have that kind of detail, there's only one thing to do: get it from somewhere else. And understanding the observations of an American poet will help.

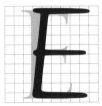mily Dickinson, the 19th-century American poet, was a keen observer of matters of color. She should, in fact, be required reading for many Photoshop theoreticians.

Although not a Photoshop user herself, she was able to put her finger on many an issue that still plagues us. The image at the upper right of this page is a romantic icon, exactly the sort of thing most professionals have to produce over and over again.

Most of the time, that reproduction winds up being—well, I'd better leave the description to Dickinson.

It tried to be a Rose
And failed—and all the Summer laughed.

*   *   *

Since our clients may not be so easily amused, it behooves us to do some technical analysis. I haven't seen the particular flower that Dickinson was referring to, of course. But I can tell you what its problem was. It had a lousy cyan plate, same as the one at the top of this page. Her operator should have blended channels to get a better one.

How can I be so certain? Because that's how it is with red roses, and that's how it is with the majority of brilliant objects. The weakest ink is the key to detail. And to understand why things work that way, one might start with the following:

> *Nature rarer uses Yellow*
> *Than another Hue.*
> *Saves she all of that for Sunsets*
> *Prodigal of Blue.*
> *Spending Scarlet, like a Woman*
> *Yellow she affords*
> *Only scantly and selectly,*
> *Like a Lover's Words.*

*   *   *

This isn't bad poetry, but as color theory it leaves a lot to be desired. The exigencies of rhyme outweighed the facts. Understandably reluctant to commence hostilities with

> *Nature rarely ladles Yellow*
> *Out of a Tureen,*

the poet found herself obliged to declare Nature prodigal of the wrong color. I cannot continue the rewrite: the business about spending scarlet is far too politically incorrect for the publisher to permit me to leave it in. I have thought, instead, about likening the way nature is with red to how calibrationists expend time and money on color management solutions that don't work, but I've had some little difficulty coming up with lines that scan. I would, however, end the poem thusly:

> *Chorus'd Nature, chanting Yellow,*
> *Sings with more élan*
> *Than Progeny of Press atonal*
> *Magenta and Cyan.*

*   *   *

Before you decide that poets should stick to poetry and Photoshop authors to Photoshop, let's cut Emily Dickinson a break.

Figure 5.1 *Two cyan plates, one with proper focus, and one that is decidedly second-rate.*

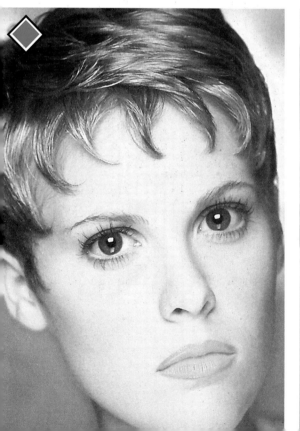
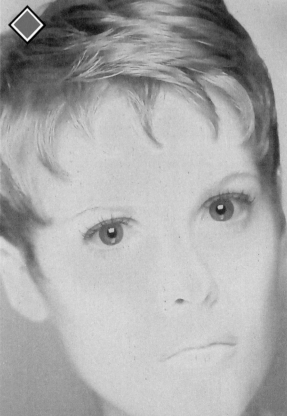

She didn't know her verse was incorrect, because she thought in the color terms some of us learned in school under the acronymous name Roy G. Biv: Red, Orange, Yellow, Green, Blue, Indigo, Violet. I don't know that there has been a lot of research done on this point, but my impression is that, of these seven hues, Dickinson is correct, nature uses yellow the least.

Today, we have buried Mr. Biv and are more inclined to think in terms of CGYRMB, a perfect color circle. In this model, red falls midway between yellow and magenta, magenta is midway between red and blue, and so on.

One might think that there would be no reason to think that any one of these six colors would be used more than another, but a quick check of the works of God and Man demonstrates how silly that view is. Red, green, and blue objects are far more common in nature than the other three. Bananas and other yellow objects exist, but they aren't that common. Bubble gum is magenta, and certain Caribbean waters are cyan, but outside of these I am hard put to come up with *anything* else that is magenta or cyan. And yet you could name literally hundreds of things that are red, green, or blue.

An interesting exercise is to walk down the street and record the color of clothes that passersby wear. I've tried this, and have found ratios of anywhere from four to ten to one in favor of RGB colors as opposed to CMY.

The point of all this poetry and palaver?

Figure 5.2 *When the two cyans are plugged into the same MYK image, the difference is impressive.*

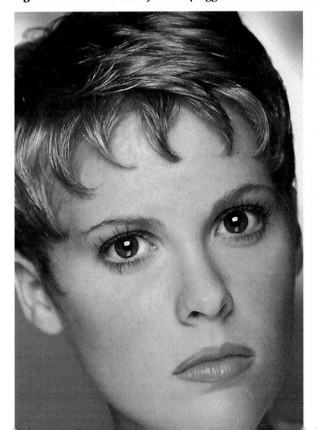 

Simply this. In the images you work with, you are far, far more likely to be working with red, green, and blue objects than cyan, magenta, and yellow ones.

To translate this into prepress language: it is extremely likely that the objects we work with will have two strong inks and one weak one, as opposed to other way around. It is that weak one, and how to exploit it, which is the focus of this chapter.

The Cavalry of Woe

CMYK, in addition to being a cockeyed colorspace, is a backwards one. Instead of choosing inks based on their positive capabilities, they have been selected for what they do *not* do. Magenta does not reflect green light; yellow does not reflect blue; cyan does not reflect red.

From this, it is not too much of a stretch to realize that much of the color correction we do is topsy-turvy: that to be effective, we have to think in color terms that are the opposite of what one might expect. When we deal with reds, we should be thinking cyan; when doing greens, magenta; and when portraying blues, yellow.

This is the religion of the *unwanted color*—the color that is the odd man out.

Because the unwanted color is so proficient at poisoning what would otherwise be a bright, clean look, it has a special importance in making an image seem lifelike. The unwanted color, even in slight quantities, is what gives an image depth.

The most obvious example of the importance of the unwanted color is in fleshtones. Regardless of a person's ethnicity, flesh is basically red. That is to say, it is a combination of magenta and yellow. There is far less cyan. Cyan is, therefore, the unwanted color.

It may be a leap of faith for you to accept that cyan is the most important color in a face. So, without further theoretical ado, we will go straight to an example. The only difference between the two images of Figure 5.1 is their cyan plates; the other three are identical.

Note that there is technically nothing wrong with the poor image. The fleshtone is within proper parameters. But the picture has gone dead. The other seems to leap into three dimensions by comparison.

When there are clearly two colors dominating, the unwanted color is so potent in neutralizing them that adding it is almost like adding black. The unwanted color, however, is not quite as blunt an instrument. Also, a much bigger range, and thus a better shape, can be engineered into the unwanted color than into either the two dominants or the black. That is just a matter of numbers: in the better version, the cyan ranges from around 5^C to 20^C. There is thus four times as much cyan in the darkest area as in the lightest. Try getting *that* with either one of the dominants.

Best of all, the unwanted color is easy to adjust—or, if need be, to create. The two dominant inks must be kept carefully balanced, otherwise areas of the face will start to get too yellow or too magenta. But it will take an enormous move in the cyan before the overall color of the woman goes to something other than a shade of red. Much can be hidden in the unwanted color, and part of the normal technique of working with faces should be calling up the cyan and seeing what improvements can be made. The picture as a whole cannot be sharpened, for example, but sharpening only the cyan is possible, and that will make a small but significant improvement.

To sum up, when trying to improve sky, the professional thinks of yellow first. To correct faces, we concentrate on cyan, and for plants and other greenery we focus on magenta.

Yet I Know How the Heather Looks

Figure 5.1 wasn't a red picture, but the most important object, the face, was red. In Figure 5.3, on the other hand, green dominates. That means strong yellow and cyan, and it means that magenta is the unwanted color.

Figure 5.3 *When the interest area is the green of a forest rather than the red of a face, the key color becomes magenta rather than cyan. At left, the original magenta plate; at bottom, a corrected version. The two color versions are identical in the CYK channels.*

The bottom halves of Figure 5.3 make clear how critical that unwanted color is. There is no difference at all in the cyan, yellow, and black plates, but the enhanced magenta seems to bring the image to life. No other channel could make such a difference in this picture. Just as in the picture of the woman no other channel could have had the same impact as the cyan.

Here, we simply use the technique of Chapter 4, steepening the curve in the magenta where the greenery is, roughly 10^M to 20^M. Also, I've sharpened the magenta channel. Notice how harsh the

result is. That's one of the happy things about the unwanted color: it's covered up by so much ink from the two dominants that we can really get away with ugly-looking things.

Of course, in real life we would do other things to this image besides tweaking the unwanted color, but that isn't the point. The message is, when confronted by such a predominance of one color, you'll get a lousy image if you *don't* take special care with the unwanted color.

If you'd like to see a similar image to compare how an unwanted-color

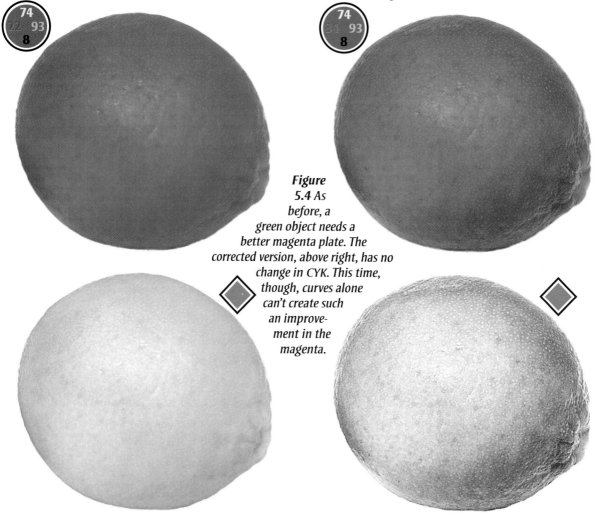

Figure 5.4 As before, a green object needs a better magenta plate. The corrected version, above right, has no change in CYK. This time, though, curves alone can't create such an improve-ment in the magenta.

move compares to a move in both dominant channels at once (and how the two reinforce one another), refer back to the grasshopper of Figures 1.3 and 1.4. And along the same lines is the tiger image of Figure 4.5. Both cater to the phenomenon of simultaneous contrast, the human proclivity to exaggerate differences between neighboring colors.

Although there is no problem handling any of the magenta plates of these images by conventional means, in many cases the need for strong contrast in the unwanted color is so compelling that we have to take

desperation measures. The normal desperation measure is to find a higher-contrast channel and blend it into the unwanted color, hoping not to throw overall color off too much in the process.

This is actually a watershed moment in this book, at least if you've been reading the chapters in order. Up until this point, the concepts have been universal. We *always* need appropriate highlight and shadow values. If we have a choice of the shape of curves, we *always* choose to have them emphasize the important areas of the image.

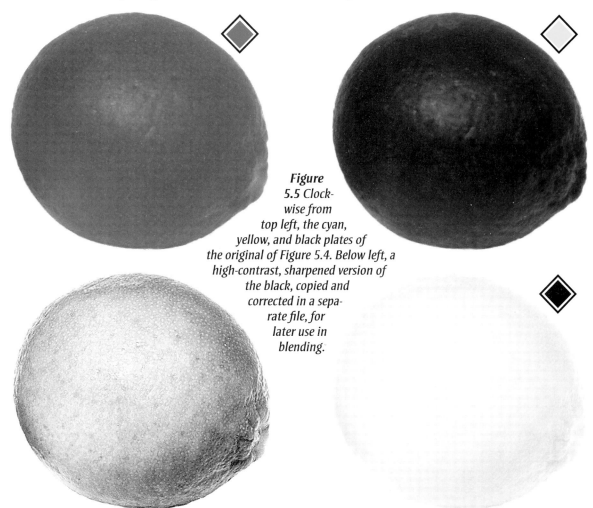

Figure 5.5 Clockwise from top left, the cyan, yellow, and black plates of the original of Figure 5.4. Below left, a high-contrast, sharpened version of the black, copied and corrected in a separate file, for later use in blending.

From here on, however, the strategies are specialized. Plate blending, unsharp masking tricks, unorthodox GCR decisions, the use of other colorspaces: these are all great responses to specific situations. Unfortunately, one has to learn what those situations are.

The Berry's Cheek Is Plumper

When everything is brilliant, nothing is brilliant. Plate blending to enhance contrast in the unwanted color is often needed when there are large areas of intense color. Fruits, vegetables, and, of course, flowers are excellent examples.

There are two main reasons this maneuver is so important. First, the human observer always tries to break apart similar colors, whereas a camera does not; therefore, humans perceive much more variation in the color of fruit than is going to be captured on film. Since our job is to remind the eventual viewer of the original subject, not what the photographer captured, we have to try to restore some of this color variation, and applying curves and sharpening alone may not do it.

Second, we want our bright objects to look three-dimensional, not like flat blobs. The right-hand lime in Figure 5.4 is a lot *rounder* than the one on the left. That's because the purer the color, the closer it seems to us. The more it tends toward gray, the further away it goes.

At the brightest spot in the center, these two limes are almost identical in color. The difference is at the edges. There, the right-hand version is grayer, less green. Those grayer edges recede, fooling us into thinking we are seeing rounder fruit.

And, not to beat a dead horse, when we have a dominant red, green, or blue object,

the way to turn parts of it gray is with its enemy, with its opponent, with the ink that is specifically designed to contaminate, poison, depurify, confound, distress, and distrain it, to wit, the unwanted color.

Once having concluded that this lime needs a magenta plate like the one at bottom right of Figure 5.4, the question is how to get there from the version at bottom left. The answer is, you don't. The original is simply too flat. Curving it won't help, at least it won't help as much as we need.

Accordingly, we need to seek assistance elsewhere. We need to find a channel with more detail and blend it into this pathetic magenta. Figure 5.5 shows the choices.

The maxed-out yellow is plainly unsuitable. The cyan is pretty flat as well, although it does have a well-pronounced hot spot in the middle. And the black? Well, at first blush it seems as flat as the magenta, but it isn't. Curving this one can bring out detail, as we will see.

The first order of business is to get a copy of the aforesaid black channel so that we can play with it. This is done by displaying the channel, Select All (Command-A); Copy (Command-C); New document (Command-N, which automatically opens a document to the same size as what we have just copied); Paste (Command-V); drop down one layer (Command-E.)

The result of all this alphabet soup is a grayscale document that is divorced from the original, meaning we can smash it all to pieces if we like.

But there is no need for such violence. Instead, what we want to do is increase contrast in the fruit, and having gone through Chapter 4, we know exactly how to do so. We create a curve that is as steep as possible in the area occupied by the lime.

And for good measure, we apply some unsharp masking afterwards. The result is at the bottom left of Figure 5.5.

This souped-up model is almost good enough to replace the original magenta plate, because the two are practically the same color. The key is understanding that contrast needs somehow to be added to the magenta. After that, how far to go is a judgment call.

With both the original file and the separate blending channel open on screen, we display the magenta channel of the original and choose Image: Apply Image. Up comes the dialog box shown in Figure 5.6. We now specify that the source is the other image and pick an opacity. Here, understanding that this is purely an arbitary decision and that you are perfectly free to think I should have gone further or not even this far, I used 75% Opacity.

Ordinarily, after a blend like this, a further correction is necessary. Blending into the unwanted color always adds detail, but it frequently changes color as well. We want a rounder lime, not a browner one. Most of our perception of color comes from the brightest area of the fruit. So we have to make sure that, after the blend, that point hasn't changed color too much. If it has, we have to apply curves to the blend plate to restore color while holding contrast.

Here, we lucked out; the color is close enough as is, another reason to favor blending with the black plate rather than the darker cyan.

If this blend seems too simple, more complicated options are readily available. We could have made two separate blending channels, one based on the cyan and one on the black, and then blended those together before blending the result in the magenta. Or we could have made a copy of the image, converted it to LAB, and used the L channel for blending. Or to RGB, and used the green. Or we could have done any of the above using Multiply as the blend mode, rather than normal.

Any of the above is a reasonable choice for dealing with this image. Giving up and leaving the magenta plate alone is not.

The Accent of a Coming Foot

The dancer's costume in Figure 5.7 looks fine in person, fine in the photograph, fine on the monitor, and lousy on the printed page. Process inks are not good at reproducing vivid colors like this red. When we bring this image into CMYK, what we get is a kind of red blob lacking most detail, since every part of the costume will be close to the limit of the press's color gamut.

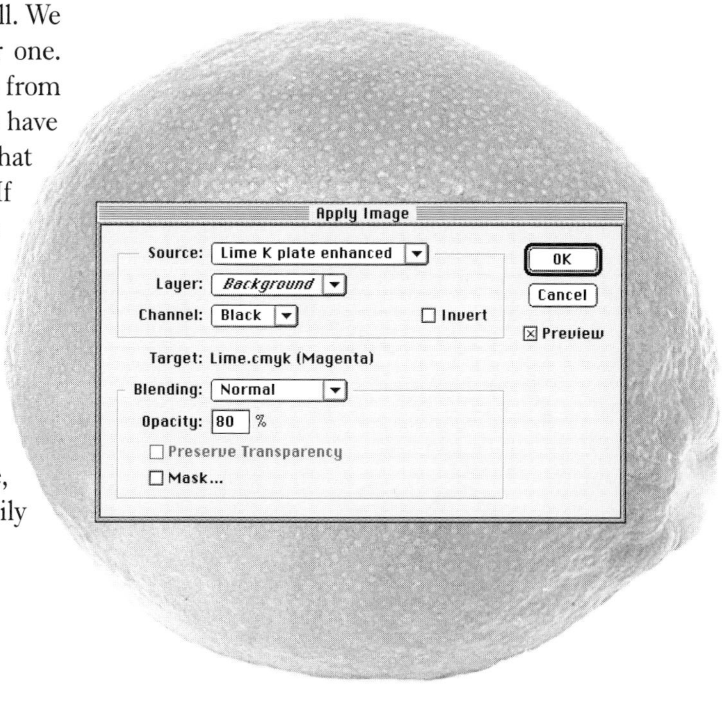

Figure 5.6 The blending process, using Photoshop's Apply Image command.

This red is made up of maximum magenta plus pretty large quantities of yellow. (If the two were equal, we would have a costume the color of a fire engine; as yellow decreases, we head toward a rosier hue.) What it will not have is very much cyan or black, because these are red-killing colors.

If we take the approach advocated in Chapter 4, the way to create more contrast in the reds should seem as risk-free as it is obvious. After all, there is nothing in the background to be harmed. There are no neutral colors, no highlights to unbalance.

Therefore, we should steepen the magenta and yellow by dropping the minimum values of them we find in the costume by 15 points or so. Magenta is probably maxed out already, but we can increase the yellow. As for the cyan and the black, we will steepen their curves by finding the maximum values within the costume and increasing them, presuming that the minimum is near zero and cannot go lower.

The problem is that when the overall effect is so brilliant, the maximum cyan and black are likely to be near zero as well. So, the impact of our correction will not be as much as could be hoped for. In fact, the poor contrast throughout is because only one of the four plates—the yellow—has any kind of detailing in it. The magenta is essentially a solid color throughout the costume and the black and cyan are basically zeroed out. In other words, three-quarters of our colorspace is not being used at all.

First, then, we should apply curves to maximize whatever small contrast we can

Figure 5.7 *When an image contains brilliant objects, look to the unwanted color. All channels have been corrected here, but the cyan move is the most important one.*

find, and along the way, make the flesh-tones more realistic. As for the costume, the way out of this mess is not to be so shockingly red throughout. Whatever the brightest part is, we should keep at the most saturated values possible, (i.e., no cyan or black at all) but we should subdue the rest. For that, we want the unwanted color, and as there is none to speak of at present, one will have to be manufactured.

In practice, we explore the image and find the brightest area. Having discovered this, we proceed to create the unwanted color. Since yellow is the only plate with detail, we create a new cyan plate that is a blend of 70 percent of the old cyan and 30 percent of the yellow.

This finagling will create a problem. There will now be a certain amount of contaminating colors everywhere in the red. The area that I have identified as lightest will have 8^C. All other areas will have more.

This conflicts with our previous goal of having the brightest area be absolutely as intense as possible, meaning no cyan or black at all. To restore these regions to brilliant red, the correction curve must move 8^C to zero. That is desirable anyway, since it steepens the cyan curve. Of course, we will steepen it further in the range of the red objects, which is the lightest part of the cyan curve. The cyan channel, before and after, is shown in Figure 5.8.

In Just the Dress His Century Wore

The interesting marbled-paper image of Figures 5.9 through 5.12 symbolizes a species particularly suited to unwanted-color moves. If an object has a pronounced

Figure 5.8 The two cyan plates of the images of Figure 5.7.

Figure 5.9 Left, the original. Center, removing all cyan sharply reduces grain. Right, increasing contrast in the cyan makes all patterns more pronounced.

grain, as this paper does, the unwanted color governs its intensity. When we want to make the grain more or less prominent, the unwanted color is the principal tool.

Although wood might be a more typical example of where we might want to control grain, the paper image has more possibilities. Images like these are sold to be used as backgrounds, for which they are very useful. Frequently we will want to make some custom variation of them. Here are a few examples.

Curve-based contrast variation in the unwanted color is the best way to affect the grain. In Figure 5.9, compare the original to a version with no cyan at all, and one with a steep contrast curve that increases cyan quartertones without adding cyan where there was none.

Unwanted colors do their work best against purer incarnations of red, green, and blue. The overall feeling of this art is less red than magenta, although the yellow plate is much heavier than the cyan. In

Figure 5.10 When the image is shifted from magenta-red to pure red, the unwanted color becomes even more prominent. Center and right, adjustments in the cyan drastically change the strength of the grain.

Figure 5.11 *Neutralization techniques. Left, a single overall reduction in saturation. Right, curves that aim for more neutral colors. Center, swapping the cyan and black plates gives less color variation.*

Figure 5.10 we make the image pure red by duplicating the magenta plate into the yellow channel. Under these circumstances, the impact of moves in the cyan is intensified. Note that one effect has gone away: a danger in working with grains is that the grain may take on the look and feel of the unwanted color. This is what is happening in the right third of Figure 5.10. Where the cyan is heavy, the pattern is becoming distinctly blue. That is not necessarily a problem with this art. If we were working

on a reddish wood, however, a bluish grain would be just as easily achievable, but far less desirable.

The center image of Figure 5.11 suggests a way of avoiding this. Earlier, I asserted that adding the unwanted color is roughly as powerful as adding black. To test this proposition, in the center image, I actually transposed the black and cyan plates. If we would like a strong grain, but don't want any of it to have a blue tinge, this is the way to go.

Figure 5.12 *Special effects. Left, increasing cyan sharply overall by blending 50 percent of magenta into it. Center, an inversion curve on the cyan. Right, using the entire available colorspace through drastic curves.*

This version is flanked by the right and the wrong way to get a less pink, more neutral effect. On the left, Image: Adjust>Hue/Saturation reduces saturation throughout the image. This floods everything with unwanted colors, and although it does make the image more neutral, it also neutralizes a lot of its appeal.

The blunt instrument of Hue/Saturation adjustment should only be used for its ability to isolate a certain color. When acting on the image as a whole, curves will always be more effective, as in the version at the right of Figure 5.11. This was treated just as we would any other image with a cast. I found areas that I wanted to neutralize and forced a gray in them. This retained plenty of interesting color variation throughout the image, since places with relatively heavy magenta, yellow, or cyan continued to display it. The only issue was where to set the highlight and shadow. This is one of the rare images that, in the interest of softness, should probably not make use of all available color space. So, I set my highlight at $10^C10^M8^Y$, intentionally retaining a slight magenta cast, and the shadow at about 50% in all colors.

Figure 5.12 shows three fanciful variants. At left, a new cyan plate that is a 50–50 split with magenta makes for a lavender image with a much less pronounced grain. Quick! How would we add more grain?

Yes, of course, this change has given us a different unwanted color. The way to add detailing would be to alter the yellow.

The center version has a flipped cyan. That is, the start of the curve is higher than the end, meaning that places that were relatively heavy in cyan are now relatively light. This is not a straight negative version of the cyan, which would overwhelm the image, but a softer variation on the negative theme.

Finally, the right-hand version is a reminder of just how much vitality we can add to any image through curves. I simply set the lightest area of each color to zero and the heaviest to around 90%.

This series of maneuvers illustrates some of the potential offered by manipulating abstract patterns. They have interest just by themselves, but they are particularly useful as backgrounds, especially if they are not too assertive.

Give the One in Red Cravat

Our last demonstration of the contrarian school of color correction is Figure 5.13. At first glance, it isn't much like the other images in this chapter, which tend toward blazing exhibitions of a single color. Here, 90 percent of the image—the door and the woman's flesh and hair—is fairly subdued. The dress, however, is brilliant red, and when we see brilliant reds we must instinctively look to the cyan plate.

The extra bite in the door comes from moves in the L channel of LAB. We'll see how to do this sort of thing in Chapter 10. But LAB techniques won't put folds in the dress. And without those folds, the dress looks like it's painted on.

This seems like just another version of the dancer or the lime. So, after the overall correction is made, we need to think about blending into the weak channel. But this one is not as easy. The dancer image was essentially all red and the lime was all green. The current image is neither. Unfortunately, this means that if we start blending into the cyan plate generally the door is apt to turn a very weird color.

We've avoided the practice for nearly five chapters, but here there's nothing for it but to make a selection, and blend into that. First, an examination of the channels verifies the problem. The cyan is terrible. The magenta is totally solid. The yellow is serviceable and is the obvious blending choice.

I've used this image in my classes and have been astounded to see professional retouchers who are insightful enough to realize that such an unorthodox maneuver is necessary, yet so set in their ways that they take half an hour to create the necessary selection mask.

Granted, the ability to make accurate masks is one of the hallmarks of the professional. If you don't have a lot of practice at this sort of thing, imagine how difficult it would be to select, for example, the hair of the woman in Figure 5.1. In such a case, we'd be looking at individual channels to try to find the best edge and doing all sorts of other tricky things.

Here, however, there is no need to spend any time at all. Just look at the magenta plate in Figure 5.14. One can hardly ask for a more decisive distinction between dress and background. All one has to do is hit the dress with the magic wand tool, and presto, a perfect selection. I feathered it one pixel from force of habit, but this is not really necessary.

Now, with the dress still selected, flip to the cyan channel, and apply the yellow channel to it. This will leave the background unaffected. I used 50% opacity.

Figure 5.13 The unwanted color at work in a selected object. An overall plate blend won't work here because it would change color too drastically in the background. By selecting the dress and blending into that, however, more detail can be built into the folds.

As happened also with the lime, this blend leaves the cyan channel temporarily too dark. Therefore, with the dress still selected, I applied a curve that brought its minimum cyan value down to what it was before the blend. I left the curve relatively steep to retain the shape of the folds.

But Graphicker for Grace

When we see a color that dominates the image, we should not be dazzled into believing that that is the one we must attack. Instead, we should be more subtle, devoting our energies to courting the color that is prominent by its absence—unwanted, perhaps, but not unnecessary, not unloved.

Admittedly, this channel blending is tricky stuff, more so than the curving of Chapters 3 and 4. The decision-making is much less automatic. It's fairly easy, I think, to know when a channel blend might be appropriate; the hard part comes afterward.

The language of color is indeed the language of poetry, and often those with a poetic bent see things that scientists cannot. The idea that there should be fewer yellow objects in nature than red, green, or blue ones is counterintuitive, but it is

nevertheless correct. Many of the ideas discussed in Chapter 2 failed because their authors did not grasp certain facts about color that were obvious to, say, Leonardo da Vinci.

Or Emily Dickinson, for that matter. How often I have been attacked, over these past years, for saying what I did in Chapter 1, that photographs taken in dark conditions generally need to be lightened even when the photographer has already

Figure 5.14
Creating a replacement for the original cyan, right. Below, left to right: the original magenta; the original yellow; a 50–50 blend of the yellow into the dress area only of the cyan; a final cyan version in which curves have been applied to the dress to lighten it and enhance shape.

MANIPULATING THE UNWANTED COLOR

✓ Areas that are predominantly red, green, or blue are peculiarly susceptible to moves involving the opponent process plate, otherwise known, somewhat inaccurately, as the *unwanted color*. In red areas, including fleshtones, the unwanted color is cyan; in greens, the unwanted color is magenta; and in blues, it is yellow.

✓ Focus-enhancing moves in the unwanted color are very powerful, roughly as effective as moving both dominant inks at once. In adding detail, the unwanted color is the most significant of the three. Steepening its curve will yield dramatic results.

✓ Many bright areas appear too flat because they lack an unwanted color altogether. In such cases, applying curves will be of little help. It is often necessary to generate a shapelier unwanted color plate by means of blending detail in from another channel.

✓ After a channel blend, restore original color by lowering the minimum value of the new channel in the affected area to whatever it was before.

✓ When trying to use bright, happy colors, consider reductions in the unwanted color rather than trying to beef up the dominants.

✓ In objects with a pronounced grain, such as woods, steepening the unwanted color will greatly intensify the graininess, but at the risk of creating an unwelcome hue. In such cases, consider means of transferring some of the role of the unwanted color into the black plate. Normally this is done by blending some of the unwanted color into the black.

✓ Zeroing out the unwanted color in the absolutely brightest area is a good way to add even more contrast to a primary color, even though letting one of the CMY colors drop to zero is normally considered unacceptable.

✓ Our perception of colors is influenced by what we see near them. To emphasize a bright color even more, increase the unwanted color in nearby areas.

✓ Be alive to the possibility that an image may offer more than one opportunity for an unwanted-color maneuver. If an ink is unwanted in one area of the image and dominant elsewhere, generally it will pay to steepen the curve in the unwanted area even if it penalizes the dominant range.

attempted to compensate. Match the art! say the scoffers. What gives you the right to think that an observer would see it differently than the camera?

A voice from 1862 answers them:

We grow accustomed to the Dark
When Light is put away.
As when the Neighbor holds the Lamp
To witness her Goodbye.

A moment—we uncertain step
For newness of the Night,
Then fit our Vision to the Dark
And meet the Road erect.

*   *   *

For all the instincts that poets have, certain things come only with experience. Appreciation of the importance of the unwanted color is one of them. For now, we should just resolve that all strongly colored red, green, and blue objects: flowers, fruits, faces, whatever—shall always have shapely unwanted-color channels in our work. In arranging this, we avoid the following Dickinsonian error of inexperience:

The good Will of a Flower
The Man who would possess
Must first present
Certificate
Of minted Holiness.

Phooey. The above is a crock. You want good flowers, you don't need any certificate. You need a good unwanted color. The certificate, plus the other three channels, plus a dollar and a half, gets you on the subway.

*   *   *

Long before the age of Photoshop, John Wiley & Sons, the publishers of this book, brought out a scholarly work on color, which offered the following wisdom:

Confusion about the elementary principles of color is very widespread, the chief reason being that words dealing with color are used very loosely in ordinary language. But the difficulty goes deeper than that. Color was an art long before it was a science, and consequently the language of color is poetic rather than factual. The words are not as a rule intended to be taken literally but rather to convey a feeling or an impression...Scientists are often infuriated by their inability to pin down an artist, or even a layman, to factual statements on subjects that might lie within the sacred realm of physics. Or, not recognizing that the artist's statements are poetic, they point out the departures from literal truth and expect the artist to retract them.

If you read about 'caverns measureless to man,' nobody supposes that a dedicated spelunker with modern surveying instruments would be unable to map them, if they existed. And if a lady with spike heels says 'My feet are killing me,' this is easily recognized as a poetic statement, on a somewhat lower plane. But if someone says 'This color has some red in it,' how are we to take it? This sentence sounds factual and objective, but probably it merely expresses that the speaker associates a feeling of redness with the color, and it might better be regarded as a poetic statement.

Indeed.

CHAPTER 6

Sharpening with a Stiletto

Unsharp masking, an artificial means of making an image look better focused, is a powerful tool, especially for larger images. How much of it should you use? As much as you can get away with, of course. By choosing which channels to sharpen, and with accurate use of Photoshop's controls, you'll be able to get away with a lot more of it.

Y ou enter the boss's office under that most tense of circumstances: you are about to ask for a raise. It is possible that negotiations will ensue, so you have to be prepared with a number. How much more money should you ask for?

The stakes are all too clear. Ask for too little, and you may get it; ask for too much, and you may get booted out of the office with nothing.

It is also clear that the amount you can get away with asking for is not fixed, but varies sharply depending on your technique. People who, during the meeting, tell the boss what a kind, sweet individual he is and what a joy to work with, as a rule can ask for more than those who imply that, were it not for their own contribution, the boss's boss would realize what an incompetent dolt he is.

And it is also clear that it depends on the character of the boss. Should you mention that another company may make you an offer at a higher salary? Some bosses respond well to this type of thing. Others, like myself, are of the crabby variety, and are apt to suggest that, should you decide to change jobs, you not allow the door to hit you in the backside on the way out.

The fact remains, you should ask for as much as you can think you can get away with under the circumstances, but the circumstances are very much under your control. This is exactly analogous to unsharp masking.

How USM Fools the Eye

Unsharp masking makes images appear more in focus. It is useful in virtually all graphic scenarios, except when we expect someone else to rescan our work, as when we are outputting to a high-resolution film recorder. Whether preparing for a large-format output device, a color laser or other digital proofer, a JPEGged file for Web use, or any type of print work, accurate USM is a big deal, and the larger an image will print, the bigger a deal it is.

Figure 6.1 *Simple unsharp masking in action. When properly applied, it can make images much more lifelike, but when overdone, watch out. Above, the raw image, below, with USM added.*

Before discussing how USM works, let's point out that it *does* work. The only difference between the two images in Figure 6.1 is the USM, but it's a pleasing difference. And this is quite an extreme example: sharpening isn't as effective when the object is basically all one color, as the car is.

In Figure 6.2, the process is put under a microscope. Where car hits background, one would expect the same nice, crisp line of demarcation between red and green we might perceive in real life. Instead, in the raw scan, top, we get several pixels that are neither fish nor fowl: dark, colorless blurs caused by the real-life line of transition being narrower than the scanner can resolve, possibly even than the film of the original photograph can resolve.

The technical workings of unsharp masking are not as important as the result, which is an exaggeration of transitions, such as where the car hits the background. USM, as the bottom of Figure 6.2 shows, puts the suggestion, the hint, of a black border, or halo, on the car's exterior. Furthermore, a second, lighter halo appears around the first. If done subtly enough, the viewer won't notice these halos when the job is printed at the proper size.

That this particular scam is highly effective at hornswoggling people into believing they are seeing stronger transitions, and thus better focus, is not a big secret. Artists have been doing it for centuries. El Greco didn't use Photoshop, but as you can see in Figure 6.3, he knew all about unsharp masking.

The Four Deadly USM Sins

As with asking the boss for a raise, the objective is to do as much unsharp masking as possible without being so obnoxious as to be counterproductive. USM is artificial, and if we overdo it, the image will look artificial as well. Fortunately, if we pinpoint, and avoid sharpening, the things that may look artificial, we can get away with more USM overall, much to our advantage.

The four problems that may limit how much USM we can apply appear in magnified form in Figure 6.4. From top to bottom, they are:

• **Color shift.** The idea of USM is to make the image look more focused, not to introduce new colors. But that is just what is happening in the first example: note the unrealistic green halo, and the brilliant, but featureless, reds breaking away from the more orange body of the car.

• **Unreasonably wide haloes.** USM only is believable when the characteristic haloing isn't obvious to the naked eye. Here, it would be.

• **Intensification of unwanted detail.** USM makes the picture look more focused, which is fine unless the things that are being focused are not things we want to see. Here, the plastic car has some scratches in its roof. Although this is real detail and not mere noise, I cannot imagine why a client would want us to emphasize it.

• **Exaggeration of grain or noise.** Random pixels in the background are being made more prominent. If we allow the image to print this way, the background will look strangely grainy.

All these problems can be finessed, provided we are willing to treat USM as a stiletto, not a shotgun. There is a lot of flexibility in how to apply it, although every

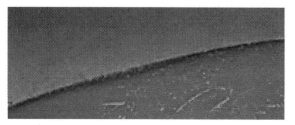

Figure 6.2 Enlarged copies of sections of the images of Figure 6.1. The sharpened version, below, shows the characteristic light and dark haloing in transition areas.

program has different strengths and weaknesses. Photoshop can do everything we need, but sometimes requires kludgy two- or three-step operations. But before discussing specific Photoshop settings, let's attack the four sins in a conceptual way.

Taking Aim at the Problems

The brilliant greens of the first example in Figure 6.4 came about because hitting an entire file with USM actually applies it to each channel individually, as though each were a black and white image.

(You should already be thinking: is that really the best way of doing things? Because we can certainly apply the filter to some channels and not others, or apply it in a different colorspace altogether.)

Recall that USM places a dark halo at the edge of the darker of two objects, and a light one at the edge of the lighter. This explains the color-shift problem: in the magenta channel, the car is darker than the background, but in the cyan, the background is darker than the car. So, at the transition just outside the car, USM darkens the cyan but lightens the magenta. This is a recipe for bright greens.

A partial solution, as hinted above, is to sharpen the weaker channel only. But for an image as soft as this one, the real answer is to eliminate channel-by-channel sharpening totally, in favor of

Figure 6.3 Desiring to have Christ's upper hand stand out more from the cross, El Greco (1540–1614) resorted to a double-haloing maneuver indistinguishable from today's unsharp masking practices.

an approach that only considers the lightness and darkness of the image as a whole, not its color.

This technique, luminosity-based sharpening, is better than the defaults of Photoshop and most other programs, though some, like Agfa's ColorExact, are clever enough to always do it this way. The second example in Figure 6.4, for all its other problems, is a luminosity sharpen, and it has none of the color shift of the top version.

If you wish to sharpen by luminosity, and you should, there are two ways of doing so in Photoshop without getting into Layersville. Easiest is if the document is in the LAB colorspace rather than RGB or CMYK. Guess what the L in LAB stands for! Sharpening the L channel is one of the many attractions of this colorspace, which we will explore in Chapter 10.

If we are in RGB or CMYK, Photoshop allows the same thing, albeit in two steps. After applying USM, choose Filter: Fade, the main function of which, as the name suggests, is to reduce the impact of the last filter applied, in this case, USM. But it also allows us to change the application method of the filter, such as to use it only to lighten or darken the original—or to act on luminosity. So, if we set the fade to 100% intensity, but Mode to Luminosity, as

in the bottom of Figure 6.4, we wipe out the color shift.

The second sharpening sin that will deter us from our goal of using as much USM as possible is the exaggerated haloing shown in the second example. Or rather, it is *one* of the halos. This points up an irritating Photoshop weakness.

USM's double haloing scheme causes a problem when one of the objects to be sharpened is relatively dark and the other is medium. The difficulty is that the car can absorb a pronounced dark halo fairly well, but the light halo at the edge of the background becomes painfully obvious.

You can try fading the filter as above using Darker mode, which will wipe out the white halo altogether, but if you are not inclined to waste time, let me tell you in advance that the image will look ridiculous if you try. No, we need to tone down the white halo, not blow it away.

The ability to control white and dark sharpening independently is an assumed feature of any drum scanner or high-end retouching workstation. But it slipped through the cracks in Photoshop, so to achieve it involves another kludge, which I will demonstrate at the end of the chapter.

Reduction of white-line sharpening would also help deal with the scratches in the top of the car. Even though those scratches are real detail and not noise, we certainly don't want to emphasize them, as is done in the third example.

The better way, though, is simply to avoid sharpening the darkest channel, which here is green in RGB or magenta in CMYK. That is where the scratches are best defined, because the background of the car will be dark, but the scratches light. By comparison, the lightest channel—red

Figure 6.4 *The four deadly sharpening sins, top to bottom: an overall color shift; halos that are too pronounced; enhancement of an unwanted detail (the scratches in the roof of the car); and exaggeration of simple noise. Below, an undocumented feature, the very desirable ability to sharpen by luminosity even when in CMYK.*

in RGB or cyan in CMYK—will have very little difference between car color and scratch.

Are you beginning to see a pattern here? Even if the image can be sharpened overall, the weak channel can usually be sharpened more. Leaving the magenta unsharpened would have virtually eliminated the problems in the first and third images, and

gone a long way toward eliminating the grain in the fourth. Meanwhile, reducing the lightening while retaining the darkening aspect of USM would have substantially improved all four of our problems.

To this point, all of our maneuvers could have been done with Photoshop's greasy kid stuff, the filters Sharpen, Sharpen More, and Sharpen Edges. I suggest you discard these popguns in favor of the vastly more flexible Unsharp Mask filter.

Are These Crops Tight Enough?

In large images, judicious USM is every bit as potent as the other big weapons in the retoucher's arsenal: appropriate highlights and shadows; good allocation of contrast; strong detail in the unwanted color; and careful use of the black plate.

Figure 6.5 Faces are the biggest unsharp masking problem. The original, bottom left, is too soft. But a careless sharpen, top, can cause the illusion of a skin disease. By avoiding the sharpening of channels that contain facial detail, the hair and eyes can be made more realistic, as at bottom right, without damaging the skin.

In smaller images, the various USM options aren't nearly as important. Small images do need sharpening, don't get me wrong, but the exact setting won't make or break quality, the way it will in large ones.

And yet, virtually all existing documentation, from Adobe's manuals to third-party Photoshop how-to books, illustrates the USM options with images the size of postage stamps.

The reason for the thumbnail approach is, of course, that it's expensive to print large color pictures in documentation. I have that limitation here, too: note the excruciatingly tight crops I've had to use to make everything fit. But it's just too hard to see the detail otherwise—and remember, if these images were printing larger, the sharpening defects would be even more evident than you see here.

A Few New Wrinkles

So far, we've discussed how to avoid exaggerating what might be termed artificiality—the grain of the film, or random noise in the image. The detail in the face of the young woman in Figure 6.5, however, is not grain, not noise, nothing artificial at all, just the natural variation of her skin. The skin of humans, even relatively young ones, is made not of alabaster, but rather of a flexible epidermoid integument, highly useful for insulation and in resisting injury, but somewhat unforgiving of acne scars, and entirely too prone to wrinkling.

What that means in English is, careless USM can make Cindy Crawford look like Louie the Lizard. While doing so would be all right with my wife and certain others, it's not too likely to be what an art director wants.

And yet, the original seems too soft,

especially in the hair. Note that even in the version with the reptilian skintone, the hair is not overfocused. The question is how to get such hair and at the same time a natural-looking, yet not overdetailed, skin.

You may think of somehow selecting the hair, or rather, deselecting the skin, before sharpening. That approach, in my experience, always falls short: one winds up with what looks like two images pasted together.

Better alternatives are to sharpen by luminosity only, which reduces the impact of the facial imperfections by not allowing them to get so red, and/or to employ a relatively high Threshold in Photoshop's USM dialog box. This will eliminate the sharpening of some of the subtler detail at the cost of limiting the sharpening of the hair. Some of the more pronounced wrinkles will still be accentuated.

But the best way of all is to finesse the whole problem by doing the deed where it can do no harm—in other words, to hit the image where the facial detail isn't. And I can tell you exactly where it isn't, by means of a simple rule that applies not just to faces, but to any image:

In all things red, green, or blue, there will be more subtle detailing in the two darkest channels than in the other(s).

A face is red. The two dark channels are magenta and yellow, if we are in CMYK, or green and blue, if we are in RGB. These are the channels we need to avoid sharpening.

USM is even more dangerous in the face of an older person, whose skin is always more irregular. The man in Figure 6.6 has pepper-and-salt hair. You wouldn't know this from the original, where it looks like a flat gray. That will never do. We must attack, but not at the cost of making him a Methuselah.

The leatherlike magenta plate of Figure 6.7 is therefore the absolutely last thing we would want to sharpen. Compare it to the cyan plate, and to the black, where the face is virtually a blank. These two channels can therefore be sharpened with a heavy hand. If there's no detail there to begin with, USM won't make it materialize out of thin air.

With the image of the woman in Figure 6.5, I didn't even bother with the cyan. The only channel I used was the black—but I really hammered it.

There is a huge advantage to doing this kind of sharpening in CMYK rather than RGB, where the weakest channel will still be heavier than either of its two CMYK counterparts.

Consider the bottle image of Figure 6.8. The noise in the first sharpening attempt is worse even than in the fourth version of Figure 6.4.

One way to sidestep this problem is to sharpen a channel that has no noise in it, such as the black. This happens frequently, especially if we have generated the black

Figure 6.6 *The older the face, the more care needs to be taken. The original, left, doesn't do justice to the man's salt-and-pepper hair. The key to the version on the right side is to avoid sharpening the magenta plate.*

plate using UCR or Light GCR. One should always take a look at the black plate to see if it can be sharpened—even if one has already sharpened the image as a whole.

And one should always look at the unwanted color as well, if there is one. Here, the image being greenish, the unwanted color is magenta. Because the background magenta is so light (and the background black nonexistent) these two plates will have less detail, and hence much less noise, than the dominant cyan and yellow.

By the Numbers

In addition to our God-given ability to apply sharpening to specific channels and not others, an acceptable USM implementation needs to give us four things:

• Control over how strong the sharpening effect is, in other words, how dark and light the halos get.
• Control of how wide the halos are.
• Some means of suppressing noise.
• Independent control of lightening and darkening.

Every application has its own way of doing these things. Two things that all seem to have in common are a dialog box that is incomprehensible to the

Figure 6.7 Dominant-color channels always have more detail, meaning we should sharpen the weak ones. Left to right, the magenta, cyan, and black plates of the original version of Figure 6.6.

typical user and a failure to document how it works and for what types of images each option might be useful.

They nevertheless have to be deciphered, and they can be, if one keeps in mind the purposes described above. In Figure 6.9, we'll compare Photoshop to Heidelberg Color Publishing Solutions' LinoColor Elite scanner-driving software.

Start with the obvious, the need to control the strength of the sharpen. Here, Photoshop uses the word *Amount* and LinoColor *Intensity*. Both terms are clear enough, except for Photoshop's insistence on using a percent sign, which seems designed specifically to bluff people into never using a number higher than 100, when 500 is the actual maximum. Anyway,

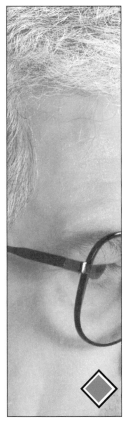

with both applications, the larger the number, the stronger the sharpen.

I doubt that most people would understand *Radius* or *Size* to refer to the width of the sharpening halos, but that's what they do. Again, the larger the number, the wider the halos. Photoshop's flexibility with this is tops in the industry; note the paucity of choices in LinoColor.

Stopping USM from enhancing noise as well as detail depends on allowing it to ignore small variations and concentrate on big-ticket items. The higher the value in *Threshold* or *Starting Point,* the less likely the filter is to exaggerate noise—but it isn't always possible to get this right. In the image of the red car, setting a high Threshold indeed will kill the noise in the background without harming the car, but the detail in the bottle image is no more pronounced than the speckling in the background.

Figure 6.8 *When background noise is heavy and detail light, a high USM threshold can't always separate one from the other. In such a case, sharpen the weak colors—here, black and magenta. Top right: the original cyan plate has noise in the background, but the black, bottom right, has none. At left, top to bottom: the original; a careless all-channel sharpen; and a version with USM applied only to the black and magenta.*

To sharpen the bottles correctly, you need to go channel by channel.

As for independent control of lightening and darkening, LinoColor has it and Photoshop should, but doesn't.

The Eyes Have It

Knowing where to sharpen is one thing, and knowing how to do it another. Time, then, to shift attention to Amount, Radius, and Threshold, the three variables in Photoshop's USM filter.

Threshold is the most straightforward. As Threshold increases, Photoshop starts to ignore variations between areas of similar darkness, in favor of bigger-ticket items. This would work to some extent in the magenta plate in Figure 6.7: there's a huge difference between a white hair and a black one, but not as much between normal flesh and an old scar. A high Threshold setting is a good way to avoid sharpening mild amounts of noise. It is somewhat less effective in faces, where the idea is not to suppress noise but to avoid accentuating actual detail.

The Radius and Amount settings define what happens when Photoshop encounters a transition area. Both settings emphasize the transition, but in different ways, as Figure 6.10 indicates.

Granted that the transition between colors in the original is razor-sharp, why do we need to emphasize it? The answer is surprisingly simple: the digital file may look great, but we print with halftone dots, and those dots are wider—a lot

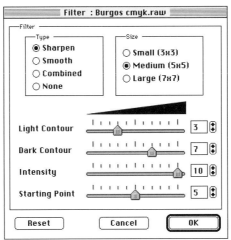

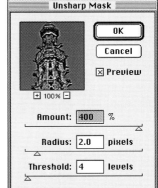

Figure 6.9 The basic unsharp masking menus of LinoColor Elite, left, and Photoshop, bottom.

wider—than the line of transition between purple and gold. Result? Blursville.

If this were a real photograph and not something generated artificially, there would be a further complication. The line of transition would also be narrower than a scanning sample. So, the scanner would add even more blurriness on top of the contribution of our lousy printing process. This, in short, is why all images need some kind of sharpening. The question is, of course, what kind.

The Radius setting, to my mind, is the most important of the three options. It regulates how wide the characteristic sharpening halo will be. The Amount setting, on the other hand, determines how ferocious the effect is, but not its width.

There is no such thing as an image that is too much in focus. The idea of sharpening is to do as much of it as possible without being detected. If we use too high an Amount, we *will* be detected, because the image will seem too noisy, even if the Radius is correct. And if we use too high a Radius, we will lose subtle detail, even if the Amount is right.

In their eternal search for mathematical verities, certain calibrationists have been known to suggest that the Radius should depend totally on the resolution of the scan. This is like saying that the larger a suitcase is, the heavier it will be. There is a certain amount of truth there, but the fact is that the contents of the suitcase have a considerable impact, and that a small suitcase filled with lead probably weighs more than a larger one filled with clothes. And so it is with images, even if we set aside the obvious fact that certain photographs have more grain than others of the same size, and thus cannot be sharpened as much.

Imagine that Figure 6.5 was a woman shown from the waist up, rather than in a tight closeup of the face. One need not be Einstein to realize that this would present an entirely different sharpening problem, because the size of the detailing would not match the original, even if the two images themselves were of identical resolution.

Accordingly, there is really no substitute for thinking. Given this tiresome necessity, here are some of the things you should think about.

Widening objects with a large Radius can be very effective. Notice that in spite of the softer face, the entire area of the eyes in the correctly sharpened image of the woman is better than in the oversharpened version. That's the Radius at work. The eyelashes are wider. So are the dark parts of the iris. And there is a hint of added weight in the eyelids, digital eyeliner, if you will.

This is all very nice, but before wheeling out a big Radius, we have to be sure that

Figure 6.10 Greatly enlarged, the differing effects of Photoshop's Radius and Amount settings are visible. A: the original. B: 200% Amount and 1.0 Radius. C: 400% Amount and 1.0 Radius. D: 200% Amount and 3.0 Radius. E: 400% Amount and 3.0 Radius. Inset in caption: the size at which the graphic would normally appear.

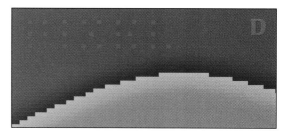

there is nothing in what we are sharpening that has subtle detail, of which big Radii are the enemy.

Small and subtle are not the same thing. An eyelash is small, but not subtle. The variations in the skin of the man are subtle, but they are not small.

In larger images, the details are more crisply defined. Hence, in principle a larger Radius will do less damage. But don't be afraid to use a big Radius on a small image, provided you have the right small image. If you don't agree, check out Figure 6.11.

Where is the subtle detail inside the bottle? Where is the big color difference between bottle and background? If you don't see these things, I don't either, and I conclude that a wide Radius will work better. Do you agree?

The character of the image, therefore, plays a much bigger role in determining the best Radius than resolution does. Ask yourself, is there fine detail or not? A person's hair, a wine bottle, the bubbles in a glass of soda: these things want a wide Radius. The bark of a tree, the skin of a fruit, a field of grass, the fabric of the soldier's uniform on the next page, all have subtle detail that a large Radius would kill.

But where both kinds of detail appear, we are forced to go with the least common denominator, and choose a narrow Radius,

Figure 6.11 *When an image doesn't have subtle detail, consider a wider Radius. Above right, the original. Below left, 250% Amount and 1.0 Radius; below right, with 250% Amount but Radius increased to 3.0.*

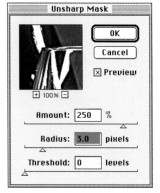

even though it is a second-best way of sharpening gross objects. We need to find a channel that does not have subtle detail. In a face, that's the black, and often the cyan, too. So, with the woman of Figure 6.5, I was able to use a Radius of 3.0 in the black channel, because as a practical matter the black contains only the eye area and the hair. And the Amount? I used Photoshop's maximum, 500%. If you hit the ball accurately enough, how hard you hit it doesn't matter.

Glitter and Be Gay

The unsharp masking filter by itself does not yield a perfectly sharpened image. The careful artist needs to work with Photoshop's sharpening *tool* as well. The tool isn't nearly as flexible as the filter, but it's highly useful in dealing with small areas, to add that last touch of believability. At the very top of the wine glass, there is a tiny sparkle of reflection on the left side where the glass touches the background. That little highlight should be sharpened. The sharpening tool will make it lighter and wider.

In fact, we don't care if there should be no dot at all in this particular sparkle. And that is the key rule for the use of the tool. Use it on anything that glints, because for such objects the brighter the better, meaning a zero dot.

More of these targets are hanging around than you might think. Let's take a quick look at the images in this chapter, starting with the young woman of Figure 6.5. She is wearing earrings and a necklace. They glint. They should be sharpened with the tool. There is a sparkle in the center of her eyes, very important in seeming to wake the face up. That, too, should be

sharpened. And, just as we should sharpen small areas where a pure white is desirable, so should we attack those where we wouldn't mind a pure black. Namely, the eyelashes, eyelids, and possibly parts of the eyebrows as well.

The older man of Figure 6.6 is not kind enough to be looking at the camera, so we can't sharpen the center of his eyes. But wire-rimmed glasses are a tempting target, especially the lighter metal of the hinge. This guy's frames are black. If they were the more typical gold, it would be even more important to sharpen them. Such glasses vanish right into the skin without it.

There are a couple of places in the stem of the wine glass of Figure 6.11 that could stand sharpening, in addition to the area pointed out previously. And the image of the soldier in Figure 6.12 has more objects that glint than Photoshop has goofy filters.

It's more than a little doctrinaire (and certainly not recommended) to sharpen only with the tool and not the filter, as I have done here, but it isn't hard. The tool is crude enough that we don't need to vary its settings much, the way we do with the USM filter. Personally I vary the brush size, but I always use 40% pressure with mode set to Luminosity.

As for the numbers one should use with the USM filter, I will admit to having been somewhat evasive. Unlike most other areas of color correction, fixed formulas and rules don't apply. A certain amount of playing around is necessary.

Also unlike most other areas of color correction, here we really have to rely on the monitor to figure out whether our sharpening settings are sufficient or

Figure 6.12 *Local areas that sparkle are natural targets for Photoshop's sharpen tool. Note how many such areas there are in the original, left. The image at right is sharpened only with the tool, not with the normally more powerful unsharp masking filter.*

whether we have gone overboard. That's a tall order, since the phosphors of a monitor don't correspond to the realities of either desktop printers or presses. We have to make the best of it, though, by being resolution-savvy. First of all, we should be viewing the image in Photoshop at 100%. Lower magnifications are unreliable on most monitors; higher ones cause needless ulcers by displaying defects that will not be visible in print.

More important, though, if our file departs from the normal rules of resolution we need to make an adjustment for it in our minds. Normal resolution, experts agree, is between 1.5 and 2 times the screen ruling, times the magnification percentage. This

book, for example, uses a 133-line screen, so normal resolution for my digital file is between 200 and 266 pixels per inch. My images here are all around 225, and I am printing them all at 100% magnification. If I were printing one at 75% magnification, that would result in a higher than normal range (225/.75=300).

When resolution is higher than normal, the printed image will appear markedly softer than it will on the monitor. When resolution is lower than normal, the printed image will appear harsher. Be warned! If, as so many people do, you scan at 300 samples per inch regardless of the screen ruling, your monitor will be lying to you about how effective your USM is.

Location, Location, Location

If you are working with large, important images, it is well worth the time to experiment with different sharpening settings. With experience, adjusting the three numbers becomes intuitive. But if you are (for the moment) uncomfortable with how they interrelate, here is a tip.

The Amount setting is a lot more obvious than the other two, so save it for last. Start with a setting of 500%, the maximum, a Radius of 1.0 pixel, and a Threshold of zero. Although this will normally seem hideously harsh, it will also show whether you are sharpening noise and/or unwanted detail. If so, start adjusting the Threshold upward.

After Threshold is set, turn to Radius. Increase it until it seems to you to be starting to obliterate needed detail rather than emphasizing it. And once you know the proper Threshold and Radius values, it's pretty easy to adjust the Amount down. But if you

Figure 6.13 *Heavy sharpening is possible provided it is done stiletto- and not shotgun-style. Version A is the raw image. B: the original heavily sharpened in CMYK. C: Version B with the sharpening reverted to luminosity. D: Version C applied to Version A in Darker mode. E: Version C applied to Version D in Lighter mode, but at 50% opacity.*

start with a proper Amount, it's not as simple to figure out what the right Radius and Threshold should be.

Brute force is no match for intelligence. The biggest gain in sharpening remains avoiding the channels with unwanted detail, allowing a much heavier sharpen of the weaker ones that add contrast.

John of Cologne's masterpiece, the spires of the great cathedral at Burgos, present a real sharpening challenge. The blurry original of Figure 6.13 (we're in CMYK here) is in desperate need of our help.

In Photoshop, the first step is to make a copy of the file, and sharpen that. I used settings of Amount 400%, Radius 2.0 pixels, Threshold 4 levels. These numbers seem frighteningly high to

the uninitiated, but in an image like this, they are justifiable—if we are careful.

Applying these settings results in the second version, which has a color shift: brilliant blues and yellows at the building edges, easily seen in the enlarged Figure 6.14. That is fixed in the third version by using Filter: Fade > Luminosity, but the

Figure 6.14 *Enlarged for detail, the five versions of Figure 6.13 show how the lightening halos of the USM filter cause the problem and how it is eliminated by a two-step application that emphasizes darkening.*

cathedral still looks like it's falling apart because of the excessive whitening.

We now return to our saved original, and put this third version on top of it, with Image: Apply Image. This time we choose Darker as the method, resulting in version four: no white sharpening at all.

Finally, we apply version three to version four, using Lighter as the method, but this time we set Opacity to only 50%. This preserves the dark areas of version four, and creates some white sharpening, but only half as much as in version three.

Some Sharply Focused Tips

It's time to apply a little USM to this chapter, to make its points a bit crisper and more sharply focused.

• **Before doing anything, look at each channel** to see which have the detail you wish to sharpen, and also which have the noise that you don't.

• If you decide to sharpen the document as a whole rather than one or two channels, **sharpen by luminosity.**

• **Think twice about about sharpening either the blue** (RGB) **or yellow** (CMYK) **channels.** These don't have much impact on overall contrast, yet generally have the most noise and are thus the most dangerous.

• **Always think about sharpening the black, and the weak channel** (if there is one), or at least sharpening them more than the others. This applies even if you've already sharpened the entire image.

• **Sharpen after tone adjustment,** if convenient. Applying a major adjustment to an image after USM can result in exaggerating the artifacts of sharpening. Furthermore, if you think there's a chance the image may be repurposed for some other printing condition later, save a copy *before* sharpening.

• **Master the Threshold setting.** If you are having trouble, set your USM Amount all the way up to 500% while previewing the image. This will make it obvious on screen whether your threshold is suppressing the noise. Once you have found the proper Threshold, you can adjust Amount to something more reasonable.

• **Be playful,** especially if the image is a large one. There are few set rules. In a large image, a little time set aside for experimentation with ever-higher USM settings can have a big payoff.

• **Be conservative.** If eventually you decide to sharpen a little more, it won't be the end of the world. But if after a series of corrections you discover that the image is oversharpened, you may wish to turn your stiletto on yourself—oversharpening is hard to fix.

• **Be greedy.** Remember the strategy of asking for a raise. There's no fixed limit. The best amount of sharpening is, the largest amount you can get away with.

KEEPING UNSHARP MASKING ON TARGET

✓Unsharp masking is an artificial method of making an image appear in clearer focus. It works by creating subtle light and dark halos in transition areas.

✓There is no fixed amount of USM beyond which one dare not venture. Try to use as much of it as possible, without making the image appear artificial.

✓The larger the image will print, the more important experimentation with USM becomes. For small images, it's OK to get by with a single all-purpose setting.

✓For overall focusing, it's best to sharpen by luminosity: either by attacking the L channel of an LAB document, or by immediately fading the sharpening back to luminosity mode.

✓For objects dominated by red, green, or blue, think about sharpening the *weaker* plates, since the stronger ones tend to have more noise. For this type of sharpening, CMYK is a much better choice than RGB, because of the presence of black.

✓The Photoshop Radius setting governs the width of the sharpening halos. This makes it inappropriate for sharpening objects with subtle detail, which it may kill. It is, however, great for objects that don't have small tonal gradations.

✓To exclude relatively small variations from the sharpening process, increase Photoshop's Threshold. This works well in faces, where there is often detail that shouldn't be exaggerated.

✓The Photoshop Amount setting, being the easiest of all to understand, should normally be specified *after* Threshold and Radius have been chosen.

✓Be alert for the appearance of any or all of the four major sharpening blunders: a color shift; excessively obvious haloing; an intensification of unwanted detail; or an exaggeration of background noise.

✓In certain images, the lightening effect of the filter will be so offensive that a multi-step approach is needed. In such a case, make one heavily sharpened version, apply it to the original in Darker mode, and reapply it in Lighter mode at a lower opacity.

✓The sharpening tool is a useful adjunct to the USM filter. Use it to intensify type, logos, eyes, and anything in the image that sparkles or glints.

Figure 7.1 *The same color can be created by many different ink combinations. Under typical dot gain conditions, Photoshop thinks the four values in each box are equivalent. These values are derived by setting CMYK Setup for Light, Medium, and Heavy GCR, and assuming SWOP inks.*

In Color Correction, The Key Is the K

Manipulation of the black plate is the most potent tool in color correction. Gray component replacement, contrast-boosting curves, and other black magic underline why four-channel colorspaces are better than those with only three.

 six-year-old, a scientist, and an electronic retoucher were each given the same test in logic. They were asked, what do the following terms have in common: RGB, LCH, YCC, LAB, and HSB?

The six-year-old said, they all have three letters. The scientist said, each is a paradigmatic construct enabling expression of empirical visual data in the form of unique normative values of probative color equivalence. The retoucher said, each is a colorspace, but not CMYK, so to hell with 'em all.

That the six-year-old gave the most coherent and technically useful response is the theme of this chapter, in which we will discover how to make a weapon of the anomaly that sets CMYK apart from and above other color models: the presence of black ink.

The techniques discussed in this chapter are not possible in colorspaces, however attractive, that have only three variables. Taking full advantage of a four-letter colorspace can avoid a lot of four-letter words.

Black is not itself a color, but rather the total absence of color. That need not deter us from using it in color correction. In fact, it should encourage us. Since black ink blots out everything, small changes in the black content of the image have a huge impact.

Let us begin the exploration of the glories of our four-letter colorspace by discussing two other three-letterers that are very poorly understood, GCR and UCR, and how to exploit them.

Until a few years ago, artists looking for quality separations did not need to concern themselves with this topic, because desktop scanners weren't ready for prime time. High-end scanners owned by somebody else produced a CMYK file, exactly what we needed to print with, and all this GCR/UCR stuff was taken care of by the time we got the files.

As the desktop revolution has progressed, it has become more common to start with files that are *not* in CMYK. If we want to print them we have to convert them into CMYK. When we do, we will need to have some plan regarding GCR.

A Hypothetical Colorspace

If this were a perfect world, we would be able to print with CMY only. In our vale of mortal sorrows, the actual inks are not quite up to the challenge. The colors that ought to be black have a reddish-brown tinge, due to the inadequacy of cyan ink.

CMY-only printing, however, isn't all that awful. People have done it for years. Certain desktop printers use CMY only, as do a couple of large-format printers. Limiting the topic to presswork, if you skip ahead to Figures 9.1, 9.3, and 15.1, you can see comparisons of printing without any black, and the CMY versions aren't so bad. So we are talking about adding a fourth ink to a mix that already works reasonably well. How much of an impact can it have?

This question is worthy of extended discussion not just because black is such a powerhouse, but because the same considerations apply if a fifth and/or sixth color is added to CMYK. Such added colors are becoming much more common in all kinds of printing devices, so much so that I've had to add Chapter 15 of this book just to discuss their ramifications.

Note how CMY, like the five other colorspaces referred to above, has three letters. As the six-year-old remarked, there's something special about that number: uniqueness.

Take RGB. We can define any color in terms of its red, green, and blue components, but we cannot define it in more than one way. Every color is unique, and no other combination of red, green, and blue can produce it.

HSB uses an entirely different model, but the result is the same. Rather than juggle values of RGB light, it assigns a basic hue, and then modifies it with a value for color saturation (purity) and another for luminance (brightness). Again, every conceivable color can be described this way, and again, each HSB color, except for pure grays, is unique.

And so on with the other color models, including CMY, and so it will be with any other three-letter system that may be developed in the future. Each color in the system has a unique value.

Adding a fourth variable to any of these will create alternate ways to make colors that were already possible. If we are talking about inks, we also will expand the gamut of colors that can be produced on press. That the fourth variable happens to be black has nothing to do with it. If the fourth color were (to suggest something off the wall) tangerine, the considerations would be the same.

Let's talk about, then, an imaginary world of CMTY. This would be very useful if we happened to represent citrus growers. Imagine the bangup oranges, grapefruits and lemons we could produce if we could back up the basic yellow and magenta inks with a hit of tangerine. We might even be able to make brighter limes, because of the strong yellow component of tangerine ink.

This concept is technically called *gamut expansion*. $0^C50^M100^T100^Y$ is a brilliant orange, impossible to reproduce with CMY, or with CMYK for that matter. Similarly, we expand the gamut in the shadows. Tangerine ink is pretty light, but adding it to CMY shadows would help a little, creating a color darker than was previously possible.

Brilliant oranges and marginally deeper shadows are not all that tangerine has to offer. It also offers *options*—options to create colors that were already possible, but to create them with different mixes of ink.

Since tangerine could be described as a mixture of lots of yellow and a small amount of magenta ink, in principle we could put it into any color that normally contains significant amounts of yellow and even a little magenta, provided we were willing to take some yellow and magenta out to make up for it.

For example, a normal fleshtone is in the neighborhood of $10^C40^M50^Y$. $10^C39^M5^T47^Y$ should be practically the same thing. So should $10^C35^M25^T30^Y$. And so should many other possibilities. Don't hold me to these numbers, I'm guessing about dot gains and other variables, but you get the idea. If we had this problem in real life we could certainly figure out the proper numbers, with sufficient precision to obtain a colorimetric seal of calibrationist certification that the colors are actually indistinguishable.

That being so, since there is no *theoretical* difference, we have to ask, is there a *practical* one? Would we put tangerine ink in fleshtones?

I will answer this quickly. Yes, we would. There would be less variation on press, a less pronounced screening pattern, and, most important, it would reduce the range of the magenta and yellow inks, which is significant for reasons more fully, er, fleshed out on pages 170–175.

Sorry for such a brusque answer, but we don't print with tangerine, we print with black, and it's time to face up to it.

Black as Tangerine

Like tangerine, black ink expands our gamut. It doesn't help at all with citrus fruit, but it enables a far deeper shadow than was possible before. And like tangerine, it gives us options. Instead of substituting for a lot of yellow and a little bit of magenta, black substitutes for all three CMY inks simultaneously.

This discussion will be a lot easier if, for the moment, we forget about such tiresome practicalities as dot gain, different printing conditions, the anemic nature of cyan ink and other obstacles to perfection.

In this best of all possible CMY worlds, mixing equal parts of the three colors, say $25^C25^M25^Y$, would result in a perfectly neutral gray. The same, in fact, as using 25^K alone. These are the extremes, but we can also split the difference: $20^C20^M20^Y5^K$ or $15^C15^M15^Y10^K$ ought to work just as well.

Furthermore, this principle could be applied to any color that contains at least 25 percent C, M, and Y. So, $75^C25^M85^Y$, which is forest green, would be eligible: we could make it $60^C10^M70^Y15^K$, among many other choices. Although forest green is not gray, it isn't pure green either. It has a gray component, which we can partially replace with black ink, the amount of said substitution, if any, being very much up to us. Hence, gray component replacement, or GCR.

Back in the real world, dot gain and relative strengths of inks dictate numbers quite a bit different from our ideals, as Figure 7.1 shows, but the principle is the same. We need not worry about the mathematics because Photoshop does it for us, whenever we change from a three-letter colorspace into CMYK.

Each time we make this conversion, we have the option of generating a little black or a lot, or somewhere in the middle. The question must be, which is best? To which, happily, there is a clear and concise answer.

It depends.

GCR: When in Doubt, Do Without

Most magazines of circulation less than several hundred thousand adhere to the Specifications for Web Offset Publications, or SWOP. Among other things, SWOP dictates that total ink values in any area cannot exceed 300, which the majority of publications adjust downward to 280. This rule exists because, at the high speeds of a web press, greater volumes of ink can cause drying problems. Worse, it can cause ink backup, which will contaminate the lighter inks and make the run inconsistent. Some titles, typically trades that print on lesser-quality paper, ask for an even lower maximum, like 260. Newspapers commonly ask for 240.

By the same token, better printing conditions imply a higher maximum. For sheetfed printing on coated paper at reputable shops, 320 is certainly acceptable, if not 340.

Enforcement of these standards is not uniform, but many magazines pay their stripping shops for a special SWOP ad inspection, and some magazine printers do the same before putting the job on press. If you are "in the neighborhood" of 280 you are no more likely to get stopped than if you go five miles an hour faster than the speed limit, but if the ink police find 300 or higher your film will bounce, and that is a lot more serious than a speeding ticket, especially if it happens late enough in the production cycle.

A traditional, pre-Photoshop separation aimed for commercial printing might yield a shadow of $90^C80^M80^Y65^K$, which sums to 315 and would therefore trash our magazine ad. And yet we don't wish to lighten the shadow; the whole point of Chapter 3 was how important overall range is.

This solves the problem of whether to use GCR. We *have* to use it in the dark areas, because for every point of black we put in we can take out three points of the others. If we adhere strictly to the 280-point rule during separation, the shadow value will be the acceptable $75^C65^M65^Y75^K$ or something close.

That GCR in shadows is effectively mandatory has two major consequences. First, Photoshop allows us to specify a maximum ink density, forcing GCR in dark areas without necessarily affecting the rest of the picture. Second, to differentiate this species of shadow-only GCR from the picture-wide varieties, there is another term for it: UCR, for undercolor removal.

You should be aware before going further that the above definitions of these terms are generally but not universally accepted. Some people use UCR and GCR to mean the same thing, or reverse their meaning. In Europe, another term, *achromatic reproduction*, is used to signify the use of heavy GCR.

We are now ready to start a two-chapter discussion of the proper values for Photoshop's CMYK Setup, which is shown in Figure 7.2. In previous versions, this dialog box was broken into two sections, Separation Setup and Printing Inks Setup.

First, contrary to what the name might indicate, it doesn't affect files that are already in CMYK. Nor does it do anything to files that originate in RGB or LAB and stay there. The only time Photoshop looks at the settings is at the moment a file is separated, which is to say, converted into CMYK. Identical RGB files separated with two different CMYK Setups will result in two different CMYK files.

For the moment, let's put everything but the GCR/UCR choice on the back burner.

For black generation, if there is nothing to indicate otherwise, use Light. At this setting, regardless of whether we check GCR or UCR, the separation will be of the

type printers have the most experience with, and which people variously describe as *no GCR, minimum GCR*, or *a skeleton black*. Black ink starts to appear when each of the three process colors is printing more than 25% and the sum of all three values is 100 or more. If the three colors get heavier the black gets heavy faster, so that the darkest area of the picture will have black values at least as high as the magenta and yellow, and, depending on the total ink limit, perhaps even the cyan.

Photoshop 5 changes the definition of Light GCR slightly, making the black plate heavier than a corresponding separation in previous versions. The definition of a UCR separation is unchanged. Therefore, there is somewhat more difference between Light GCR and UCR in Photoshop 5 than previously was the case. I think there are very mild technical advantages to using Light GCR in preference to UCR as a general rule.

Either one, however, is certainly a skeleton black, which is mandatory for many of the curve-based corrections described in Chapters 3 and 4. There, several examples required an increase in black throughout the image. These increases added depth, but did not make the pictures muddy. With a skeleton black, there's little if any black ink in colored areas, so such a muddying effect can't happen.

Of the other four GCR options, "None" gives, as the name suggests, no black plate at all. Use it if you are intending to print CMY only. "Maximum" wipes out CMY altogether in neutral areas and is therefore unusable for most images; who needs a shadow of $0^C0^M0^Y95^K$?

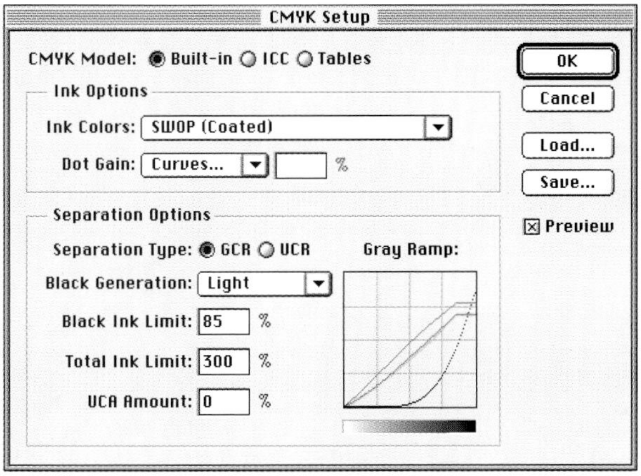

Figure 7.2 These are good all-purpose defaults. For details on the dot gain curves, see Chapter 8.

It does have one specific use, which I'll discuss shortly.

The "Medium" and "Heavy" settings, though, are perfectly workable. It therefore behooves us to inquire whether there may not be certain cases where they would be preferable.

Remembering that there is no theoretical difference between using one variety of GCR and another, there are two ways in which one may actually be superior. One is to control problems in the pressroom. The second is to make our life as color correctors easier.

When More Black Is Better

This is not a book about printing, so why do we concern ourselves about pressroom problems? Because printers are, if possible, even less inclined to take credit for their own screwups than prepress people are. Instead, if the job looks lousy, they will blame the photographer, the art director, El Niño, and, most especially, us. Worse, the client sometimes falls for this pap, or even comes to the same erroneous conclusion without any help from the printer. Preventing pressroom mistakes is therefore very much in our interest.

Black is by far the most powerful ink, and once on press, the presence of additional black has several pluses and several minuses. If the pluses seem to match what we want to accomplish with our picture it will pay to use GCR.

The most obvious way GCR can help is as a defensive measure against some of the problems caused by a variation in ink density on press. Presses and pressmen are not precision instruments, so this happens all the time. If you are operating some kind of CMYK digital printer, it may be easier to avoid such a problem, and some of these comments about black may not apply.

The nice thing about black is that it is perfectly neutral. The more black contained in any color, the less possibility that overinking of cyan, magenta, or yellow will affect the basic hue. The bad thing is that if black itself is overinked, it is much more noticeable than any of the other three.

The shish kebab of Figure 7.3 would consequently be a very bad picture for GCR. The visual strength of this image depends on retaining detail in the three-quartertones. If we engineer a lot of black into these areas and the pressman overinks, the detail in the meat will close up and image quality will fall into the flames.

You may say, suppose we don't use much black, wouldn't it be just as likely that the cyan or some other color would print too heavily, achieving the same muddy mess? Yes, surely there could be too much cyan, but it wouldn't be nearly as bad. Each process ink darkens much less than the equivalent amount of black. And as for a cyan cast, in areas this dark our eyes are not particularly sensitive to colors. We would perceive added darkness, not blue meat.

Figure 7.3 In images with critical detail in dark areas, GCR should be avoided. An unexpected overinking of black could ruin the image otherwise.

From which, we derive:

• **Rule One**: When the most important part of the image is dark, stay away from GCR.

The teddy bears of Figure 7.4 present a neutrality problem. No matter how careful we are, there is always the possibility that for any of a number of reasons an ink may run too heavily on press and we will wind up with bears that are supposed to be white or gray but instead are pink or green.

We cannot stop a determined pressman from doing this to our job. We can, however, make it a lot harder for him by using lots of GCR. The more black in the bears, the less prone they are to acquire an offensive off-color.

A less well-known extension of this rule involves items containing a grain, such as the image that is the background of Figure 7.1, or many types of wood. The grain of reddish or brownish wood can become blue rather easily. To prevent this, use higher GCR. Distinguish these cases, though, from the marbled-paper image shown back in Figure 5.9. In that image, if the grain takes on the hue of the contaminating color, it isn't such a bad thing.

• **Rule Two**: When the most important part of the image is a neutral color and it is lighter than the

Figure 7.4 Where major parts of the image are light and neutral, GCR helps guard against the possibility of color variation on press.

equivalent of 50 percent black, use GCR to guard against disaster.

As will be pointed out in Chapter 15, GCR is also useful when producing a duotone effect with process inks. If we are trying to get the look of a green duotone, we will actually use three inks: cyan, yellow, and black. No matter how good our separation is, if yellow or cyan is overinked, parts of the image may not have the uniform green tint we want. But the more black we use, the less pronounced the effect will be.

• **Rule Three**: when creating a process tritone or quadtone, use Heavy GCR.

Allowing Flexibility on Press

Sometimes color fidelity is so critical that we resort to all kinds of horsing around on press. The best-known examples are mail-order clothing catalogs. If a shirt prints in slightly the wrong shade, tens of thousands of dollars worth of merchandise will be returned by angry customers who believed the book.

In such stressful cases, pressmen and art directors do not rely on contract proofs, but

Figure 7.5 When creating an artificial drop shadow, don't forget GCR principles. The shadow should be partially black, to avoid color variation on press, but it shouldn't be all black, or there may be problems with trapping or an obvious line where the shadow ends.

on a real shirt that they hold in their hands as they try all kinds of inking shenanigans to match it.

This is not the time to use GCR, because black neutralizes everything. The more black ink, the less leeway there will be to make artistic changes on press.

• **Rule Four**: When you are expecting careful help for a critical color match during the pressrun, GCR is a hindrance.

These rules can conflict. I once had to work on a clothing catalog where the designer decided that each item should be lit in such a way that a shadow was thrown onto a light background.

As recommended above, the separations were done with minimal GCR, but the shadows handcuffed the pressmen. Any effort to color-correct the clothing caused the shadows to take on an offensive cast.

Careful technique by the artists preparing the catalog could have minimized the problem. After arranging for the liquidation of the designer, they should have created two sets of separations, one with light GCR and one with heavy. Then, they should have created composite images, using the lighter GCR for the clothing and the heavier for the shadow. The point being, of course, that if the shadow is anchored by black ink

it does not matter what gyrations may be occurring in the other three plates.

The same principles apply if you are creating drop shadows using the nifty implementation of Photoshop 5 found in Layer: Effects > Drop Shadow, as shown in Figure 7.5.

This doesn't mean make the shadow *entirely* black. If you do this, you are asking for trapping problems, and asking for a highly visible line of demarcation where the shadow fades into the background. A little bit of black goes a long way. I know some very good pressmen, but none who can make black ink print other than a shade of gray.

• **Rule Five**: When creating a drop shadow, specify around a third as much black as CMY inks.

Project design can also affect GCR desirability if there are areas near the image that require heavy coverage. Ink gets hard to control when a lot of it hits the paper at once. So, if our image is going to be placed on a solid black background (as you may recall seeing in Figure 2.2), bet on the black coming down too heavily in the picture itself. Naturally, if one is fortunate enough to know about this before converting to CMYK, one uses less GCR.

Other hints that the black may be hard to handle are very bold headline type, or text type that contains fine lines, Bauer Bodoni being the most glaring example. Any of these factors may motivate the pressman to hike the flow of black ink.

• **Rule Six**: If there is reason to fear heavy black inking on press, avoid GCR.

Repeatability with GCR

Since black ink minimizes hue variation, if the same image appears more than once, there is a good case for using GCR.

This principle seems so obvious that we may forget 95 percent of the things it applies to. An image doesn't have to be a photograph. A flat color will behave the same way. And many designs call for repetitions of the same color, usually a pastel, in large background areas.

Light colors scarcely seem like the place one would want to introduce black. But if we are trying to insure fidelity from one page to the next—as, for example, in a company logo—it can be an excellent idea.

• **Rule Seven**: When repeatability from page to page is an issue, don't forget GCR principles, even when specifying colors in linework and flat tints.

Many people wonder why we use a K to stand for black. Mainly, it's to avoid confusion: in the pressroom, cyan is customarily referred to as *blue,* so B is ambiguous. But K is more elegant, anyway. It stands for *key,* and indeed it is the key to the final major uses of GCR.

Black is the key for registration, meaning that the other three colors are supposed to be adjusted to agree with it and not vice versa. When a job is printed out of register, then, the culprit is almost invariably one of the other colors.

This suggests an application for GCR in the growing volume of work for lower print-quality applications, especially newspapers. Because of the speed of newspaper presses, misregistration is common. A beefy black will minimize it. Warning: before trying this, make sure you understand newspaper dot gain—it is greater than in other forms of printing, and if the black is too heavy the outcome will not be pleasant.

• **Rule Eight**: Where misregistration is likely, use a heavier black to control it.

The K is the key, not just in registration but in color correction generally. As the most powerful ink, it can add detail and contrast, muddy or clean up colors, and bulk up shadows in ways that three-letter colorspaces can only envy. So,

• **Rule Nine**: Before making the conversion to CMYK, ask yourself: do I want to correct this image, and can the black plate be of use?

That is a rather deep rule.

The Planned GCR Correction

There are several easy and efficient correction methods that use GCR as an accomplice. The first is for images that need focusing or definition.

Kodak Photo CD scans are the best example. Like other scans made with a wide-open profile determined by machine readouts, they are almost invariably too soft. This dictates more use of unsharp masking than one would like. But since these are customarily opened not in CMYK but in LAB, we can specify whatever GCR setting we like on the way to CMYK. If we choose Light black generation, we will get a black that includes only transition areas and anything darker. We can now exaggerate the black plate with curves, normally by boosting the quartertone point. This adds snap to the picture in a less obtrusive way than oversharpening. And it can't be done with any other GCR setting: had we used Medium or higher, there would have been black in the lighter colors, and they would have dirtied up when we applied the curve.

This boosting of black, at least through the quartertones, is so common a remedy for listless images that it, if there were nothing more, would justify using Light GCR as our standard method of converting into CMYK. If the images are produced on a drum scanner that is going to give good contrast and sharpness all the time, there is a better case for using more GCR, but that is not really a Photoshop issue.

This kind of process can also work in reverse, to give depth to an image that is too brilliant, or too dominated by a single color. In Figure 7.6, we'd like to establish more shape in the apple. At first blush,

this seems like the same problem we dealt with in the lime of Figure 5.4. There, we attacked the unwanted color, magenta, making it steeper and more detailed.

That image, however, had no background to speak of. Here, messing with the magenta will be fine for the apple, but it may turn the background purple. A better way is to hit the black—but without GCR, that won't work either. In Figure 7.7, compare the original black plates of a Light and a Heavy GCR. A curve applied to the light one would have almost no impact on the apple. In most images, that's what we want. Put black in light greens, and if black heavies up on press, we get mud.

Here, however, that *is* what we want, because it will make the apple seem rounder. And we need no help from the pressman; we can do it ourselves by separating with Heavy GCR and then bumping up the black in the manner shown, first checking that there is no black in the brightest spot of the fruit. Here, it was necessary to move the starting point of the curve slightly to the right, as shown in Figure 7.7, to do that.

Figure 7.6 *Bright objects like this apple need a quick falloff in color saturation if they are to appear round. The corrected version, right, starts off with Heavy GCR, followed by a curve that increases black.*

Putting Snap in Neutrals

When the interest areas of an image are predominantly light and neutral, we, as per Rule Two, use GCR to prevent press error. But that's not the only reason. There are uses for it even if we are going to a large-format printer, or to an Iris proofer, where we know that there will be no wild swing in inking.

Figure 7.8 is a reprise of an example in the first edition of this book. Except, I didn't do it as well as I should have, because I didn't keep that thought in mind.

What I did say was true enough. I pointed out that an image where the main subject is neutral, as the statues are, suggests a black correction. In most pictures we don't mind picking up a little extra color, here we want to stay subdued. Unfortunately, when one expands range, one

usually livens up color—unless, that is, we are talking about the black plate.

I added that there are two possible approaches. As the background is heavier than the statues, one could write a black curve that emphasized either the statues alone or both statues and background.

Increasing contrast in the original black was clearly better than nothing, but I had a smarter alternative available. I should have said to myself, this will work a lot better if I can engineer more detail into the black plate before I play with it. I should therefore have taken the image out of CMYK temporarily, changed CMYK Setup to a heavier GCR (this time, I used Medium) and *then* applied my curve to the black after returning the image to CMYK.

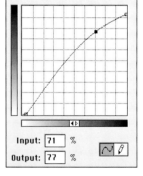

Figure 7.7 *One normally avoids excessive GCR for fear that colors will become muddy. Here, however, that is what is needed. Bottom left, the original Light GCR black; bottom right, a Heavy GCR equivalent. When the curve shown is applied to the Heavy GCR version, it produces the corrected image of Figure 7.5. Note how much darker the bottom right version is at the sides of the apple. This will seem to force them to the rear, making the fruit appear rounder.*

Input: 71 %
Output: 77 %

Figure 7.8 *Top left, the original image; top right, a conventionally corrected version. Bottom left, the same idea, but with a heavier black plate to start with. Bottom center: the original black plate, generated with Light GCR. Bottom right: the black of the version at bottom left, which had been reseparated with heavier GCR.*

Photoshop on the Razor's Edge

This is the first of several examples of how to use the GCR decision to place detail in areas that can conveniently be attacked. Next, we'll turn to something mundane, yet troublesome if not dealt with correctly.

In Chapter 6, we discussed how to avoid accentuating unwanted detail in a woman's face. That accords with current aesthetic practice: in advertising, the vogue is for women's faces to have an unnaturally perfect complexion. With men's faces, this doesn't apply, but men have a different problem: a five o'clock shadow.

At the top of Figure 7.9, that defect is present in all its glory. We may well be asked to give these gentlemen a digital shave.

One way of reducing the beard is to take the pencil tool and repeatedly sample surrounding facial areas and drop them into the individual whiskers. To me, this seems like an invitation to carpal tunnel syndrome, not to mention death from ennui. Something more straightforward is clearly necessary.

The easiest place to find the whiskers will always be in the cyan and black plates, which are much lighter than the other two. In a normal black, it will be easy to erase the whiskers, because it doesn't contain much other detail. We can even use the eraser tool, if we like.

That may be enough in certain cases, but not in others. The man at right has much coarser hair than the man at left does. To get his whiskers acceptably light, we may need to work with the cyan plate as well, but there's a problem. If we somehow eliminate the beard in the cyan, what will remain are *red* whiskers. So, how to avoid the scruffy look?

Using the Blur, Despeckle, or Dust & Scratches filters, which are more or less the opposites of adding noise and sharpening, will soften the whiskers, but also the face. They can therefore be used only in moderation.

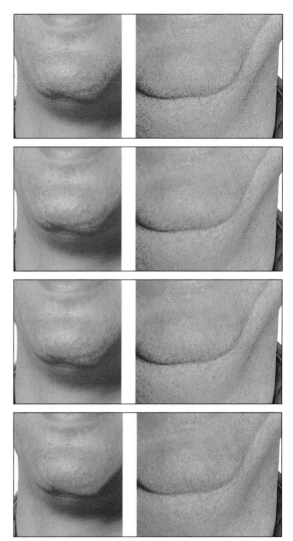

Figure 7.9 *Men's whiskers are often exaggerated during scanning and when unsharp masking is applied. Above: the original image, followed by three relatively automatic ways of correcting. Below: the original cyan plate.*

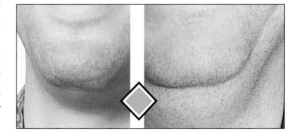

The second and third versions of Figure 7.9 both have had the whiskers excised from the black plate. In the second version, I set the airbrush tool to Lighten, 75% opacity, wide brush, and opened the cyan channel. There, I found the darkest skin except for the whiskers themselves, and by clicking on it with the Option/Alt key held down, selected it as the foreground color. Then I brushed over the area that needed a shave. This method reduces the darkness of the individual whiskers without doing anything to the rest of the face. To counteract the problem of the whiskers turning red, I also ran the Image: Noise>Despeckle filter on the magenta channel only.

The third sample uses blurring only. I ran the Image: Noise>Median filter, Radius 1.0 pixel, on the cyan plate and the despeckle filter on the magenta. Then, I added five points of noise to each one.

The fourth sample, which looks to me by far the best of the bunch, also took by far the shortest time. I wanted the stubble where I could get at it conveniently, so I reseparated the image with Heavy GCR. The whiskers landed in the black plate and I erased them. End of story.

If We Shadows Have Offended

In the Chinese tapestry image of Figure 7.10, the fly in the ointment is the shadow area, which is not even close to being dark enough. Normally, this would call for us to trot out some kind of curve to accentuate the heaviest blacks.

To use curves, however, we need a base image at least somewhere close to what we are trying to achieve, not on some other continent.

This is a most unsatisfactory image. Lighting conditions were not right when the photograph was taken. As a result, instead of the shiny black background that usually characterizes these wall hangings, we get a translucent, flimsy-looking silk fabric, the shadow of a shadow, if you will.

As matters stand, the black is at least 30 points too light everywhere. And, in the left side of the image, certain dark areas

Figure 7.10 *At top, the original suffers from poor shadow density. The corrected image uses a false reseparation to generate a stronger black plate.*

contain only 15^K, which is maybe 45 points lower than we would like.

A standard curve might work, but it also might exaggerate the difference between the left and right sides of the image. It may seem like we are left with the tedious alternatives of local selection, or blending the cyan plate, which has a decent shadow, into the black. That strategy would risk contaminating the lighter areas of the picture with black, and those areas, at the moment, are pretty good.

Now that we are GCR experts, there's a more effective option: a false reseparation. Using Image: Duplicate, make a copy of the image, and convert it to LAB. Change CMYK Setup to UCR, a black ink limit of 85%, and the ludicrously low total ink limit of 215. Photoshop doesn't know that no printing conditions on this planet require this low of a limit; it assumes we knows what we are doing. And we now bring the copy back to CMYK.

The black of this monstrosity will have heavier shadows, because whenever the sum of the CMY values would otherwise reach 180 or so—which happens throughout the black parts of the silk—extra black will have to be generated instead, to stay within the absurd total ink limit of 215. At the same time, the lighter areas of the black plate will be unaffected, since we specified UCR rather than GCR. This confines the damage to areas that exceed the total ink limit we specified in CMYK Setup; the bright colors in the fabric won't change.

The CMY plates of this new separation are quite worthless and should be given the burial they deserve. But when we replace the original black plate with the black from the second separation, surprise, we suddenly have a decent piece of art.

Do Your Eyes Glaze Over?

The theme of a false reseparation has another major use, although depending on your work, you may not be affected. And the use is—well, are you suddenly having trouble reading this text?

The subhead above, and these two paragraphs of text, are not set in the conventional way. Instead of forming the letters with solid black ink, I am giving them the value of a shadow, as if they were a photograph, 80^{C}70^{M}70^{Y}70^K.

So much for the demonstration. Obviously, having three extra inks back up the black type is not a particularly successful notion. Neither is the concept of breaking up the black plate into halftone dots. Notice that the effect is much worse in the text than in the subhead.

This is because of the presence of fine lines in the text typeface. Trying to print these accurately with a 133-line screen is like trying to drain a lake with a slotted spoon, especially because the fine lines are horizontal and the screens of the three heaviest inks are angled.

Without such fine lines, the subhead can handle this kind of black fairly well. It's not quite as dark as it should be, but this is because the shadow value is designed to be light enough to protect delicate detail, which type doesn't have. But if we increased the weight of all four inks, we could probably get by.

Switching back to images, the overwhelming majority resemble the subhead more than the text. So, in a case like Figure 7.10 we are better off with a balanced four-ink shadow than with one constructed of black alone. This is why we stick with Light, Medium, or Heavy GCR, not Maximum, for the overwhelming majority.

Those words *overwhelming majority,* naturally, imply an exception. And the exception is images that for some reason have something in common with the text type, namely, fine lines that should print in black. One such category of images appears frequently in this book. Can you name it?

Yes, indeed. I am referring to screen grabs such as Figure 7.2. Note the fine black lines around the dialog box. Printing these as a standard shadow would be about as successful as my earlier experiment with the text type. When reproducing cartoons, which tend to have fine black lines, we run into the same problem. Figure 7.11 is a more difficult example.

Assume that the client insists on greater prominence and legibility for the small type elements at the bottom and the black line that borders the green type at the top. Right away, we should be thinking of Maximum GCR, to get solid black in the type.

Yet, this image is made up of dull colors, where large amounts of black are generally a poor choice. The consequences of unpredictable ink coverage argue strongly against vast amounts of black anywhere *except* in the area we're trying to emphasize.

Accordingly, we really need two separations, one with Light and one with Maximum GCR. If the original starts out in RGB or LAB this is ideal, but even if we are given a CMYK file, such as the top half of Figure 7.11, to start with we can still fix it as follows:

•   Make a copy of the original (which in this case has Light GCR) and convert it to LAB.

•   Change CMYK Setup to Maximum GCR, 100% black ink limit. Convert the copy back into CMYK.

Figure 7.11 *Images where fine type is critical become candidates for a two-step process involving Maximum GCR followed by a blend with a standard separation.*

• Still working with the reseparated copy, using the lasso tool, make a quick and dirty freehand selection of the woman and the flower, and delete this entire area from the image. The selection doesn't have to be at all accurate, as long as it doesn't delete any of the type. The idea is to prevent any of this area from being overwhelmed by black ink during the eventual blend.

• Apply a curve to what's left of the black plate by moving the top right point to the left, thus darkening the shadow. The idea is to get the type areas to be close to 100^K. The rest of the image, other than a big hole in the middle of it, will now be too dark; ignore this.

• Copy this overly dark image to the clipboard. Paste it on top of the original, making it a layer.

• Activate Layer: Layer Options as shown at the bottom of Figure 7.12. As set up, it tells Photoshop to replace the bottom layer with the top *only* where the black plate of the top layer is heavy, meaning, only in the areas we care about.

There remains one slight problem: the image now needs to be trapped—which brings up another important use of GCR.

Staying Out of Traps with GCR

Trapping is desirable when two totally different colors butt one another. Without trapping, a disagreeable white line can occur if the job should happen to be printed out of register.

For example, suppose that for some stupid reason it was decided that the background of this page should be magenta, the text type black as it is now, but that the subheads should be printed in cyan. If the magenta stops at exactly the point it hits either kind of type, we are

asking for trouble. If it does, and the registration of the two colors on press isn't perfect, a white hole will appear on one side of the type and a darker overlap on the other.

Figure 7.12 *The progress of beefing up the type. Left side, the black plate, top to bottom: the original with Light GCR; a second version with Maximum GCR; the final merged product. Below, the Layer Options dialog box set up to accept only the type from the second black version. Right side, the cyan plate. Top to bottom: the original; after the version with Maximum GCR has been merged in; after running Photoshop's Trap filter.*

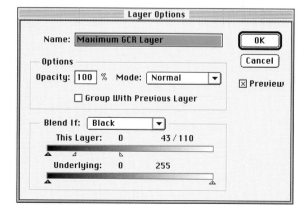

To guard against such an ugly occurrence, the cognoscenti build in intentional overlaps—some of the time. In the case of the cyan headline, we would make it slightly fatter so that it would overlap the magenta background. With the black text type, we would not interrupt the background at all, but just print right on top of it.

As you may know or suspect, learning how to trap isn't especially easy. Fortunately, in most of the work discussed in this book, it's unnecessary: photographs rarely need to be trapped at all.

The reason is, before trap is necessary, there has to be a knifelike edge between two colors that have very little in common, such as pure magenta and pure cyan. In a photograph, those two things almost never happen at the same time. Edges tend to be somewhat indistinct, and colors somewhat subtle, meaning that any two neighboring colors probably share certain common values and a white line or even a relatively light one cannot appear.

With Maximum GCR, however, this is no longer the case. Now, black elements, such as type, will

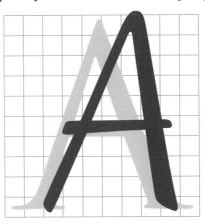

Figure 7.13 *When all graphic elements share large amounts of color (here, cyan) trapping is unnecessary.*

have virtually no CMY component and thus may have nothing in common with their colored neighbors.

In Figure 7.12 note what is happening to the cyan plate after the Maximum GCR type is merged into it. The body of the type is now nearly blank. It thus is possible, if the black is sufficiently out of register, for the dreaded white line to appear.

It's not totally obvious that this is a trapping situation, because a very slight overlap already exists. But I think it makes sense to do it, particularly since Photoshop makes it so easy. Image: Trap offers us a dialog box that allows us to specify the width of the desired trap, in pixels. I chose the minimum, one pixel, and got the result on the bottom right of Figure 7.12.

A mild trap like this has virtually no impact on the rest of the picture. The only trick is knowing where it's necessary.

Finding the Real PMS Equivalent

As previously noted, if you never use Maximum GCR, you'll probably never have to trap a photograph. But because most readers occasionally have other kinds of trapping problems, I'm reluctant to let the subject drop, because Photoshop can be a big help in solving them.

Being lazy, I think that the best way to avoid trapping problems is to avoid situations that require building a trap. Figure 7.13 is an enlarged version of the drop cap that appears on the first page of this chapter. It was constructed in Adobe Illustrator, not Photoshop. In this design, no trap is necessary. There is no possible turn of events that can result in a white line. The background grid is cyan, but both letters have a significant cyan component.

Suppose, though, that the background letter were not a bluish gray, but a gray, period. Now, it's a trap situation, if you happen to be an idiot. An idiot says that gray is a shade of black, and constructs it entirely out of that ink. And, as there is no black ink in the grid, trapping becomes necessary.

You would not, of course, do this, because you are not an idiot, and you know the theory of GCR. You realize that you can make a gray just as well with the CMY inks as with black, and a CMY gray will have enough cyan in common with the grid that trapping will no longer be an issue.

That was an easy exercise, but are you willing to carry it further, into a case where there is nothing gray? Let's assume that it's the Christmas season, and the client wants us to print with red and green. Only, we are given Pantone Matching System equivalents, which we have to match with process inks. Let us say PMS 179 for the red and PMS 342 for the green, and that we need to print green type on a red background, or vice versa.

Chances are, we aren't doing this job in Photoshop, but we could if we liked, because the PMS process equivalents are built in, as Figure 7.14 shows (to get there, double-click on either the foreground or background color at the bottom of the toolbox, and choose Custom from the next menu.)

All other professional-level programs have these values built in as well, and they will all give PMS 179 a value of $0^C79^M94^Y$. PMS 342 will be, as seen in Figure 7.14, $100^C0^M69^Y43^K$. And we have a trapping problem. The two colors have only 69^Y in common. Yellow is a very light color. A bright yellow line appearing between relatively dark green and red is no good.

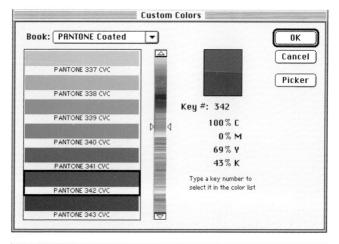

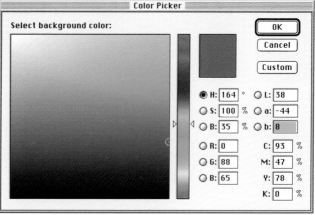

Figure 7.14 *Pantone Matching System formulations aren't necessarily the best for trap avoidance. Above, locating the nominal CMYK values in the Custom Colors submenu of the Color Picker. Below, using LAB equivalents to find a definition of the same green that uses magenta rather than black ink.*

Those may be the numbers Pantone recommends, but GCR theory tells us that there are many other ways of making the same green—and if we make it with magenta ink, rather than black, the green and the red will have enough in common that we can forget about trap.

Here is where Photoshop can help us in a way that other applications can't: it will tell us the equivalents. To find out, call up the Color Picker by double-clicking on

Figure 7.15 *Because one color may have several CMYK equivalents, canny users can eliminate many trapping headaches. Above left, the green type, pursuant to a Pantone definition, has a great deal of black and no magenta. Unfortunately, this means that the red and the green do not have enough in common. If the magenta prints out of register (above right) an obvious yellow line appears. But by redefining the green to a rough equivalent that uses magenta in lieu of black (lower left), such a yellow line becomes impossible. The worst that can happen is a pink line (lower right). The upper left version requires trap, the lower left does not.*

either the foreground or background color in the toolbox. This time, rather than clicking Custom, enter Pantone's CMYK values for the green in the bottom right.

The Color Picker works not only in CMYK but in the three other colorspaces that are the subject of this section of the book. So, when we enter $100^C0^M69^Y43^K$, three equivalent values automatically appear, namely, $0^R87^G65^B$, $38^L–44^A8^B$, and $165^H34^S100^B$. Whether you would know offhand that any of these colors is a green, let alone the same green, is entirely irrelevant. What you already know is that in these three colorspaces, these values are unique. But in CMYK, they aren't, thanks to what might be called tangerine theory.

If we enter a CMYK value in the picker, Photoshop has no choice about what RGB, LAB, and HSB numbers to represent it with. But what if we start out by entering the number in something *other* than CMYK? How does Photoshop then decide which of the infinite number of CMYK equivalents to use?

That's up to us. So, we close the Color Picker, and open CMYK Setup. We change the black generation preference to None. Then, back to the Color Picker, where we enter the known LAB (or whatever, it shouldn't make a difference) value and see what Photoshop gives us for CMYK. As the bottom half of Figure 7.14 indicates, the answer is $93^C47^M78^Y$.

THE POWER OF THE BLACK PLATE

✓Although black has no color of its own, it is the most powerful of the four process inks. Generally, adding black has as much impact as adding all three of the other colors simultaneously.

✓At a minimum, there needs to be enough black to give depth to shadow areas. That is the traditional method of making a color separation. There are, however, instances where more black is desirable.

✓CMYK is unique in that most colors can be expressed as more than one combination of inks, depending upon how much black is being used. This is the principle behind gray component replacement.

✓Any time an image goes from another colorspace into CMYK, we have to make a GCR decision. Unless there is a reason to do otherwise, use Light GCR, which will yield a minimum, or skeleton, black.

✓SWOP dictates that the sum of all four ink values not exceed 300, but most publications request a 280 maximum. This effectively requires use of GCR in shadow areas. This species of GCR has its own name, undercolor removal, or UCR.

✓When the most important part of an image is neutral, using heavier GCR can avoid problems on press.

✓For cartoons, critical fine type, and anything else that requires fine black lines, consider one separation with Maximum GCR merged into another with standard settings, using Layer Options to limit the merge to the black areas.

✓Contrast-enhancing curves in a skeleton black plate are an excellent way of adding focus to an image. The most common adjustments are an overall increase, or a boost in quartertone values.

✓Applying unsharp masking to the black plate only is often very effective in creating better definition, without some of the drawbacks of using it on all four plates.

✓Information gathered from Photoshop's Color Picker can be helpful in finessing trapping problems. Most CMYK colors can be expressed in many ways, so one chooses the numbers that avoid the necessity of trap.

Armed with this information, we go back to the application we were using, plug in the new green value, and call it quits. Since the red and green now share 47^M78^Y, a reasonably dark orange, the trap problem vanishes, as illustrated in Figure 7.15.

Incidentally, even if you don't have a trapping problem, you should use this approach to find PMS equivalents. The CMYK values that Pantone suggests assume finer printing conditions than most of us have. Assuming that we aren't printing on coated paper on a sheetfed press, using these values will give us a color that is unnecessarily dark, in comparison to its spot-color cousin.

To correct this, read the LAB values just as we did above, *and then type the same values right over themselves.* This will force Photoshop to recompute the colors using current CMYK Setup assumptions for dot gain and ink balance, and will result in a more accurate match, no matter what kind of GCR you have chosen.

It All Fits Together

If we are working in CMYK, we are well served to know what CMYK is all about. This example, where Photoshop knowledge is found useful even in a job that seems to have nothing at all to do with Photoshop, holds a lesson.

Note, also, how it is helpful to know equivalencies in other colorspaces. In the next four chapters I'll try to show how they all fit into a pattern, and how they can be exploited.

Other difficult corrections are possible by correct use of dot gain curves and of the various ink limits. At the end of Chapter 8,

we'll have a look at the toughest conversion yet, a last-ditch effort to save important detailing in the shadows.

This concludes our current exercises, but not our exploitation of the awesome power of black ink as an enhancement tool. Once you master it, you will feel as much pity as I do for the scientists who, with no personal experience in color correction, preach that one should only manipulate images in a three-variable colorspace, and that GCR decisions should be made on the fly by the output device.

If ever you are forced to work under such straitened systemic circumstances, you will be able to produce pretty good color if you have become proficient at writing curves.

But if pretty good is not quite good enough for you, accept that your perpetual punishment for acceding to a three-variable colorspace will be color that can only be pretty good, forever. Through eternity, a voice in your mind, whispering ever so softly, will torment you by repeating the biggest secret in professional color reproduction. As you wail and gnash your teeth over your lack of a good image backbone, over your inability to hold neutral colors, over the missing definition, the highlights that cannot be highlighted, the voice will continue to haunt you; and whatever your color correction talents, however close you get to the sacred territory that is better than pretty good, you will continue to hear it. And you will know and understand, even without the voice, that if you wish to unlock the cell of your pretty good prison, that if you wish to be set free into a better-looking world, the lifeless, gray door *can* be opened—and the key is the K.

CHAPTER 8

Managing Photoshop's Separation Settings

Separating a file into CMYK was never easy, and Photoshop 5 introduces many complications. Keeping things under control depends on understanding a sad, paradoxical law: the more you try for perfection, the farther away from it you'll get.

merican football is played on a rectangular field roughly 50 by 100 yards, exclusive of the end zones. The field in the Canadian version of the game is about 10 yards wider in each direction.

The larger field mandates certain rule changes. For one thing, Canadian teams have a twelfth player. There are only three downs, rather than four. Although the passing game is emphasized, the same plays work in both games, and the same skills differentiate the star player from the mediocre one.

A football fan therefore adjusts easily to watching either version of the sport. But suppose that the differences were much greater. Imagine a kind of football played on the side of a hill, rather than on a flat surface, and on a trapezoidal, rather than rectangular, field, with a brook and a few trees in the middle of it.

Once you realize that in such a game the set plays and strategies of conventional football no longer necessarily work, you are well on the way to understanding why so many people have trouble making decent color separations. To be more precise, they are having trouble translating scans (or digital captures) into CMYK.

For that matter, we are starting to need new types of separations that involve different flavors of CMYK (as for both a newspaper and an annual report) or devices that use more than four inks or toners in an effort to get snappier color.

Prepress professionals don't have a whole lot of experience in solving this problem. Until recently, most separations were done on drum scanners that converted to CMYK on the fly. An RGB file never existed, so the question of whether the CMYK file looked like the RGB never came up.

Jumping to the conclusion that making the conversion must be easy, if only one spends enough on color-measurement devices and software, various parties have hyped "solutions" which, quite predictably, the market has emphatically rejected.

As I argued in Chapter 2, the reason these products haven't flown is not a lack of sophistication, or inadequate computing power. The whole concept is wrong. Those whose quest is the perfect separation algorithm are chasing rainbows, setting traps for unicorns.

Indeed, the perfect separation method is a mythical creature, but one with a substantial sting: the closer one tries to get to it, the farther away it seems to be. This chapter will try to explain why, review the changes in Photoshop 5's color defaults, and suggest how to adjust them to deliver better results.

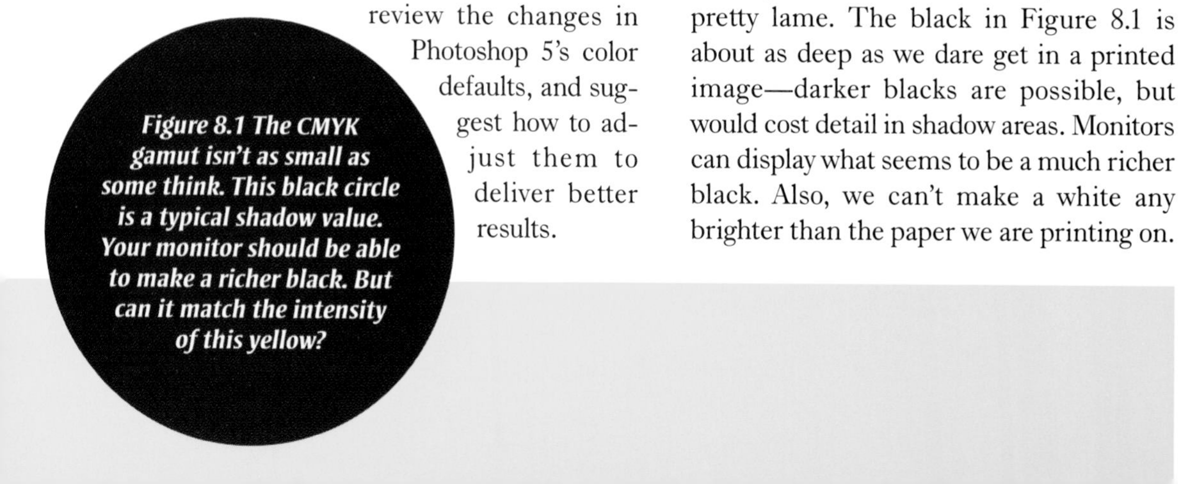

Figure 8.1 The CMYK gamut isn't as small as some think. This black circle is a typical shadow value. Your monitor should be able to make a richer black. But can it match the intensity of this yellow?

Decisions and Damage Control

As with football, trying to translate between colorspaces is only hard when the rules they play by are radically different. A monitor and a transparency have slightly different gamuts (the monitor can get a richer blue; the film can achieve better secondary colors) but these differences in what colors can be had are small in the overall scheme of things. So it isn't difficult to create RGB files that more or less match the chrome. It is also easy to adjust one professional digital proofing system, such as Iris, to match another, such as Approval, or to match a digital proof to a traditional film-based contract proof such as a Matchprint.

Going from RGB to CMYK is not nearly as simple. Some people say that this is because the playing field is smaller, naïvely ignoring that it is tilted as well. Let's take a quick survey of what RGB can portray that CMYK can't—and vice versa. For this, you will need your imagination, because while I can tell you what colors aren't possible in CMYK, for obvious reasons, I can't *show* you.

The differences can (and should) be divided into two categories: color and contrast. Contrast is mostly a matter of how bright and how dark the white and black points are. In this area, CMYK is pretty lame. The black in Figure 8.1 is about as deep as we dare get in a printed image—darker blacks are possible, but would cost detail in shadow areas. Monitors can display what seems to be a much richer black. Also, we can't make a white any brighter than the paper we are printing on.

Because there is less of a darkness range available, the CMYK practitioner needs to emphasize contrast. In football or hockey, a larger playing surface rewards speed and finesse, and a smaller one favors physical strength. CMYK is much the same thing.

But the playing field, in addition to being smaller, is also weirdly shaped. The popular knock against CMYK is that is lacks the the color range of RGB. In most respects, that's correct. But in others, it has more. Let's contrast the capabilities of a monitor to those of commercial printing.

The building blocks of each are different. A monitor's phosphors are red, green, and blue, highly convenient if pure red, green, or blue appears in the image. On press, red, green, and blue are each mixtures of two inks, which is a disadvantage. On the other hand, CMYK is well equipped to produce pure cyan, magenta, and yellow.

Especially yellow. It's technically the purest ink, and under good printing conditions, a stronger yellow is available than can be had in real-world RGB. Can your monitor match the intensity of the patch of yellow shown in Figure 8.1? Solid magenta and cyan also can be as intense on paper as they are on a screen.

As these colors get lighter, however, CMYK has more trouble with them. Bubble-gum pink is a shade of magenta, so you might think that you could portray it as well in print as on a monitor. No way. As colors get lighter, they get represented by smaller and smaller dots, and accordingly, larger and larger quantities of blank, featureless paper. The monitor has no such dot structure, and can create much more appetizing-looking bubble gum.

And the notorious weakness of print work is that cyan ink does not mix well with

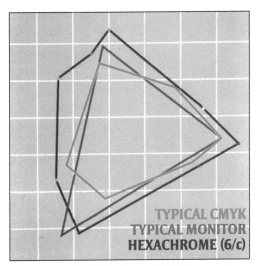

TYPICAL CMYK
TYPICAL MONITOR
HEXACHROME (6/c)

Figure 8.2 The tilted playing field. A comparison of the gamuts of a generalized CMYK versus that of a typical monitor and of six-color printing. Note that in spite of CMYK's terrible weakness in the blue corner (lower left) it is still capable of certain colors that a monitor can't reproduce.

magenta. Therefore, although reds and greens in CMYK are somewhat worse than those available in RGB, the blues of CMYK are *far* worse—the clearest example of the tilted playing field.

Figure 8.2 shows one manufacturer's conception of the gamut differences, contrasting the capabilities of a monitor, normal CMYK, and a six-color process.

To summarize the differences: in CMYK we have better yellows, about the same magentas and cyans, but lousy reds, worse greens, and disastrous blues, in comparison to RGB. As the colors get lighter, everything changes in favor of RGB, except the CMYK disadvantage in blues is minimized. Also, CMYK lacks contrast generally.

That is a clear case of playing by different rules. When the differences are this complex, beware of anybody saying they have a foolproof conversion.

A Question of Aesthetics

The aspen forest of Figure 8.3 speaks starkly about the injustices of CMYK. It's an outstanding image—in RGB. It loses a lot in translation to the printed page.

In the original, the sky is lighter than what you see here, but also much bluer—a

Figure 8.3 Brilliant blues are the major weakness of the CMYK colorspace. The sky in the RGB original of this image is an almost luminous blue, a blue that can't be reproduced in print.

nearly luminous, icy, gorgeous light blue. I have more chance of playing tackle for the Edmonton Eskimos than of reproducing that color accurately in this book.

On the other hand, part of the reason the blue is so striking in the original is that it plays off against the bright yellows of the leaves, a CMYK strength. We are not at the limit of yellow ink yet. I can make those leaves yellower still, brighter than they were in the original. But *should* I?

Granted that we can't match the original or even come close, there are many ways to try to make the best of this bad situation. Should we

- Tone down the yellow, to keep the relative balance with the blue?
- Ratchet the yellow up, to accentuate the contrast between yellow and blue?
- Wipe out any yellow or black ink in the sky, which will wipe out detail as well, yet make the sky seem bluer?
- Increase cyan ink in the sky, to make it bluer, albeit darker?
- Or, is the answer none of the above, but rather the image just as it appears here? Not too likely: this separation was done in Photoshop 5 using the default setting, which is not good for this type of image.

I suggest that this is a problem without a solution. Some images will look better if we make the colors more vivid. Others will not. Human beings make such aesthetic decisions routinely, and accurately. Profiles and other algorithms are rather bad at it.

The EIAM and the PCCM

Now, let's consider a general approach to converting a document from RGB into CMYK. I will kick off by proposing a method so preposterous that you may have trouble recognizing its intrinsic logic.

Here it is: for every RGB color that can be faithfully reproduced in CMYK, do it. For every color that can't, do something completely random, such as translate it into lime green. Because of this uncertainty, I dub this approach EIAM, which stands for, Every Image an Adventure Method.

EIAM has, to put it mildly, distinct disadvantages. For example, if it is used to convert the aspen forest image, the sky will become lime green, which is unlikely to please our client.

If this sounds very radical and unreasonable, it is, but no more so than the team it's up against. That opponent, the PCCM, tries to force the two colorspaces into the same shape, so that the brightest red, say, in RGB becomes the brightest red possible in CMYK, with all other reds being toned down to accommodate it. PCCM normally features some artificial color-measurement device measuring swatches such as the one shown earlier in Figure 2.3. To the extent that actual images are used to try to match the two colorspaces, they tend to be grossly atypical ones, such as Figure 8.4.

Hence, the name I have chosen for it: the Politically Correct Calibrationist Method. PCCM is the wishy-washy approach of finesse and compromise, just as EIAM is the blunderbuss method of brute force and hope for the best.

Before you write off EIAM for what it did to Figure 8.4, remember that this particular image was a setup for PCCM, specifically composed to present virtually every kind of technical difficulty that the separation process can encounter. Photoshop's "Olé No Moiré" and Kodak's "Musicians" are similar. Critical detail exists in both highlights and shadows, there are out-of-gamut colors everywhere, there are neutral colors that must be retained, every hue is in use, there are fabric patterns prone to moiré, and there are subtle shadings even in the most brilliant colors.

You could spend a lifetime in the graphic arts and never work a live image that has all of these characteristics at the same time. If you ever encounter one of these monstrosities—don't hold your breath—PCCM is definitely the best way to separate it.

But it succeeds in this unusual case at a considerable price. Think about the critical color, blue. In the original RGB, we have certain blues that are simply too brilliant to be duplicated in CMYK. We have some other bright blues that *could* be duplicated, if we made them as blue as possible, which is what EIAM, the steamroller, would do.

PCCM, the great compromiser, trying to retain some distinction between the two kinds of blues, tones both of them down—along with every other blue down the food chain.

That works well enough in this particular image, but what if there were no brilliant blue in the original? Then the compromise would be pointless. We would be toning down our in-gamut blues for no reason. Here is where EIAM, which does no toning down of anything, would have a decided advantage.

Despite its calibrationist, match-the-art aura, PCCM guarantees that we will *never* match the art—all colors will be toned down, and all images will look flatter than the original.

EIAM, on the other hand, is for the high roller. If the art can't be matched, catastrophe! But if it can, EIAM will do it, and in those images it will outscore PCCM.

A General Law, Sad but True

Which of my two proposed methods of separation is better depends very much on your definition of *better.* If the definition is, which method produces more *acceptable* images, obviously PCCM wins: it is stolid, stodgy, and free from ridiculous errors.

It is also a recipe for mediocrity.

Suppose, though, that the question is, which method works better *most of the time?*

Guess what! Most images don't contain out-of-gamut colors. And for all those that don't, that silly EIAM will kick butt, as it does in the Goya painting of Figure 8.5. How good can political correctness be, when an *absurd* method gets palpably better results on the majority of images?

EIAM *is* absurd. In real life we don't deliberately sabotage images, the way EIAM would to anything that contains an out-of-gamut color. So, if forced to choose one or the other, we have to pick PCCM, because even if we are dissatisfied with its results, we can perhaps fix them, which is more than can be said if EIAM starts dispensing lime-green pixels all over the place.

But intermediate approaches are possible—and very, very practical. Confronted by an out-of-gamut color, EIAM drops back 15 yards and punts. It is content with a totally unacceptable image. We can, however, visualize a smarter method with all the advantages of EIAM. Such a method would fake it by substituting for out-of-gamut colors not lime green, but something close

Figure 8.4 The separation approaches described in this chapter as the EIAM (top, creating areas of lime green wherever it can't match a color) and the PCCM (below, toning down everything to accommodate the brightest shades.)

to what the colors actually were. Granted, a lot of detail might vanish in these areas as a result.

With PCCM, we have acceptable color 100 percent of the time, but if its color isn't bad, neither is it good. With pure EIAM, we have a better image than PCCM maybe 60 percent of the time. The other 40 percent of cases are disastrous, full of lime green and totally unacceptable.

The less ridiculous version of EIAM described above does better. Now, we may beat PCCM 70 percent of the time. An additional 10 percent of the time the image

will be acceptable, yet not so good as PCCM's. The remaining 20 percent remains, well, unacceptable.

The time has now come to state the law that governs all transformations from one colorspace to another. It is a sad law, a rock-and-a-hard-place law, but an uncompromising, invariable one. Here it is:

The better the algorithm does on the typical image, the more prone it is to do something really objectionable to ones that are not typical.

Interpretation: our choice really depends on whether we want something to be good, or whether we don't want it to be bad. The difference explains a lot about why people have such strong feelings about the separation process.

Figure 8.5 *Goya's famously ugly portrait of the queen of Spain doesn't contain any colors that can't be matched in CMYK. Therefore, EIAM, left, wins this competition.*

For one thing, it explains why so many people accuse Photoshop of making "bad" separations. What is meant by that is that Photoshop, like its relative EIAM, sometimes uncorks a real howler, changing blues to purples with great elan and losing detail in out-of-gamut colors. If you see enough of these stinkers, admittedly you may think that Photoshop itself is what stinks. But all it is doing is following my law: since it generally makes good separations, it frequently makes bad ones.

The law also explains why, after ten years of endless hype, workflows that allow correction only in RGB, with the CMYK conversion done on the fly at the last minute, have been such a total flop. All such methods have been PCCM-based—which means that for the majority of images, they will not do even as well as the idiotic EIAM, let alone a more sophisticated variant, such as Photoshop. (I am not attacking here those who do *some* corrections in RGB, only those who do *all* correcting there and assume the conversion will miraculously be perfect.)

This workflow's advocates have so far offered us applications that are expensive and hard to learn. Considering that they also don't provide separations as good as Photoshop's most of the time, it adds up to a pretty severe market handicap.

Photoshop 5's Four Setup Boxes

The changes in color handling made in Photoshop 5 are the most significant in the program's history. Before designing our own separation method, we need to go over the new options, and how they compare to those offered in previous versions.

Photoshop 5.0 was booby-trapped by defaults that, without warning, altered the colors in existing files. Faced with a user revolt, Adobe released a patch, version 5.0.2. It, and version 5.5, don't change 5.0's color structure, but add a color "wizard" who tries to help you find appropriate settings. This crutch makes it less likely that you will wind up with something really stupid, such as the 5.0 defaults.

I say, to hell with the wizard. Learn what the settings mean, and change them to what best suits you. I also say, if you are not familiar with ICC-based color management, or if your workflow functioned well with earlier versions, leave it turned off. Instructions on how to do so are on page 27. The new features do have merit for certain operations and you may wish to experiment with them later.

Edit: Color Settings breaks down into the following four subsections.

• **RGB Setup** has no specific equivalent in earlier versions of Photoshop, although it is related to what was previously called Monitor Setup. The function is to establish an "RGB workspace" that is "device independent," a whimsical notion that would have done nobody any harm—if only every user really understood how it worked.

• **CMYK Setup** combines two previous dialog boxes, Printing Inks Setup and Separation Setup, adding the option of separating using ICC profiles, and a useful new way to edit dot gains in specific inks. All the defaults *look* like those of earlier Photoshops, but this is a clever device to lull us to sleep. With these defaults, Photoshop 5 yields much lighter separations than past versions. So if we were happy with the way things were, we have to act.

• **Grayscale Setup** replaces, with different terminology, the checkbox "Use dot gain for grayscale images" previously found in Printing Inks Setup. Unlike the other three options, there's nothing dangerous about this one. If we intend to print black and white images, we choose Black Ink. If we are intending the files to go to the Web or otherwise remain viewable on screens, we choose RGB.

• **Profile Setup** is entirely new. This is the enforcement arm of color management. It looks for ICC profiles, if you let it, on incoming files, and will alter their colors on the fly, if you don't stop it. It will embed ICC tags in the Photoshop files you save, inviting other applications to alter them later, unless you change it.

This is an ugly situation. Not so much because we can't control our own settings, but we now have little idea what settings our clients are using, and why. In a worst-case scenario, a client with a foggy understanding of these matters may inadvertently start making major color changes to files that started out correct.

Choosing the CMYK Settings

"We have had reports," said an Adobe white paper on color management that accompanied the beta release of Photoshop 5, "that the separations from Photoshop 4 tended to run a little on the dark side."

Considering that almost everybody who writes about color management feels compelled to obscure everything with clouds of gobblydegook, one can enthusiastically endorse such a clear description of the problem. We do not need to discuss tristimulus values, histograms, delta-E, Neugebauer equations, or the hyperbolic cosecant of the cube root of the number of companies that have gone out of business peddling color management solutions. What we need to discuss is, the images are too dark.

"A little on the dark side," while pretty good English, leaves an important question unanswered, namely, too dark *for what?* Because Adobe forgot to ask itself this question, Photoshop 5's defaults were changed in a way that causes problems for anybody who is used to the separations generated by earlier versions.

Adobe blamed this lamentable darkness on the dot gain settings of earlier Photoshop versions, which it therefore changed in Photoshop 5. But it did so in a crazy way. Rather than simply altering the default dot gain number, it kept the same number but changed what it meant, except with its Eurostandard settings, where it changed both. This disenfranchises anyone whose workflow was based on the numbers valid in earlier revisions of Photoshop.

A technical description of the phenomenon of dot gain would be the most difficult topic in this book, worse even than the spec for the LAB colorspace. Please understand that I am sparing you Murray-Davies equations and other gory details because I am merciful by nature, and that the following summary is not just smoke-blowing.

The truth about dot gain is, we know it exists, but that's almost all. We don't have agreement on how to measure it, we don't have agreement on what causes it, and we don't have agreement on where it is worst. We do know that the same image printed on different paper usually seems to be darker on the cheaper stock. Similarly, the more a press is built for speed, the less it is built for quality. Very fast presses usually seem to print darker than more conservative ones.

Even these sketchy rules have exceptions, however. About the best we can say for sure is, if the image is going to print on newsprint, it will seem darker than it would on better papers. Consequently, we have to, by hook or by crook, produce a *lighter* final image than usual, if we are intending it to appear in a newspaper.

Everything else is a matter of probabilities. Sheetfed presses are slower, and therefore usually seem to print lighter than web (rollfed) presses. Bet on this by assuming a lower dot gain for sheetfed printing—just don't bet your life.

It's especially a matter of probabilities because in the pressroom, dot gain changes not just minute by minute, but one can commonly have different dot gains at the same moment on the same unit of the same press. Where the press form is large, the outside pages of a signature frequently suffer higher dot gains than those printed on the inside. Similarly, on web presses especially, pages printed on the inside of the paper roll tend to have two or three points more dot gain than those printed on the relatively smoother side of the paper on the outside of the roll.

Whether or not you followed that last paragraph, it should be clear that this is very much a by-guess-and-by-gosh adjustment. It's possible to do it all in one's head, not changing any Photoshop settings but simply producing lighter separations and hoping for the best.

Most people, however, find it more sensible to adjust the dot gain percentage in CMYK Setup.

For a file that is already in CMYK, changing things in CMYK Setup doesn't alter the file—but it does alter what we see on the screen. If we raise the dot gain setting, Photoshop tries to give us a better idea of what the printed result will look like, by darkening the *preview* image.

For a file that is in RGB or LAB now and forever, CMYK Setup is also irrelevant. The only time that it makes a difference is when a file *enters* CMYK, at which time Photoshop takes it into account.

We saw everyday examples of that in Chapter 7. In several cases, we started with a conventional light black plate, only to discover that we really wanted to use more GCR. So, we took the files out of CMYK in order to bring them back in again, at which point the setting in CMYK Setup would make a difference.

The same can be done with dot gain. Suppose we have an image that is in CMYK, prepared for a magazine, but we need it to appear in a newspaper. One way to solve the problem is to convert the file to LAB, set the dot gain higher and the total ink lower, and reconvert to CMYK. This works, because the LAB image more or less matches the original magazine CMYK. When we reset dot gain and convert, Photoshop correctly supposes that we want to retain that same darkness, and lightens the image to compensate. We may not notice, because it also darkens the screen image to compensate for the lighter digital file.

It would be very wrong to raise the dot gain setting first and then convert to LAB. If we did, the preview of the CMYK would get very dark, and Photoshop would think it had to match that darkness in LAB, and we'd be in a whole peck of trouble.

Pick a Number, Any Number

So far, there has been no mention of any particular dot gain *number*. This is because there is little agreement on what the numbers mean, but especially because the numbers don't mean the same thing in

Photoshop 5 that they did in previous versions. Photoshop 5's separations are lighter.

In Photoshops past and present, the default dot gain is 20%. If you don't know what that figure is supposed to mean, the chances of your being able to deduce it by logic are nil. I therefore am privileged to inform you that, for reasons best known to others, the dot gain figure is the number of points—not the percentage—by which a 50% dot appears to increase. In other words, a 35% dot gain means that a 50% dot would appear to the viewer to be 85%.

Try figuring out a way to measure this, and you'll understand why the specific number has little meaning. Where dot gain is high the printing is more than a little irregular, so that densitometers have a tough time getting a handle on it. Furthermore, there's the best-behavior-syndrome problem. Like many people with a prepress background, my customary manner of speaking contains, as a grammarian would put it, certain substandard usages. You will not find any of these in this book, because I have cleaned up my act, knowing that the editor will delete such peccadillos anyway.

It should not come as a great shock to learn that pressmen behave in the same way when printing swatches that they know are about to be measured for the purposes of checking press quality. The very fact that they are printing sample sheets calls into question whether the samples are representative of real printing conditions. You can bet that they won't be *worse* than in real life.

There is also the lack of any history. In the days before desktop publishing, there most certainly was no consensus on what

"35% dot gain" meant. So, although we didn't admit it, we guessed. We made arbitrarily lighter separations and told the world that we were being scientific about it.

The bottom line is, 35%, 20%, or whatever, are almost random numbers. We try them out, and if the resulting separations look too dark, we raise them. If they look too light, we lower them. To the extent that a standard exists for what a 20% dot gain separation is, it was the standard of Photoshop—or, of Photoshops before version 5.

Changing the definition was most unnecessary because, as the above discussion suggests, no matter what the defaults are, we probably want to change them. 20% is different in Photoshop 4 than it is in version 5, but in either case, the resulting seps are indeed a little on the dark side—for printing on plastics. For waterless printing with a 600-line screen, both of them are a little on the light side.

As for what Photoshop's default dot gain number should be, one might as well ask what the default waist size should be for the pants of each Photoshop user. *Any* setting is going to be too dark for certain uses and too light for others. The box on Page 148 will get you started, but if you care about quality, you have to experiment.

Don't fall for the old line about asking your printer, either. Most printers have no clue what their dot gain is, I regret to say. And, even if they think they know it, they are likely to understate it, for two very understandable reasons. First, if they tried to measure it, the press sheet that they measured is itself suspect, and real-life conditions are probably worse. And perhaps more important, higher dot gains suggest poorer printing, so the printer has a strong motivation to embellish the truth.

Taking Your Best Guess at Dot Gain

Some pressmen can tell what kind of a dot gain a certain paper will have by running it along the underside of their tongues. If learning that method sounds too difficult, try using the following in Photoshop's setups. If you go to more than one type of output, you'll need more than one set of dot gains. This is for presswork only. As for ink-jet, dye-sublimation, or toner-based color printers, the technology is changing quickly and each device is different, so you'll have to fend for yourself. After setting the base figure, remember to lessen cyan and increase black dot gain (see page 151).

These recommendations are conservative, because we are far better off overestimating the dot gain than we are underestimating it. If the pressman has to adjust ink to match our proofs, we want him adding ink, not substracting and making everything look mangy. These values assume coated paper. Because Photoshop 5's computation of dot gain varies from that of past versions, suggested values are listed for both. These are starting points only. Obviously, as you see more results from a given process or press, you'll be able to tweak these numbers (down, usually) to get more accuracy.

Waterless sheetfed printing If handled properly, this is the highest quality offset printing available. Set your dot gain for **6%** (Photoshop 5) or **16%** (previous versions).

Sheetfed offset The standard for short-run jobs. Use **11%** (Photoshop 5) or **20%** (previous versions).

Default If you haven't got a clue where the job is going, assume web offset conditions. It's a lot easier to darken a file if you must than it is to lighten it; similarly, pictures that print too light are less objectionable to most people than overly dark ones. **17%** (Photoshop 5) or **24%** (previous versions).

Web offset These high-speed presses are quite variable. Start with **17%** (Photoshop 5) or **24%** (previous versions). If the press has on-line ovens (heat-set offset), subtract two points.

Gravure Unless you are printing hundreds of thousands of copies, you won't run across this technology. If you do, assume that the dot gain is somewhat lower than normal web, tempered by the fact that the paper is probably cheaper. **17%** (Photoshop 5) or **24%** (previous versions).

Eccentric substrates. If you print on plastic, metal, fabric, fertilizer bags, cardboard, canvas, or the like your dot gain will be high, but there are few rules beyond that. Try **40%** (all versions)

There are a number of factors that would modify these recommendations. If any of them apply to you, make the following additions or subtractions.

The stock For supercalendared (ultrasmooth) uncoated paper, **+3**. For standard grades of uncoated paper, **+5**. For high groundwood uncoateds (you should be able to perceive tonal variation in this paper), **+8**. For newsprint, **+12**.

The film If your job is imaged on positive film (common practice in Europe, but not the U.S.) **−3**.

Direct to plate If your job is going to a commercial press—not a hybrid such as Xeikon or Indigo— and the plate is imaged directly from your digital file, with no use of film, **−3**.

The halftone screen Unless you are printing waterless, if your job is using a 175 LPI screen, **+1**; if higher **+4**; if a stochastic screen **+8**.

While it pays to try to get it right, remember that all this is guesswork. Normal pressroom variation is at least four points in either direction. At least two more points could be blamed on the inaccuracy of your monitor. So, a 10 or 12 point total variation, which is huge, is possible, though uncommon.

If you are trying to figure out the dot gain of a press, be sure to have at least half a dozen image samples, preferably printed at different times. Remember, a press is extremely variable. If you calibrate to a single printed image, that's certain to be the one that ran while the head pressman was out for a beer or on the day some lamebrain spilled black ink in the magenta fountain.

Plus, there's the impact of the monitor. We adjust the dot gain setting until the monitor matches the printed samples. While all properly calibrated monitors should show approximately the same colors, there is certainly no guarantee that the dot gain I set for 22% using my monitor shouldn't be 20% or 24% on yours.

So, there are no right answers for the overall dot gain number. But for the other separation settings, there are definitely some *wrong* answers—and Adobe has found them. If your seps seem a little on the dark side, while faulty overall dot gain is a suspect, it's more likely the fault of certain other CMYK Setup defaults. Here's how to do better; this fleshes out the recommendations shown earlier in Figure 7.2. (In Photoshop 4, the first four of these are found in Separation Setup and the last one, along with the overall dot gain value, in Printing Inks Setup.)

• **Ink Colors**. The default is SWOP coated. As my work almost invariably is printed to SWOP standards on coated paper, it makes no sense for me to change this. It may for you.

The stock of most magazines, and of this book, has a chemical coating that resists moisture, thus making the paper less absorbent. Less absorbency, less dot gain.

If your seps are going to a newspaper, you can still use SWOP coated in this

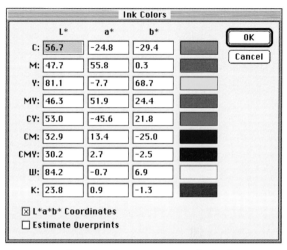

Figure 8.6 *Photoshop's separation method relies on its profiles of the four inks and what happens when they overlap one another. Edit these values at your own risk.*

choice, although you'll have to raise dot gain to 30% or so (35% in previous versions). However, it's probably better to switch to SWOP newsprint. Photoshop bases its separation on its ideas of what colors result when certain values of ink overlap. The newsprint setting assumes muddier colors, which is correct. This yields a slightly better newspaper sep in my tests.

If you don't believe this, you can call up (by choosing "Custom" under "CMYK") the dialog box shown in Figure 8.6, and examine the ink descriptions. Photoshop 5 lets us specify values in LAB, rather than the opaque xyY method of previous versions. If you print with nonstandard inks, you may need to use it, but it is still very much an experts-only feature.

As to the other Ink Colors defaults, I will not pretend that I have carefully examined every one; I don't know if anybody ever has. But, if I were printing to something non-standard, or if I were doing work in Europe, I'd move away from the default.

• **GCR Method**. As discussed in Chapter 7, a heavier black does not necessarily imply a change in the color of the image. Photoshop's default, a "Medium" black, is heavier than the traditional standard, but not incorrect—until you pair it with an erroneous computation of black dot gain. For most images, you'll have better luck changing GCR to "Light."

• **Black Ink Limit.** Whether they use inks, toners, waxes, or dyes, all output devices fail to hold detail when the aforementioned colorants reach a certain heaviness. The worse the output device, the lighter the point at which the failure will occur. For a number of reasons, the failure point for black can be quite low. In many applications even a coverage of 80^K is likely to print as solid; even the finest presses occasionally fail at 90^K. I recommend an 85% maximum black for virtually all print conditions. Anything between 80 and 90 makes sense. Photoshop's default, 100%, is a recipe for mud.

• **Total Ink Limit.** This will vary with intended use. The default is 300, which is the SWOP standard. If your conditions are of better quality than this, the number can go up. If worse, it'll have to go down.

This limit is theoretical. You are unlikely ever to see such a number in a live job. Therefore, you are safe in setting it 10 points higher than the actual maximum that your job requires. If you leave it at 300, for example, 300 points total ink will only happen when the original RGB or LAB file is absolutely black, meaning values of $0^R0^G0^B$ or 0^L. It's extremely unlikely that anything in your files will have these values, so as a practical matter you will never see CMYK total inks of more than 290 or perhaps 292.

Do remember, though, that this limit doesn't protect you once the file is in CMYK. If you correct aggressively after the conversions, your relations with the ink police are in your own hands. If you show up with a 330 shadow where the limit is 300, good luck convincing them that it *used* to be 300 before you fixed it up.

• **UCA.** We haven't discussed this option before, because in Photoshop's implementation, it makes little sense to use it.

UCA (for undercolor addition) artificially adds cyan, magenta, and yellow to the shadow. This would only make sense where the normal shadow value is much less than the total ink limit, which in itself doesn't make sense. The only way this would normally occur is if GCR were set to Maximum and/or maximum black were set to 100%. Neither of these settings should be used for a typical image.

If you are trying for a darker shadow, it makes much more sense to set a low black limit—80% or so—and, after separation, apply a curve that brings 80% black into the nineties. This method, unlike UCA, boosts contrast in the shadows, and would therefore almost always be preferable.

• **Channel by Channel Dot Gain**. There's a major improvement in Photoshop 5, but in implementing it, a skeleton came tumbling out of the closet. Photoshop has been operating on a false assumption, one that accounts not just for the muddy look but for some magenta casts.

In the early days of Photoshop, the programmers apparently mixed up the concepts of ink purity and dot gain. They decided that the relative impurity of cyan ink, which we have discussed so many times in this book, actually means that cyan has a higher *dot gain* than the other inks.

This is completely wrong. In real life, black usually has the highest dot gain and yellow the lowest. To correct for this in Photoshop 5, you need to have set overall dot gain first. Then, change Dot Gain from "Standard" to "Curves." In each of the four CMYK curves, enter a new number at the 50% point. For magenta and cyan, enter 50% plus the overall dot gain (66%, if you have set dot gain at 16%). For black, enter four points higher than magenta and cyan, and for yellow, two points lower. If you are using Photoshop 4 or earlier, you can do approximately the same thing by changing Printing Inks Setup>Color Balance to the following values: Cyan 1.0; Magenta .95; Yellow 1.0; Black .92.

The Photoshop 5 method of fully adjustable curves for dot gain is superior. If most of your work goes to a single printer, you may find that certain tweaks are helpful. For example, magenta dot gain often seems higher in the quartertone than in the midtone. If you see this occurring, you can compensate by putting an additional point in the magenta dot gain curve. Assuming again 16% overall dot gain, this second point might raise 20 to 34, leaving the 50 to 66 point alone.

If you are using earlier versions of Photoshop and want to make such an adjustment, you're out of luck. In fact, with Photoshop 5, one could actually do serious color correction, along the lines of the examples in Chapters 3 and 4, by altering the dot gain curves for every image. Although this is very clever and will work, it's also nuts. Why forego all the flexibility, cancellability, interactivity, and previewing of the normal method of applying curves? Better to stick with a single shape of dot gain curve and do the fancy stuff elsewhere.

If you are dead set and determined to make use of these curves, and if your work prints in a newspaper or other high dot gain environment, here's a tip. Use the curve shape shown in the bottom half of Figure 8.7. When dot gain is high, the effect is more noticeable in the quarter- to midtone range and less in the shadows. With the default curve shown at top, too much detail will be lost in the mid- to three-quartertone in the conversion.

Is It Really a Problem?

Here's the good news about Photoshop 5's changes in the method of handling RGB. If your final destination is CMYK—and if you live on a desert island and never interact with anyone else—you can simply ignore the RGB changes, even if you are one of those benighted individuals who does a lot of color correction in RGB.

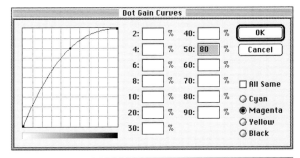

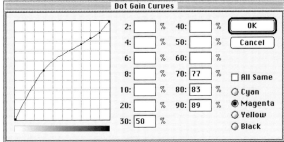

Figure 8.7 When dot gain is extreme, as in newspaper printing, the normal curve model (top) is somewhat inadequate. The custom curve at bottom is usually more accurate—but remember, it's all basically guesswork.

The bad news is, you probably do not live on a desert island.

Photoshop 5 implements ICC profiles as an RGB default. There is no need to be paranoid about this; there were de facto RGB profiles in previous versions, and nobody seems to have been the worse for it. To understand the changes, and their dangers, we should probably discuss the old way first.

In a way, there are different kinds of CMYK, and in a way there are not. $20^C40^M60^Y$ on newsprint doesn't look much like $20^C40^M60^Y$ on fine coated paper. Calibrationists are very scornful of this, and refer to CMYK as "device dependent," a phrase they seldom comprehend.

And yet $20^C40^M60^Y$ is, in a way, invariable. The numbers are constant, regardless of where they are being printed. Only the *appearance* changes.

However, since appearance is what we are selling, we'd better take it into account. We're willing to accept that the image will look worse on a newsprint—up to a point. There is no reason to have it print radically darker. Since most people rely on the monitor to give at least a general impression of what the final product will look like, it makes eminent sense for Photoshop to provide an easy method of making the screen display images darker or lighter.

Similarly, it makes perfect sense to have an easy way of making the actual images (as opposed to the monitor display) darker or lighter automatically.

Photoshop accomplishes both of these things by changing its CMYK profile. Whether it's the built-in Photoshop profile or an ICC profile is in principle irrelevant.

The question is, should something similar be going on with RGB files? There, the answer is much less clear. No two monitors are identical, so the same file displayed on both will appear slightly to moderately different. But this is true whether the file is in RGB, CMYK, or even LAB. This variation in monitor performance has historically been controlled by adjusting the brightness and contrast dials, use of the Gamma utility that shipped with previous versions of Photoshop, or more sophisticated proprietary methods.

None of these adjustments had any effect on the conversion between RGB and CMYK, but certain other adjustments *did*. These adjustments were found under File: Color Settings > Monitor Setup. A change in parameters there would not alter an RGB file, any more than a change in dot gain parameters would alter an existing CMYK. But, just as a change in dot gain would alter the RGB-to-CMYK process, so would a change in Monitor Setup.

As a result, until Photoshop 5 it has always been the case that, if you gave me an RGB file and told me to separate it to, say, 20% dot gain, Light GCR, 85% black limit, 300% total ink, I would probably have gotten a slightly different CMYK result than you would have if you had done it that way yourself. This is because my definition of RGB probably varied from yours.

It is highly non-obvious that this constituted any kind of problem. If I were going to color-correct your file, then the slight difference in the CMYK I started with would be inconsequential. If you were going to take charge of the process, why did you give me an RGB file in the first place?

If it *were* a problem, there was a very easy way out. You could have converted your file to LAB before you gave it to me. That takes variations in Monitor Setup out of the picture, and assures that our results would be identical.

Have you ever heard of anybody doing this? I certainly haven't. Adobe must have, however, because it has determined that this is such a horrible state of affairs that it warrants trashing the entire RGB structure of Photoshop. RGB, it asserts, needs to become "device-independent."

RGB and the Desert Island

The most obvious way to implement this quixotic decision without hurting anyone would also have been the simplest: eliminate Monitor Setup as part of the conversion equation, and allow it to affect screen display only.

A less happy, but still workable, method would be to allow users to define RGB by means of an ICC profile that is at least somewhat similar to the former default.

Instead of either of these logical paths, Photoshop 5 makes the new profiling system a *default*. It makes it rather difficult to change back to the old way (for instructions on how to do so, see page 27), but far worse, it encourages users down the line to alter our color unexpectedly.

This still would not have been so bad, if the definition of the default RGB had some remote relation to past practice. Instead, as nearly as I can surmise, Adobe convoked a committee and charged it with finding out what would be the worst, most unreasonable, and most inconvenient definition to inflict upon us. Maybe this was a clever ploy to force everybody to learn more about color. I'm not sure.

After lengthy consideration, the committee determined that, due to its restricted color gamut and general incompatibility with anything else, the worst possible

choice would be a definition called sRGB, which was accordingly made the Photoshop 5 default. The howls of protest from users who were sandbagged by this unexpected switch were the principal reason for the release of 5.0.2, with its color wizard.

sRGB is a standard suggested by Microsoft and Hewlett-Packard, with the fanciful idea of someday having everybody who accesses the Web see precisely the same colors, regardless of what monitor they use.

In constructing such a chimera, one needs to assume the impossible, that the variations in individual monitor performance will somehow vanish, but more than that, one has to use a least-common-denominator approach, assuming the worst because that is what many Web surfers have.

We will probably be seeing a lot more of sRGB in the future. It's catching on as a standard for consumer-level color products. Professionals can use it as well, but it certainly wouldn't be one's first choice. It's particularly poor in blues and cyans, which are already our biggest problem.

Furthermore, its gamma is 2.2. That's the default Windows uses for monitors, but in the Mac-centric world of professional publishing, it is decidedly nonstandard. For those needing a translation, sRGB assumes a cheap monitor that displays the midrange of colors too dark, almost the equivalent of high dot gain in CMYK.

This is not news to Adobe. In May 1998, as Photoshop 5.0 shipped, one of its top color architects wrote as follows about his program's new default: "Actually, sRGB is only recommended for those that don't know better (or never do anything other than Web work)."

Do you have a problem with this?

The result has turned out to be exactly what I predicted at the time: a chaos of competing RGBs, rather than just one. The entire professional world shifted away from sRGB, but not all changed to the same definition. How could they? Photoshop 5 offers an alphabet soup of nine alternatives, plus you can create your own variant, as several prominent users have done.

In Chapter 2, I defined calibrationism as the ability to be so deluded by what seems to be science that one is blinded to the obvious. Anyone can make a mistake. To trash a nearly universal standard in favor of such an every-man-for-himself situation is a blunder, no matter the rationale. But to replace it in the name of device independence, that takes a calibrationist.

So far in this book, we've stuck pretty much with CMYK color correction, but we're about to get heavily into LAB. My style is to use these two colorspaces a lot more than I do RGB. If you wind up agreeing and adopting this style, the choice of RGB definition isn't all that important; you could even get by with sRGB.

This is because, in principle, the RGB setting doesn't have an impact on what happens in CMYK. Suppose you are used to a workflow of scanning RGB into Photoshop 4, doing a certain amount of work there, and then converting into CMYK.

Photoshop 5.0's default, on opening an RGB file, changes its color values, lightening it to compensate for the fact that it is now designated as being in sRGB. This sounds worse than it is, because the minute that the file leaves RGB (like, if you convert it to CMYK), Photoshop imposes a counter-correction, leaving it in more or less the same condition it would have been had sRGB never made an appearance.

There is more than a little irony in all this correcting and counter-correcting. This is exactly the type of move that calibrationists have previously condemned as horribly destructive. They have therefore advocated color-correcting in RGB rather than LAB or CMYK, on the grounds that the RGB data, having never been converted, is more pristine. Now that a couple of extra conversions have been thrown into the process, this mathematical wisdom has suddenly been rendered inoperative.

My tests suggest that there's no serious loss as a result of these conversions: throwing a file back and forth repeatedly damages it slightly more than moving in and out of RGB and LAB, and slightly less than moving it in and out of RGB and CMYK.

Accordingly, at least in principle, your workflow is unaffected by the change. Provided, that is, you live on a desert island.

Minimizing the Damage

There are certain users for whom an ICC-profile based workflow will be a help. If you can't see a reason why it would be a help to *you,* you are in the vast majority.

Regardless of which group you are in, you must concede that if a mistake occurs—that if, somehow, an incorrect profile is applied at an inappropriate time—then any advantage of the new method is lost a hundred times over.

And, considering that you, as a reader of this book, identify yourself as being well above average in sophistication, let me ask you: how easy do *you* find the material in this chapter? This entire area has proven itself much too difficult for the typical user. For people who do not understand the theory behind it, mistakes are inevitable.

In Chapter 7, we talked about using GCR as a defensive measure against press error. Similarly, we now need to configure our systems to defend against the incompetence of others who may have to deal with our files.

We start with RGB Setup, the particulars of which have gotten a lot more debate from color management aficionados than the subject really warrants. For the workflow described in this book, which emphasizes CMYK and LAB, none of these settings have a big impact—unless you do something stupid.

• **RGB.** The question here is whether to stay with something similar to past practice—Apple RGB, Monitor RGB, or an RGB saved out of a previous version (to do so, open the older version, go to File: Color Settings > Monitor Setup, and hit Save. This file can now be loaded directly into Photoshop 5's RGB Setup.)

The alternative is to specify an RGB with a wider gamut. This may help you if a lot of your images have details in bright colors, especially blues. It's almost certain to help you if you are outputting to a device that only accepts RGB input, such as a film recorder or many Epson printers.

The problem with these arises if you ever pass your RGB files on to someone whose knowledge of color management is suspect. If that person fails to understand that you have chosen one of these alternative RGBs, you are in for a peck of trouble.

Accordingly, look to your own workflow. If you never exchange RGB files with anyone other than trusted colleagues, go ahead and try ColorMatch RGB, or, even more aggressively, Adobe RGB (erroneously called SMPTE–240M in Photoshop 5.0.) If not, or if you're working with people who don't use Photoshop 5.x at all, use one of the more conservative RGBs.

• **Gamma.** 1.8 is the Macintosh default (under Windows, it's 2.2), and therefore is the setting used by the majority of professionals. There are very mild advantages in the separation process; somewhat greater ones if you do a lot of channel blending. 2.2 is certainly workable but if your orientation is CMYK I'd stick with 1.8.

• **White Point.** Similarly, most professionals, particularly in the U.S., use 5000K as a white point. Many people now believe that 6500K may offer advantages. I don't believe either choice will significantly affect your workflow. If you do a lot of work with fleshtones, there's a minor advantage to 5000K. It will force more of a blue component into the face, which can be convenient later on. But personally, the main reason I use 5000K is that it is what the majority uses, not because I really think it's better.

• **Primaries.** Unless you have a particular plan in mind, stick to the primaries defined by the choice under RGB.

• **Display Using Monitor Compensation.** Because this option, inexplicably, affects the display of CMYK files, it must be kept checked if you have chosen anything other than Monitor RGB.

Now, the options of Profile Setup:

• **Embed Profiles** The problem with embedding profiles is that it invites other applications to alter your files. This can be disastrous, particularly since some applications, like QuarkXPress, ignore the profiles, while others, like Adobe PageMaker, not only notice them but may act.

Properly designed applications, however, won't act if they don't find a profile at all. To that end, I strongly recommend that you turn *off* embedded profiling *unless* you have a specific reason to have it on. That reason normally would be that you have decided to adopt a profiled workflow.

• **Assumed Profiles.** If you have decided to abandon the profile approach, choose None throughout. If not, choose Monitor RGB.

• **Profile Mismatch Handling** Even if you are anti-color management, you should probably check "Ask When Opening" rather than "Ignore." If some client hands you a file with an embedded profile, it's a good idea to know that the profile is there; whether you choose to make use of it is another story. Unless you are a solo practitioner with no possibility of receiving files from foreign sources, the default, "Convert to RGB Color" seems to me an undue temptation to fate.

Should We Use CMYK Profiles?

Unlike the chaotic RGB situation, here the only chaos is the change in dot gain values, which we've previously discussed. ICC profiles can be used for CMYK, but they are an *option,* not a default, which is what should have been done in RGB.

Embedding these profiles in CMYK documents can be right for certain users. Using them for conversions into CMYK also has certain advantages along with certain disadvantages.

First of all, an embedded profile suggests that you are open to the possibility of having your file altered automatically somewhere down the line. For most people, that's a bad decision. If you have prepared an ad for magazine use, and now it has to appear in a newspaper, prepare it for that purpose yourself, if you care about quality.

But such quality takes time. If you don't have a lot of it, but still have to prepare your images for more than one purpose, ask yourself if the purposes are of equal importance. For example, I sometimes lecture to large audiences, using a projection system. I may therefore need to repurpose some of the images in this book. I am certainly not going to do this by means of having one RGB master file modified by two sets of profiles; that would cost quality in the book. The lecturing is, for me, far less important than the book, so if there is a compromise to be made, I'll make it there. Either I'll generate the presentation files directly from the book files, or I'll embed profiles into the book files and convert the presentation files based on those. Either way, I've put my emphasis on making good book files, in accord with my own priorities.

But there is a flip side. Suppose you're a realtor. You have pictures of thousands of houses

Figure 8.8 *ICC profiles can't be edited from within Photoshop 5, but if you have a program that can do it, like Kodak's ColorFlow, you can generate very specialized conversion methods. Below, constructing a profile that finds dark greens and makes them brighter.*

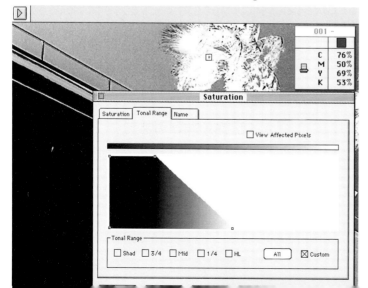

Figure 8.9 Three methods of separating a subject that is outside the gamut of what can be accurately reproduced. From left: the Matchprint Euroscale ICC profile, set to Absolute Colorimetric; the same profile set to Perceptual; a normal Photoshop separation. Note the tradeoff in all three: the more detailed the rose is, the less attractive are the green leaves.

that are currently on the market. The age of Photoshop is very good for you, because advertising in color is highly profitable. If only one or two additional houses are sold as a result of your use of color, it's well worth the cost.

Therefore, you print a weekly catalog. But you also post the images on your Web page. Which of these is more important?

Well, since either one could generate a sale, I'd say they're *both* very important. So, if you are interested in optimal quality, I'd have to say, do two sets of images, custom correcting each one.

That, of course, is ridiculous. With thousands of images in play, you can't afford to horse around with them individually. And this makes you a prime candidate for ICC-based color management.

You are a prime candidate not just because this method lets you generate two sets of reasonably good images automatically, but because you have a unique application, for which custom profiles may offer some benefits.

Your images are not all shot by professional photographers. They are not all shot on sunny days. And yet, for the purposes of selling real estate, you want happy colors—

in some cases. You want blue skies and green lawns. But in other cases, you don't. Brick houses shouldn't be bright red. Pink houses should not be shockingly so.

If that is your agenda, Photoshop's built-in engine isn't as powerful as a well-run custom profile generator. In Figure 8.8, using Kodak's ColorFlow profile editor, I'm trying to demonstrate this, measuring an image that appeared previously as Figure 3.9. That original had a problem typical of real estate images. It had palm trees that were a very dark green. My new profile will, if it finds that color, make it a lighter, happier green in all future images. This can't be done with Photoshop alone.

ICC profiles offer an additional advantage in CMYK conversions: each one gives us a choice of the PCCM *or* the EIAM approach. The term *perceptual* is used to describe PCCM, where all colors are subdued slightly to make room for out-of-gamut interlopers. *Absolute colorimetric* means EIAM, modified to try to approximate out-of-gamut colors rather than turn them lime green.

Figure 8.9 is a reprise of this old argument about tradeoffs. The rose, which was originally out of gamut, is best in the perceptual profile version. The leaves, which weren't, are better in the colorimetric. And Photoshop's version falls somewhere in the middle in terms of contrast.

The flip side? There is no technical argument against using ICC profiles, provided they're properly prepared. Unfortunately, these profiles are often dashed off with a quick pass of densitometry and zero quality control. Having seen so many really poor profiles, I'd be inclined to test any third-party product before using it.

One of the biggest disadvantages of using prebuilt profiles is that it's difficult to improvise. Altering a profile is a pain. Also, the Kodak product shown here costs a stiff

$2,500, although several cheaper packages were introduced in 1999.

For things like Figure 8.8, where we're trying to do something that isn't possible otherwise, there may be a case for it. But most tweaking doesn't fit that description.

For example, in February 1998 the magazine I write for switched printers. I immediately saw that all my images were printing darker than I was expecting. In Photoshop 4, I opened Printing Inks Setup and raised dot gain from 25 to 26. Time elapsed, 15 seconds. If I were using an ICC profile, I'd have needed some way to edit it, which would necessarily be much slower and more expensive, but wouldn't be any better.

Figure 8.10 Images with critical detail in the darkest area, as this woman's sweater, are a major problem, particularly where dot gain is high. Often the only way to get an enhanced version (right) is to do some kind of custom separation followed by a contrast-enhancing move in the black plate. (In this correction, it's assumed that the only objective is to improve the clothing.)

Figure 8.11 In dark neutral areas, cyan, magenta and yellow have to be suppressed for the image to stay within the total ink limit. Therefore, the contribution of the original CMY channels to the detail in this clothing is just about nil, and everything will depend on the quality of the black plate.

Dot gain is hardly the biggest thing that Photoshop's engine addresses more easily than a profiled workflow does. How about GCR decisions?

Don't get me wrong. With something like ColorFlow, you can design a profile with any kind of GCR, black ink limit, or total ink limit that you fancy. It seems improbable, however, that one would make 20 or 30 such profiles to cater to every possible black generation need.

And yet, for serious retouching, we can't live without that control. We spent a large part of Chapter 7 discussing why this is so, but let's close out this chapter with one last example of why one needs to have flexibility in GCR decisions.

How to Hold Shadow Detail

Figure 8.10 originated as an LAB image. The left-hand version was converted into CMYK using the pure defaults of Photoshop 5, dot gain 20%. Please assume that the woman's face, pallid though you may find it, is acceptable. Instead, our job is to bring out detail in her sweater and jacket, and secondarily in her hair.

That's easier said than done. Shadow detail is notoriously difficult to enhance.

A glance at the individual channels in Figure 8.11 indicates who's to blame: it's the ink police. They insist that the sum of all inks be 300 or lower, even in the darkest areas, such as where the jacket meets the chin. Without the ink police, those areas would be in the 90s in the CMY channels. But the ink police exist. That important CMY detail has to be suppressed, held down to between 70 and 80, to let the black be as dark as usual without going over that tiresome 300 total.

The bottom line is, in terms of achieving the goal of more shadow detail, the CMY channels are worthless. We live and die by what happens in the black. If we can make it a *lot* better than the original, we win. Otherwise, the client will look for somebody who knows GCR better than we do.

The basic strategy is clear. If everything is going to depend on the black, then we'd better come up with one that has excruciatingly high contrast. To do that, sooner or later we are going to have to apply an excruciatingly steep curve to the black plate.

With the default black, that is simply not going to happen. We can't increase the shadow value because it's nearly at 100^K already. We can't decrease the lightest point of the clothing very much, because the black plate is carrying detail in both hair and face, and such a curve would blow those away.

We therefore have to forget this particular black and try some alternatives. When the situation is as desperate as this, many rules go by the wayside. We will also forget about the normal shadow of $80^C70^M70^Y70^K$. Increased contrast in the black takes priority; the longer the range in the black the more contrast it will have. We must plan on a black shadow value in the mid-90s, with the other inks coming down to compensate. We will worry about that at the end, ignoring the ink police in the interim.

Figure 8.12 shows nine alternatives, some of them very unlikely. There are obviously an infinite number of others, times an infinite number of permutations, because we could take the black plate from a single separation and the CMY plates from a different one, or we could mix and match even further.

To start with, we try four basic variants, each with 85% maximum black. Note the similarity between UCR and Light GCR. The Medium and Heavy GCR versions we can reject out of hand. They carry too much detail elsewhere, and that will be an obstacle. We want to clear the decks, to have nothing in the way of our eventual contrast-building curves.

Figure 8.12E is something entirely different, a black generated by one of Photoshop's supplied ICC profiles, Euroscale Matchprint (perceptual). This profile permits a maximum shadow of 95%, which

accounts for the high contrast in the clothing. But in principle, it's a lighter black generation even than Photoshop's built-in UCR setting; compare the darkness of the eyes to that of Figure 8.12E.

Next, another brainstorm. The dot gain setting alters contrast in the black plate. If we separate with a false dot gain setting, we will definitely have to trash the CMY files. But it may be worth a try.

Where more dot gain is assumed, Photoshop needs to deliver a *lighter* separation, to compensate for the expected gain on press. Therefore, it's no surprise that Figure 8.12F, at 40%, is so much lighter than Figure 8.12G, at 10%.

That extra lightness came about because Photoshop dropped the midtone of the reproduction curve more for 8.12F. Therefore, the lighter half of the curve became flatter, and the darker half steeper, and you know the rest. The lower dot gain version is absurd; it hurts contrast just where we want to gain it.

It looks to me, though, that Figure 8.12F has just lost too much detail in the lighter area to be usable, no matter what the CMY plates look like. So, as a first serious try, I'll invest in yet another separation, with the 20% dot gain we want, but UCR, 100% black allowed. The reason for these

Figure 8.12 With difficult images, it sometimes makes sense to try several separation settings. At right, black plates generated by nine different CMYK Setups. Which would you prefer to start with? Version A is at 20% dot gain, Light GCR, 85% maximum black, 300% total ink limit. The others vary from these settings as noted: B: UCR. C: Medium GCR. D: Heavy GCR. E: Bypassing the Photoshop engine altogether and using the supplied Matchprint ICC Profile. F: 40% dot gain. G: 10% dot gain. H: 35% dot gain, 65% black limit. I: UCR, 52% black limit.

Figure 8.13 *The two black plates that produced the alternate versions of Figure 8.10. When coverage in the other three channels is so heavy, there is no need to fear a very harsh-looking black.*

thing is, I set the maximum black to 52%.

With the maximum black that low, it's possible to apply a really drastic curve to boost contrast. Furthermore, with the black so constrained originally, a certain amount of shadow detail is forced into the CMY plates.

When almost everything rides on the black plate, one may as well go for broke by trying to sharpen it. Chapter 6 teaches that a large sharpening Radius is the enemy of subtle detail, and there's a lot of subtle detail in the fabrics. So, I went with a Radius of .8 pixel—but an Amount of 500%, and a zero Threshold.

The eyepoppingly harsh result is shown next to the default black in Figure 8.13.

settings is, I want to be able to plug an entirely new black into the image, I want to affect non-shadow areas as much as possible, and I want to accommodate a very high black value in the shadows.

Now, yet another separation, the black of which is shown in Figure 8.12H. I raised the dot gain setting to 35%, and I cut the maximum black to 65%. The plan was to boost contrast in it with a curve, and then paste it into the black channel of the separation I just made.

Nice idea, and probably worthwhile in slightly different circumstances, but here it didn't quite work. There is still not sufficient detail in the black to hold shape in the hair. Back to the drawing board.

Figure 8.12I uses the principle of substituting an easier problem for one that is more difficult to solve. In this version, I used 20% dot gain once more, and UCR so as to limit the amount of detail the black carries in light areas. The unorthodox

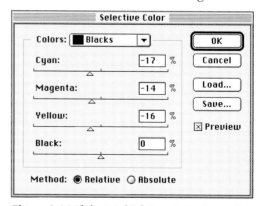

Figure 8.14 *If the total ink in a CMYK image is illegally high, this move in Image: Adjust>Selective Color can get you off the hook.*

MANAGING THE SEPARATION PROCESS

✓CMYK and RGB have drastically different color gamuts. CMYK has better yellows and sometimes better magentas. As against that, it has very poor blues. Because of these differences, a perfect separation algorithm is a contradiction in terms.

✓The better a separation method is at handling exceptional situations, the worse it will be on the average image. Conversely, the better the method does on average images, the more likely it is to do something really bad on occasion.

✓Dot gain compensation, a critical feature in making a separation, is radically different in Photoshop 5 than it was in past versions. The percentages no longer have the same meanings, and now yield much lighter CMYK files.

✓Although there is no one correct number for dot gain, several other Photoshop CMYK Setup items aren't suitable for high-quality work and should be changed.

✓In principle, changes in Photoshop's RGB method don't affect files that are destined for CMYK. However, the new default, sRGB, is undesirable for anything but work destined for the Web.

✓Certain users can benefit from the use of embedded profiles. If you aren't sure you're one of them, you probably aren't. In that case, you are probably better off disabling Photoshop's color management.

✓There is no theoretical objection to separating either with Photoshop's built-in engine or with an ICC profile. The question is, how good is the profile, not what format it's in.

✓A disadvantage of separating with ICC profiles is that small tweaks to the algorithm are time-consuming and require special software, which at the moment is rather expensive.

✓Where shadow detail is critical, consider separating with a low black limit and then applying a contrast-boosting curve to the resulting black plate.

✓For knowledgeable users, the exact method of separation—except for black generation—is nearly irrelevant. Almost all images still need correction once they get to CMYK, and small variations in the initial file won't make a difference either to quality or the time needed to make the changes.

Certainly, I could not have dreamed of sharpening the other channels to this extent, but why should I want to? They don't have detail in the areas of interest.

And the problem I substituted for the one I solved by this approach? Well, the printer of this book won't allow me to show it to you, because the shadow under the woman's chin is $87^C79^M82^Y94^K$, 42 points higher than SWOP allows.

Compliance can be arranged by means of Image: Adjust>Selective Color, as shown in Figure 8.14. Choosing Blacks as the target, I reduce sharply the quantity of CMY inks. The reason for the slight imbalance is that I judge the shadow should remain slightly brown, rather than neutral.

What Is the Impact?

One of the few good things that can be said about the Photoshop changes described in this chapter is that at least they force us to think. The result of the thinking ought to be a realization that, for all the palaver about the perfect separation process, there really is no such animal.

One method is better on certain images and another on others. But usually, the exact method is almost completely irrelevant. We have two perfect examples in this chapter.

In the Goya painting of Figure 8.5, and the rose of Figure 8.9, we can probably agree on which versions are better—but we should also agree that none of them is acceptable. Both Goyas need more detailing in the queen's clothing just as the image we just worked on did. All three roses need more shape just as the rose at the beginning and end of Chapter 5 did. So we need to correct them.

In doing so, it does not make the slightest difference which of the alternate versions we start with. The impact of the separation algorithm is absolutely zero in these cases. The PCCM version of the Goya looks a little worse to start with than does the EIAM, granted. But the correction techniques would be identical on the two. Only the numbers on the curves would vary. Neither would be in any way more difficult than the other. Neither would take more time. Neither would have the smallest advantage in quality once we were done.

There is no point in avoiding the easy changes that make the separation more accurate, such as increasing Photoshop's dot gain adjustment when separating an image for use in a newspaper. But an accurate separation only goes so far.

If there really were one best way to convert into CMYK, it would have been discovered a long time ago. Meanwhile, there are many reasonable variations within Photoshop and elsewhere. If you don't particularly care about image quality, it won't much matter which one you use. If you do care, and if you know the right way to get there—well, then it won't matter much, either.

RGB Is CMY

Nowadays most files start in RGB and end in CMYK.
What happens in between is up to us. Each colorspace has
its partisans. To decide which is more effective, one has to
appreciate their differences. But to appreciate their differences,
one has to understand how alike they are.

tourist, visiting New York for the first time, stops a native
and asks how to get to Carnegie Hall. The New Yorker
replies, "Practice, practice, practice."

Being from that neck of the woods myself, I take the same intoler-
ant attitude toward color correction. This accounts for a lot of missing
material in this book.

For example, I see no purpose in discussing the Sharpen filter.
Although it can improve certain images, the Unsharp Mask filter is
much stronger and more flexible. The sooner we get comfortable with
it, the better our images will be, and the more we practice with it, the
more comfortable we'll be.

Similarly, but more provocatively, this is the only text on Photoshop,
to my knowledge, that doesn't discuss the Levels command. Same
reason: there's nothing wrong with Levels, but curves are more
powerful. Why waste time learning the second-best way? If you want to
learn to swim, jump into the deep end.

The same reasoning applies—sort of—to the choice of colorspace.
This book covers a lot of things, but our principal tool is curves.
Anyone who is serious about print quality has to know how to write

CMYK curves, because, as the last chapter pointed out, there's no such animal as a perfect separation process. So the more practice we get, the better. That's why, up until this point, we haven't even considered the uses of the two other colorspaces that Photoshop offers us for options.

Although it will take three chapters to get there, let me cut to the chase. LAB and CMYK are so different that each one can do things the other can't possibly accomplish.

Figure 9.1 *Above, a normal separation of an RGB file. Below, the individual RGB channels pasted into the CMY of a blank CMYK file and printed without a black plate.*

RGB, however, is *not* that different. That is the problem and also the potential. If you take the doctrinaire position that you will never apply a curve to an RGB document, there's no reason you can't get top-quality color. The same cannot be said of LAB, and still less of CMYK.

It is tempting, then, to say, forget RGB, for the same reason you should forget Levels. But there are a couple of flaws in this logic, of which the biggest is the following.

If you know CMYK, you *already* know RGB. If you know RGB, you know CMYK.

And if you realize why they are really the same, you will know how to exploit their differences.

Enter the Ink Police

In RGB, the lighter a channel is, the more of that color is supposed to hit the viewer's eye. In a picture of a rose, for example, the red channel will be very light.

In CMYK, the lighter a channel is, the less of that ink will appear. The function of the ink is to prevent reflection of a certain color. Cyan prevents reflection of red. In a picture of a rose, for example, the cyan channel will be very light.

Similarly, where the red is dark, the cyan will be dark. Where the magenta is light, so will the green. Where the blue is dark, so will be the yellow. RGB is CMY, and they even make it easy for us by putting the letters in the proper order. R=C, G=M, B=Y.

Figure 9.1 shows just how similar they are. The top is a normal separation of an RGB file. The bottom is a weirdo: it's the red pasted into the cyan, the green into the magenta, the blue into the yellow, and no black at all. No, the two images are not identical, but they aren't all that far apart, either, in the overall scheme of things.

Before discussing this, let's consider Figure 9.2, which shows the RGB channels plus their CMY equivalents after a normal Photoshop separation. Note the family resemblance but also the differences. The cousins, red and cyan, are both approximately the same color, but the red has much more contrast. And the green similarly, in comparison to the magenta. But there is an unusual wrinkle. See how, in the magenta, the hair is completely washed out, lighter than the faces, whereas in the green, things are more normal.

That's the long arm of the ink police. In making the separation, CMYK Setup called for the maximum sum of all four inks in the darkest areas to be 300, in deference to the above-mentioned gendarmerie.

The faces don't approach this number. Although they are dark in magenta and yellow, even if they printed at 100% in both, it still wouldn't bother the flatfeet, because cyan and black are each less than, well, five-oh. So, 300 is impossible.

Figure 9.2 The individual RGB channels are similar in color to their CMY cousins. But they have more detail in the highlights, and more weight in the shadows. The unusual effect in the children's hair in CMY is the result of a total ink limit for printing. The color channels have to be restricted to make room for a heavy flow of black ink. Otherwise, the limit might be exceeded.

The hair is another story. It's a neutral color—strong in all four inks. Thus, it arouses the curiosity of the ink police. With black ink floating around 70, a sum of 300 is very achievable. Accordingly, the natural darkness of the CMY inks has to be suppressed, and the black carries all detail, just as it did in the final example of Chapter 8. There, that detail was critical. Here, we'd probably ignore the issue.

The parrot of Figure 9.3 was given the same treatment as Figure 9.1. The left version is a normal separation; the right version is blackless, and consists of the RGB channels pasted into their CMY cousins. But these two renditions are much closer to one another than was the case in Figure 9.1. Also, here one could actually make the case that the right version is the better of the two. When you understand why, you'll be on the road to the proper use of RGB.

Enter the Dot Gain Curve

RGB has no ink police. It also has no dot gain. When an image moves into CMYK, Photoshop suddenly has to cope with both factors. This explains not only the washed-out hair of Figure 9.2, but also why the bogus version of Figure 9.1 is too dark yet that of Figure 9.3 is not.

Since dot gain will cause darkening on press, the image must be lightened as it

Figure 9.3 *Like Figure 9.1, the right-hand version has no black, and the RGB channels have been pasted directly into their CMY counterparts. This time, though, the two versions are much closer in overall color. Do you understand why?*

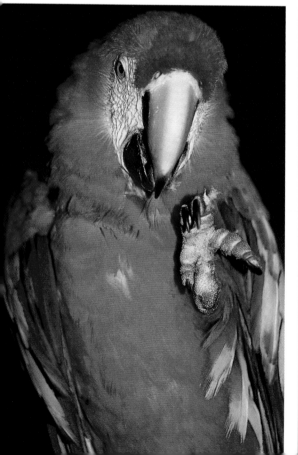

goes into CMYK. The worse the printing condition, the greater the dot gain, and the more lightening Photoshop has to do to make up for it.

Unless we decide to exercise the new Photoshop 5 ability to make custom dot gain curves, the lightening will be accomplished by a curve that drops the midtone, where dot gain is theoretically heaviest. This is the "black cat" curve of Chapter 4.

Such a drop in the midtone flattens the light half of the curve and steepens the dark half. The normal consequences of curve application have not been suspended. The steeper the curve, the more the contrast. *The separation process, by its nature, suppresses highlight detail.*

In Figure 9.1, the bottom version is darker, because there never was any such lightening, and because the image is rich in midtones. But notice how much better the definition of the chairs against the beach is. That's the extra highlight detail at work.

Not such a big deal here, perhaps, but it's more significant in Figure 9.2, and absolutely critical in Figure 9.3.

In a face, the cyan plate gives most of the contrast. We shouldn't put up with one as lame as that shown in Figure 9.2. The red channel shown is much better than the cyan, not just because the lightening curve suppressed highlight detail in the cyan but because the red does some of the shaping work done by the black in CMYK.

Figure 9.4 *The two cyan plates of Figure 9.3. The one on the right is also the red channel of the RGB original.*

In a red parrot, the cyan is even more important, and that's why the right-hand version of Figure 9.3 is more detailed in the red areas. Its cyan plate—the original red channel—is better defined than that of the normal separation.

Have you figured out why overall darkness is not the issue in the parrot that it was in the beach scene?

The lightening routine is strongest in the midtones—and this bird doesn't have any. The red areas, for example, are very heavy in magenta and yellow, very light in cyan, and nonexistent in black. The other brilliant colors are similarly all highlights

Figure 9.5 Contrast-enhancing curves work better when the original object of interest falls in a narrow range, as the orange object does at upper left. Given the longer range of the purple object at upper right, an overly drastic curve would be needed (lower right) to achieve the same benefit as in the lower left curve.

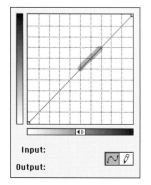
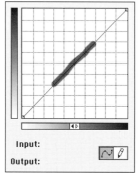
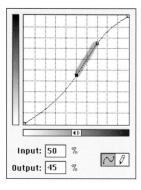
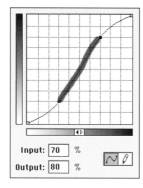

and shadows, with nothing in the middle.

Figure 9.4 shows the difference in the cyan channels. Not much of a competition, is it? Well, the successful retoucher is a thief. If Chapter 5 has convinced you of the critical nature of the cyan plate in red objects, your logic will convince you that this opportunity for felonious misappropriation of the version on the right cannot be passed up. With Image: Apply Image, copy the red channel from one image into the cyan of the other. There is no law against mixing colorspaces during channel blends, and this is the first of many times I will recommend it.

Exit the Subtlety

To summarize, RGB channels always appear to have higher contrast than their CMY counterparts, especially in the lighter half. In the darker half, they may show detail that has been arrested in CMY by an overly zealous ink police.

There's a lot to be said, then, for using RGB as a resource for blending. In other areas, the news isn't nearly so good. Figure 9.5—another round of that old refrain, the steeper the curve, the more the contrast—shows why.

Assume that we are trying to improve a certain object in a certain channel of a certain image, and at the moment, it falls in the orange area of the top left curve. We react by steepening it, as at bottom left.

Now, suppose that the object, whatever it is, falls in the longer purple area of the top right curve. Our approach has to be the same, but we are unlikely to be as effective.

The bottom right curve is the only way to make the purple area as steep as the orange one was. That is a violent curve. We are unlikely to be able to get away with that

Figure 9.6 *Should this image be corrected in RGB or CMYK?*

in real life. The gentler twist in the orange one probably won't affect overall color, but in the purple one it probably will. The orange curve will diminish contrast slightly in the rest of the image. The purple one will run over it with a steamroller.

Some type of compromise is clearly necessary. We will steepen the purple curve, but not as much. This will improve the object. It will not improve it as much as the orange curve does.

The moral of this exercise is, the shorter the range of the object, the more effective our curve corrections, and the less likely we are to punish some other area.

For all the reasons we've just discussed, the RGB channels are *always* longer and higher in contrast than their CMY cousins.

This doesn't mean curves don't work in RGB. If all we want to do is set highlight and shadow, there is no reason to avoid RGB. And more ambitious moves are possible. But if you're thinking of one, think CMYK. More channels, more better.

To illustrate, lets try a correction first in RGB, then in CMYK. Figure 9.6 shows the Beverly Hilton. It's a moderately complex image, with a fair number of colors we'd like to keep close to neutral, and two objects we would like to improve: the stone facade, and the detailing in the shadow areas. Let's give it a shot, first in RGB.

Since this is our first full-fledged RGB correction, let's review the concept. Instead of using percentages, we use values of 0 to 255. The higher number indicates a larger amount of that color of *light* hitting our eyes. Thus, the higher the number, the brighter.

For example, the highlight here, which I take to be on the roof of the car, is $255^R255^G228^B$. Neutral colors are easier to define in RGB than in CMYK: all we need is three equal values. Here, they aren't. There's too much red and too much green. Green and red light add up to yellow, so the car has a yellow tinge, as if you didn't know this by looking at it.

Other colors that should be more or less neutral, but aren't, in order of increasing darkness: the front of the awning is $217^R196^G194^B$, too red. The hotel at rear is $189^R171^G180^B$, a magenta cast. The stripes of the flag at left are not white but purple: $155^R136^G177^B$. And the shadow, in the archway, is slightly orange, $34^R29^G24^B$.

Short of converting the image to grayscale, we're not going to be able to get all of these mini-casts out of there no matter what colorspace we write curves in. But we want to move in that direction, while setting highlight and shadow at the same time. Here, I'd suggest values of 248 in the highlight and 20 for the shadow. While we're at it, we'd like to arrange for the facade to fall in steep areas of the three curves. I measure it as $147^R121^G118^B$ in its lightest area and $79^R65^G57^B$ in a moderately dark one.

In looking at the curves of the top half of Figure 9.7, remember that they are set up with dark in the top right corner, to emphasize their similarity with CMYK. I'll discuss each one from darkest to lightest, that is, from top right to bottom left. The parts of the curve in which the facade and the shadow detail fall are highlighted.

The red needs to be heavier in dark areas, so I move the top right point to the left. The next two points on the curve attempt to force the facade into a steep area of the curve. You may well argue that this is not particularly steep, but getting more of an angle is easier said than done. We don't start with a whole lot of detail in the arch-

way and the darkest areas of the windows. All that detail falls between the *first two points,* in other words, in an area that has become flatter, something I did reluctantly and am certainly not going to do any more of. So that second point goes no higher.

Can the third point go lower? Not unless you want the hotel and the stripes of the flag to go blue. So, no further progress. The fourth point suppresses red in the awning and the fifth adjusts the highlight.

The green curve is simpler and also more palatable. The first point adjusts the shadow just as in the red. The second puts more green into the awning, neutralizing it. That's good, because it makes the entire top three-quarters of the curve steep. That curve covers the facade and the shadows, both of which appreciate the attention. But we can't add further points to try to isolate them, unless we want a green hotel and green stripes in the flag.

The blue curve is bad news. It flattens the first half of the curve, losing contrast in both facade and shadows. But there's no alternative: both the hotel and the flag are too

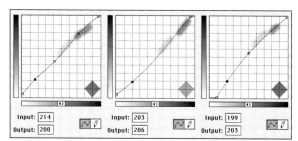

Input: 214   Output: 200   Input: 203   Output: 206   Input: 199   Output: 203

Figure 9.7 *The longer ranges of objects hamstring those who try to target them with RGB curves. In this image, extra snap is desirable in the building's facade (yellow range on curves) and in the shadows beneath the awnings (blue range.) In RGB, these ranges are consecutive, in addition to being slightly longer. In CMYK, they are much easier to get at. The key channels here are magenta, where the two ranges overlap, and black, where they are distinct. In both channels, it's possible to steepen these ranges dramatically without damaging color balance. No such opportunity exists in RGB.*

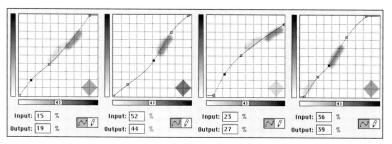

Input: 15 %   Output: 19 %   Input: 52 %   Output: 44 %   Input: 23 %   Output: 27 %   Input: 36 %   Output: 39 %

blue, and we have to bring the center point up to compensate.

Taken as a whole, these curves yield the improved image at the top of Figure 9.8. There is more snap, and the facade's color isn't as close to that of the hotel as it was. Overall balance is much improved.

Making images better is pretty easy. The question always is, however, how much better could they have been? Let's do the same image from scratch, but in CMYK.

Curtain Up on Contrast

Choosing the same sample points as before, the highlight is $3^C2^M15^Y$. The awning is $16^C21^M16^Y$, the hotel $28^C29^M18^Y$, the stripes of the flag $42^C44^M6^Y1^K$, and the full shadow $73^C69^M76^Y58^K$. The light point of the facade is $45^C49^M43^Y3^K$ and the dark point $66^C66^M70^Y27^K$.

In CMYK, the range of the facade is therefore around 20 points out of a possible 100. In RGB, it's more like 70 out of a possible 256. Not to bore you with the arithmetic, but the range in RGB is about 25 to 30 percent longer than in CMYK. Furthermore, in CMYK we can exploit the black to build shadow detail, without having to worry about whether it throws the neutrality of the image off.

Best of all, for those of a piratical bent, in CMYK there is a region of the curve that rarely is

Figure 9.8 Top, the correction done in RGB with the top curve of Figure 9.7. Bottom, done in CMYK using the bottom curve. Note the added contrast in the facade and shadows.

important. In shadows, the CMYK colors don't exceed 80%. In RGB, without a black ink to establish darkness, shadows have to be much higher.

The cyan curve here is similar to the red, as might be expected. But the top half, where the facade lives, is steeper, because there is now no need to guard against loss of detail at the very top of the curve, as there was in RGB.

The magenta is even more of an improvement over the green, for the same reasons. In the magenta, the top fifth of the curve contains little of value and can be flattened. But in the green, the top fifth of the curve carries most of the shadow detail in the image. In the magenta, the shadow and the facade inhabit the same area of the curve; an improvement to one improves the other.

Figure 9.9 *When brilliant objects lack detail, a blown-out RGB channel, like the red below, is frequently the culprit. After some plate blending, the original, top, gains detail, center.*

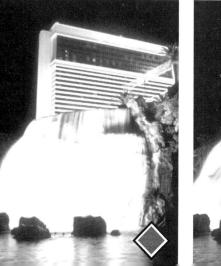

The yellow parrots the blue. Yellow being by far the weakest ink, one need not go overboard in trying to build contrast with it.

As often happens, critical elements can be isolated in the black. The first steep area contains the facade. The second has all the shadow detail. There is a small area between them that contains nothing of value. That gets flattened in the interest of steepening the other areas still more.

The RGB correction is nice, sure, but it can't compare with the CMYK either in the facade or in the shadows. Don't think this is some kind of sharpening legerdemain, either: all three versions used the same separation parameters, and all were sharpened equally—in CMYK—as the very last step.

At this point, it's useful to review the five major weapons in our arsenal, and how the capabilities of RGB and CMYK stack up:

- **Setting overall range**. This is easy in either colorspace.
- **Steepening interest areas within a curve**. As we have just seen, CMYK is much better at this.
- **Working with the weak color**. CMYK's version is always weaker than its RGB cousin, making it easier to improve with virtually no risk of changing the overall color of the image. Moreover, black can often be used as a *second* unwanted color.
- **Unsharp masking**. This is more or less a subset of the last item. The unwanted color and the black can generally be sharpened heavily in CMYK, because they don't usually have as much noise as their darker RGB counterparts.
- **Manipulation of the black plate**. As RGB doesn't have one, CMYK wins in this category by default.

Exeunt the Flat Channels

Because of the presence of black, the three remaining CMY colors are subtler than their RGB relatives. Red makes more of a statement than cyan, green is more potent than magenta, and blue is certainly more powerful than yellow.

This is a two-edged sword. On the one hand, complicated, finely-tuned corrections such as the one we just did work better in CMYK. On the other, when there is something seriously wrong with the image, attacking with curves is a better option, but it isn't as good an option as using LAB, which we'll cover in the next chapter.

Blending, however, is an important use of RGB—and it isn't a one-way street. Whenever you see an RGB image with brilliant colors, you should keep this in mind.

Consider the red chest of the parrot in Figure 9.3, or, better yet, since we've dealt with this subject several times, consider a rose. The shape of the flower, and thus the success or failure of our work, depends on the cyan plate. The detail in the cyan is in the lightest area. When we convert to CMYK, we apply a dot gain compensation curve that suppresses such light areas.

How clever does that sound?

Not that the compensation degrades the image, mind you. In principle, press conditions will counterbalance the curve, and the printed piece will more or less reflect the original.

The problem is, it was a lousy photograph to begin with. The photographer didn't capture as much detail in the rose as we now need.

How do I know this? Because there isn't any other species of photograph of roses. For reasons stated in Chapter 5, they *all* need some kind of contrast boost from us.

Since the idea is to wind up with a nice cyan plate, the direct approach is to blend something with more detail, commonly a copy of the original red channel, into it.

But this isn't the only way, and it isn't necessarily the best way. Remember, we postulate that the image didn't have enough contrast to begin with. That means that the original red channel of RGB is itself too weak. And if that's the case, and a blend is going to be necessary, why not consider getting it over with in RGB?

This isn't always possible, because it can throw off the other colors of the image too drastically. But changing the red now will have more of an impact than changing the cyan later. And if a problem exists in one of the RGB plates, it will proliferate into at least two CMYK plates, if we let it.

Therefore, I recommend that, if you are starting out in RGB and you have an image with bright colors, you check the individual channels to see if you can do now what you would otherwise have to do later. Figure 9.9 is a demonstration.

With lighting this harsh, it's hard to know what the numbers should be. The black sky is properly neutral, $15^R16^G14^B$, but there are few other clues. Let's ignore that issue, and assume that our client's main objection is a lack of detail, particularly in the waterfall and in the bright sign at the top of the hotel.

And, assuming we are starting in RGB, since this image clearly has bright colors, we should check out the individual channels shown in Figure 9.9. This shows what we might expect: in an image this yellow, the blue channel is very dark. Consequently, it has stronger highlights than do either of the other two (particularly the blown-out red).

If the idea is to get a better waterfall, it's pretty clear where to find it. If the idea is to find and replace a channel where there isn't any detail, it's pretty clear where that is as well.

The brightest spot in the water starts out at a yellowish $255^R255^G233^B$. The first step should be to shove the bottom of the blue curve to the right, lightening it slightly, so that the highlight is only about half as yellow as before. The purpose of this move is to add contrast to the waterfall, prior to blending.

Then it's just a question of how much to blend. I chose 30% of the blue into the red, 33% into the green. The exact numbers are governed by the color balance one wants. Darkening the red—which is what we are doing, as much as we are adding detail—is the equivalent of adding cyan ink. That pushes this image toward green. Darkening the green channel, on the other hand, makes the image warmer. You'd probably choose different percentages than I did.

This is not the approach for every image. Under certain circumstances, it wouldn't even be the right one for *this* image. We specifically assumed that the issue was the waterfall and not the trees, which we permitted to lose detail. That's frequently a bar to channel blending.

But where the brightly colored object is silhouetted or pretty much isolated from everything else, this RGB maneuver is very strong, and it's more effective than if done in CMYK.

On the other hand, the final move in this image can't be done in RGB. After converting the image to CMYK, I took advantage of the lack of detail in the dark sky and water. Since there's nothing much to lose there, I made them even darker, along the lines

RGB AND CMY

✓The crucial point in deciding whether to use RGB or CMYK is understanding that they are very similar. The red channel will resemble the cyan, the green the magenta, and the yellow the blue. The black is *sui generis*.

✓CMY channels seem lighter than their RGB cousins, because in the RGB-to-CMY conversion, a lightening takes place to compensate for dot gain on press. Also, in the deepest blacks, the CMY channels lack detail. This is because they have to be suppressed to make room for black ink and stay within the total ink limit that print shops demand.

✓RGB channels have more detail in highlights than their CMY counterparts. Since highlight detail in the unwanted color is vital (see Chapter 5) it frequently makes sense to use the RGB cousin channel to blend into the unwanted color channel in CMYK.

✓Objects in RGB files always have longer ranges than in CMY, owing to the absence of black ink.

✓For curve-based corrections of typical images, CMYK has many advantages over RGB. There is a much greater chance that several important objects will fall into the same range on a single curve.

✓For corrections of very poor originals, in principle RGB is better than CMYK, but LAB is better yet.

✓Problems with lack of detail in brightly colored objects can often be traced back to one poor channel in an RGB file, which then proliferated into several CMYK plates. In such a case, since plate blending will eventually be necessary anyway it is advisable to blend while still in RGB.

✓To avoid banding of gradients after the RGB-to-CMYK conversion, consider blending one or more of the original RGB channels into its CMY cousin.

✓In general, images that are headed for an RGB output device, such as a film recorder, can remain in RGB. By-the-numbers curves will work well enough, because not as much strengthening of detail (and sharpening) is needed in positive color film than in the narrower gamut of the printed page.

suggested way back in Figure 1.7, by putting more black ink than usual in the shadow.

This one is a busier image, and such a darkness move might muddy things up in undesirable places, but there's an easy workaround—in CMYK. Open the black curve, lock the bottom half of it with anchoring points, and bring the shadow point sharply to the left.

Know your colorspaces—and your colorspace conversions—and many such convenient tricks will suggest themselves. Blending an RGB channel into its CMY cousin, for example, is suggested by our knowledge of the workings of dot gain, a topic one might have thought irrelevant in this chapter.

Similarly, do you ever have problems with gradients that are created in RGB developing harsh bands when converted to CMYK, especially in deep, rich colors?

You shouldn't. If you think back to the discussion of EIAM in the last chapter, you'll understand why it's happening. Those colors are out of the CMYK gamut, and Photoshop is improvising. As for fixing it, now that you know the why, the how becomes obvious: find the CMY channels with the problem, and replace them with their RGB cousins.

What about RGB Output?

This book presupposes that eventually your files have to become CMYK. But what if the eventual destination is a film recorder, the Web, video, or a printer that requires RGB input? In that case, input may be RGB, and output as well. Is there a need to leave the womb at any time?

If you are going to a film recorder, the answer is an emphatic no. The major advantages of CMYK are targeted corrections plus better control of unsharp masking. These things are not helpful if you are imaging a high-resolution chrome. Sharpening is, in fact, a bad idea; suppose somebody blows the image up to poster size and finds sharpening halos an inch wide?

Similarly, we don't need to force contrast into a chrome; that decision can be left to the person who takes it into print. A pansy that is too pallid on the printed page packs plenty of punch in a positive.

As for the other cases, sometimes added snap is needed and at other times it isn't. If you find that RGB curves can't deliver it, take advantage of another RGB strength: you can convert from RGB to and from LAB as often as you like, within reason, without any loss of detail. That is more than can be said for CMYK. And we are about to go into the virtues of LAB.

If we were restricted to one colorspace for corrections, it would have to be CMYK. If we were restricted to two, one would certainly have to be LAB, which brings a lot to the table because it is so different. In that case, the choice of the second wouldn't be that big a deal. CMY is RGB, remember? So, we'd choose whichever was our final output space—if we had to choose.

Fortunately, we have no such restriction. We can pick whatever we like whenever we like. The choice should be made on the basis of effectiveness, not political correctness. To someone who thinks in this fashion, not only is CMY merely another form of RGB, but all colorspaces are one.

HSB Is LAB

For those who have tried to boost contrast in an image but come up with an unwelcome color change instead, here's a solution: a colorspace that keeps the two separate. LAB, powerful enough to be called the patron saint of lost causes, also happens to be the best space for general retouching.

one shall part us from each other, goes the most breathtaking love song in all of opera, *One in life and death are we: all in all to one another, I to thee and thou to me.*

That this particular gem rears its head in the most unlikely setting possible, right after the lowest slapstick in a Gilbert and Sullivan comedy, does not diminish the impact of the lines that follow:

> *Thou the tree, and I the flower;*
> *Thou the idol, I the throng;*
> *Thou the day, and I the hour;*
> *Thou the singer, I the song.*

Or, to rephrase it more in keeping with our time, you are the words, I am the tune, play me. Whichever you like, the metaphor is so effective because it likens the lovers to things that nobody in their right mind would wish to consider as separate items.

Like, for example, color and contrast. So far, these items have been as inextricably intertwined as anything on Gilbert's little list. Every correction shown so far has involved both. Every channel in CMYK, every channel in RGB, affects both. And certainly, every one of us needs to be able to control both.

But considering color and contrast together has a downside. How many times have you tried to boost the detailing in a color picture, only to give up in disgust because you threw the colors off? There is also the matter of how clients react to our work. Many opinions are possible about color—but not about contrast. After all, when was the last time one of your clients complained because your image wasn't foggy enough, or because it seemed to carry too much detail?

This chapter introduces two colorspaces that do what RGB and CMYK do not, namely, keep contrast and color isolated from one another. That is an extraordinary advantage to have—on certain kinds of images. On other kinds, the old reliables do better. With a little bit of judgment, we can have the best of both worlds.

Dicky-bird, Why Do You Sit?

Of the two, LAB is by far the more important, but it gets that distinction by default. Since Photoshop 2, there hasn't been full support for HSB, although a couple of important vestiges of it exist. LAB, on the other hand, is supported almost as completely as CMYK and RGB.

Figure 10.1 shows why it is unfortunate Photoshop no longer lets us work in HSB. For this, I wheeled out my copy of Photoshop 2.0.1 and opened up one of the images used in Chapter 9. I then converted it to HSB (don't try this with Photoshop 5!) and what you see here is the S channel.

You may ask what this exercise proves. I would answer, not much, unless we have to mask this bird, and in that case this particular channel is going to be a much better start at making the selection than any alternate method.

But enough crying over spilt birdseed. Let's define how these two specimens work.

HSB stands for Hue, Saturation, Brightness. Users of Heidelberg Color Publishing Solutions' LinoColor product, a leading scanner-control package, encounter a different acronym: LCH, for Luminance, Chroma, Hue. The two mean the same thing, and you can use the commentary in this chapter to help run LinoColor, except you can go even further because in LinoColor you can write curves in HSB.

The L of LAB stands for Luminance. The letters A and B don't stand for anything in particular. The colorspace is more formally known as CIELAB, for Commission Internationale de l'Eclairage, an international color standards body, or as L*a*b*, which differentiates it from previous LAB incarnations. Adobe has chosen to refer to it as Lab color, although it has nothing to do with a laboratory, and as if the A and B were not the separate channels they are.

In both of these colorspaces, one channel—the L in LAB and the B in HSB—carries all the contrast, and none of the color. These channels, therefore, can be seen as black and white renditions of the color image. The other two channels define the color, but in radically different ways.

The underlying color in HSB is set by the H channel. It can be red, green, blue, or anything else. By this strange definition, the skin of a young child has the same H as does a fire engine: both are almost pure red, not tending toward yellow or magenta. The child's skin is *lighter,* meaning that it would be different in the B channel, but it also differs in *saturation,* the S, which is the most important channel for our purposes because it allows us to play certain games that aren't easy in CMYK or RGB.

Saturation defines the purity of the color, or how vivid it is. One could describe it as how much the color tends toward neutrality. Another way would be in terms of the presence or absence of the unwanted color. If we were reproducing a fire engine, we would use virtually no cyan ink, so we would say the color was a completely saturated red. The child's face is lighter, but it is also less saturated. Although cyan ink in a face is limited, it's there.

A less saturated red than a child's face is the color known as brick red. Less saturated than that is brown—which is a species of red—and less saturated than that is gray.

In Figure 10.1, where lightness equates to saturation, the parrot consists of highly saturated colors, hence the strong definition of the bird's outline.

When Happiness Is Unwelcome

LAB's handling of the two color channels is even more difficult to understand than the HS of HSB, if possible. Here goes.

The L, as we know, is simple—it's just a black and white version of the image. The A is an *opponent-color* channel. At one extreme it is magenta, at the other, green, and in the middle it favors neither one.

The B is just like the A, except its opponent colors are yellow and blue. If it falls in the middle, it is neither yellow nor blue, and if both A and B are in the middle then the overall color is neutral. Otherwise, the overall color is determined by a highly nonintuitive interplay between the A and B channels. If you can get past this obstacle, LAB is a more powerful color-correction space than HSB. But at least one of them has to be part of your arsenal. If you use Photoshop 5, it has to be LAB. Let's set the

Figure 10.1 *In the early 1990s, Photoshop allowed files to exist in HSB. Above, the S channel of a Photoshop 2.0.1 document. It would be nice if Photoshop 5 offered a comparably easy way to mask this parrot.*

table with a couple of corrections that would be troublesome in RGB or CMYK.

When an image starts out flat, a correction in CMYK or RGB tends not only to add contrast but to create brighter, cleaner colors. If you go back and have a look at the corrections of Chapters 3 and 4, you'll see what I mean. In all of those images, the happier colors make sense.

Indeed, most images *do* look better with brighter colors. The problem is, quite a few do not. The glass of seltzer in Figure 10.2 is one of these. It needs a twist of something (I favor a curve rather than a lemon) but

certainly not any accentuation of color. Yet it needs a violent correction: the rear lip of the glass is almost invisible in the original.

This subject is a nasty one to shoot and a nasty one to scan. Even in the pallid original, there are flashes of yellow at the bottom of the glass and other traces of color in the seltzer itself. Plus, assuming that the original, slightly reddish, background, is what is wanted, that's a delicate color, easy to screw up.

In short, any correction, let alone the big one we need here, risks letting the color get out of hand. Unless, of course, we have a channel that doesn't affect color at all.

Saturation and Apparent Distance

Ecclesiastes remarked, Is there any thing whereof it may be said, See, this is new?

If you are looking at the concept of LAB curves with trepidation, take what the preacher said to heart. We've already used HSB and LAB principles, even if they weren't called that at the time.

The role of the unwanted color, to which we devoted Chapter 5, is largely a saturation issue, particularly as illustrated in Figure 5.4. There, the idea was to get a rounder-looking lime by forcing more magenta into the sides of the fruit. This pushed them away from green and toward gray—in other words, it desaturated them.

Similarly, in Chapter 6, we noted that unsharp masking sometimes introduces weird, objectionable color variations, as in the first version of Figure 6.4 and the second version of Figure 6.14. These can be wiped out by using Filter: Fade> Luminosity after sharpening. Which is, of

Figure 10.2 *The hopelessly flat original, top, needs more contrast, but not more color. This makes it ideal for an L channel move, bottom.*

course, an LAB move all the way. It's the equivalent of sharpening the L channel only.

Before entering 15 pages of hard-core LAB, let's dispose of the two main relics of HSB: the Adjust Hue/Saturation command, and the sponge tool. In principle, the main use of Adjust Hue/Saturation is to isolate a single color and make some kind of alteration, without having to go through the annoyance of selecting it. If you want the parrot's feathers in Figure 10.1 to be more of an orange color, this command, shown in Figure 10.3, is ideal.

Hue/Saturation is analogous to Image: Adjust/Selective Color, which also selects a target color, but uses a CMYK model to correct it. I find Hue/Saturation a little more intuitive and Selective Color a bit more precise, so I use Hue/Saturation when I am guessing at what may be right and Selective Color when I think I know for sure.

Selective Color has always had the advantage that we can choose Blacks, or Neutrals, as our target, which really helped in the correction of Figure 8.10. Hue/Saturation gains a big advantage in Photoshop 5: the ability to point to a color of our choosing as the target, rather than just "Reds" or whatever. This is a big help in avoiding the typical problem of these commands, which is having them affect unintended areas that happen to be somewhat close to the color of what we were trying to change.

The other big problem with both Hue/Saturation and Selective Color is that a lot of people use them too soon. The presumption is that most faulty color will be corrected by setting the basic numbers with curves. If those numbers are correct and you *still* have a problem with a particular color, then by all means trot out one of these commands. But don't do so before a

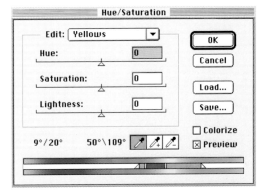

Figure 10.3 *Photoshop 5's revamped Hue/Saturation command allows precise definitions of the target color. Here, the command is set to affect oranges, but to have the impact fade out in the reds more rapidly than it does in the yellows.*

general correction. If you think that the parrot isn't orange enough, maybe it's the correct color and you just don't like it, or maybe it's because the image has a blue cast. Until you find out which it is, don't act.

A more powerful use of HSB is in creating the illusion of distance, which is critical in product shots, as well as any other image containing a foreground object with a pronounced color.

It's that old human vision thing again: the more saturated an object is, the closer it appears. Or, more importantly, the more desaturated it is, the more it recedes.

In a case like Figure 10.4, that makes certain moves obvious. If we want to emphasize the man, we should tone down the background. The best way to do that is to desaturate it. So, in the right half, the background (selected first, obviously) gets hit with a desaturation hammer by the Adjust Hue/Saturation command. Does not the man now appear much closer?

At times, of course, we can't get away with such skulduggery. What if the client *liked* that background color and didn't want us to change it?

In that case, we indulge in a trick very reminiscent of unsharp masking. Setting the sponge tool to Desaturate mode with a low pressure, we create a gray halo around the man, as in the left half of Figure 10.5. Note the extra pop as opposed to the right side, which moves in the opposite direction. If we are subtle enough, we'll sneak in under the viewers' radar. They don't usually notice USM, remember.

Modified Rapture

While it's nice to understand the theory behind desaturating with the sponge tool, the fact is, it is superfluous. The capability already exists, in LAB, further proof of the essential similarity of the two colorspaces.

I first have to give you a brief introduction to LAB curvewriting, which should definitely have a warning label saying, *Closed track! Professional driver! Don't try this with your own vehicle!*

As a further disincentive, the numbering system in LAB is specifically designed to discourage the tourist. The actual values are diagrammed in Figure 10.6, but let's go over each channel.

The L is easiest to understand. Normal rules apply: the steeper the curve, the more the contrast. Increasing steepness in critical areas of the L curve is extraordinarily effective at bringing out detail. About the only hangup is that the numbering system appears backward: 100 represents an absolute white; 0 an absolute black. An L channel range of between 95 and 8 or 10 is sensible for most work.

The L correction of Figure 10.2 is analogous to similar moves in other colorspaces. We start by measuring the highlight, which has an L value of 93, just underneath the lip of the glass, and also in the ice cube. This is one of two images in this book (the other is Figure 3.3) that do not have a shadow. That is, there is no point that we really want to portray as particularly dark. The current darkest area is in the center bottom of the glass, 43^L.

The liquid itself has only 12 points of range, from 92^L to 80^L. That, obviously, is

Figure 10.4 *Saturation is closely related to our perception of depth. When the background is desaturated, right, it seems to recede and the man seems to come forward.*

the area we seek to steepen. So we slide the lower left endpoint to the right, creating a lighter than normal highlight of 98^L. This decision seems justifiable on the grounds that there is almost no detail in the very lightest areas.

The process continues by adding a point in the quartertone and raising it sharply. This, in conjunction with the endpoint move, makes the first quarter of the curve, where the liquid resides, quite steep.

The third point is more debatable. Its positioning depends on how dark we want the pseudo-shadow to be.

Finally, remembering that LAB is the sharpening space of choice, we sharpen the L channel. And, remembering the principles of Chapter 6, we use a wide Radius (3.0 pixels here) in doing so. The bubbles are what we're trying to enhance, and they have no detail for USM to blow away. Furthermore, there is no objection to a wide halo around the bubbles. Quite the opposite: it will make them seem more pronounced.

Both the Simple and Quadratical

The reverse of the seltzer correction is one that affects color only. To do this, we need to discuss the baffling numbers of the A and B channels, which are laid out in Figure 10.6.

The A starts with magenta at the light end of its curve, and ends with green at the dark end. Just to be difficult, the numbers go from +128 at the magenta endpoint to –128 at the green. In the middle is zero. The B is exactly the same, except magenta is replaced by yellow and green by blue.

Somewhat shockingly, about half of the real estate of these curves is worthless for printing. LAB is an academic colorspace, designed to encompass not just the colors of print, not just the colors of a monitor or of film, but of everything—even fluorescent colors. A value of plus or minus 90, let alone 128, is out of gamut even for the best print conditions. Plus or minus 70 is about as intense as can be used.

This extravagant way of describing colors has two very good ramifications for

Figure 10.5 *When it isn't possible to desaturate the entire background, a gray halo around the foreground object often works well, left. At right, a counter-correction that brings the background closer to the man.*

those brave enough to correct in LAB, and two very bad ones. The first good thing is, there is no such animal as a color cast so bad that LAB can't zap it. Slight moves in the curves have huge consequences. When the original is somewhere near where you want it to be, think CMYK. When it's on some other continent, think LAB.

The second good thing is that it's easier to control neutral colors in LAB, because we need only balance two channels, not three. As long as we have 0^A0^B or thereabouts, it won't matter what the colorless L value is.

As against that, the very power of the A and B channels means that using them to correct is approximately the biggest and darkest dynamite factory an unwary artist can blunder into with a lighted match. One wrong move with an AB curve,

and it's curtains for the image. Thank goodness Photoshop 5 allows multiple levels of undo!

The second bad thing is, you can forget about using LAB as your *only* colorspace. It's powerful, but inaccurate. There is no way to fine-tune the numbers precisely enough for the best quality. Although for the purposes of this chapter I'm taking the LAB documents into CMYK and blithely printing whatever Fortune furnishes, in real life one has to plan to make minor adjustments in RGB or CMYK after the LAB maneuvering.

It's a reasonable position, therefore, to leave the A and B alone, while concentrating on the vastly more intuitive L. And yet, there is one simple AB correction technique that works on a whole lot of images, Figure 10.7 being one.

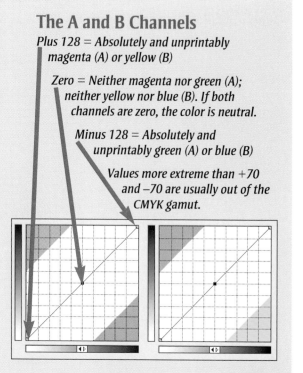

Figure 10.6 *The numbers are challenging and counterintuitive, but anyone wishing to work in LAB must learn them.*

The L Channel
100 = Completely White

Zero = Completely Black

Typical range should be white = 95, black = 3-5. (If you are worried about losing shadow detail, choose a lighter black value.)

The A and B Channels
Plus 128 = Absolutely and unprintably magenta (A) or yellow (B)

Zero = Neither magenta nor green (A); neither yellow nor blue (B). If both channels are zero, the color is neutral.

Minus 128 = Absolutely and unprintably green (A) or blue (B)

Values more extreme than +70 and −70 are usually out of the CMYK gamut.

The normal questions don't become irrelevant just because we are in LAB. Highlight? Easily found. $95^L1^A-1^B$, in the left eye of whatever this creature is supposed to be. Shadow? $7^L1^A-1^B$, in the black paint at top left. Neutrals? The shoes, which also are close to 0^A0^B throughout, although there is considerable variation in the L. And fleshtones? None.

For once, then, all the numbers seem to be good at the outset. The highlight is light enough, the shadow is dark enough, and both are neutral. The shoes are correct. And, in my view, no one part of the image is so much more important than the rest that it's worth fooling around with the shape of the L curve so as to gain contrast in one area and lose it elsewhere.

So, we are stuck with the L channel just as it is. Does that mean we just close the file? I suppose we could; there's nothing technically wrong with the image. But it seems to me that the colors suffer from tired blood, and I'd like to wake things up a bit. So I'll turn to the curves in A and B.

By now the refrain, the steeper the curve, the more the contrast, needs no more repetition. But what about the case of a contrast-free channel, a channel that contains color information only? In such a case, the steeper the curve, the more the *contrast between colors,* the more variation between one color and its neighbor.

The LAB definition of neutrality helps us out. In CMYK and RGB, the concept of neutrality is changeable, transitory. If we alter any curve, we have to recheck the neutral points to make sure nothing has changed. And if Channel X is too low with respect to Channel Y, we don't know whether to raise X, lower Y, or both. The channels depend on one another.

But in LAB, neutrality is absolute. If, in a color that is supposed to be neutral, the A or B channel is nearly zero, that value is correct, regardless of what is happening in either or both of the other two channels.

In this image, *both* the A and B are correct for neutrality, which means that the midpoints of their two curves are absolutely correct, unchangeable. And yet, we'd like the curves to be steeper, to pep up the color.

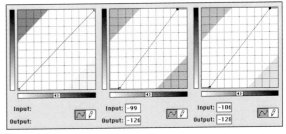

Input: Output: Input: -99 Output: -126   Input: -106 Output: -128

Figure 10.7 *In this original image, top, tonal range is correct, but the colors are too subdued. The curves above intensify them.*

The solution is to pivot the entire curve counterclockwise around the midpoint. To do so, move the top right point to the left, and then the bottom left point to the right until the curve—er, the straight line—goes right through the center point, leaving it unchanged from its original value, as in Figure 10.7.

A Combined Approach

Correcting only the L or only the A and B is reasonable. But there are plenty of occasions for some kind of combined approach. Overly flat images can get quite colorful if corrected in CMYK or RGB. Usually, that's what we want. Granted that there are a few cases like the seltzer of Figure 10.2, where we don't want any color increase at all, there are a lot more of the class of Figure

10.8, where the colors are subtle. We would like slightly more saturated reds, not canyon walls the color of fire engines.

In this image, we start with a light point of $77^L5^A–5^B$ in the foreground river. That's a bias toward magenta and blue, which, taken together, adds up to a tilt toward purple. Do you believe this is logical? The shadow, such as it is, is in the foreground rocks, $31^L4^A–8^B$, another purple. There are no known neutral colors or flesh-tones in the image. The objects of interest are, in my opinion, the red rock formations. In the L channel, they fall in a narrow range between 55 and 40.

The overall L range of the original is thus only 46 points, which explains why it is so dreadfully flat; Figure 10.7, for example, started with a range of 88.

Figure 10.8 *This original starts out too flat, but the normal technique of opening range in CMYK or RGB might make its colors too bright.*

While LAB is made to order for the sub-optimal image, we shouldn't try to hit a five-run homer with it. This image has a lot of subtle detailing in the darker areas. If we force the shadow to a value of 10 or darker, it's likely that the blunt instrument of L correction would inflict some collateral damage. Instead, my plan would be to leave LAB with a relatively light shadow, intending to darken it after the conversion to CMYK.

Hence, the L curve shown in Figure 10.9. Note the steep area right where the canyon walls occur, near the center of the curve.

As for the A and B curves, I think they need to be steepened to bring out more color, in much the same way as was done with the graffiti image. But there, the neutral colors were really neutral to start with. Here, they aren't.

A neutral color, to reiterate, is anything with 0^A0^B. One or two points of difference is insignificant. But both the measured highlight and shadow of the Grand Canyon image are at least four points off in both channels. The problem is, we're not sure, from the context of the image, that our measuring points *should* be neutral.

In both the light point in the river and the dark point in the rocks, the A value is

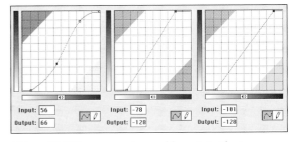

Figure 10.9 *The curves above add range in the L channel, plus a slight boost in all colors. The corrected image is below.*

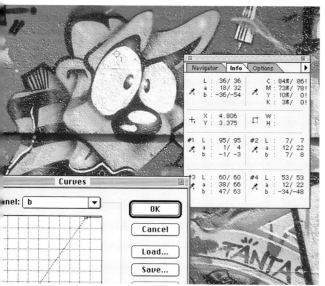

Figure 10.10 *A danger of correcting the AB channels is that they may create colors outside of the CMYK gamut. The exclamation points in the Info Palette indicate that the new colors can't be matched in CMYK.*

positive. This means, tending toward magenta rather than green. Shadows are normally neutral, but I can certainly believe that a shadow in the middle of red rock could itself have a magenta tinge.

But what about the water? Does it make sense that it could be more magenta than green? Not to me, it doesn't.

The B analysis is more straightforward. Here, both original numbers are negative, so both highlight and shadow are tending toward blue, rather than yellow. In the water, brackish though it may be, I can certainly buy more blue than yellow. But not in those rocks. Yellow, maybe. Neutral, maybe. Blue, impossible.

Therefore, I conclude that the original values are wrong, and that we need to move toward green in the A channel and toward yellow in the B.

In writing the AB curves for the graffiti image, we had to make sure the new curves

crossed the center point exactly where they did originally, because we knew that the original neutral colors were correct. This time, we know the original center points are *wrong*. So, we make our new A curve cross the center line a little higher than the midpoint—high being the green direction—and the new B cross lower, lower being yellow.

The question may well be raised, how do I know what angle to use for the new AB curves? Truth to tell, I *don't* know. It's a purely subjective decision. This differentiates it from the techniques shown in Chapters 3 and 4. I *am* sure that the handling of the L channel is correct. I *am* sure that neutralizing the highlight and shadow is correct. But how colorful to make the image, that's something on which reasonable people can vary.

The Advantages of AB Correction

Such straight-line corrections in the AB channels belie by their simplicity the concept that LAB is only for the brave. There are, in fact, a couple of everyday uses in which this technique is simpler, faster, and better than the CMYK alternative.

• **For newspaper use**. Normal scans don't quite cut it when prepared for newspapers. There are a number of reasons, but one of the biggest is that colors don't seem bright enough. That's because newsprint is not white. Every bright color is contaminated by the underlying dreariness of the paper. To compensate, brighter originals are needed. The formulas in this book for a fleshtone, for example, would be too gray for newsprint use: we would have to cut back on the cyan values.

The most flexible way of accomplishing this, while still correcting for neutrality, is with straight-line curves in the AB.

- **For a series of smaller images**. This book is biased in favor of wringing the maximum possible quality out of an image. Some images are simply not worth that attention. And the smaller an image is to be printed, the less noticeable all these tricks are anyway.

Furthermore, in small images we are apt to want bright, happy colors. The typical example might be a realty catalog, showing many different houses or interior shots. The client is sure to be looking for blue skies and green lawns, whether they existed in the original photograph or not. For this kind of work a quick correction and sharpen in LAB is effective and efficient, allowing us to process hundreds of images in a single shift. It's true, we have to forego finetuning the images in CMYK, but for this kind of work, who cares? If this were a magazine cover, we'd be sure to have the highlight in perfect balance. For a thousand-image weekly, close is good enough.

Photoshop 5's improved Actions capabilities allow us to be even faster. For this kind of work, write an Actions script that opens the RGB image, converts to LAB, applies Auto Levels in the L channel, sharpens the L, steepens the A and B, converts to CMYK, and saves as a TIFF file. If

Figure 10.11 The original, top, needs a color boost, but a careless correction in the A channel can result in something like the middle image. The bottom image helps out the greens without creating candy-colored reds.

you want to go further, have three different such scripts, each with a more drastic boost of the colors, and decide which one to apply after a quick examination of each image.

• **For conversions into RGB**. Nowadays, it is more likely than ever that a CMYK file may have to go into RGB for some reason. Maybe an image that was prepared for a print advertisement now has to go to the Web, maybe it needs to go to a desktop printer that can only take RGB, maybe it's going into video or some other kind of multimedia presentation, whatever. The problem is, RGB has a wider gamut of colors available, but Photoshop has no clue whether to use them.

In other words, suppose we have a blue in the CMYK file that is about as bright as we can get in that blue-deficient colorspace. Should we match that blue exactly in RGB? Or should we punch it up to be the brightest blue possible in RGB?

This is very much a case-by-case decision, but once you have made it, the easiest

way to implement it is to convert the CMYK image into LAB, apply straight-line corrections to the AB, and then move into RGB.

There's one thing to be careful of. It's easy to go overboard in LAB and create colors that are out of the CMYK gamut. If you do, you will be relying on the tender mercies of Photoshop's separation method when you finally convert to CMYK. That method, as discussed in Chapter 8, isn't too kind to out of gamut colors. So, when correcting in LAB, keep an eye on the Info palette. When exclamation points appear in the CMYK equivalents, as they do in Figure 10.10, you've gone too far.

Reshaping the AB Curves

There are variations on this straight-line approach. We can decide we want to hit the yellow-blue B channel without touching the magenta-green A, and vice versa. We can use different angles on each one. Or, in special cases, we can depart from the straight-line shape altogether.

Figure 10.11 is the kind of image that requires an LAB move, for the grassy hillside if nothing else. In the original, there's not the variation in the greens that a human observer would see. Clearly, we'd like to steepen the A curve. Also, the blues of the lake, mountain, and sky are too much alike. Perhaps steepening the B will help that.

The highlight of this image, at several places in front of the foreground houses, is $95^L1^A0^B$. The shadow, in the train or the black cows, is $6^L-6^A2^B$. There are no neutral colors or fleshtones to worry about.

Although the highlight and shadow values in the L channel are correct, we need to reshape the curve. Entirely too much unused real estate falls between the highlight

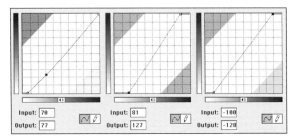

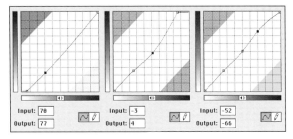

Figure 10.12 The LAB curves that produced the center and bottom versions of Figure 10.11.

and the second lightest area of the image, which is the grass or the lake. We need to flatten that area of the curve so as to allocate more contrast to the rest of the image.

The B value in the shadow is all right, but the A is biased toward green. So a first approach is to use the same AB curves as in the graffiti image, but to make the A curve cross the center line lower than the midpoint, so as to move the A away from green and toward magenta.

This results in the middle version, which is a whole lot better than the original, but has a problem: we are starting to get candy colors in the roofs of the houses at right. The grass is also turning a bright yellow, although it is gaining color contrast. And the sky seems to have become reddish as well.

These difficulties could have been avoided. The colors we are really interested in enhancing are greens and blues. What's the point of beefing up the reds?

It's time, therefore, to move away from the straight-line approach in the AB curves. Since magenta and yellow, which together make red, live in the lower halves of their respective channels, what we have to do is lock the lower halves of the curves in place, then steepen the upper halves as in the bottom of Figure 10.12.

There's a third possibility, which I haven't illustrated. Suppose we decide that the red component is so annoying that, instead of keeping it constant, it should be *suppressed?* Well, in LAB, that's easy. Instead of leaving the lower halves of the curves constant, we move up the lower left endpoints, giving us flatter lower halves of the curves but steeper upper halves.

And occasionally one finds an image that seems so hopeless that only a radical AB move can come to the rescue. That kind of thing is for the truly ambitious, and beyond the scope of this chapter, but you'll see an example at the end of Chapter 11.

The Best Channels to Blur

The problem of colored noise in originals has always been around. Photographs taken under poor lighting conditions or with very fast film, sports photography being the most prominent example, often display such noise.

But it's gotten worse recently. Many digital camera backs occasionally throw in a disturbing colored flare at the edges of objects, and certain desktop scanners do the same thing. These artifacts are difficult to get rid of—unless you use LAB.

For the same reason that the L channel absorbs sharpening well, and is thus often our first choice, the A and B can accept blurring. This is a much better method than using a blur filter (or the Median, Despeckle, or Dust & Scratches filter) on an RGB or CMYK channel.

The reason is obvious. The last thing we want to do is defocus a channel that contributes to the contrast of an image, even if it's the weak yellow plate. Blurring the yellow may be better than nothing but it certainly isn't as good as blurring a channel that doesn't carry detail.

In Figure 10.13, the corrected blue channel seems to have lost the noise but not any contrast: it remains sharply focused. However, as the color image indicates, one shouldn't overestimate the effect of noise in the yellow plate (which is, recalling Chapter 9, what the blue becomes in adult life). The picture as a whole isn't improved nearly as much as you might expect from looking at the channel in isolation.

Blurring the A and B is especially useful for the class of images that has the most noise of all—the prescreened original. We'll go into that in Chapter 14, but suffice it to say here that even a quick AB blur of a prescreened original goes a long way toward eliminating moiré.

A Declaration of Independence

LAB is, without qualification, the best colorspace in which to retouch.

By retouching, I am not referring to the common variety of removing scratches and dirt. You can attend to such simple stuff however you like. I am talking about serious moves away from the art, or the restoration of large damaged areas. The reason is not that LAB is device-independent, but that it is channel-independent.

Figure 10.14 represents the sort of thing I'm talking about. Can you guess what's wrong with this image?

This photo was taken one fall day in the Canadian Rockies. We had stopped for a break when we were visited by this handsome specimen, who desired to know whether there was anything in the car that bighorn sheep like to eat. My father, sitting in the passenger seat, quickly produced a camera, and you see the result.

Unfortunately, the car window was not completely rolled down, which accounts for the wide blue line running diagonally across the picture. My father thinks that the picture is therefore a total loss, for which he blames me. A lot he knows.

The blue band is a big problem, but it certainly isn't the only one. Even if we could eliminate the color cast in it, the underlying image would still be out of focus. In fact, the defocused area extends well below the obvious blue line.

Worse than that, the entire bottom half of the image is the wrong color. It's slightly too blue, to judge by the appearance of the animal's bottom half.

As you may have gathered, in bleak circumstances like these, one calls on the patron saint of lost causes, namely, LAB. With it, one can get from Figure 10.14 to Figure 10.15. Without it, it's very difficult.

Inventorying highlight and shadow values has to be confined to the top half of the image, since the color in the bottom half is suspect. For highlights, I find $97^L 1^A – 5^B$ in the bare mountain, $94^L 2^A – 8^B$ in the clouds. It makes sense that the clouds might have a blue cast, but not the mountain.

For shadow, in various deep areas of the trees I find $7^L 0^A – 7^B$. Conceivably, the color of the trees might be throwing off the B reading here, although you'd think it would affect the magenta-green A first. Just to be sure, therefore, we measure the inside of the sheep's ear at $9^L 4^A – 9^B$. There's no excuse for this to be blue, so, since every reading we've taken has been to the north of zero in the B channel, it must be concluded that the image has a blue cast.

The L and A values seem good in highlight and shadow, so there's no point in changing them. But before going any further, I think we should shove down the B curve, pushing it away from blue and toward yellow, by moving the top right endpoint down.

That accomplished, we need to find out just how bad the damage in the bottom half of the image is. For that, we'll need a close look at each channel. The findings are somewhat surprising.

The L channel, first of all, was badly defocused in the diagonal blue stripe, and also to some extent for about a quarter of

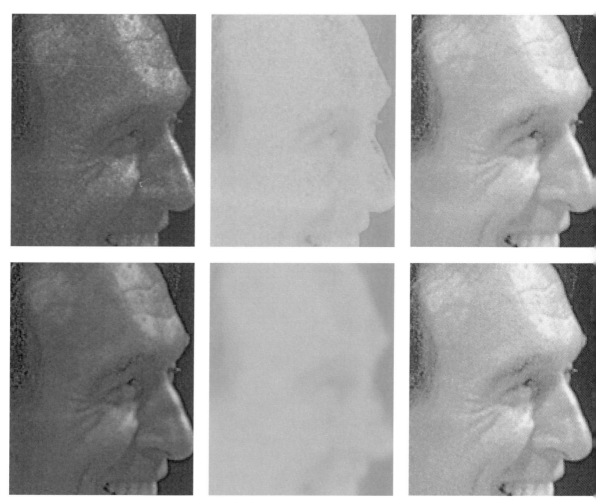

Figure 10.13 *Blurring the A and B channels is a nearly cost-free way of reducing colored noise. Above left, the man shows heavy noise in the blue channel of an RGB original. Above center, after conversion to LAB, the B channel is also noisy. After blurring the B, bottom center, and reconverting to RGB, the new blue, bottom left, is almost noise-free. At right, the color image, before and after this correction.*

an inch below it. The defocused area was not, however, significantly lighter or darker than what surrounded it.

I was scarcely able to detect any damage to the A channel at all. Even when I experimented with an extremely steep curve, no diagonal line showed up. This diagonal line, it seems, is pure blue, not tending at all toward magenta or green, or toward darker or lighter.

Of course, this means that the B channel has more problems than a Mac SE running Photoshop 5.5. Figure 10.16 shows the diagonal stripe clearly. To create it, I made a copy of the B channel, and applied an extremely steep curve to it, trying to have mostly whites and blacks.

As you can see, I also inverted it. Normally in the B yellow is light and blue dark. Not here. I flipped the values. I needed the blue to be *light,* because it was my intention to use Figure 10.16 as a mask.

But before applying it, we have to attend to the color problems in the bottom half of the image. It's clearly too blue, but it's hard to say *how much* too blue it is. The sheep's body, which is in the blue area, isn't going to match the face for color anyway. The gravel is blue, but who knows what color it's supposed to be. Nor are the plants much help, because the foreground plants seem to be of a different species than the lighter plants above the diagonal line.

At the extreme right of the image, just above the line of damage, is a clump of plants that seem to be of the same species as those in the lower half of the image. Measuring their values, they are equal in L and A, and around four points less negative (meaning more yellow, less blue) in the B.

The next step, therefore, is to activate the lasso tool, and draw a line, freehand, just under the top of the diagonal line throughout the width of the image, then extending the selection to encompass the entire half of the picture that is below the damaged area.

The reason for the freehand selection is that irregular selections are tougher to detect than those based on straight lines.

Figure 10.14 *There seems to be a diagonal blue line across the center of the image. Can you guess the cause? How would you fix it?*

I doubt that this is a big factor here, since much of the damaged area is going to be replaced altogether, but what the heck.

Having made the selection, the next step is to apply to it the same curve that previously was applied to the entire image, moving the B value 4 points toward the positive, moving the lower half of the image away from blue and toward yellow.

The first application of this curve could have been done in CMYK. It might have changed the overall lightness and darkness of the image, or the balance of red vs. green, but at least the image would be internally consistent.

The second move, no. If the magenta-green balance had changed, the bottom half would not have matched the top half. Without LAB, in my opinion, this would have been a very difficult correction. Not as difficult, however, as the next adventure, restoring the damaged area itself, which is well nigh impossible without LAB.

A Bit from Here, a Bit from There

You may never have had to repair damage caused by a car window before, but you've probably had to do similar things, hopefully in not such a large area. Everybody has their own favorite method of doing this,

Figure 10.15 *In correcting images with physical damage, LAB is usually the best, because its three channels operate independently of one another.*

Figure 10.16 *The A and B channels can often be the foundations for effective masks. Here, an inverted, contrast-enhanced copy of the B channel isolates the area of damage.*

but all techniques boil down to the same thing. We somehow have to replace the damaged part with detail cloned from the remainder of the image.

The downside with doing so in CMYK (and RGB similarly) is that we can't just pick up the cyan from the left corner of the image, the magenta from the right, and the yellow and black from somewhere else. No, we have to clone all the channels simultaneously. That means that everything we paste in has to match its surroundings not just for detail, but for color.

In LAB or HSB, this ghastly difficulty goes away. We *can* clone the channels from three different areas if we like. Here, we only have to replace two channels, because the A is correct as is. We do this in two passes, vastly easier than trying to do it all in a single operation.

First, the B. Since the channel viewed by itself is very difficult to comprehend, open the Channels palette, click on the B, but then click the eye icon to the left of the LAB row. This will display the

entire image, while making it impossible to alter anything except the B.

It would probably be acceptable to just slather this area with B values from elsewhere in the greenery, using monstrously large brushes of the rubber stamp tool. But why take chances? It's so easy to make a mask for this (that is, if we know our LAB). So, we return to Figure 10.16, which was made prior to all these shenanigans, and load it as a selection into the main image. Now, we can slather away, confident that we are only painting new B values into damaged areas and not elsewhere.

Having done this, we remove the mask. A detail-free channel like the B can be

Figure 10.17 *The advantage of repairing damage in LAB is that serious cloning only has to be done in one channel, rather than three or four. Above, a section of the original L, showing the defocused area. Below, the L channel just prior to conversion to CMYK.*

Quick & Dirty
LAB and HSB

✓LAB and HSB are similar in that they separate color from contrast. Each has one channel that contains all the detail and two that contain all color information.

✓Photoshop doesn't support HSB to the extent it does the other three colorspaces, but certain other applications do, so it's important to understand it.

✓The Adjust Hue/Saturation and Adjust Selective Color commands are useful, but they should be applied *after* all other color corrections.

✓Desaturated objects seem to recede into the background. Therefore, desaturating with either the sponge tool or by use of Adjust Hue/Saturation on a selected area can be a good way to deemphasize one object so as to promote another.

✓For noisy images, digital captures with flaring colors, and prescreened originals, consider blurring the A and B channels, which deadens the defects without harming contrast.

✓Setting overall range with the L channel is easy. This is the method of choice when an image is flat but should not contain vibrant colors. Opening range in CMYK or RGB tends to intensify colors, which is desirable—most of the time.

✓Because LAB has an enormous gamut, color corrections are imprecise but very powerful. Any color cast, however severe, can be eliminated in LAB.

✓Steepening the A and B curves by pivoting them counterclockwise around the curve midpoint is an easy and effective way to liven up colors generally.

✓Edges are often better defined in the A and B channels than they are in any channel in RGB or CMYK. Although they always have to have contrast added, they are often a good starting point for creating masks.

✓It's easier to control neutrality in LAB or HSB than in CMYK or RGB, where neutrality depends on the interaction of several channels. In LAB, if the A and B channels have a value of zero, that's a neutral no matter what the L is.

✓For complicated retouching, LAB is much superior to either RGB or CMYK, because the channels are completely independent. A new area can be defined based on different samples from each LAB channel, whereas in RGB and CMYK all channels must be copied simultaneously.

pasted in undetectably through a soft-edged mask; the L cannot. Furthermore, the mask did not allow working on the animal, which was too yellow in the original to be included. So we have to clone more B channel there, sans mask.

The beauty of correcting the L is that we don't have to worry about color at all. That has already been taken care of by our moves in the B. All we need do is pick up detailing from greenery anywhere in the image and start cloning,in any of a variety of ways, ending with the bottom version of Figure 10.17.

The last issue is the sheep itself. The body can be rebuilt in the same way as the greenery, but there is next to no definition of the animal's edge. That's not something that can be picked up elsewhere. Unsharp masking won't help, either: USM needs to find an edge before it can enhance it.

Recalling the example of Figure 6.3, and mindful that what's good enough for El Greco is probably good enough for us, if there aren't any USM halos available, let's make 'em. My way is to use the paintbrush tool, single-pixel brush, method Darken, L channel only, L value of 25, pressure 15%. With that, I draw in subtle edges where animal hits background. Afterwards, I reverse this process, with a light edge where both animal and background are relatively dark.

This hint of an edge can finally be unsharp masked—with the sharpening *tool,* not the filter.

After darkening the animal's muzzle with the burn tool, set to midtones, L channel only, we switch over to the A and B. To get the muzzle to the proper color, we clone the A and B from some other likely area in the animal's coat.

Also, the blue cast of the gravel in the foreground is the sort of thing we usually need the sponge tool for. We would like it more neutral, more gray, less blue.

As noted earlier, LAB has this capability, too. Set the foreground color to anything neutral—that is, to any color with 0^A0^B. Now, activating the A and B channels only, with the airbrush tool set to 50% pressure, we paint over the gravel. Every time the airbrush passes over it, the gravel gets more gray, but detail is unaffected.

After this, we can at last leave LAB for the more comfortable ground of CMYK and a final tweak of the highlight and shadow values. This step is always necessary in view of the inherent inaccuracy of LAB corrections.

This chapter barely scratches the surface of what's possible with LAB, other than to make the point that it's a lot more than most people think, and well worth the effort to master. Don't be frustrated by its intricacies: that frustration will dissipate the very first time you execute a retouch or a color correction that wouldn't have been possible in another colorspace.

Master LAB, and for you, there *will* be no bad originals. It probably can't be your primary workspace, but once you appreciate the virtue of divorcing color from contrast, it's one you will never part from. The serious retoucher, joyful yet respectful, sings to the imperious colorspace:

> *I the stream, and thou the willow—*
> *I the sculptor, thou the clay—*
> *I the ocean, thou the billow—*
> *I the sunrise, thou the day!*

CHAPTER 11

All Colorspaces Are One

Though they approach problems in unique ways, each colorspace can make the basic corrections. Go beyond basics, and certain changes are more effective in certain colorspaces. The professional has to be ready to change color models quickly, but unwilling to do so when it isn't really necessary.

BTSS is the acronym for a nutritional disease that I happen to suffer from, as do many other computer artists. It manifests itself when we are confronted with interesting menus in restaurants. It generally results in serious cases of indigestion. The full name is Eyes Bigger Than Stomach Syndrome.

My doctor has had a lot to say to me about the necessity for restraint in this area, and no doubt she is right. The problem is, in our health-conscious society, we can't afford to take a bite of every dish that passes by, nor a drink of every beverage. And it seems silly to have dessert in between the appetizer and the main course.

In the last four chapters we have seen enough colorspace goodies to set anyone's mouth watering. The question is now one of restraint, of knowing when one is enough and when we have to take a nibble out of several. All will do the same job, but for certain images, certain spaces leave a much better taste in the mouth. I will illustrate with a series of images of good things to eat.

Often enough, we can enjoy all the advantages of a given colorspace without ever actually entering it. Suppose, for example, that we have just presented a client with a first proof of some chocolates that look

like the upper left rendition of Figure 11.1. Not too surprisingly, she screams at us that the image is flat, lifeless, and unappetizing. Now what?

It would seem we want to fix this image in LAB. The client objects to the lack of detail, not to the color. No matter what colorspace we're in, we plan to make the chocolates land in steep areas of the curve in every channel. Right now, we're in CMYK, and the lower left version shows the danger. After the curves of Figure 11.2, more detail is certainly there—and so is a new color.

If we were instead to convert to LAB, we could use the same kind of curve in the L channel to get the same extra detail without the offensive color shift. But who needs extra work? We can, in effect, work in LAB even if the file is CMYK. All we need do, after applying the curves that generated the off-color image, is apply Photoshop's Filter>Fade command, choosing 100% as the opacity, and Luminosity as the method. You do remember, naturally, what the L in LAB stands for.

Figure 11.1 *The original chocolates, above, are correct for color, but lack snap. A normal CMYK contrast enhancement begets the version at lower left, correct for detail, but now the wrong color. Fading the curves back to luminosity creates the final version, lower right.*

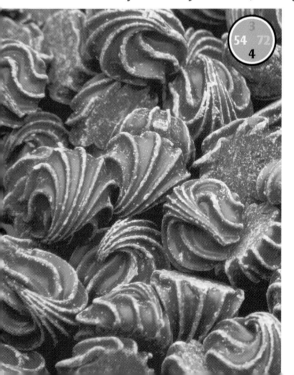

This kind of move isn't limited to CMYK, and it isn't limited to this one command. Images where the color is right and the contrast is wrong are very common. Such is the case with the raspberries of Figure 11.3.

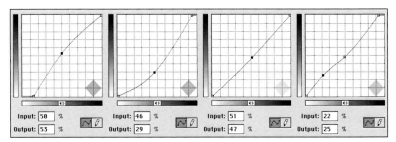

Figure 11.2 *The curves that generated the off-color lower left version of Figure 11.1.*

This time, we start (and finish) in RGB. The versions have been converted to CMYK for printing purposes, but I've done no tweaking beyond the default settings.

One's first impression is that this is just a variation on the chocolates theme. The berries are properly red at the moment; all we need do is increase contrast by means of curves. This, of course, is done exactly as it would be in CMYK, by making sure that the berries fall in appropriately steep areas of the three individual curves. And, of course, the problem is exactly the same as it would be in CMYK. Chances are, the berries won't stay the same color.

The chocolates were easier because we assumed that a client had already approved the overall color. Here, let's assume that we have no such approval, and that although the color looks good now, we are open to small changes to go along with the big change in contrast.

Under these circumstances, I'd suggest doing the correction on a separate layer. Begin with Layer: Duplicate Layer, putting a copy of the RGB image on top of itself. With this second layer active, apply RGB curves that steepen the range in each channel that affects the berries, leaving sharp, but off-color, fruit. If you like, apply USM as well.

In the Layers palette, shown in Figure 11.4, I changed the mode from Normal to Luminosity, which accomplishes the same thing we did with the chocolates. As it happens, I quit right there, which means I could have done exactly the same thing with an Adjustment Layer.

Using a true layer, however, opens up room for experimentation. It's possible that we might think that the berries should move just slightly in the direction of the corrected color but move strongly toward its contrast. We'd accomplish this by keeping the contrast layer in Normal mode, but turning down Opacity to 10% or so. Then, we'd add a third layer, duplicating the second, but 100% Opacity, mode Luminosity. Or an infinite number of permutations.

Back to the Unwanted Color

If you think you have seen this raspberry picture before, you have. It just wasn't a picture of raspberries, but of a lime, in Figure 5.4. The subject in both cases is brightly colored fruit. The choice is something that looks natural, or like a large blob of ink.

If you feel like exercising the first choice, there is an easy recipe. As Chapter 5 was at pains to point out, the shape of a bright red, green, or blue object depends almost exclusively on the unwanted color: magenta, in the case of a lime; cyan, for raspberries.

Figure 11.3 As with the chocolates, the original raspberries, top, are correct for color, but very flat. The corrected version, below, uses LAB techniques even though the file never leaves RGB.

Very interesting, is it not, the way that all colorspaces treat the image differently and yet achieve the same thing?

The objective with these fruits is always to create more of a range of saturation. They must be kept bright in the foreground areas, but have to fade rapidly toward gray at the edges—in the case of the raspberries, at the edges of the individual cells that make up the fruit.

The values at the left of the leftmost berry, which are highlighted in the color circles, demonstrate. They're a touch grayer in the corrected version.

These numbers show why the cyan and black plates are so critical in bright red images. Both the magenta and yellow are in the high 90s. Confronted with that heavy a flow of ink, dot structure in these two plates will not hold up when the job gets to press.

In the lime image, we used a brute-force approach of blending more detail directly into the magenta plate. With the raspberries, a different strategy got the same result, as Figure 11.5 shows. The new cyan plate is superior to the original.

Figure 11.5 is a useful contrivance known to professionals as a *prog,* or in this case, a partial prog, short for progressive proof. It allows us to assess the impact of various plates, and here it shows that we may be able to see detail in the magenta plate on the monitor, but it won't hold up when ink hits paper. Everything will depend, therefore, on how good our cyan and black are.

Figure 11.4 Photoshop's Layers palette offers Luminosity as an option, even when the base document is not in the LAB colorspace.

The prog also recalls one of the major limitations of calibrationism alluded to in Chapter 2. If these were real berries and not just an image, the relatively dark area we've been talking about would still be extremely red. If we were able to somehow pick up this small area of berry and transport it into a picture of something else, that piece of berry would likely be, and by far, the reddest thing in the image.

In such an imaginary second image, it would be nuts to portray that red with as much cyan and black ink as in the corrected version of Figure 11.3. If we did, all reds in the new picture would have to be even more desaturated to show they weren't as red as the berry. A face, for example, would have to be made very gray, because we certainly can't have a face the color of a raspberry.

And so, to reiterate the point that fouls up so many beginners and so many calibrationists, context is everything. The color of the darkest part of a raspberry is *different* in a picture that does not contain the brightest part of a raspberry. Don't listen to anybody who tells you that if it's the same piece of fruit it ought to be the same color. That logic works well for colorimeters but not for human beings.

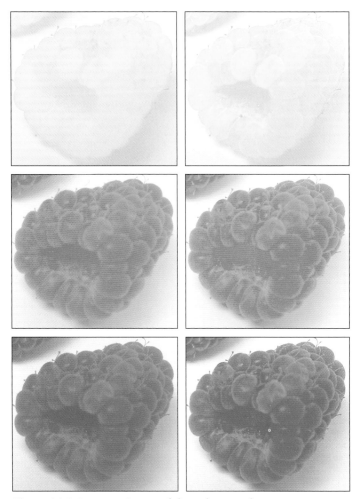

Figure 11.5 *A progressive proof shows how much more impact the RGB correction had on the eventual cyan plate than it did on the magenta. In any event, the magenta prints so heavily that it can contribute little detail. Left side: the original cyan, magenta, and cyan plus magenta plates. Right side: the same from the final image.*

Having decided what needs to be done, all colorspaces are one. If we are using LinoColor or some other software that supports curve correction with HSB, we write a longer saturation curve. If we are working in LAB, we steepen the L curve in the raspberry range, darkening (and thus desaturating) the edges that way. If we are in CMYK, we can blend into the cyan plate to get the extra contrast. And in either CMYK or RGB, we can use HSB principles by working with the sponge tool to desaturate the edges, or LAB principles in either of the ways shown in Figures 11.1 and 11.3.

Figure 11.6 The assignment here is to silhouette the arm and rose, get more detail in the flower, correct the blown-out area at the top of the arm, and eliminate the reddish shadow at the bottom of the watch.

Planning the Colorspace Attack

It happens so often that we can enjoy the benefits of one colorspace while in another, that it's worth a look at some examples where we *can't* get by with such a method.

Figure 11.6 represents a simple kind of LAB-based retouching coupled with a difficult kind of RGB. Please assume that for this job, we have to silhouette the arm, glove, and rose, for placement on some other background.

A quick look indicates the following irritating features of this assignment:

• The detail in the rose stinks.

• There is a blown-out area in the top of the arm.

• The arm and glove should be easy to silhouette because they are so different from the background, but the rose itself is another story.

• On the lower part of the watch there is a reddish shadow caused by the roses at bottom. But since said roses are going to be deleted, the shadow won't be logical, and will have to be eliminated.

Which of these problems suggest various colorspaces?

As for the bottom of the watch, clearly it's LAB. The idea is to change color, not contrast, and since LAB separates the two, that's where we want to be. The top of the arm is probably CMYK. In the original, that part of the arm is actually green; magenta is nearly zeroed out, lower than the cyan. The likely solution is a plate blend.

At this point, we may have an HSB issue. If we blend with yellow, the likely candidate, the green leaves will also gain magenta. The green will therefore be desaturated, and we'll have to fight back.

The question of detail in the rose is a matter for both RGB and CMYK. The green channel is probably very bad in RGB. Also once we separate and compensate for dot gain, the cyan plate will need work as well.

And the selection mask? Well, I'm on deadline for this book now. I need a lengthy procedure to make this mask the way I need a case of eight-inch floppies. And so it will be done in LAB.

To generate a mask quickly, there needs to be a strong differentiation between the objects we're keeping and the background. Figure 11.6 doesn't answer that description. Figure 11.7 does.

You might think we would be working on the A channel, but that doesn't have the differentiation we need. The rose isn't that much more magenta (excuse me, magenta-as-opposed-to-green) than the background. It is, however, very much more yellow-as-opposed-to-blue. And so, the key is the B—the curve shown in Figure 11.7 actually inverts the channel. It isn't too tough to break an orange background away from a blue rose. There are umpty-eight ways to make a mask from here: I used Select: Select Color Range to grab the orange, which I then deleted. From there, it's easy to remove the black parts of the background and to fill in the interior parts of the glove and arm.

Preparing the Plate Blends

Setting the mask aside and returning to the original—of which I have a copy both in RGB and LAB—the question becomes, how hard do we fight for detail in the rose? As is common with roses, the green channel is solid black. We may also decide to apply curves to the red and blue channels, where there is detail. Depending on how badly this throws the color off, we may decide to go into LAB to restore it. There is no cost in doing this, since the move from RGB to LAB is essentially lossless. But, we don't have to do it if we don't want: we can stay in RGB with a luminosity layer if we like.

There wasn't a convenient way to strengthen the red channel, so I used the red to stamp a

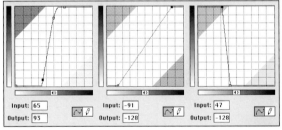

Figure 11.7 Since the background is to be eliminated, a mask is needed. It's much quicker to construct one when the background and the foreground object are sharply different. In Figure 11.6, they aren't. Here, an application of LAB curves (above) creates an orange background and a blue rose. Bottom, the final mask.

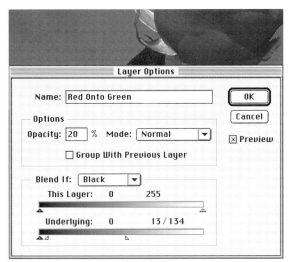

Figure 11.8 Applying the red channel to the green to get more detail in the rose. The bottom slider limits the effect of the blend to the darkest parts of the green channel but has the blending effect taper off in lighter areas, rather than ending suddenly.

little contrast into the green channel's rose. To do so without affecting anything else, I made a copy of the green and pasted the red on top of it, establishing a layer. Then, with Layer: Layer Options (Figure 11.8) I limited the paste to areas of the green channel that were originally quite dark.

Note the split triangles in the bottom of the dialog box. This valuable feature avoids an obvious cut-and-paste line by gradually fading the blend as the image gets lighter,

rather than cutting it off suddenly. To split the triangles, hold down the Option (Alt) key while selecting them.

Once this blend was done, and after some slight curving for more contrast, the color of the rose was a little strange. So I saved a copy of the image and converted it into LAB, giving me two separate LAB files along with my RGB one. I pasted the L from the new one into the old one, retaining the red color, and then discarded the new LAB document.

For the retouch of the red shadow, since we happen to be in LAB, we open the Channels palette, click and Shift-click on the A and B rows and on the eye icon to the left of the LAB row. In this way, we are ready to correct the A and B, while the L remains off limits.

The rubber stamp tool is not such a good idea in an image like this. There's too much color variation in the shadow areas of any part of the watchband we might choose to copy. Instead, I'd vote for the paintbrush tool, selecting a golden color from the side of the watch and painting it over the red shadow. With the L channel unavailable, this will affect color only, not contrast.

Now, a standard conversion into CMYK. Two plate blends seem necessary here. First, about 20% yellow needs to go into the magenta, so as to add pinkness to the lightest areas of the arm. This blend must be in Darker mode so that the magenta component of the rose doesn't get lighter.

And, as usual, we need to strengthen the unwanted color, the cyan. The way to do this is by blending in some of the red channel from the RGB document that I saved a copy of earlier. Which

Figure 11.9 After a plate blend to put more magenta in the arm, the leaves of the flower have become too gray, left. This is corrected with a Hue/Saturation move, right. The additional detail in the rose at right comes from a blend of the red channel into the cyan.

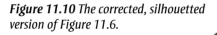

Figure 11.10 *The corrected, silhouetted version of Figure 11.6.*

brings up a tip that has already come in handy twice in this image: when working in several colorspaces, save one copy in each one. You never know when you'll need to borrow a channel.

After the plate blend into the magenta, the leaves were, as shown in Figure 11.9, too gray. To fix that, I opened Image: Adjust Hue/Saturation, chose Greens, clicked on the leaves to indicate that this was the color I wanted to affect, and increased saturation.

With the sharpening tool, I sharpened the watch and the buttons on the glove, but even here a relic of LAB was necessary. Sharpening in Normal mode would have yielded a bright watch—but a white one. By turning the mode to Luminosity, the yellow color was preserved.

Finally, I loaded the mask of Figure 11.7 and hit the Delete key, which eliminated the background and left Figure 11.10.

Nature Rarer Uses Yellow...

Our final riff on the bright-fruits-and-vegetables theme adds a major complication: no unwanted color. Remember Emily Dickinson's philosophy of color allocation in Chapter 5? The huge majority of natural objects are red, green, or blue. That means,

in CMY terms, two strong inks, and one exquisitely important weak one.

The pepper of Figure 11.11, however, is not red, not green, not blue. It's yellow: one strong ink, *two* weak ones.

That makes it harder to handle. Ordinarily, moves in the weak plate can't override the basic color established by the two dominants. But if only one ink is dominant, moves in the weaker two *can* change color. So, blending into the cyan and magenta channels is unlikely to work.

Let's start in RGB. Examining the individual channels in Figure 11.12, we discover two worthless voids and a decent green.

One thought might be to treat this image as we did the raspberries. Apply a contrast-enhancing curve to the green, then try some blending into the red and blue, ending with a layer arrangement that affects luminosity only, retaining the original yellow color.

Since all colorspaces are one, let's use LAB terms to describe what just happened. We have replaced the L channel—even though the file itself never entered LAB.

Once we realize that replacing the L is the point of the exercise, we may well ask ourselves why we are driving from New York to Boston by way of Dubuque. Let's make a copy of the image and convert it to LAB. Look at the original L channel in Figure 11.12. Pretty rancid, right? Got any ideas of where we could find a better one?

That's right. We replace the L channel with the green from RGB. Unorthodox, perhaps, but no less sensible than blending an RGB channel into a CMY one, which we've seen many times.

As with all such blends, we have to be careful with overall weight. The green is slightly heavier than the original L, so it has to be lightened. The way to do this is to find the lightest part of the pepper in the original (91^L) and, with a curve, lighten the point in the new L until it matches. Naturally, we make sure this curve is steepest in the range of the pepper.

The difference between the two versions of Figure 11.11, therefore, is less than a minute of work: one plate blend, one easy curve, convert to CMYK, and print.

Examining the Luminosity Values

The idea of blending into the L channel, as in this pepper image, is a creative response to a specific problem. Most of the time, one doesn't have to go to this much trouble. Occasionally, one has to go to considerably more.

To say that Figure 11.13 has some problems is to say that it is occasionally cold in Antarctica. Let me first reiterate that the policy of this book precludes sabotaging images in order to make the correction more impressive. I *paid* for this image, and this is what I got.

The preflight analysis: well, some situations are almost too grim for words. Ordinarily, we don't decide whether an image has a color cast without verifying it in the Info palette. Here, we can make an exception. We can also make an exception to the usual rules about checking highlight and shadow numbers, until we get slightly deeper into the correction process.

Now that you are a multi-colorspace maven, however, you should be able to recognize the following color: $255^R 245^G 26^B$, which can also be expressed as $95^L - 16^A 83^B$ or $4^C 0^M 90^Y$. Whichever way you like it, it's a

Figure 11.11 *Yellow objects are tougher to correct by plate blending than red, green, or blue ones because they have two weak inks rather than one.*

brilliant yellow, entirely suitable for the brightest portion of the pepper of Figure 11.11—but, as a fleshtone, about as close to what we need as Los Angeles is to the planet Saturn.

Nevertheless, that is the current value in the young woman's left arm. The immense blown-out area is but one of many obvious problems, including the lack of detail in the face; the desirability of holding detail in the dark brown garments; the necessity to keep good shape in the hair; the overall cast; and the lack of differentiation between fleshtone and background.

Making something acceptable out of such a disgrace to the scanning profession will be challenging, but it can be done—see Figure 11.14—if you know your colorspaces. Without them, forget about it.

A number of these issues have shown up in other corrections in this book, although not, thankfully, all at once. The immediate thought is that this is so similar to the pepper that some RGB plate blending would be in order. But it is still going to have such a ghastly color cast that an LAB correction will probably be needed. Some special separation technique may be needed to hold the detail in the clothing. Whatever correction method we use will probably destroy the color of the eyes and lips; and we still haven't

even discussed what to do about the holes in the arms.

In deciding that question, a good way is to examine luminosity values. That's done by measuring the L channel, which can be done even though we're not in LAB yet. With the eyedroppers in both sides of the Info palette, set the palette so that its first half reads Actual Color (RGB, at the moment) and the second half LAB.

In this way, we learn that the arm is around 97^L, and the next lightest area, the steps under her left hand, are 85^L. I believe that this makes no sense at all and that this becomes one of the very rare images that requires a local selection, which means we need a mask.

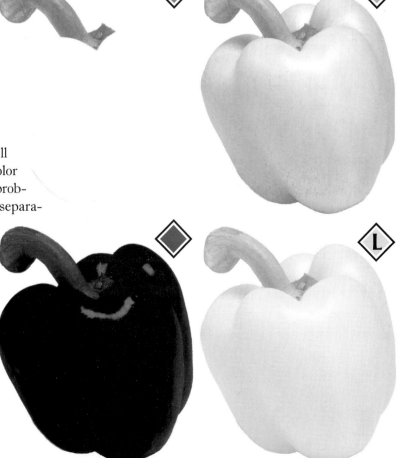

Figure 11.12 *The original red, green, and blue channels from Figure 11.11, plus the L channel from a copy of the image that was converted into LAB.*

Finding the Right Mask Channel

Although this is the third time in three chapters we've needed one, this is not a book about how to make a selection mask, any more than it's about monitor calibration. Nevertheless, certain techniques come up quite often—especially for those who know their colorspaces.

In situations like these, eventually we hope to cobble together a reasonably accurate selection, which we then load in Quick Mask mode. Then, using any of Photoshop's painting tools, we touch up whatever parts of the mask aren't correct. Finally, we Select: Save Selection, to store the mask as a separate, nonprinting channel of the base file or as a separate Photoshop file, which I prefer because it saves disk space.

The question is, do we want to spend 30 seconds on this mask touchup, or 30 minutes? The key to avoiding the latter is having a decent start point, the key to that is knowing where to find edges, and the key to that is colorspace knowledge.

Selecting this woman is more difficult than it was to isolate the rose, because here the cast is so bad that the background is practically the same color as the woman's flesh.

For getting the outlines of the woman's clothing, almost anything will work. I'd use Photoshop 5's magnetic lasso tool myself. It might also get the shoes and parts of the legs, but it will definitely have trouble with the hair and the arms.

For those, we either need to draw the mask ourselves or find some channel that has already done the work for us. For example, suppose the background steps in this image were blue. In that case, the cyan plate would have enough definition between arm and steps that it could be used as the start of a mask. But they aren't, and it doesn't.

In images like this, with a bias toward certain colors, the best source of masks is often the A or B channel.

Figure 11.13 *The pervasive yellow cast is but one of the technical problems with this original.*

We can't use them directly, because they are too flat, too gray. But we can copy them to new documents, increase their contrast, and find the edges that way. The B channel has a good start at isolating the hair and arms.

The Steps, Step by Step

Fast forward. We have a mask. We start by examining the RGB channels, and, because this picture is so dreadfully yellow to start, they resemble somewhat those of the yellow pepper. That is, the red is washed out, the blue is too dark, and the green looks nice. You can follow the progress of this correction along in Figure 11.15.

To aid in planning, it pays to make a copy of the image and convert it to LAB, to see whether we can pull the old replace-the-L-with-the-G trick. Not here: the two channels are similar. But either one can be used to engineer more contrast into the red and blue channels. Right now, these two are pretty sad.

Whichever we choose (I stuck with the green) we should make a copy of it and increase contrast, as we have done with several other images previously. Then, we blend it in—I used 50% in each channel—to the weak red and blue.

Now, a conversion to LAB, where the curves shown in Figure 11.16 attack the cast. We've tried to stay away from oddly shaped A and B curves in the past, but there isn't much choice here: we need to slam the brightest yellows, but if we do this by moving the straight line of the B curve to the left, the brightest areas of

the steps will become bright blue. Frankly, we have more than enough problems to solve already.

Note that we don't want to go overboard in darkening the L channel. There's delicate detail in the hair. That calls for something with rather more finesse than the clumsy L. Nor do we sharpen at this point: too much noise in the fleshtone,

Figure 11.14 After forays into four different colorspaces, the image is much improved.

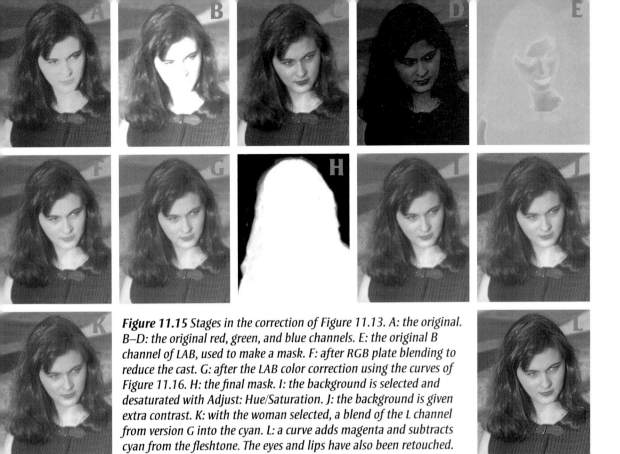

Figure 11.15 *Stages in the correction of Figure 11.13. A: the original. B–D: the original red, green, and blue channels. E: the original B channel of LAB, used to make a mask. F: after RGB plate blending to reduce the cast. G: after the LAB color correction using the curves of Figure 11.16. H: the final mask. I: the background is selected and desaturated with Adjust: Hue/Saturation. J: the background is given extra contrast. K: with the woman selected, a blend of the L channel from version G into the cyan. L: a curve adds magenta and subtracts cyan from the fleshtone. The eyes and lips have also been retouched.*

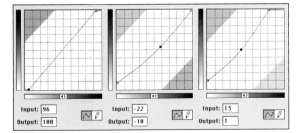

Figure 11.16 *These LAB curves reduce the yellow cast without turning neutral areas blue-green.*

noise that's present in the L but won't be in certain channels in CMYK.

With this in mind, after applying the curves and saving a copy of the LAB file, we cross into CMYK, using the same trick as in Figure 8.12: a relatively low black ink limit of 70% to give us room to steepen it to gain contrast in the clothing and hair.

Now, the differentiation between woman and background. Loading the mask, which makes it impossible to alter the woman, we open Adjust Hue/Saturation and kill most of the cast in the background by reducing saturation overall. Then, an LAB-like move: we apply CMYK curves that bring the lightest areas of the steps to a near-highlight value and establish a shadow in the cracks, then Filter: Fade back to Luminosity so that there will be no color shift.

Then, we Select: Invert Selection, flipping the mask so that we can work on the woman, but not the background. Two items require attention: we need a better cyan plate and we need to fill in the holes in the arm. These were the exact issues we faced in the rose image, but they're worse here.

The cyan problem is solved by applying the L channel from the LAB file we saved two paragraphs ago. That's close to what we did in the rose image, but we won't be

ALL COLORSPACES ARE ONE

✓Although the style of correcting varies in different colorspaces, the result is usually the same. When dealing with a brightly colored object, for example, the desired result is a strong plate in the unwanted color. It seems as if this is a strong argument in favor of CMYK correction. In fact, moves in the other three colorspaces will eventually create a strong unwanted color, even if they don't do so directly.

✓Increasing contrast without altering color is usually associated with the L channel of LAB. However, the technique can be duplicated in CMYK or RGB by either fading curves to luminosity or by using a correction layer in Luminosity mode.

✓When making moves in several colorspaces, it's helpful to save one copy in each. You never know when they can be used for a blend.

✓As a practical matter, there is no loss of image quality in converting between RGB and LAB. The conversion into CMYK is lossless; the conversion from CMYK into LAB loses a small amount of shadow detail, which is easily compensated for.

✓When confronted by a difficult image, a sensible approach is to list all of its problems and think about which colorspace is most advantageous for treating each one.

✓If you need masks for silhouetting or any other purpose, a lot of time can be saved by finding the correct colorspace. With three Photoshop colorspaces, there are ten possible channels, and one of them is likely to have the edge definition needed to get started on a mask.

✓Working in Color mode in RGB or CMYK is essentially the same as working in the A and B channels of LAB. However, in many images it pays to work in LAB because the two channels can be handled differently. For example, in noisy images the noise is typically more yellow-blue than it is magenta-green. This means that the B channel of LAB should be blurred more than the A.

✓Don't go overboard with the use of multiple colorspaces. The majority of corrections don't need them. The mark of the professional is not just understanding the colorspace concepts, but knowing when a desired correction can only be done in a certain manner in a certain colorspace.

able to blend the yellow into the magenta, as we did there. This time, the yellow is too flat, thanks to the original cast, and mixing it into the magenta would kill facial detail.

Instead, with the woman still selected, we apply a curve to the magenta that does nothing but bring the zero point up to 15%, ensuring at least that amount of magenta in the arm. At the same time, we lighten the cyan slightly, compensating for the darkening that took place in the blend, while retaining the additional contrast.

At this point, we're ready to apply unsharp masking, but only to the black and the cyan, for the reasons discussed in Chapter 6.

Finally, the local retouching. We try to restore natural coloring to the eyes and lips. With all these corrections, it would be a miracle if these features were anything like the colors they're supposed to be.

A Reality Check

This is the second time in one chapter that we have visited four colorspaces in a single correction. This time, only the HSB move has a reasonable alternative. I could have desaturated the background with curves in any colorspace (I'd choose LAB, where just flattening the AB would do this.) The Hue/Saturation command seems easier to control, particularly in a case like this where the decision is a totally subjective one, not relying on numbers.

Eliminating use of the other colorspaces is another story. For many images, the plate blending in RGB can be omitted in favor of later moves in the L channel. Here, that wouldn't work. If we did an immediate conversion into LAB, we'd need to boost the quartertone in the L channel so as to add detail to the woman's face. But if we did

that, we'd clobber detail in the clothes and hair. There is some chance we could get the job done in CMYK instead, but it would certainly be much more difficult. By far the easiest method is what we did, correcting the original red channel with a blend.

Similarly, although the added snap that the L move added to the hair could have been arranged elsewhere, there's no good substitute for the AB curves. When the color cast is this severe, it's nearly impossible to remove outside of LAB.

Finally, the tricky separation, followed by the boost in the black and the blend into the cyan channel, is only for those who can handle CMYK. I'm not aware of any way to accomplish the same result in either RGB or LAB.

This is, therefore, an experts-only kind of correction, which is what one might expect for an original of this quality. But the real mark of the expert is knowing that this kind of maneuvering should be saved for the really exceptional kind of image, of which this is one.

For the typical image, the techniques discussed in Chapters 3–6 work nicely. They may be enough for many users or for those who, like professional photographers, have good control over the quality of the images they start with.

The professional retoucher, however, is assumed to be capable of producing professional quality not just out of ordinary images, but out of those that are seriously flawed. If you can't do this, but consider yourself a professional, perhaps your approach is what's seriously flawed. Keeping in mind the strengths and weaknesses of all four colorspaces, and all ten Photoshop channels, will cure that, just as surely as it cured this seemingly ineradicable cast.

The Resolution Issue, Resolved

Many important concepts in scanning, retouching, imagesetting, and printing are lumped under the universal term *resolution*. And many of these very different types of resolution are measured by the same ambiguous acronym, *DPI*. At times, a high resolution is necessary. At others it's a complete waste of disk space and computing power, if not an outright quality-killer.

Graphic arts is notorious for its ambiguous terminology. *Trap* can mean a prepress technique or a pressroom anomaly. *PMT* describes a variety of scanner or a type of positive proof. *Shadow* means one thing to a photographer and another to a retoucher. A typeface called *Gothic* is a bold sans-serif—unless it is a medieval blackletter, such as Old English. Even *red* means something different to a pressman than it does to the rest of the world.

But of all the semantic snares we set for the unwary, the most insidious has to be the innocent-sounding *dpi*, which plagues us throughout our process and sometimes is used as a synonym for a second bugaboo, resolution.

Consider all the different things that DPI connotes, and understand why novices—and some experts—get confused. 300 DPI may be a type of scan or a laser printer. 2,400 DPI may connote a different type of scan or an imagesetter. 72 DPI may be a monitor's resolution or a newspaper's screen ruling.

In choosing the various flavors of resolution for a certain job, it's silly to assume that bigger is better. Unnecessarily high resolutions, at best, eat storage space and bog down networks. If we are not so lucky, they

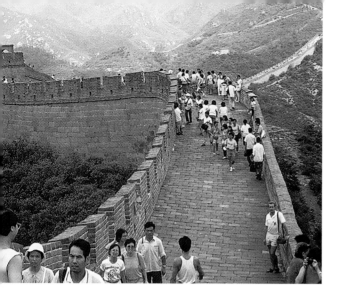

may bring a RIP to its knees, or worse yet, produce poorer quality than if we had used the proper resolutions to begin with.

And what are these correct resolutions? They depend on the job, but they also depend upon each other.

First of all, even defining *resolution* is not that easy. It means, more or less, how far apart the smallest distinct parts of the subject of discussion are. Frequently, these small parts are all of the same size, as in the individual pixels of a Photoshop file. But in nondigital parts of the process, they aren't, as in the case of film grain, which is, one might say, the resolution of film, or the halftone dot, which might be termed the resolution of a printing press.

Figure 12.1 suggests what happens when we print without enough press "resolution," in other words, with a halftone screen that is too coarse. The grainy-looking center image is more appropriate for newspapers than for a book. The smaller the dots, the less obtrusive they are, and the more the final product looks like the original photograph it is supposed to recall.

Anyone who thinks that if a fine screen is good then a finer one must be better, is a moron. The finer the screen ruling, the smaller the dots, but the smaller the dots, the more difficult they are to print properly. If the dots are on the cusp of what the press can tolerate, the following irritating things happen:

• Darker areas start to plug up, resulting in a perceived lower maximum shadow.

• The minimum acceptable highlight dot goes up; at some point, a dot simply becomes too tiny for the plate and the

Figure 12.1 Top, an image printed at press resolution (oops, screen ruling) of 133 dots per inch; center, at 65 dpi; and bottom, at 300 dpi.

blanket to hold. Overall, the highlight will become inconsistent.

• The image will begin to appear soft as transition areas become less distinct.

• Dot gain will appear to increase.

Now, at what point does all this unpleasantness start to kick in? In newspaper printing, as a rule it happens at about 100, so most newspapers print with an 85-line screen, and 65-line is not uncommon. Some, however, do use a 100-line screen, and I know of at least one that has successfully used 120 lines.

As paper starts to get a little better and as we migrate to commercial presses, the tolerance goes up. Reasonable uncoated papers can easily hold a 120-line screen, and there can be some success with 133. Magazines that use coated paper generally use 133, and some try 150.

High-quality commercial printing, such as annual reports, uses more expensive coated papers and usually is done at 175, sometimes even 200. And waterless offset, a relatively new approach, appears to make it much easier to hold small dots. There have been successful uses of a 300-line screen, and even higher, with this technology.

The sad truth is that many printers overstate their own capabilities. A large part of my career has involved preparing color ads for reproduction in national magazines. Most magazines will accept either 133 or 150. My observation is that overall the ads printed at the coarser screen have had a considerable quality edge.

Many people get fooled by their contract proofs, which are far easier to control than a press. The bottom version of Figure 12.1 looks just fine on mine. On press, assuming I can slip it by the printer's preflight department, I predict an unholy mess.

This will be the first of several examples of how too much resolution can be harmful. Most people assume that the reason an excessive resolution would be counterproductive pertains exclusively to the press.

It doesn't. All resolutions depend upon one another. Too fine a screen may cause more quality problems with the imagesetter than the press.

Out of Spots, Dots

The term DPI stands for dots per inch. In printing, that's just what we are describing, dots. Infuriatingly, this is the one instance where the term DPI is *not* frequently used; most reserve it to describe situations in which it would be just as accurate to say bananas per inch as dots. But in talking about presswork, people don't say 65 DPI, but a 65-line screen, and they abbreviate it as 65 LPI. Yet we have dots, not lines.

To find out how those dots get there, we need to discuss another kind of resolution.

Whether from a $300,000 imagesetter or a $300 laser printer, the halftone dots we've been talking about are made up of tinier dots. How tiny those tiny dots are governs how effectively the bigger dots can be drawn. The size of those tiny dots, which I will henceforth refer to as *spots,* represents the resolution of the device.

We've barely begun, and already the terminology is tripping us up. This will never do. In the first edition of this book, after griping about it over several paragraphs, I caved in to the conventional and used DPI indiscriminately. No more. I am older and more set in my ways now. This time, I'm taking a hard line. Where appropriate acronyms don't exist, I will invent them. And, as you can see, I'm using SPECIAL TYPE to set the various acronyms off.

I shall therefore, use DPI to describe a dots-per-inch screen ruling, but never to describe measurements that don't involve dots. The rest of the world can use sloppy terminology and be damned, for all I care. You don't like it, buy a different book.

End of rant. A modern imagesetter, if made in the United States, usually has a resolution of at least 2,400 DPI—oops, 2,400 *spots* per inch. If made elsewhere, the usual resolution is at least 2,540, which happens to be 100 spots per millimeter. Note that spots, unlike dots, never vary in size. They are either off or on.

The spots are too small for most of us to see, which may make them just about the right size to construct halftone dots with,

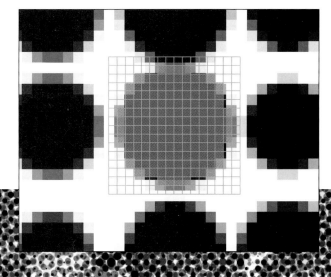

as Figure 12.2 shows. But it may not: the size relationship between spot and dot is critical, and if it's out of whack, quality will suffer. To know what "out of whack" means, we have to consider yet another species of resolution, the ability of the human eye to resolve differences in color and tonality.

Nobody really knows how great that ability is. Some reputable sources suggest that typical humans can only perceive around 2,500 different shades of color. On the opposite extreme are folks like myself who say that some individuals are capable of differentiating a million or more.

For realism, whatever printing method we choose should be able to portray at least as many colors as typical humans can perceive, and preferably quite a few more, in case we start moving things around with curves. We need to be able to make very fine adjustments, therefore, in the size of the halftone dot. The smaller the imagesetter spot is, the more flexibility we'll have. On the other hand, constructing dots out of spots is not a trivial calculation. Having spots that are too small will snarl the most powerful RIP.

Figure 12.2 *Dots and spots: Below, a blowup of Figure 12.1 shows its dot structure clearly. The imagesetter constructs each dot, inset, by turning spots off and on in a grid. Here, the grid has 256 such spots available for each dot, which is just right—in theory.*

It certainly makes sense to have at least 200 different sizes of dot available, probably more. If the halftone dots are at 150 DPI and the imagesetter resolution is 2,400 SPI, this will be possible.

150 is $\frac{1}{16}$ of 2,400. The spots that the imagesetter can potentially paint will be rectangles where each side is $\frac{1}{2400}$ of an inch, or .00042". Those rectangles will be exactly $\frac{1}{16}$ of the maximum width of the halftone dot. There will be 16 rows of rectangles across and 16 columns down, for a total of 256 rectangles. Depending upon how many of these actually get painted, there are 256 possible darknesses of the halftone dot, or 257, if you count zero.

256, is, coincidentally, a key number in yet another kind of resolution.

The Blind Man's Eyeglasses

Tonal information also has a resolution, in a manner of speaking. An original photograph is said, rather inaccurately, to be *continuous-tone*. Digital files aren't. They only can portray a certain number of varieties of tone, frequently 256. Printable Photoshop files have 256 VOT *per channel,* which is why so many different colors are possible. A standard RGB file can accommodate 16,777,216 different colors, this being 256 to the third power.

To add to the exponential chaos, a second term, bit depth, is often used in preference to VOT, with different numbers that mean the same thing. A 256 VOT file is also known as an 8-bit file. In keeping with the spirit of the rest of this chapter, it gets a more precise name, 8 BPC, for bits per channel. This refers to the computer storage space required per pixel, in this case eight binary bits:

eight zeros or ones. With eight zeros or ones the total number of possible variations is two to the eighth power, which is, conveniently, 256.

Most scanners and some other devices can operate at higher bit depths. A 12 BPC scan has 4,096 VOT. Some manufacturers would have us believe that a greater bit depth implies better scan quality. Don't believe it. If a scanner can't see detail in shadow areas, a 12 BPC scan won't help. We may have 4,096 VOT, but in this case, VOT stands for varieties of trash. To see why, let's compare the work of three very expensive pieces of hardware.

Dots & Spots: a Glossary

Much confusion is caused by the use of a single term, *dpi,* to refer to wildly different genera of resolution. In an act of rebellion against this practice, different abbreviations will be used in this chapter. Unfortunately, in some cases, I have had to invent them. Here is an alphabetical list of the acronyms you'll find here. These don't agree with industry practice, and there is no suggestion that you should use them. But at least they are more accurate than calling everything dpi.

BPC Bits per channel, in a digital image file.

BPI Black or white bits per inch, in a bitmapped graphic file.

DPI Dots per inch, in a halftone screen.

PLD Total pixels in the long direction of a digital file.

PPI Pixels per inch, in a digital file.

SPI Spots per inch, the smallest area that can be marked by an output device such as an imagesetter or film recorder.

SSPI Scanning samples per inch.

TPC Total pixel count of a digital file.

VOT Varieties of tone, sometimes called levels of gray, the maximum number of shades of gray in a single channel of a digital file.

For the past quarter century, drum scanners have been the standard for those desiring the highest quality. They continue to be the best today, but not by much. Their photomultiplier tubes have certain advantages over the charge-coupled device technology used in flatbed scanners and professional digital cameras. CCD devices are particularly vulnerable to a loss of detail in the darkest areas.

They've been getting better, though. Five years ago, no scanner costing less than $10,000 was even remotely in the same quality league as a drum scanner. Today, $2,500 buys a very strong desktop unit that, if not capable of the same enlargement, is almost as good otherwise.

To assess the state of the technology, in 1996 I arranged a shootout between a drum scanner from the early 1980s and two professional-level (i.e., they cost about $50,000 apiece) CCD units. I refrain from naming the products, because all three vendors make better scanners today.

Anyway, the idea was to have expert operators of each scanner try to milk the most from a dozen moderate-to-difficult chromes. They were given identical printing and sizing specifications. If they did not like the scans for any reason they could do

them over. When they were satisfied, all 36 versions would be assigned random letters and proofed next to one another. The proofs would go to a panel of ten experts who, working in separate light booths, would evaluate which of the three versions of each original was the best, without knowing which ones came from where.

I expected this exercise to prove that the CCD scanners had basically caught up. It didn't. Of 120 first-place votes, Brand X (you and I know it's the drum scanner, but the jurors didn't) got 98, Brand Y 12, and Brand Z 10. In 7 of the 12 contests, Brand X swept all ten votes.

Figure 12.3 is one of those in which the vote was unanimous. I'm showing a piece of it, then enlarging it, and then applying a drastic contrast-enhancing curve to it, so that we can evaluate just how well these three beasts are holding the shadows.

This is easiest to judge in the three right-hand versions. The problems are the center of the tree and the car beneath it.

Brand X is the only one that is having any luck with the car. If you look hard, you can even see that the taillights are red. In the tree, which is darker still, it's a lot more of a struggle. Brand X is obviously at its wit's end, but it is still a drum scanner, and

Figure 12.3 *The ability to retain shadow detail is a major test of a scanner. Opposite, normal-size reproductions of scans of the same original by, left to right, Brands X, Y, and Z. Above, the shadow areas magnified (left) and with contrast in the shadows greatly enhanced (right). Top to bottom, the Brand X, Y, and Z scans.*

a cut above the other two in such shadow areas. Brand Y posterizes the inside of the tree, whereas Brand Z freaks out. The whole center of its tree is featureless.

The final output of these scanners is an 8 BPC file, but all three interpolate that down from an original with more data. Brands Y and Z are 12 BPC scanners. Brand X is analog; its original scan is a series of voltage readings that in principle carry an infinite variety of tonality. More modern versions of this scanner are fully digital, and also give 12 BPC files.

So, Brand Z can portray 4,096 levels of tonality in each channel. A fat lot of good it did. In this image, endowing the scanner with extra bits is like handing a blind man a pair of eyeglasses. If Brand X were an 8-bit scanner, yea, verily, if it were a *six*-bit scanner capable of only 64 VOT, it would still have the best version here. If you're buying a scanner or a digital camera, forget this bit depth balderdash, and look at a few tough samples.

Comes the Quintillion

The above discussion is no endorsement of drum scanners. Experts looking at these images closely found enough difference to say that Brand X was better. I concur, and so do you, presumably. The question is, though, how *much* better? Going back to the real originals, the smaller versions in Figure 12.3, I'd have to say, a little better, but very little.

So, while the drum scanners have a theoretical advantage, in real life it doesn't amount to much, at least not in comparison to a mid-five-figure CCD scanner. In a race like this, the difference is going to be the jockey, not the horse.

Of even less practical significance is the use of the extra bits in Photoshop. If we have a scanner that can save files with more than 8 BPC, Photoshop 5 can work with them to a limited extent. We can apply curves and the rubber stamp tool, but not filters, before converting them to the 8 BPC that all output devices require.

Theoretically, this is tempting. When we apply a curve to an image, we reduce its VOT, for the following reason. Suppose we have a B/W file with 256 VOT. It happens to

Figure 12.4 Theoretically, working with 16 bpc should give smoother transitions, even though the file must be reduced to 8 bpc for printing. In practice, it doesn't work that way. At left, a file from a high-end CCD scanner, originally at 16 bpc. Opposite page, RGB curves are applied that are many times more violent than the norm. Top left: the curve applied to the 16 bpc file, which is then converted to 8 bpc; top right, the original converted to 8 bpc first before the application of the same curve. Bottom: the blue channels of the two files, which should show the greatest advantage for 16 bpc. A histogram would show the difference, and if the image is blown up to three or four times its size, the 16 bpc image looks better—but can you see the difference here?

Spots, Dots, & Tonality:
DPI vs. SPI vs. VOT

	IMAGESETTER RESOLUTION (spots per inch)					
	300	600	1200	2400	3600	
65	21	85	256	256	256	
85	12	50	199	256	256	
100	9	36	144	256	256	
120	6	25	100	256	256	SCREEN (dots per inch)
133	5	20	81	256	256	
150	4	16	64	256	256	
175	3	12	47	188	256	
200	2	9	36	144	256	

Figure 12.5 Realistic photographic images are impossible if the output device can't generate enough varieties of tone. For professional work, one needs at least 100 vot, and many would say at least 200. Here's how many levels of tone imagesetters of various resolutions can theoretically produce at some common screen rulings.

be a picture of a white cat, so we jack up the center point by, say, 10%. Originally, 128 of our tones fell below the midpoint, and 128 above it. But now, we have stretched the light tones, and compressed the dark ones. Only about 115 real tones now fill the first 128 available spaces. On the other hand, there will be 141 real tones competing to fill the second 128 spaces. The surplus has to be discarded. Hence, only 243 real tonal values remain of the original 256.

If we work, instead, with the extra bits, this criticism will not apply. Photoshop's options (under Image: Mode) are 8 or 16 BPC. While no scanner extant gives 16 meaningful bits, if we start to fool around in LAB or do various other things, it's possible that we may fill those extra bits up with something other than garbage.

This makes our file size twice as large. It also gives us, shall we say, a bit more information. To be precise, each channel now has a resolution of 65,536 VOT. How many

discrete CMYK possibilities can this produce? The answer is so impressive that I can't bear to use numerals, I have to just say it. Eighteen quintillion, 446 quadrillion, 744 trillion, 73 billion, 709 million, 600 thousand, that's how many.

If we apply a curve to such data, we still throw away a few of these possibilities. We will miss this about as much as Bill Gates misses the quarter he spends on his morning newspaper.

For those calibrationists to whom a good-looking histogram is more important than a good-looking image, this cinches it. We must work in 16 BPC whenever possible, to avoid that fearful bogeyman, data loss.

To be honest, I used to think that there was merit in this belief. I thought, if the curves we apply are extreme enough, that extra information could help.

The more I've played with extra-bit files, unfortunately, the less I've been able to justify the extra processing time and disk space. In fact, I've been unable to see any practical difference at all, even under extreme testing conditions.

The left half of Figure 12.4 is an 8 BPC file; it has to be or I wouldn't be able to print it. But it was originally a 12 BPC file produced on a high-end CCD scanner.

On Page 225, the image goes through a torture test. This is not a color correction, but a drastic curve applied to open everything up in much the same manner as was done in Figure 12.3. I did this in two ways, with two copies of the 12 BPC RGB file. In the left-hand sample, I applied (and saved) the curve to the 12 BPC file, and then converted it to 8-bit CMYK for printing here. In the right-hand version, I first went to 8 BPC, then applied the curve, then converted to CMYK.

Theoretically, the version on the left should be superior. But as a practical matter, is it? The detail-filled blue channel should show the difference more than the composite original.

The calibrationist response to this is that the difference can clearly be seen in the image's histogram, and it can. That of the left-hand image is smooth and beautiful. The one for the right-hand image looks like a comb. (As a matter of policy, I refuse to include histograms and similar irrelevancies in a serious book, so you'll just have to take my word for it.)

When we start printing histograms alongside our final work, then the eventual viewers will know for sure how bad our work actually is. Until then, they will have to rely on how the images *look*. To me, they look the same.

The obsession that some have with the extra bits matches their paranoia about switching from one colorspace to another. Both are cases of Bill Gates worrying about losing quarters. 256 VOT is more than enough for practical color work. 100, or even 80, is quite sufficient, although one would like more in black and white. Remember, in an RGB file, even 100 VOT produces a million different colors. That may not be 18 quintillion, but let's not be piggy.

By all means, if you are planning to apply 20 different curves consecutively to a certain image, do it with an extra-bit file. And if you sometimes take images out of CMYK so as to work on them in other colorspaces, or if you are an aficionado of ICC profiles, try to limit yourself to no more than ten or twenty conversions per correction.

In real life, you are not going to do either of these things. Don't worry about histograms. Worry about making the image look good. 256 VOT is far more than enough—for photographic images, that is. But if you are making gradations, you have to look at resolution in yet another way.

And the Band Played On

Banding in gradients has been a headache since the first days of PostScript. In the middle of what seems to be a smooth gradation, there is a systemic burp, a sudden, annoying jump from one tonality to another, ruining a job.

"How can this possibly have happened?" shrieks the hysterical artist, "when I specified 256 steps for the blend?"

Two ways. The first one was discussed in Chapter 9: an RGB blend with colors that are out of the CMYK gamut. The other is, of course, a resolution problem.

If a blend goes from say, 10 percent gray to 20 percent, the output device will only have about 25 VOT available. It won't matter whether the input has 256 or 256 million VOT. Furthermore, some of the 25 are probably not available, due to rounding error, so, banding is likely to show up, especially if the blend covers a wide area on the page.

In principle, an output device that can create 256 VOT itself has exactly enough resolution. In practice, that isn't quite true. The dots are angled, which can reduce the number of spots available. More important, although both file and imagesetter are at 256 VOT, the two 256s won't line up exactly. Certain values that are different in the original file will result in identical dots, and certain dots that are theoretically possible will actually be inaccessible.

So, how many VOT are actually available at 150 DPI on a 2,400 SPI imagesetter? Chances are, 220 or so. If all we print is photographic images, neither we nor any-body else will be able to tell the difference between 220 and 256 VOT. If, however, we start introducing gradations, it may make quite a difference indeed.

Banding can be defeated by adding a small amount of randomization (noise) to the digital file. This is why photos don't band: there is always enough natural noise to obliterate the problem.

Other methods of overcoming banding are to use an imagesetter with a higher resolution or to reduce the screen ruling. 150 DPI blends on a 2,400 SPI imagesetter tempt fate. 133 DPI blends are more reliable.

Figure 12.5 shows how many VOT are ac-tually available at normal DPIs for some common SPIs of laser printers and image-setters. I'd avoid any number under 150.

This is why photographic reproduction on laser printers is so lousy, even on today's better 600 SPI units. And yet there's a reso-lution paradox. This book is imaged on a 2,400 SPI platesetter. If we were to substitute output from a 600 SPI laser printer, the images would be a joke—but few people would notice that anything was wrong with the *type*. How can the same resolution be so terrible in one case and so nearly unde-tectable in the other?

The Resolution That Isn't There

Unlike the images we've been considering so far, type contains no grays, only black areas on white paper. The type still has to be painted using the same imagesetter spots, but now it's much easier. The glory of PostScript is that it allows certain kinds of graphics to have an entirely different variety of resolution, to wit, none at all.

Objects that can be described in terms of curves or other mathematical shapes

(and typefaces can be so described) eventually need a resolution. An image-setter doesn't print mathematical concepts, only spots. But a RIP's whole function is to map out those spots, and when a file comes in saying, "I am a bunch of curves, map me however you think best for your imaging engine," not only can the RIP do this, it can do so much more smoothly than if the file already carried its own bitmap.

Since type and similar line graphics contain no grays, only blacks and whites, Figure 12.5 is not relevant. The only question is, how many spots per inch does the printer need to construct the curves and fine lines of text type accurately?

Older laser printers, which generally have a resolution of 300 SPI, produce type that's obviously inferior to what you're reading here. At 600 SPI, the type is pretty good—one has to look closely to see the difference between it and type output from a 1,200 SPI imagesetter, which, in turn, is indistinguishable from 2,400 SPI without a loupe.

When it's necessary to scan type or other graphics because digital versions don't exist, yet another kind of resolution comes into play. We now have a file that can be expressed in bits per inch, each bit being either white or black. If a 600 BPI file is sent to a 600 SPI printer, the printer's RIP has to remap it. The results will not be quite as good as if a resolution-independent file were sent to the same printer.

So, at what resolution should one scan type and other line graphics? There isn't clear agreement. Half again the resolution of the output device is my rule, to a maxi-mum of 1,800 SSPI—scanning samples per inch.

If you've ever wondered why type always looks fuzzy in a photograph, it's that old devil resolution again. In Figure 12.6, you will observe that 300 BPI is inadequate for type—and most color images are scanned at less than 300 SSPI. The type in such images isn't quite as jagged as the example, because screening tends to soften images, but it still will be pretty bad.

One way to make it better, naturally, is to scan at a higher resolution. The higher the scanning resolution, the softer and smoother the curves will be. The problem with that is, so will everything else.

When scanning type only, excessive resolution eats up disk space, overburdens the imagesetter, clogs up communication, and is generally a complete waste of time. Other than that, it doesn't hurt. But with a photographic image, too much resolution, in addition to the shortcomings enumerated above, actually *does* hurt. Which of the two images of grass in Figure 12.7 do you like best?

If we want something that looks like blades of grass and not AstroTurf, the bottom version seems clearly better. But it's the lower-resolution scan! Doesn't high resolution equate to more detail?

Of course it does. But here, we don't want detail, we want the *illusion* of detail. That's what the bottom one provides. Let me try to explain how and why.

The bottom image's resolution is approximately four scanning samples per halftone dot. That's in line with the conventional wisdom, which is that it should be between 1.5 and 2 times the screen ruling. The dots are roughly ⅓₃" apart, the scanning samples roughly ⅟₂₆₆". That squares up to four samples per dot: two across, two down.

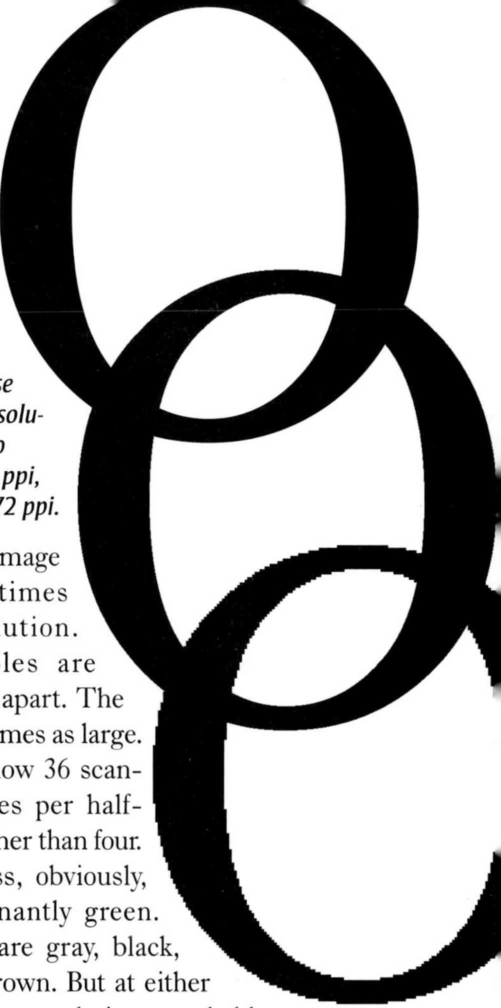

Figure 12.6 How much resolution is needed for smooth-looking type and similar graphics? These letters have resolutions of, top to bottom, 1800 ppi, 300 ppi, and 72 ppi.

The top image has three times this resolution. The samples are roughly ⅟₇₀₀" apart. The file is nine times as large. There are now 36 scanning samples per halftone dot, rather than four.

The grass, obviously, is predominantly green. Parts of it are gray, black, yellow, or brown. But at either of these scan resolutions, probably three out of four samples will find green.

In the lower resolution image, therefore, which has four samples per halftone dot, the chances are that three of them will be green, but sometimes all four will be green, and sometimes zero or one. In such cases the resulting dots won't produce green.

In the higher resolution version, with 36 samples per dot, this is far less likely to happen. It is conceivable that three out of four samples may not be green. It isn't conceivable that 27 out of 36 samples—which is the same ratio—will be something other than green. A rule of mathematics: the more samples, the less variance from what the law of averages predicts. If we flip a coin four times, it may well come up heads

Figure 12.7 Does resolution equal detail? The top version seems soft, even though it was scanned at three times the resolution of the bottom version, and takes up nine times as much disk space. In areas of one color, like the grass, the higher the resolution, the more even the color will become.

three out of the four, although two heads is more likely. If we flip four *hundred* times, 300 heads couldn't possibly happen.

The higher the resolution, the more uniform the color will be: the closer it will approach whatever the average color of the grass is. There is a lot more variation in the lower resolution version. That variation, or action, suggests the blades of grass that our imagination is telling us are actually there.

In scanning, moving to a lower resolution is a move toward action and variability.

This is a fine concept, but if the resolution gets too low, the image will become harsh and jagged.

A higher resolution is a move toward smoothness and consistency. This is also a laudable goal, but if it gets too high, the image will look soft and defocused.

It follows that there is no one "correct" scanning resolution. A woman's face generally should be scanned at a higher resolution than a man's, because we accept more roughness in a man's face. An image of furniture requires more resolution than does grass, because furniture has diagonal lines that shouldn't look too harsh. A damaged, noisy, or prescreened original also is helped by higher resolution. And, certainly, if you think there is a good chance you'll be upsizing the image, give yourself some extra resolution in the original scan.

Many people, refusing to believe that too much resolution can hurt, obdurately scan everything at 300 SSPI. This explains why so many newspaper photographs look so soft. It also makes the vendors of disk drives very happy. File size increases with the square of the resolution. If, for magazine work, you go with 250 SSPI rather than 300, your files will only be ⅔ as large—and quality will probably be *better*.

Resampling and the Rogue Dot

The foregoing discussion concerns scanning resolution, expressed in SSPI. The resolution of the Photoshop file is not necessarily the same kind of resolution. We express this in PPI—pixels per inch. A pixel is the smallest building block of a file. You can see them clearly in Figure 12.8.

When a raw scan is opened directly in Photoshop, at that moment the SSPI equals the PPI. That equality does not necessarily continue, because at some point the scan may get *resampled.* Plus, with many desktop scanners, what seems to be the raw scan isn't any such thing: it may already have been interpolated.

Photoshop itself allows us to change the number of pixels in a file, using the dialog box shown in Figure 12.10, accessed by Image: Image Size.

When the Resample Image box is unchecked, changing the numbers changes only the nominal size of the image, not any data. A 4"×6" file at 150 PPI is exactly the same as a 2"×3" file at 300 PPI. One changes size without resampling for the sake of convenience. For example, images in Photo CD format start at a nominal resolution of 72 PPI. They have more than enough pixels to use for this book, provided I place them in the page layout file at a quarter of their nominal size, which would make their effective resolution 288 PPI. To avoid this hassle, I change resolution to 250 PPI, without resampling. That, I know, will make the image close to the size I need.

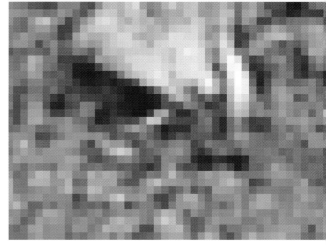

Resampling *down*—that is, throwing some of the data away—is appropriate when there's more than enough for whatever use you intend. It's ridiculous to post a 5-megabyte image file for Web viewing, just as it's ridiculous to use a 15-megabyte file for the top half of Figure 12.7.

To resample down, check the resample box, and enter a lower size, resolution, or

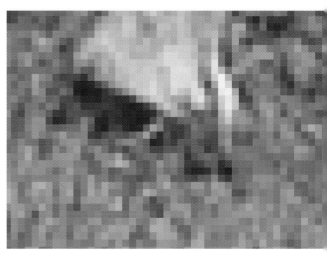

Figure 12.8 What passes for detail is often nothing more than variation. Pixels in the top two images (blowups of the two images of Figure 12.7) seem to have the same amount of variation, but this is an illusion. If the high-resolution version, top, is downsampled to match the resolution of the middle version, the result is the image at bottom, which is much softer.

SOME RESOLUTIONS ABOUT RESOLUTION

✓ Many different kinds of resolution are often described by one ambiguous term, *dpi*. Photoshop users have to know what each kind of dpi means.

✓ Excessive resolution is often as harmful as not having enough. This is true in the screen ruling of a printed image, and in scanning, where too much resolution yields an overly soft result.

✓ Graphics prepared in vector programs such as Adobe Illustrator, Macromedia FreeHand, and CorelDraw, are resolution-independent: the output device will draw the graphics in the optimal fashion. The same goes for type. Once imported into Photoshop, though, the graphics are turned into pixels and lose this attribute.

✓ The choice of screen ruling shouldn't outstrip the capabilities of either the press or the imagesetter. If the imagesetter isn't capable of at least 150 varieties of tone at a given screen, go to a coarser screen.

✓ The industry consensus is that scan resolution for an image that is to be printed at same size should be 1.5 to 2 times screen ruling. As the screen ruling goes up, the effect of inadequate resolution goes down.

✓ Scanning at a relatively high resolution guarantees smoothness and consistency. If overdone, however, images become soft. Lower resolution is a move toward action and variability. If overdone, however, images become harsh and jagged.

✓ Type and other line graphics should generally be scanned at 1.5 times the printer or imagesetter resolution, or greater.

✓ Many manufacturers of scanners and digital cameras trumpet how many bits per channel they capture. This is very interesting but has little bearing on the critical question, which is how accurately the device sees into shadow areas.

✓ Photoshop 5 allows several operations on files that contain 16 bits of information per channel. Although many scanners can provide such files, it is questionable whether there is any advantage to working on them in this mode.

✓ When forced to work with an image that has inadequate resolution, upsampling the file in Photoshop can help, provided that certain retouching techniques are used afterwards.

both. But keep two things in mind. First of all, unless you're positive you'll never need to print the image at a larger size, save a copy of the original. Down-sampling is a one-way street.

Second, realize that a downsampled image isn't equivalent to an original scan of the same PPI. The downsampled version will be softer, like the third version of Figure 12.8.

The lower the resolution, the more chance of a rogue dot, an area where the scanner picked up really atypical information, which will translate into a halftone dot that looks out of place, almost like a speck of dust. The greater the density of scanning samples—resampled or not—the less likely this is to occur. And the higher the screen ruling, the less noticeable a rogue dot is.

The conventional wisdom is that resolution should be 1.5 to 2 times screen ruling times magnification. If your images have been downsampled you really don't need that much (1.3 to 1.7 ought to do it). Also, with screens of 175 DPI and up, or stochastic screening, you can get by with less.

Sometimes, unfortunately, we have to work with an original that doesn't have enough resolution. In such a case, resampling *up* doesn't add any quality to the image. However, if you want to make the best of this bad situation, an upsampled image can be corrected using many of the techniques that apply to prescreened originals (Chapter 14) and older, damaged art (Chapter 16).

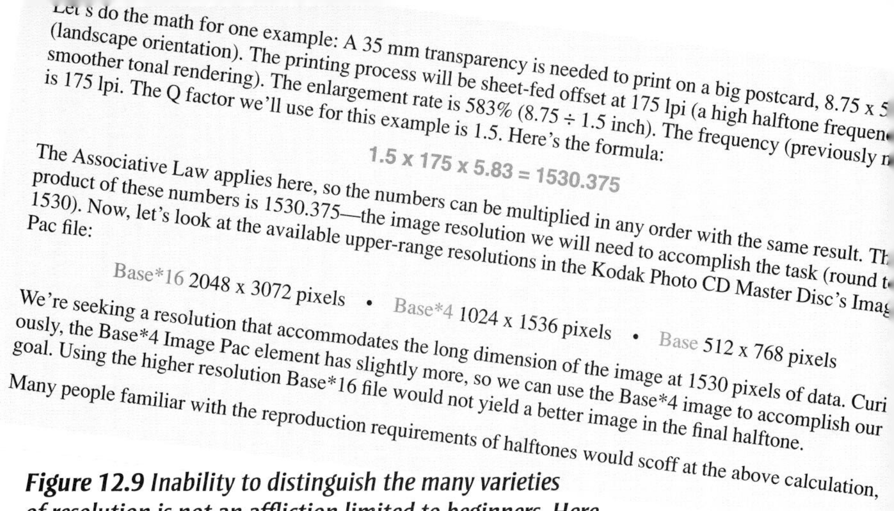

Let's do the math for one example: A 35 mm transparency is needed to print on a big postcard, 8.75 x 5 (landscape orientation). The printing process will be sheet-fed offset at 175 lpi (a high halftone frequency smoother tonal rendering). The enlargement rate is 583% (8.75 ÷ 1.5 inch). The frequency (previously n is 175 lpi. The Q factor we'll use for this example is 1.5. Here's the formula:

$$1.5 \times 175 \times 5.83 = 1530.375$$

The Associative Law applies here, so the numbers can be multiplied in any order with the same result. Th product of these numbers is 1530.375—the image resolution we will need to accomplish the task (round t 1530). Now, let's look at the available upper-range resolutions in the Kodak Photo CD Master Disc's Imag Pac file:

Base*16 2048 x 3072 pixels • Base*4 1024 x 1536 pixels • Base 512 x 768 pixels

We're seeking a resolution that accommodates the long dimension of the image at 1530 pixels of data. Curi ously, the Base*4 Image Pac element has slightly more, so we can use the Base*4 image to accomplish our goal. Using the higher resolution Base*16 file would not yield a better image in the final halftone.

Many people familiar with the reproduction requirements of halftones would scoff at the above calculation,

Figure 12.9 Inability to distinguish the many varieties of resolution is not an affliction limited to beginners. Here, Kodak gives users some incorrect, and quality-damaging, advice on how to use Photo CD, based on a misunderstanding of two types of resolution.

Millions and Millions of Pixels

The concept of PPI is closely related to another species of resolution: total pixel count. Film recorders, digital cameras, and certain types of scans express their resolution in terms the total number of pixels per image, not per unit of measurement, probably because their vendors like to impress people with a lot of zeroes. A high-end digital camera may have a resolution of 20,000,000 TPC, but it is less bulky to quote it as 5,000 PLD by 4,000 PSD—pixels in the long (short) direction.

Throwing around all these types of

Figure 12.10 The Photoshop resampling dialog box, accessed under Image: Image Size.

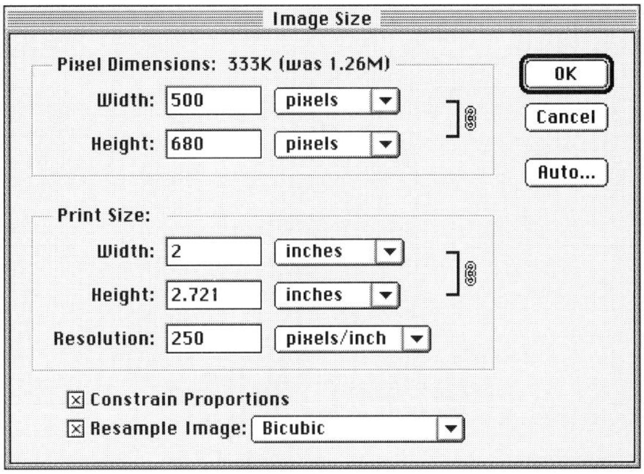

resolution can be confusing even for experts. If your head is swimming, take heart: even Kodak sometimes doesn't fathom these distinctions, as Figure 12.9 shows.

This gaffe, excerpted from a Kodak document on how to prepare Photo CD images for press, offers the following example: given a 35 mm original (1½" wide), which of several Photo CD resolutions should we choose, if we intend to print the image 8¾" wide at a 175 DPI screen?

The author of this document observes that "Many people familiar with the production requirements of halftones would scoff" at his answer. That is definitely correct, but not for the reason he thinks. We scoff, instead, at those who are so busy with Q factors and associative laws that they miss the basic concepts. Here, Kodak has mixed up two kinds of resolution. Let's try to help the Great Yellow Father out.

Kodak suggests 1.5 here for the ratio of resolution to screen ruling. This is certainly reasonable. The magnification factor is 583%; the screen factor is 175. Multiply the three together, and the answer is 1,530.

Since one of the possible Photo CD resolutions has a width of 1,536, Kodak concludes that it is nearly a perfect fit, and that this is the resolution of choice.

But no, as the doctor said to Hercule Poirot. No, no, and again no! That is an explanation that will not hold water!

The desired resolution of 1,530 is in pixels *per inch*. The Photo CD alternative of 1,536 is in pixels *in the long direction*. The original being 1½" wide, we need to multiply that 1,530 by 1.5 to get an appropriate PLD. Since Kodak's choice of 1,536 is too low, we need to go to the next higher alternative, which is 3,072 PLD.

That 3,072 figure gives us the happy ratio of 2.0 times the screen ruling. 1,536 would yield a 1.0 ratio, and print quality would go down the tubes, Kodak's feelings to the contrary notwithstanding.

Some Final Resolutions

The genesis of this chapter was a magazine column I reluctantly wrote in response to the requests of novices who didn't understand the difference between the "DPI" of scans and laser printers. I began with the idea that it was a throwaway, for beginners only. Once I read the first draft, however, it struck me that this is the most baffling and confusing topic I've ever written about— even though it doesn't even touch monitor resolution, the resolution of Web images, or of film recorders. That was when I decided to highlight each occurrence of phrases like yet another species of resolution.

Like many professionals, I had made the mistake of assuming that this was all intuitive. After observing just how many highlighted phrases there were (and after reading an extraordinary volume of correspondence after the column appeared), I had a much better understanding of why some artists find themselves buried under a blizzard of soft images, jagged edges, strangled networks, and unhappy RIPs.

The way to resolve one's resolution difficulties can be simply stated: don't ask for too much, don't provide too little.

You may find it easier to do that if you refrain from using that deceptive DPI term.

Declaring that we will never let those three deadly letters pass our lips is probably impractical. I don't really advocate that. But even if you *say* DPI, don't *think* DPI. Keeping the true meaning in mind is one of the best resolutions you can make.

CHAPTER 13

Keeping the Color
In Black and White

When color images move into black and white, they lose contrast—in some places. Those who can predict where the contrast will be lost can correct for it in advance, before a fatal conversion to B/W discards it forever.

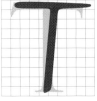he ease with which we can produce and manipulate color images on the desktop has made some of us view the whole idea of black and white as antique, primitive, foreign, even contemptible.

Though it may be all of these things, we cannot ignore it, because black and white printing is not going away. Adding color printing units to web presses is not a cheap proposition. Even though many newspapers have added color to certain pages in the last few years, we can expect that the majority of pages will remain monochrome for years to come. Many other printed products have the same problem.

This unpleasant reality causes us color publishers a considerable technical problem. We frequently have to produce materials that will print in color in one publication and black and white in another. Often the black and white version is more important than the color one.

Even when color is readily available, there are frequently sensible artistic reasons to use black and white as a foil. There are significant examples of this throughout the history of our culture. While it is incongruous to mention Steven Spielberg in the same sentence with Michelangelo, the greatest masterpiece of each involved the intentional use of monochrome when color was not only readily available but also cheaper.

Good conversion to B/W is also a prerequisite for effective duotones, which will receive a full airing in Chapter 15.

Digital conversion of color photographs to black and white is a recent phenomenon. Until about 1990, color separations were so expensive that nobody would do one if the end result was to be black and white. Furthermore, there were a lot more black and white originals then than today, when almost all photographs are in color.

Since few people have experience doing it, few people do it very well. The job is much tougher than it looks.

Figure 13.1 *Certain types of contrast convert well to black and white, but other varieties completely dry up.*

The Fatal Flatness in B/W

Color pictures almost invariably appear flat when they go to B/W. A lot of the contrast we saw in the color original is gone, and we can no longer distinguish some of the subtler details. Recognizing this, a photographer making a B/W print from a color negative will almost always use some kind of high-contrast filter. We have some even niftier desktop tools to get rid of the flatness—provided we understand what is causing it.

Eventually, we have to ask Photoshop to make a mode change into grayscale. In doing so, it uses a weighted-average method based on RGB values, even if the image we are converting is in CMYK. Each new B/W pixel, in the Photoshop algorithm, gets approximately 60 percent of the value of the green component of the RGB, 30 percent of the red, and 10 percent of the blue. As usual, some calibrationists, seduced by anything that seems to have a mathematical formula in it, claim that this will always give the most "accurate," and hence best, rendition of a color photograph.

Figure 13.1 is a little test of this assertion. Let's see what happens when we convert this "picture" to B/W using this infallible formula.

In a proper conversion, the B/W image should be crisp and legible. The viewer should be able to form a mental picture of what the color image must look like. If these are our objectives, we have obviously failed miserably. What went wrong?

In a B/W world, there is only one kind of contrast, which can be called lightness, luminosity, or dark vs. light. If the original color image has this kind of contrast, we are in good shape. This is

Figure 13.2. A default conversion of this image to B/W will have difficulty holding contrast in the bear's fur and in the red background.

what is happening in the right-hand third of our checkerboard. The B/W conversion of this third is entirely reasonable.

When we convert, however, we lose completely two other kinds of contrast. In the left third of our checkerboard there is a huge contrast in colors. In the middle third the contrast is there not because of color difference but because of purity difference. We easily distinguish the muddy green at the bottom from the clean one at the top. As color and purity variation are irrelevant in B/W, however, our attempt to convert these parts of the picture was not exactly crowned with success.

Figure 13.1 really is a picture of the HSB colorspace, discussed in Chapter 10. One third varies in hue, one in saturation, one in brightness. It's useful to think of B/W in terms of HSB—we just have to remember that H and S are now worthless.

If we start with the bottom version and try to correct it, we will get nowhere fast. We have to do something, but whatever it is, it has to be done to the color version, before we make the switch to black and white. This is a most important concept. A good 4/c image can produce an unacceptable B/W one. Sometimes it takes an unacceptable 4/c image to produce a good B/W one.

Planning the B/W Conversion

Our assignment will be to take five color pictures of various subjects and create the best possible B/W representations of them. Per our normal policy, no selections are permitted. We will limit ourselves to moves that affect the image as a whole. The general approach will be similar in each case.

The first step is very obvious. Unfortunately it is also very hard. We have to visualize what is going to go wrong when our color perception is taken away. It takes a close look at the *color* to realize what we will be missing in the B/W.

We must identify which parts of the picture are likely to convert well, and which are not. In Figure 13.2, our first challenge, we will have no problem with the bear's nose standing out from her fur. That is strictly lightness vs. darkness, and it will look just fine in B/W.

On the other hand, the bear's coat will suffer for sure. Most of what we take for contrast in the color version is a subtle variation in the red and yellow shading in her fur. Ditto for the background rocks: we see contrast in the purity of the reds

there, and a lot of it will simply disappear in B/W.

Our second step, therefore, will be to formulate some method of exaggerating the contrast in the areas we expect to have trouble with. In effect, we will intentionally louse up the color.

Our principal tool will be, as always, curves. There is more flexibility than usual, though, in that we no longer have to worry about keeping grays neutral. When they get to B/W, they *will* be neutral, believe me. Also, we need not be too careful about highlight and shadow values. Once in B/W, we will be able to correct these easily with a supplementary curve. We can also make liberal use of plate blending to emphasize certain details, since what happens to the color balance makes no difference.

The third step will be the actual conversion, and any minor tonal range correction that's needed once we are in B/W.

Figure 13.3 *Parts of the original CMYK channels of the bear image of Figure 13.2.*

Those of us in need of ego gratification usually add a fourth step, which is to go back to the original, uncorrected color picture, convert it to B/W exactly as is, compare the result with the corrected B/W version we just made, and pat ourselves on the back for the improvement.

Back to the bear.

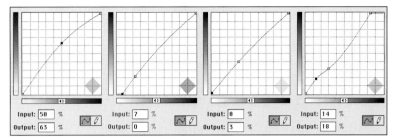

Figure 13.4 *Prior to converting to B/W, it's generally a good idea to pump up contrast in the color channels. This curve to the image of Figure 13.2 is designed to bring out detail in the bear's fur.*

Fuzzy Wuzzy Needs Some Hair

The first order of business is always to examine the individual channels. With this bear, we start in CMYK, which is usually better because of the presence of the powerful black channel. But RGB can be an important part of the conversion process as well.

Sometimes, we will try to build contrast in one with a blend from another. Whether that's part of our agenda or not, we should have zero tolerance for a poor channel. As you can see in Figure 13.3, we really don't have one.

Compare the cyan to the magenta. If forced to choose one, I say the magenta is better, but they each are making a contribution. The cyan has detail in the shoulder that is missing in the magenta.

Similarly, the yellow, though flatter than either the cyan or magenta, has depth that the others don't in certain areas. Therefore, none of the three can be discarded.

To add contrast to the bear, we have to steepen the range she occupies in each curve. We would do that even if the image were staying in color, except that we can go much further now. Spots of color are already starting to appear in inappropriate

places in the fur, and further contrast will make them worse—if this is going to stay in color. If we are intending to go to B/W, however, we care not a fig for this.

The whitest part of the bear is her forehead. The darkest parts of the fur are in the areas where we see traces of red, yellow or blue shading. What we need to do is to increase the difference between the lightest and the darkest, thus providing a bigger range of colors, and hence more detail and contrast.

The bear's forehead is a perfect highlight of $5^C2^M2^Y$. That shouldn't go much lighter, so we'll have to make the dark spots darker.

Measuring the red spots above her left rear leg, the yellow spots in her midsection, and the bluish area near her neck, we observe that the predominant color—whether it is magenta, cyan, or yellow—is in the neighborhood of 30%. We need to push those values up.

In this set, the most important curves (Figure 13.4) affect the black and the magenta. Changing the black, the most powerful tool we have in color retouching generally, is even more prominent in B/W conversions. Beefing up the black accentuates detailing, such as the darker areas of the rocky background in this picture. Such

Figure 13.5 *Above, a default Photoshop conversion to grayscale of Figure 13.2. Below, a conversion using the techniques described in the text.*

a tactic should be semi-automatic when converting from CMYK to B/W. The exact move depends on the image.

Correct handling of the magenta plate is the key to this image. I am so anxious to steepen the range that is originally 10^M to 60^M that I am willing to obliterate all magenta less than 5^M, and have little difference between 80^M and 100^M. In this way, I have drawn a rather vertical curve and have gained detail in important areas at the expense of areas I care nothing about.

Manipulating the cyan and yellow is largely a reaction to the moves made in the magenta and black. I have, as described earlier, intentionally blown out the magenta highlight; there are now areas that have no magenta at all. That would not be acceptable if the picture were to print in color, but as our goal is B/W, it is irrelevant.

However, we must be sure that we don't allow anything like it to happen in the other colors, or we may find ourselves with areas in the final B/W that have no dot. To guard against this, I add slightly to the highlight values in cyan and yellow. The yellow adds so little contrast to an image that I am willing to do this; in the other three channels, I will insist that the curves remain as steep as possible in the light end.

Applying these curves to the color picture creates a horrifying result. The background turns cranberry, and the bear becomes every color of the rainbow, making us wonder whether she is a polar bear or a grizzly who has just trashed a paint store. I won't even show how bad it looks, because what matters is how it looks after we change it to grayscale.

And there, strange to say, it works.

So, compare the two B/W images of Figure 13.5, one converted without correction,

one with the curves of Figure 13.4 applied to the color first. One is much more alive than the other. Every detail of the picture is snappier. The uncorrected version might strike us at first as a reasonable rendition of the 4/c—but to those who know, it is, er, bearly acceptable.

A Change in Luck

Figure 13.6, an even more ferocious-looking member of the animal kingdom, presents the problem of the bear in reverse, and to complete the theme of opposites, we'll do the correction in RGB.

This is a tougher image right from the start because of the nearly total lack of shadow detail. In an image consisting almost entirely of shadow areas, this is somewhat of a drawback.

Examination of the three channels (Figure 13.7) shows that the best kitten is in the red and the worst in the green. We can't kill the green channel altogether, though, because it has the best shape in the basket.

I chose to blend the red channel into each of the other two using Screen, rather than Normal, for mode. Screen lightens the image, but it is especially effective at exaggerating shadow detail. It's the opposite of the more commonly used Multiply mode, which darkens but especially increases highlight contrast.

I made the new green channel a 50–50 blend with the red. For the blue, I used 70% of the red and 30% of the former blue.

Prior to converting to grayscale, I applied curves to each channel to further exaggerate contrast in the shadows. In color correction, one black cat is much like another, so the red and blue curves look much like the black cat curves in Figure 4.2. In the green, I moved the highlight

endpoint until the reflection in the basket reached 255^G, as bright as possible. Since the other two channels had little detail in the basket there was no point in such a move there.

The same sharpening settings have been applied to both the corrected and the default version.

Preserving the Tartan

Continuing our program of increasingly difficult images and more dangerous species of subject, we turn now to Figure 13.8. Instead of working in either CMYK or RGB, this time, we'll need both.

In addition to the question of whether the colors of the kilt will be sufficiently

Figure 13.6 *This original image, top right, is so lacking in detail that a default conversion, bottom left, is sure to disappoint. Some RGB channel-blending plus contrast-enhancing curves prior to the conversion results in the much more satisfactory version at bottom right.*

differentiated, this image, even in color, starts off with some grave technical difficulties. For example, the woman has no nose. Also, there is very little shape to her sweater.

It's plain that the sweater has a cyan cast in the original. It's too dark to detect in the composite image, but in the individual channels of Figure 13.9, see how much darker the sweater is in the cyan than the magenta. The black plate, despite being too light, has potential for shape in the sweater, but the other three are hopeless.

For an image so woefully lacking in snap, we should consider a move discussed in Chapter 9, namely, the use of RGB channels to blend into their CMYK cousins.

After duplicating the file and converting the duplicate to RGB, the blue channel comes as a pleasant surprise. A detailed face, nice kilt, crisp hair. There isn't enough difference between the background and the woman, but it's a good start.

The yellow plate has nothing to recommend it over this blue, so we replace one with the other. The green is also better than the magenta, but I would be afraid to make a total replacement, for fear of the sweater darkening too much. So I select a 50–50 blend of the two.

The cyan channel has problems, but the red doesn't have solutions. There's really no better detail in the face; the sweater is darker, and we don't need the extra contrast in the kilt. So, forget the red.

Now that we have a CMYK document, here's my recipe, and my reasoning:
• In the magenta and yellow channels, reduce the highlight by moving the lower left endpoint of the curve to the right. The blending I've done has made both channels slightly too dark.
• With the black channel, move the top right point to the left until the very darkest fold of the sweater is at 100%. This is to milk every drop of contrast possible out of

Figure 13.7 *The original RGB channels of Figure 13.6.*

the sweater. 100% is, of course, too dark to print with, but we're not yet scot-free.

• Blend 50% of the blue into the magenta. This is to get better detail in the face, and to lighten the red parts of the kilt.

• Make a copy of the blue channel to a grayscale document. Then, apply the curve that goes up in the quartertone, but down in the shadow. The idea is to create a channel that saves contrast in the face, yet lightens (and kills detail in) the sweater.

• Blend this new channel, at 10%, into the cyan. This will help the face, which is currently a disaster. Don't worry about the loss of contrast in the sweater. I've already hung my hat on the black channel for establishing that.

• Blend the original blue channel into the black, at 8%. Again, this adds depth in the face, and backs the sweater off 100% in the shadow, without doing too much violence to detail.

• Sharpen the channels individually, because each one has different characteristics. The Amount is discretionary—I used 200% throughout—but the Radius and Threshold have to vary. I used a Radius of 1.0 in the cyan and magenta, but 1.3 in the black, which has less background detail. In the cyan and black, there is so little background noise that there is no need for a Threshold, but as is usual in pictures of faces, there is undesirable variation in the magenta. To avoid sharpening that, I set a Threshold of 10. The yellow channel, as usual, should not be sharpened at all.

• Convert to B/W. Enjoy the comparison.

What to Lighten, What to Darken

There is plenty of color in Figure 13.10, but it is all relatively light, and full of the kind of contrast that is great in 4/c and terrible in B/W. The dark windows will certainly convert well, and the bricks will be moderately

Figure 13.8 A more complicated conversion creates extra detail in the black sweater and the face, right. The center version is a default conversion.

Figure 13.9 *The key to the extra depth in the corrected version of Figure 13.8 is the black plate of the CMYK document. The idea is to change the original black (left center) to something much snappier (right center). This is done by first curving the original black so that the darkest point goes to 100%, then blending in a percentage of the blue channel (upper right) to add detail to the face and to bring the shadow values down slightly. Meanwhile, the weak magenta and yellow originals (below) are largely replaced by their RGB counterparts. The cyan also gets a blend from the blue, to pick up facial detail.*

Figure 13.10 *This image is full of the kinds of contrast that cause headaches when converted to B/W.*

successful, though some of the color-related contrast in the bricks will vanish.

In order of importance, the major problems are:

• The sign over the door is likely to disappear into the background bricks.

• In the color image there is great contrast between the light blue shutters and the red bricks, but this will go away in B/W.

• Maintaining some semblance of life in the doors.

• Helping out the bricks.

The shutters vs. bricks problem raises the interesting issue of which should wind up darker. If we want differentiation in B/W, we will have to make a choice.

In such cases, set up the Info palette (using its eyedropper tools) so that it reads LAB as well as the actual color, currently CMYK. We find typical values of 73^{L} in the

blue shutters and 71^{L} in the bricks. The readings in the A and B channels, being color-related only, are irrelevant. Since, in the L, a lower number is a darker one, we start off with the bricks being very slightly darker than the shutters. We need to exaggerate this difference before it vanishes in the conversion to B/W.

Inspection of the individual plates (Figure 13.11) shows bricks in all plates, but the sign is heaviest by far in the yellow, and the shutters are concentrated in the cyan.

In image enhancement, there is a time for delicate instruments and a time for sledgehammers and crowbars. This is one of those latter instances.

The fastest way by far to make an object darker is to get some black ink into it. Therefore, my first step was to blend 20 percent of the yellow into the black. The

black was now much darker overall, but more importantly, it had a pronounced sign. Since this move also put some unwelcome black in the image highlight, I wrote the curve shown. This blew out the black where it wasn't wanted, but steepened the area in which the bricks and the sign fell.

This left less black than before in the bricks, so to compensate, I increased magenta above the midtone, but I killed the magenta highlight. This made the light areas even whiter and thus gave more contrast to the bricks.

Next, I went to the magenta and increased contrast by lightening the highlight and darkening the bricks. In the magenta, the shutters were already much lighter than the bricks, and this move exaggerated the difference, just as planned.

Figure 13.11 *Left, top to bottom: the original cyan, magenta, yellow and black plates of Figure 13.10. Bottom right: the black after 20% of the yellow was blended into it, followed by an application of the curve at right.*

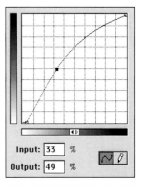

Input: 33 %
Output: 49 %

But not enough. The idea being to get shutters much lighter than the windows, I blended 50% of this magenta into the cyan, where the shutters were strongest. This left the cyan plate with shutters and bricks roughly equal. Since in the other three plates the bricks were much darker than the shutters, I called it quits there and converted to grayscale.

Looking at the final results in Figure 13.12, you must agree that there would be no hope of ever correcting the top image to equal the one at the bottom.

If you want your B/Ws to look their best, you must logically also agree that initial corrections must be done in color. Taking it further still, you must also agree that the quality of Photoshop's CMYK-to-grayscale conversion is really a secondary issue.

Recall that all we are doing when we go into grayscale is forcing our image into a smaller colorspace of drastically different shape. It is precisely analogous to an RGB- (or LAB)-to-CMYK conversion, where the data is forced into a colorspace that effectively has no blue.

If you concur that the corrected B/Ws in this chapter are overwhelmingly superior to the default conversions, you have become an anti-calibrationist.

The KISS Principle

In our final example, Figure 13.13, it would be hard to imagine a stronger contrast than between the red flowers and the greenery behind them. It would also be hard to imagine a more obvious case where one would wish to avoid a default conversion to B/W.

Figure 13.12 *(opposite) A default conversion of Figure 13.10, top, and one using the methods advocated in this chapter.*

This particular image starts in RGB. We plainly have to do something to break the flowers away from the background, but what to do isn't obvious at first glance.

Confronted with a close call like this one or like the blue shutters against the red bricks in Figure 13.10, changing the settings in Photoshop's Info palette to read LAB values is a big help—usually. Not in this case, however. The L values are between 45 and 48 for both. This explains the ghastly lack of contrast in the default conversion.

Any sort of calibrationist approach to this image is dead on arrival. We have to, as W.C. Fields once remarked, take the bull by the tail and face the situation. Either we are

Figure 13.13 *Converting this image properly depends on differentiating the bright red flowers from the grass.*

  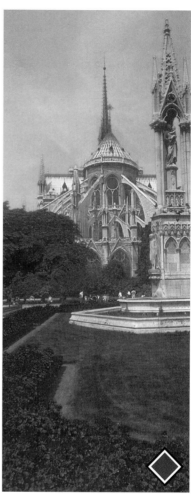

Figure 13.14 The original RGB channels of Figure 13.13. It's comparatively rare for one channel to be superior to the others in every respect, but that's what's happening here.

going to have to make the flowers darker than the background, or lighter.

The choice is presented starkly by the red and green channels of Figure 13.14. To me, the whitish flowers of the red look very bogus. In fact, I can't find a single area in which I prefer the red to the green. And the blue is clearly out of the question.

Since the green channel is better in every way, what's the big problem? Just copy it to a separate grayscale document, set highlight and shadow, sharpen, save,

and print. Figure 13.15 is a 30-second correction. (I've applied the same sharpening settings to the default conversion.)

Keep It Simple, Stupid. Working with the green channel alone is an old scanner operator trick. Occasionally, as here, it works, but it usually isn't the best way. In the image of the black kitten, you will recall, the green channel was the *worst* of the three.

It would be pretty stupid, as this example shows, to assume that every B/W

CONVERTING COLOR INTO BLACK AND WHITE

✓There are times when we *have* to use black and white, and times when we *want* to. B/W can be a very effective foil for other color images. Until recently, it was unheard of to take a digital color image and convert it to monochrome. Now, with most images coming into our computers in color, it is commonplace.

✓Any time an image goes from color to B/W viewers complain that it loses contrast. This is inaccurate. The image loses those types of contrast that are associated with color, but it fully retains light/dark distinctions. A color image of a black cat in a blizzard will convert to B/W with spectacular success.

✓Conversion candidates should be examined carefully for the kinds of contrast that *don't* convert well. Different colors that are of roughly the same lightness (e.g., the reds and blues in the flags of various nations) will reproduce as nearly the same shade in B/W. Similarly, different saturation values of the same color are readily distinguishable in CMYK, but not B/W.

✓Having identified the areas of a color image that will not convert well to B/W, apply correction curves or other methods that will exaggerate the differences, forcing different colors further apart.

✓Before the conversion, examine each plate of the CMYK image individually. Often one or more plates are very flat. If curves will not suffice to add contrast, think about blending in portions of other plates to add definition. The black plate, in particular, tends to have more shape than the other three and is a good candidate for blends.

✓Photoshop's default conversion to B/W takes no account of the individuality of the image. If we were not allowed to color-correct before conversion, it would probably be the best formula. As matters stand, however, practically every image can be improved by CMYK or RGB moves before going to B/W.

✓Don't worry about strict adherence to highlight/shadow settings in making the first correction. These can easily be fixed once we get to B/W, but whatever contrast we lose on the way will be gone forever.

✓RGB images often should go to CMYK first before conversion to B/W, so as to get the benefit of moves in the black channel.

Figure 13.15 *A default conversion, left, and one based on the green channel of Figure 13.14.*

conversion requires the prestidigitation needed for the woman in the kilt. But it happens sometimes. Consider for a moment the bag of tricks in that image. We had strengthening of the unwanted color (Chapter 5); sharpening of different channels at different settings (Chapter 6); a significant black-channel maneuver (Chapter 7); and an RGB-to-CMYK blend (Chapter 9).

Do you see why B/W conversions are so challenging? The art of turning color into black and white requires thinking, just as the art of correcting color does. The effectiveness of the result depends upon the effectiveness of our imagination.

Math, Moiré, and the Artist: A New Angle on Descreening

Whenever two patterns overlap in print, a weird-looking interference is possible. Mostly this happens with prescreened originals, occasionally with patterned objects. Usually, moiré can be avoided by keeping two words in mind: thirty degrees.

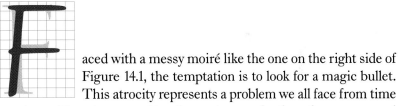

Faced with a messy moiré like the one on the right side of Figure 14.1, the temptation is to look for a magic bullet. This atrocity represents a problem we all face from time to time, although we would rather not: reproduction of a prescreened original. People recommend all sorts of magic bullets for dealing with it. Frequently the bullets wind up in their feet.

Can you guess what I did to correct the file to produce the resounding improvement shown at the left?

Nothing. I did nothing at all.

The two versions are exactly the same. They access the same file, are cropped identically.

For identical pictures, that is rather a dramatic difference in print quality. It indicates that prescreened originals present some unique problems, many of which can be solved by keeping two words in mind: thirty degrees. That's the real magic bullet.

Before getting into descreening technique, we'd better have a quick review of what this screening stuff is all about.

Limiting ourselves for the moment to black and white, successful reproduction depends on achieving a full range of tone: whites, blacks, dark grays, light grays, medium grays. Unfortunately, we have no gray ink to work with on press, merely black ink and white paper.

A little legerdemain is therefore in order. By subtly laying down smallish quantities of black ink in conjunction with showing smallish amounts of white paper, we can fool the viewer into perceiving gray.

There are several ways of doing this. Randomly placed dots will work. If such dots are intended to be readily visible, we call the result a *mezzotint*. If they are too small to be seen easily, we call it a *stochastic screen.*

Overwhelmingly, though, the printing industry uses some kind of regular pattern of ink coverage that gets darker or lighter to portray different shades of gray. Nowadays that pattern is almost invariably one of dots that vary in size but not in distance from one another. The pattern is called a *screen;* the number of dots per linear inch is the *screen frequency* or *ruling.* A higher ruling implies better print quality: the pictures of Madeleine Albright are screened at 65 dots per inch, which is more appropriate for newspapers than a book. (In this book, the normal screen is 133 DPI.)

The dot pattern is modestly more pronounced if the rows of dots are exactly horizontal and vertical with respect to the

Figure 14.1 The moiré in the image opposite is absent in the version to the left. What's the secret that makes this corrected version so much better?

page. Therefore, it is customary to angle them. The exact angle makes not a whit of difference, unless the picture is being printed with more than one ink—or unless we are trying to reproduce a prescreened image.

The Thirty Degree Solution

Most of us have some kind of vague comprehension that cyan, magenta, yellow and black are customarily printed at four different screen angles. It is normally completely irrelevant whether we know what those angles are or why. If, however, we are going to be working with prescreened originals, understanding the theory of angling is critical.

inks can be 30° apart from one another. If an ink were angled at 90° (i.e., the row of dots is perfectly horizontal) it also would be 0°, since a row of dots would also be perfectly vertical. We could have a second ink at 30° and a third at 60°, but we'd have to scramble for a fourth angle.

Fortunately, yellow is so much lighter than the other three colors that it really doesn't matter what its screen angle is. (For want of anything better, it's usually set at 0°, the same orientation as the page.) As long as the cyan, magenta, and black are 30° apart from one another, we're home. Conventionally, the magenta is at 75°, the black at 45°, and the cyan at 15°, but it's the 30° relationship of the three that's important, not these particular numbers.

Now, back to Secretary Albright. The original appeared in a newspaper that uses the above angles. Its black is therefore at 45°. My scan captured its dot pattern, and although I may not have had the original exactly straight when I scanned it, the pattern probably is somewhere between 43° and 47°.

On top of that, we impose this book's black screen, which is also angled at 45°. This is why the right image resides in Moirésville. The left version is vastly better, because instead of two screens at around 45°, there is one at 45° and another 30° away at 15°. The book's angle didn't change. The image's did.

This demonstration should convince you that if you are dealing with prescreened B/W originals, you will improve quality decisively by rotating them all 30° on the printed page. Regrettably, that is a somewhat unrealistic method.

Whenever two regular patterns are superimposed on one another, there will be some kind of interference, or moiré. The moiré can range from spectacular, as in the right half of Figure 14.1, to almost unnoticeable. Obviously, we prefer the latter. However, if we print all the CMYK inks at the same screen angle, we are guaranteed to get one of the former variety.

Color printing has been around long enough for a lot of experimentation. In that time printers have learned that, while a lot of angle combinations work, the most reliable is one where they are 30° apart.

The Photoshop convention in referring to angles is that a vertical line would be at 0°, a horizontal one at 90°. If you think about it, you will realize that only three

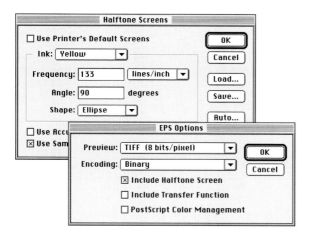

Figure 14.2 *The two steps in embedding a screen angle in a Photoshop file: background, the Screens submenu of Edit: Page Setup; foreground, saving an EPS file.*

Confronted with a moth that persisted in trying to throw itself into a lighted candle, archy the cockroach remarked, "why do you fellows pull this stunt/because it is the conventional thing for moths or why/…have you no sense [?]"

Take it to heart. The 45° black angle is, indeed, the conventional thing. But the mountain need not come to Mohammed. If the original art and the new screen both have the same angle, and you can't rotate the original art, rotate the screen.

If we save the image in EPS format rather than the more customary TIFF, we are allowed to choose a screen angle and/or frequency that will override the imagesetter's default. If we want our Albright image to be oriented vertically but not have that revolting moiré, all we have to do is set the black screen angle to 15° or 75°, either of which is that magic 30° away from the original screen.

The method of embedding angles is shown in Figure 14.2. The first step is File: Page Setup>Screens, to enter the frequency and angle of the screen we've

decided to use. Then, when saving the file, choose Photoshop EPS as a format, and the second dialog box shown will pop up automatically.

Changing screen frequencies and angles can be devastatingly effective. It can have devastating effects of an entirely different nature if you or somebody else later picks up the image and uses it for something else. Photoshop issues no warning that an EPS file has embedded screens.

Therefore, you should issue your own. Name the file *albright.screens.in* or something else that unambiguously indicates what is going on. This practice is likely to save your local police department a lot of money, because they will not have to figure out which of the frustrated subsequent users was the one who murdered you.

PageMaker 6.5's Print>Color Options allows us to change the angle and frequency in the same way, without the dangerous practice of embedding them in the image file. The print menu of QuarkXPress 4 has similar features, but earlier versions of the program do not.

Embedding a Screen

With black and white images, we should feel free to embed screen rulings that minimize moiré. With color images, there is considerably more risk, and this should be an experts-only tactic. But in B/W, nothing much can go wrong if we change the angle to 15° or 75°, which are optimal if the prescreened original was at 45°, as it almost always is.

But while doing this, we ought to think about screen *frequency* as well, because this is another case where prescreened originals should be treated in a way completely foreign to what we are used to.

The image of President Clinton in Figure 14.3A illustrates why we should not be overly intent on destroying every dot. Although it's an uncorrected scan of a prescreened image, and I haven't fiddled with the angles, the moiré is scarcely noticeable. It is in fact scanned from the same newspaper as the Albright image.

The only variable is that Albright is rescreened at 65 DPI, whereas Clinton is at the standard 133. The coarser the patterns, the worse the moiré. The finer we make the output screen pattern, the better off we'll be.

The flip side is, the smaller the dots, the less controllable they are on press. If the printer can't hold dot integrity, the picture will start to go blurry. Ordinarily, that is a terrible thing, but in the case of a prescreened original, it's a good thing. Ordinarily, we trust what the printer says about maximum screen ruling—but not when we're trying to fight a moiré.

Magazines, for example, recommend a 133-line screen. If you are submitting a prescreened B/W piece, however, I recommend that you embed a 150-line screen—and with a black angle of 15°, not 45°.

There is an interesting test of this on the facing page. One of the Clinton images has a 200 DPI screen, which the printer of this book would likely have a heart attack over if he knew in advance it were there. Web presses like the one that is slated to print this book are not meant for such abuse; even the finest sheetfed presses using the best stock have difficulty with 200-line screens, as do imagesetters.

There's a similar example in Chapter 12, but that one (Figure 12.1) uses a finer ruling, an unscreened original, and a color image. Here, there's a lot more of a case for it. This set of images has already printed in four different magazines, moiré avoidance being a major concern worldwide. In the original article that accompanied them, I predicted that Figure 14.3B had a good chance to be the best of the bunch when ink actually hit paper.

So far, the results are, better in two magazines, worse in one, about the same in the fourth. How'd we do here?

Thirty Degrees Again

In addition to the angle of the original and that of the imagesetter, there is a third angle that must be taken into account: the angle of the scan.

Scanners take their samples in a perfectly horizontal pattern, or, to make it consistent with previous terminology, at an angle of 90°. They are not exempt from the 30-degree rule. Just throwing prescreened art into the scanner, as I did with the Albright image, is highly inferior. For best reproduction, the scan must be angled as well. If the original is mounted straight up and down, there will be an unacceptable 45° between its screen pattern and the angle of scan. We therefore rotate the original by 15°. Whether the rotation is clockwise or counterclockwise is irrelevant in a B/W image; either way, the scan angle will be off by 30°, which is just what we want.

Angling the scan is one of the more common magic bullets being offered for your delectation by various authorities, most of whom recommend trial and error. If the original is as bad as it can possibly be, angling it can't make it worse, I'd have to agree. But why guess? Why choose a random angle, when the 30-degree rule suggests there is one that is better than all others?

Instead of popping the original into the scanner at an angle chosen by Providence because you are desperate, pop it in at 15° because you are confident.

All this horsing around with angles and frequencies will solve most of your B/W descreening problems. These easy steps may give you all the quality you require out of a prescreened original. If so, there is no need for you to read further. The rest of this chapter is for the folks who have time to spare and need to make rescreened images look not just OK, but as good as possible.

Figure 14.3 *Different approaches to a prescreened original. A: an uncorrected scan. B: the same file with a 200-line screen embedded. C: the same image scanned and corrected with the methods recommended in this column. D: the same file with 150-line screen at a 15° black screen angle. E: version A treated with an automated range correction and descreening routine.*

Those Dots: Rules and Exceptions

Any attempt at further improvement starts with the realization that the dot pattern is a two-edged sword. On the one hand, it prevents us from adding contrast to the image by threatening us with a ruinous moiré if we try. On the other, it holds all the detail. We don't need to eliminate it, just subdue it somewhat as we add range overall.

Exactly how much to play down the dot pattern is an image-by-image decision. I'll give you a recipe that usually works, but you may have to modify it in certain cases. Before I give you that recipe, here are some general concepts:

• Always scan prescreened art at the highest possible resolution, then resample it down. Very high scan resolutions are usually bad because they make images overly soft, but if the original has a pattern, softness is just fine, thank you.

• Learn to read the angles of the original. This takes practice, especially when dealing with color. Examine the original under a loupe, and imagine a box, or an L-shape, as shown in Figure 14.5. Rotate it until straight rows of dots match its sides, and you'll know the angle. With few exceptions, you'll find that black is at 45° and that cyan and magenta are at approximately 15° and 75°, respectively. But it isn't always so, particularly in older publications or those printed in Europe. Once you have verified the angle, use the 30-degree rule in both scanning and imaging.

• Build yourself a scanner template, with a line showing you where 15° is. Admittedly, you will never set the angle perfectly in a scanner, but why be off by five degrees?

• Don't use unsharp masking. The whole problem with prescreened originals is they are *too* sharp. Generally we want to blur them to some extent, and it is possible, nay likely, that we may want to go into local areas with the sharpening tool thereafter. For example, a person's eyes or jewelry will lose sparkle during the blurring. This should be attacked with the tool, but not an overall filter. If you blur so much that you have to sharpen globally, the sharpening is a bandage to put over the magic-bullet wound in your foot.

• Don't use an automated descreening package, such as those used by certain scanner-control software. Some, like the routine illustrated in Figure 14.3E, are pretty good, but none will give the same quality as careful human intervention.

There are some successful descreening algorithms for film, but once ink hits paper, there are enough variables to make automated descreening mediocre at best.

And now, the recipe. First, go back to the Albright moiré, and convince yourself that it isn't as bad as you first thought. Her jewelry is fine as is. Her dark dress and the background are also more or less acceptable. The really disgusting moiré happens only in the face. That is very typical. It's the middle range of the picture we need to worry about, not the two ends.

Second, break the image into two parts in your mind. On the one hand, the dots, which have detail, on the other, the white space between them, which does not. We definitely have to reduce the difference between the two, but doesn't it make sense

Figure 14.4 *Deemphasizing the dots is best done in separate lightening and darkening steps. A: a blowup of part of Figure 14.3.A, with contrast increased. B: a Gaussian Blur on a copy of version A. C: the blurred version B applied, Darker mode, to version A. D: the Dust & Scratches filter run on a second copy of version A. E: version D applied, Lighter mode, to version C.*

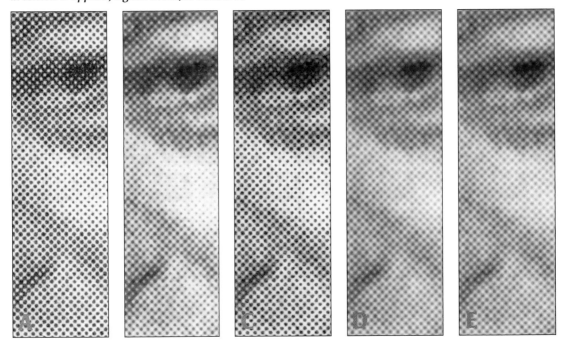

to handle these two hugely different phenomena in two different ways, rather than with a single cataclysm?

With these thoughts in mind, you may follow what happens in Figure 14.4.

• Take your properly sized and rotated grayscale scan and increase its contrast to your taste, ignoring the fact that this makes the dot pattern worse.

• Make two duplicates of the resulting image, which I will refer to as Copy A and Copy B.

• Going to Copy A, apply a Gaussian blur filter at Radius 1.0. This will fill up the white space, which we want. It will also badly damage the dots, which we don't. Not to worry.

• Back to the original. With Image: Apply Image, apply Copy A in Darker mode. This will not affect the dots, which will necessarily be lighter in Copy A than the original.

• Trash Copy A, and turn to Copy B. Apply a curve to bring up the highlight to a minimum of a 20 percent dot.

• With the newly darkened Copy B, apply Photoshop's Dust & Scratches filter, radius 1. This will diminish the dots but hold their shape more or less, except for the lightest dots, which will be history.

• Back to the original. Apply Copy B, this time in Lighter mode. The point of the earlier darkening of Copy B now becomes clear. The lightest fifth of the original will be unaffected by this move— Copy B is guaranteed darker. The big action will be in the midtone. Copy A will have brought up the background, and Copy B subdues the dot pattern without killing it altogether.

• If it seems appropriate, increase contrast again.

Figure 14.5 *Finding the screen angles can be tough, especially in a color image. Below, an enlarged scan of a printed image. Above, the original digital image with a perfect screen imposed. To find the cyan angle, for example, imagine an L-shape, and angle it until the lines of cyan dots follow it both up and down. Insets: the two cyan plates, showing how much detail is lost because of printing and rescanning.*

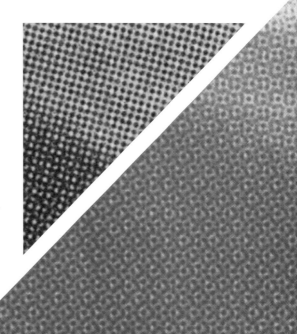

If you can proof the image before actually going to press with it, be conservative with the above recipe. It's a lot easier to reduce moiré on the second pass than to restore detail.

Figure 14.6 *Striped shirts are notorious for being subject to moiré, as in the original above. This is commonly—and wrongly—blamed on screening. As the enlarged sections of the cyan plate below show, moiré was already present, thanks to the scanner.*

The Good Old Days

If the 200-line screen, which we know to be ridiculous, is even close to being acceptable, that's a strong vote in favor of using 150 or even 175. This is a fairly risk-free technique with B/W originals, less so with color. Prescreened color originals are easier, in the sense that the dot pattern is not as pronounced, but they are also harder, in that we have to spend a lot of time worrying about the possibility of goofy colors creeping in.

The age of Photoshop has given us so many advantages over traditional methods that it is somewhat sobering to hear that the old way was better. Our forefathers would merely stick the prescreened original into a process camera and "fineline" it. The result would then be merged by hand into the final film for the job. In other words, they would let the original screen also be the final screen. We, having no choice in a PostScript world but to screen

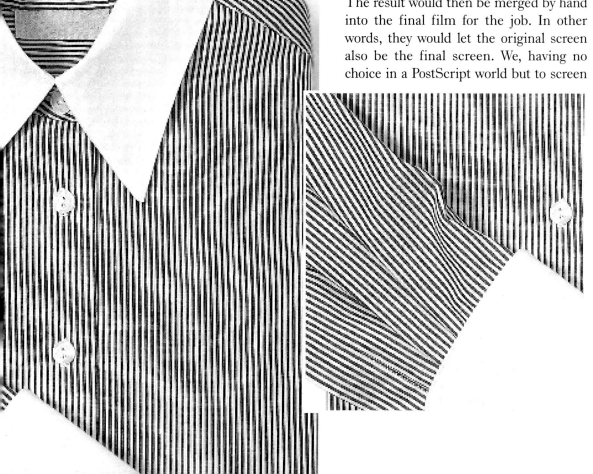

the original again when we place it in our pages, are not so lucky.

That camera method doesn't work if the original screen is drastically different from the final desired one, as in the Clinton image, which was originally 65 DPI yet needs to match the 133 of the rest of the book. In such a case, the traditional high-end method is to scan at an extremely high resolution, which we can do to some extent with our desktop scanners, and to scan just slightly out of focus, which we can't. We can never equal the quality of starting with a continuous-tone original, true. But *acceptable* quality? I think so. The Clinton series, remember, is done at same size from an original printed in a 65 DPI newspaper. That's about as bad as it gets. How unreasonable is the corrected version?

It would be nice never to have to work with prescreened art, but it sometimes can't be avoided. Original photographs get lost or damaged; historical photos are only available in printed form, and so forth. It would also be nice to have some of the high-end tools of the past to deal with them. But we can make do.

A Pattern of Deception

Moiré isn't limited to cases where an original is already screened. Whenever two or more patterns overlap, unusual things can but do not always occur, as in Figure 14.7. These sub-patterns are interesting, but they aren't exactly what we want to see on the printed page.

We who work with print are particularly vulnerable to this disagreeable interference patterning, because in reproducing artwork, we generally impose a pattern ourselves, in the form of rows of tiny, evenly spaced dots, otherwise known as a screen ruling. If there is also some kind of pattern in the original art, such as the striped shirt of Figure 14.6, ugly things can happen.

There is, however, a third potential contributor. As the enlarged sections of the cyan plate demonstrate, the moiré is already an integral part of the image, courtesy of the *scanner*. Even a stochastic screen, which has no pattern, would not help at this point.

The mathematics of moiré are moderately complex. But for our purposes, one grand oversimplification will do. Remember the lesson of the black and whites we just did. Assuming two straight-line

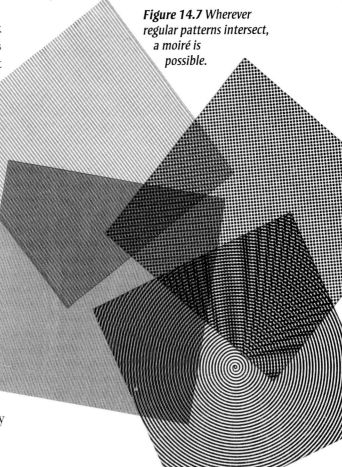

Figure 14.7 *Wherever regular patterns intersect, a moiré is possible.*

patterns, having them 30° or 60° apart from one another is best; the same angle, or 90° apart, is worst.

The vertical stripes of the shirt have an angle of 0°, disastrous because the scanner does its thing at an angle of 90°, leaving the deadly 90° difference.

If you don't believe that this is the cause of the problem, have a look at the sleeve. I measure it at 126°, a very happy 36° away from the scanning angle, and, by gosh, there isn't a moiré!

The moral is that striped shirts only produce moirés when the scanner operator falls asleep. Here, all that had to be done to avoid moiré was to rotate the original by 30° prior to scanning it, intending to reverse the rotation in Photoshop later. By using that angle, the stripes would have been at –60° with respect to the scan and the sleeve at 66°, both of which are nearly optimal.

Color images are a little easier to descreen than black and whites, and also a little harder. Easier, because moirés will ordinarily not be in all plates. Harder, because if one or more plates has a serious moiré, image quality will suffer even if we

Figure 14.8 Top left, an original digital file as printed in a magazine. Bottom left, a scan of the actual printed result done as though it were an ordinary piece of reflective art. Bottom right, a different scan of the printed piece using an automated descreening package. Top right, a reproduction of the printed piece using the methods advocated in this chapter.

can't easily see the moiré in the image as a whole.

And the same, because they are still subject to the 30-degrees-is-best rule; because the idea is to subdue the dots without wiping them out entirely; and because with reasonable care one can get much better results than by using some sort of automated descreening program.

To illustrate, in Figure 14.8 I'll work with an image I used in a magazine article. Naturally, I have the original file, which is shown for reference. Every version with a B in the upper right is actually a scan from the printed magazine.

The image of the shirt had a subject moiré—there was a pattern in the shirt proper, having nothing to do with the printing process. In principle, there is no such pattern in the woman's face, but the fact that it has been previously screened introduces not one, but four patterns, one for each CMYK ink. We need to compensate for that during reprinting, but especially during scanning.

The Unimportance of Yellow

Figure 14.9 has a moiré, but it isn't a prescreened original: it's the same file as the original in Figure 14.8, but with something strange going on with the screens. I have swapped the magenta and yellow angles. The purpose of this is not to prove that random screen angles don't work as much as that we shouldn't get terribly agitated over the fate of the yellow plate.

A reminder: only three inks can have angles 30° apart. Naturally, we let those three be our darkest inks, cyan, magenta, and black. The yellow is a singleton; conventionally it is sandwiched between the magenta and the cyan, 15° away from either

and 45° away from the black, but in reality the yellow angle is irrelevant.

If you don't believe this, have a closer look at the misangled version. Can you explain why there is moiré in the background and the hair, but not so much in the face?

This magenta plate isn't 30° away from anything. But the angle is only relevant if there's something to conflict with it. Cyan and black are doing a good job of that in the background. But the face is almost entirely magenta *and yellow,* and yellow isn't strong enough to create a moiré.

Given the normal angles of 15° for the cyan plate, 45° for the black, 75° for the magenta, and 0° for the yellow, if we mount a prescreened original in a scanner at the usual angle, 90°, *none* of the screens will be 30 degrees away from it. We therefore should mount at an angle, but what that angle should be is open for discussion. For the same reason that only three printing inks can be 30° apart from one another, only two can be 30° away from the scanning angle. Which leaves us with some choices to make.

Figure 14.9 the original file printed with magenta and yellow screen angles reversed (note the color variation from the original, although the files are identical!)

The best scanning angle for prescreened color is usually 45°, which is 30° away from both magenta and cyan. Black and yellow will unfortunately thus be at relatively bad scanning angles.

The importance of these choices is demonstrated starkly in Figure 14.10. This scan was made at a 45° angle and then rotated back to vertical in Photoshop. Shown, greatly enlarged, are the resulting RGB channels.

The red and green channels are shaped by the cyan and magenta components, respectively, of the original. Do you see the characteristic 15° angle of the dots in the red, and the 75° angle in the green?

The dot structure, however, is crisp and well defined. Compare that to the blue channel, which is based on the yellow component of the original. Moiré has struck! As, indeed, mathematics suggests. The yellow screen angle is zero; rotating the scan as I did places it at 45° relative to the scanner, which is not good.

This plate will hurt quality, but we'd much rather have a good cyan and magenta than a good yellow. We can recover from a bad yellow, as I'm about to demonstrate. If we don't take care in choosing the scan angle, though, we'll have *every* channel looking like the blue one does in Figure 14.10, and that will be a mess.

Resolution, and Other Resolutions

With that mathematical introduction out of the way, let's first resolve not to accept the atrocities shown in Figure 14.8 of either a normal scan or an automated descreen. Both have too many problems to repair. The first has an incipient moiré nearly everywhere; the sledgehammer applied to the second has blown away detail.

Let us further resolve that this is not to be an all-day affair. With unlimited time, one can reconstruct almost anything.

Finally, let us remember that the dots that make up this image may not be much, but they're all we have as far as detail goes, and we can't afford to damage them. That means, no festivals of resampling, blurring and resharpening, no added noise, and no other sledgehammers. Instead, let's:

• **Scan at maximum resolution, and at the proper angle.** The high resolution softens the image. Of course, you should also downsample it to the desired resolution before printing; see Chapter 12 for guidelines. The proper angle keeps the moiré manageable. For monochrome images, the proper scan angle is 15 or –15°; for color, 45° is usually best, sacrificing a little in the black channel in the interest of better cyan and magenta. In certain darker images, –15°, which sacrifices magenta, or 15°, which sacrifices cyan, may work better. Figure 14.11 puts the choices in graphic form.

• **Convert the image to LAB, and blur the A and B channels.** This is a critical step. LAB separates color from contrast, and the A and B define color only. Blurring the A and B eliminates the big color transitions that dots of colored ink cause, without damaging detail in the image. Note how much better the blue channel above is once this blurring is done and the image is reconverted to RGB.

Choose a Gaussian blur value that will eliminate the dot pattern in the channel, which you should be able to see easily. The amount of blur will usually be more in the B channel than the A. Here, I used a Radius of 1.4 in the A and 2.0 in the B. Because of

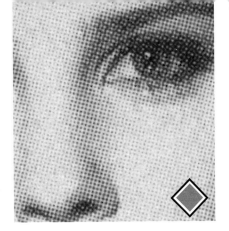
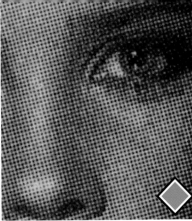

the need to use two different Radii, doing this in RGB or CMYK and fading back to Color mode isn't an adequate substitute.

• **Create a black plate immediately.** Make a copy of the LAB document as is, and convert it to CMYK. You may discard the CMY channels if you like; this version of the document is useful only for its black. The idea is to preserve all the detail possible in the black—the next step will suppress some of the dot pattern in the other plates, but the black is the backbone of the printed image, and we want it to be as close to the original in detail as possible.

• **Reduce the dot pattern in the L channel.** Returning to the original LAB document, open the L channel and descreen it as though it were a black and white image, using the same recipe described in our discussion of the Clinton image of Figure 14.3.

Figure 14.10 The angle of scanning is critical in dealing with prescreened color originals. A 45° angle is optimal in most cases, and will give the best possible capture of the cyan and magenta dots. Above, greatly enlarged, are the red and green of a 45° scan. Note the excellent dot structure in the red, which is based on cyan, and in the green, which is based on magenta. Below left, however, the blue channel has a bad moiré. This happened because the blue is based on yellow, and 45° is a poor angle for yellow. Had this image not been scanned at an angle, in all probability the red and green channels would look like this as well. Below right, the same blue channel after the document had been temporarily converted into LAB and the A and B channels blurred.

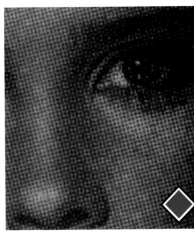

• **Correct color and convert.** How you go about this is up to you, but if you are able to set range using the L channel of LAB, that's the best way for a prescreened original. All the rescreened versions in Figure 14.8 suffer to some extent from color hot spots, which an L correction wouldn't exaggerate.

• **Replace the black plate.** Since some degradation will have taken place in the last two steps, replace the new black plate with the black plate that was generated earlier.

• **Ask yourself, where is detail unnecessary?** In more places than you might think. In the current picture, we'd like to hold detail in the hair, the eyes, the eyebrows and eyelids, the lips, the earrings, and the garment. But that only amounts to a small fraction of the image's

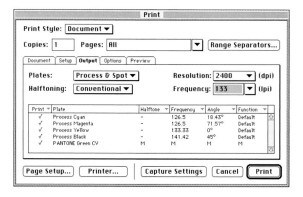

Figure 14.11 The graphic below shows the conventional 4/c screen angles, and offers some suggested scanning angles. Not every image-setter, however, uses precisely these angles. In any application that is capable of loading Post-Script Printer Descriptions (PPDs), we can read what a specific imagesetter will do. Above, a menu from QuarkXPress 4, which, unlike past versions, allows default screens to be overridden.

geography. If the skin and background, which cover a much larger area, somehow got smoother, that would be just fine.

Accordingly, if you are comfortable with the use of masks, make a copy of the picture and blur it. Then, merge the two versions together, masking out the portions of the original that have critical detail. If you are uncomfortable with this method, an alternative is to use the blur tool to soften up the face.

The best technique of all, in my opinion, is to place the original as a layer on top of a blurred version. Then, by Layer: Add Layer Mask>Reveal All, establish a mask on which you can, in effect, airbrush in detail from the bottom version. We'll talk more about this technique in Chapter 16.

In the corrected version in Figure 14.8, you can, if you look carefully, detect graininess in the hair, which needs detail. The woman's face, which does not, is smooth.

•**Consider manipulating the screen angles.** In a black and white image, as we've seen, the original screen is almost sure to be 45°. It's virtually automatic, therefore, to change the output screen to 15° or 75°, assuring there will be the magic 30° difference.

The argument also applies (albeit less strongly) to color work. In finely detailed or color-neutral images, it pays to make, for example, the cyan output angle something other than the angle of the cyan in the original. In a case like the image of the woman, which is not very subject to moiré in the first place, I wouldn't recommend it.

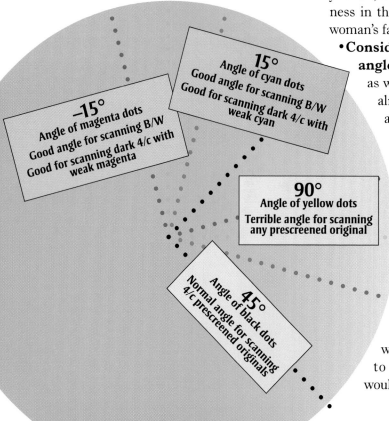

MATHEMATICS, MOIRE, AND THE ARTIST

✓Whenever two regular grids are imposed on one another, some type of interference pattern will result. This interference is somewhat unpredictable. It may be unnoticeable, or it may cause an obvious moiré.

✓When we print anything that contains tone, we impose a pattern, or screen ruling. If we scan a printed piece and try to reprint it, we impose a second pattern on top of the one that is already in the image, and moiré is the likely result.

✓Patterns are much less noticeable when they are offset from one another by 30°. This rule applies just as much to the pattern of a striped shirt as it does to a row of dots.

✓Reprinting a prescreened black and white, without intervening, will cause moiré, because there will be two sets of screens, each with an angle of 45°, which is the conventional black angle.

✓Photoshop, QuarkXPress 4, and PageMaker allow us to override normal screen angles. In the case of a prescreened black and white, we would substitute a new output screen angle of 15° (or 75°), to stay 30° away from the screen that is part of the original art.

✓The cyan, magenta, and black inks are customarily printed with screen angles 30° apart from one another. There is no room for a fourth such offset, but this doesn't matter, as the yellow is too light to create any moiré.

✓The 30-degree rule also applies to scanning. The original should be mounted 30° away from the screen angle of the most prominent ink(s). A prescreened or patterned original should never be mounted perpendicular to the scanner, as other art would be. After the scan, rotate the file back to vertical in Photoshop.

✓In correcting a prescreened file, the goal is to tone down the dot pattern, not eliminate it. The dots are what define all detail. If you can no longer see the dots, the image is too soft. For best results, consider the file as two separate images: one containing the dots, and one the white spaces between them.

✓Don't apply overall unsharp masking to a prescreened file. If the file needs it, you have probably blurred the image too much in a needless effort to kill the dots. Use the sharpening tool if needed on critical areas such as eyes.

A Self-Fulfilling Prophecy

My statement that the correct angles are 15°, 30°, 75° and 90° isn't quite accurate nowadays. Each imagesetter has different characteristics, and manufacturers recommend slight differences not just in angle, but in screen frequency as well.

The imagesetter that set the original of Figure 14.8, for example, runs its cyan at an angle of 18.43°, not 15°, and at a frequency of 126.5 lines per inch, not the 133 the magazine advertises. The black is at the normal 45°, but at a frequency of 141.42 DPI. If you feel the need to swap angles, I suggest you just swap the magenta and cyan, which will be simple and effective. If you are ambitious, there will be cases where a more aggressive approach will work.

It is true that, in a perfect world, we would never have to work with a pre-screened original, any more than we would have to repurpose an indexed-color image from the Web for press, any more than we'd have to restore a 19th-century photograph,

or take a 2-megabyte file up to poster size. But today we get asked to do this kind of thing more than ever before.

It would be nice never to have to work with prescreened art, but it sometimes can't be avoided. Original photographs get lost or damaged; historical photos are only available in printed form, and so forth. It would also be nice to have some of the high-end tools of the past to deal with them. But we can make do.

A number of practitioners assure us that it is impossible to get adequate results from such originals. They they proceed to make this a self-fulfilling prophecy by first scanning at the wrong angle, followed by an obliteration of the dots, possibly with some unsharp masking thrown in, and finally outputting the whole mess at the wrong screen angle.

Those dots are your friend. They become your enemy only if you allow them to moiré. Remember the magic words—thirty degrees—and they won't.

Multitones and Extra Plates: The Fifth Color Follies

CMYK is normally enough, but additional inks represent an opportunity—an opportunity either for better color, or big headaches. Here's how to construct duotones, with extra inks or by simulation, and how to make sure they'll print properly.

O ne of the most striking graphic arts advertising campaigns in recent memory likened most scanners to a box containing four crayons. The advertiser's scanner, meanwhile, was represented as a box filled to overflowing with crayons. Doubtless the success of this campaign demonstrates that we computer artists are children at heart. Give us enough crayons, and we'll be happy for months.

Children with too many crayons can yield to temptation. It works that way with adults, too, even when there is only one extra crayon to play with rather than a boxful. That is the case we will now explore: the promise and the perils of preparing a job when an extra ink is available on press.

Sometimes this extra ink is a color we pick ourselves. More commonly, it's one our clients pick for us, because it's the color of their logo or some such thing. Either way, there's an extra crayon available, and it can usually be exploited, even if it's not the particular crayon we would have picked ourselves.

Most of the time, this extra ink is a fifth color; sometimes it is a second color; occasionally a sixth color; on extraordinary occasions, a seventh or greater. For now, please imagine a hypothetical world in which the extra ink is a *fourth* color.

We are so accustomed to thinking of printing in CMYK that we attribute mystical powers to these inks. And indeed, cyan, magenta, and yellow do have a spark of the divine in them, for they are the direct opponents of the three colors of light upon which all human color perception is based, namely, red, green, and blue. This is a long way of saying that when attempting to print in full color with only three inks, the only rational possibility is with CMY.

As you can see from Figure 15.1, printing with CMY only is highly feasible. It has in fact been done that way in many settings for many years. If you would like to do so, before bringing an RGB or LAB file into CMYK, open CMYK Setup, and choose None under Black Generation.

If we are given an fourth ink to play with we can do better, but there is no particular reason for that extra crayon to be a black one—in fact, black is not the fourth color we'd have in the best of all possible prepress worlds.

The bride's gown is pretty good in CMY, but the dresses of the women on either side of her exhibit the two major problems that afflict CMY-only printing. First, the darkest areas of the image lack bite. The black dress is brownish. And the lack of a dark ink to use as a backbone causes the whole image to lack snap.

Second, we can't get very good deep blues in CMY. The blue dress here seems pallid in comparison to the red flowers.

A moment's thought about this makes it fairly obvious that the ideal fourth ink would be deep blue, which would solve both problems at once, unlike black, which handles the first but not the second.

And yet, we all use black. A further moment's thought explains why. We use black because that is what's given to us. Most jobs involve type as well as images, and type ordinarily prints in black, not deep blue. The printer therefore tells us, black is there, take it or leave it.

If there is going to be a *fifth* color, the ideal one is no longer deep blue, because black has fixed up our problem of light reddish shadows. Probably the best choice is some kind of lighter blue or cyan—but beggars can't be choosers.

Printers and Pricing

Getting an additional color to play with can be cheaper than you think. Many printers will negotiate with you. To understand why, let's take a look at their economics.

To even be capable of more than four colors, the printer has to lay out considerable bucks. A press with five printing units doesn't cost 25 percent more than one with only four, but it's pretty close, and four-color conventional presses start at around half a million dollars—and that's for the teeny-weeny ones.

There are philosophical differences in pricing. Some printers want anybody who uses that fifth unit to pay a share of that big capital investment. Others take a more liberal view: they regard the additional units as a promotional expense, a means of differentiating themselves from the competition. They are very happy when we use five colors because they think it makes it less likely we will take our next job to some service bureau or quick printer. So they give us a break. Similarly, many printers buy those extra units because they have particular large clients who want that capability. If so, the printer may regard any additional five-color printing as so much gravy.

Certain fifth-color expenses will always be around. There definitely needs to be a fifth set of plates, for one thing. But some savings are possible.

The Pantone Matching System that almost all printers use is a recipe method. If we specify PMS 230 or whatever, the printer doesn't just have this on his shelf, nor does he order it specially from Pantone. Instead, he consults his recipe book, which tells him how to whip up this color using some combination of the 14 primary Pantone inks that he does have on his shelf: so much Rhodamine Red, so much White.

Naturally, he has to pay somebody to sit there and do the mixing. He will also have to mix up more ink than will actually be used, and the remainder will be thrown away. Neither of these expenses will be necessary if we specify one of the basic Pantone inks, like Rubine Red, Reflex Blue, or other equally useful ones.

Furthermore, some unfortunate press-man is going to have to wash down the fifth unit, getting rid of the residue of whatever ink was in there last. This is no high-tech operation; he uses a hose. After that, he scrubs down the unit with a towel. When our pressrun is finished, he or some other unfortunate will repeat the washup proce-dure. All this takes a while, and during this time, the unit cannot be used for anything else, such as printing five-color jobs for other clients.

Reasonably enough, printers expect us to pay for this down time—unless there isn't any. There won't be, if we can piggy-back our job on top of another that uses the same fifth color. Opportunities to do that are more common than you think. There is no law against asking your printer if you can get a price break by sharing a color that somebody else is already paying for.

The Greater Gamut

The argument for using extra inks is that more intense colors are possible than with CMYK only—in most cases.

CMYK, as previously noted, has a problem with blues, due to the decrepitude of cyan ink. Also with greens. Reds and yellows aren't so bad. Fire-engine red can be portrayed in CMYK just about as well as with a custom-mixed red ink.

Figure 15.1 To understand what a fifth color adds, consider what a fourth color adds. Above, a separation optimized for printing with cyan, magenta, and yellow only. When the image is reseparated allowing for the use of black ink, below, the results are better.

If CMYK is so good with red, you might think it would also do well with pink, which is a close relative, a tint of red, if you will. But it does rather poorly. It makes the pink with a dot pattern of magenta and yellow inks. A lot of white paper shows through. To get a truly shocking pink, we are better off mixing up a special ink. The same goes for virtually any other pastel color.

The screen pattern is also a strong argument for a custom ink for type, especially small serifed type. Small type that prints, say, $20^M 65^C 100^Y$ is going to look very, very fuzzy next to the same type printed in one hit of green ink.

These factors explain why custom inks are so common in consumer packaging work. In commercial printing, using more than six colors is rare. In packaging work, 12- or even 15-color printing isn't unusual.

Fifth colors are often used to solve real-life press problems as well. Or, to be more precise, real-life design problems.

A common design error is to try to have a black, rather than a white, page behind photographs. That is, the design calls for solid black ink (and possibly traces of other inks as well) everywhere that there is no type or picture.

Why is this an error? Because as a practical matter, such a design can't be controlled on press. The designer surely wants the background black to be rich and dark. The black ink pouring rapidly into the background to accomplish this comes out of the same ink unit that has to print the black component of the images. It is simply not possible with present press technology to prevent this black from coming down too heavily, and the pictures will look muddy, as (I assume) happened back in Figure 2.2.

Yet pictures knocking out of a black background can be so striking that you or your clients may not wish to give up on the idea so easily. A partial solution, if you can figure out how to do it, is to create a CMY-only separation like that in Figure 15.1 and add only the merest wisp of black to the shadows. But a much more elegant and effective way involves a fifth color—which, as it happens, is also the fourth color. We will print in CMYKK, with black ink in two units. The second unit will be used for the background only. Not only does this eliminate the problem of contamination of the images, it permits a beautiful, rich black background, because in addition to full coverage from the extra black unit, we can afford to add 30% or 40% more coverage from the first black unit. With two hits of black ink the results can be very dramatic.

The most seductive, tantalizing, and—you guessed it—most difficult use of additional colors is to beef up the quality of standard color separations with them. The concept can be illustrated even in black and white.

You will, I trust, agree that the bottom version of the image in Figure 15.2 is the better of the two—but why?

Assume, please, that this is a two-color job. We have black, of course, and we have purple, because that is our client's corporate logo color. The client has no interest in making the photographs have a purple cast. Does that eliminate the possibility of using purple in the photographs?

Clearly not. It can be used for the highly desirable purpose of adding shadow depth and definition. I've simulated the purple here with process colors, but the way this would be done is as follows:

- Create a blank CMYK file that is exactly the same size as the finished B/W file.
- Copy the B/W file and paste it into the black channel of the CMYK document. Also, paste it into the cyan channel, leaving the magenta and yellow blank.
- Apply the curve shown to the false cyan channel. This wipes out anything in that channel that was going to print at less than a 60% dot. It also exaggerates contrast in everything darker than that.
- Save and output the image. Inform the printer that the plate that comes out labeled "cyan" is actually purple.

Pretty easy, no? If you are printing in two colors, that's the way you should handle all your B/W images, in my opinion, regardless of what the second color is. Note how similar the effect of added depth is to what happened to the image in Figure 15.1 when we added black.

Practicing Safe Hex

Adding additional inks to a standard separation is an idea whose time has come. Its merits are undeniable, but the tools are primitive, and four big problems are waiting to bite us, namely:

- **Screen angling and frequency**. As we saw in Chapter 14, it's been tough enough for the industry to figure out how

Figure 15.2 When an additional ink is available, images can be subtly improved. Do you agree that the bottom image is superior? It's the doing of a second color, based on the black but with the inset curve applied, restricting the effect of the second ink to deepening the dark areas of the image.

Input: 60 %
Output: 0 %

to print with *four* inks without getting an offensive moiré. A fifth color is a further complication.

• **Figuring out how to output the dang thing**. This has gotten a lot better with Photoshop 5, but still, none of the major desktop packages were designed by people who had any clue that foolhardy folk like ourselves would be thinking of making 5/c seps.

• **Proofing limitations**. There isn't any method of making a proof, in most cases. Even if there were, given printers' lack of experience with this, how reliable would it be? What happens on press may come as a surprise—a nice one, we hope.

• **Great expectations**. Adding a fifth ink potentially gives a better-looking product, and sometimes a much better-looking one. If you try to force *potentially* and *sometimes* to become *always*, your fifth color will probably drive you to a fifth of something else, and your printed piece will look worse than if you had forgotten all this lunacy and stuck to CMYK.

The first commercial attempt at such "hi-fi" printing that I know of featured red, green, and blue inks in addition to CMYK. Why the proponents thought seven-color printing had the slightest future in an industry where there are few 7/c presses, I cannot imagine.

Six-color, that's another story. There are plenty of six-color presses around, so a 6/c scheme, of which Pantone's Hexachrome is by far the most prominent example, can be taken seriously.

There's no right answer to what the additional colors should be. If I were designing a 6/c system, I'd add a light blue and a light red to CMYK. That would cure the problem of not just blues but also pastels: an extra hit of light blue ink would make the dresses of both women on the left in Figure 15.1 more vivid.

Instead, Pantone has added orange and green, and slightly reformulated the CMY inks. They don't do quite as good a job with pastels as my suggested inks do, but they allow really brilliant colors, brighter sometimes than our monitors can display. (To get an idea of Pantone's claims as to how big the Hexachrome gamut is, turn back to Figure 8.2.)

Orange and green have another advantage: they eliminate problem 1, the angling issue, for reasons I will get to shortly. Pantone has rightly attacked problems 2 and 3 head-on. It is vigorously lobbying software vendors to include Hexachrome capabilities, and offers a plug-in for Photoshop that will automatically generate Hex seps from an RGB file.

Similarly, many contract-proof vendors are now able to make Hex proofs. How accurate they will be remains to be seen, but this is a big plus for the process.

Problem 4 for the moment has the upper hand over Pantone and its adherents. Adding orange and green to CMYK does not compare in importance to adding black to CMY. And, as we have seen, that addition of black, while very desirable, will not make us or our clients turn handsprings with amazement at the magnitude of the improvement.

Nevertheless, here's what a top Pantone official says: "This raises the bar for printers everywhere. The broad applicability of Hexachrome…will create an environment where four-color will always look like a poor relation in contrast. In a side by side comparison, Hexachrome will always look superior."

Not in a lot of the samples I've seen, it doesn't. In one magazine comparison, Hex looked worse.

That is the fault of the users, not Hex itself. If you start with the assumption that any Hex rendition must look vastly better than CMYK, and attempt to force it to happen, the devil will smile. With a picture of an orange, Hex can leave CMYK looking totally tepid. With a picture of a salad, if you try to flex your Hex, you'll buy yourself the radioactive greenery that has been a common problem in Hex promotional materials.

But, properly handled, it can work. Now. Will it catch on? I doubt it, at least not in a big way. Printers didn't buy those very expensive fifth and sixth units to sit idle in the hope that Hexachrome would one day come along. No, customers were paying good money to put other inks in those units. Not just inks: many jobs are varnished, and varnish uses a unit and counts as an ink. A 6/c press can't run Hex and varnish at the same time. Or even, heaven help us, Hex plus Scratch 'n' Sniff.

There should, in fairness, be less call for custom inks when printing Hex, because

Specifying the Color We Want: The Pantone Matching System

If we are lucky enough to be able to afford printing with additional inks, we need a way to be able to communicate exactly what we want the additional color to be. "Light green with a pinch of an aqua feeling, not too cheesy," may sound precise to you, but to a printer, it's, well, kind of gray.

The standard way of coping with this confusion is the Pantone Matching System, a numbered grouping, with accompanying sample swatches (below right) of around a thousand colors. Several of them might answer the description of our aqua-ish green. All we need do is look at our swatch book, call up the printer, say "PMS 3258" or whatever, and hang up the phone. Although the printer won't have such a weird color on the pressroom shelf, Pantone issues instructions on how to mix it from combinations of 14 primary Pantone inks. It's simple and effective for printer and client.

One common source of misunderstanding arises when one specifies a PMS color and then attempts to emulate it with CMYK inks, rather than having the printer mix a separate ink for use as a fifth printing color. Photoshop, like most other desktop publishing applications, lets us do this. We can select PMS 3258 directly from the color picker. If we place that color anywhere in a CMYK file, Photoshop will insert the values that Pantone says will give the closest match—in this case 60^C34^Y.

The problem arises if you have seen true PMS 3258 somewhere and suppose that 60^C34^Y is exactly the same color. It's not. The real thing is more intense, since it's a solid color, not two screened applications of pale inks on white paper. Because cyan ink is so poor, matching most blue, green, or purple PMS inks with CMYK is impossible. One can get something of the flavor of the color, nothing more. For the closest match, one must also consider dot gain (see page 132).

In the swatch book at right two versions of each color appear side by side. One shows the specially-mixed ink, one the closest CMYK equivalent. Be sure you know which one you're asking for.

Figure 15.3 *A common CMYK dilemma: the brilliant blue of the racecar above is a corporate color. If used in advertising, it is likely to be accompanied by type or logos printed in the same color, but with a custom-mixed ink that gives a far more intense blue, so much so that the client may object to the picture printing so tepidly. The solution is to add some of the blue ink into the CMYK image.*

the odds are much greater that Hex can match whatever color is wanted. Pantone suggests that we explain this to our clients. Good luck doing that, say I.

Beefing Up the Blue

Let us therefore proceed to the topic of how to improve the CMYK separation if a certain fifth color is available.

For this exercise, assume we are working with the image of a blue racecar shown in

Figure 15.4 *Establishing a spot color channel in Photoshop 5. This capability is absent from earlier versions.*

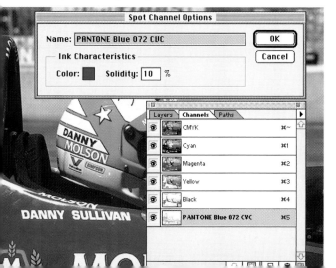

Figure 15.3. Take my word for it, in the original the blue is far more intense than portrayed here, to the annoyance of our client. (It's out of the Hexachrome gamut, too, for that matter.)

Fortunately, blue being the corporate color of this particular client, we have been authorized to use blue ink for various headlines, logos, and whatnot. We will clandestinely borrow some of this blue to help out our image.

This is not for those who spook easily. Anyone who tries this in real life is a desperado. You can stop reading now, if you like. But if you are truly obsessed with getting the best possible color, and are determined to ignore my warning, there is nothing for it but to attack the four major problems, starting with screen angles.

As discussed in Chapter 14, CMYK practitioners have found out the hard way that it pays to have the angles of the screens in cyan, magenta, and black plates offset 30° from one another. Contrary to what you read in many texts, the yellow screen angle doesn't matter: the ink is too weak to cause a moiré.

Blue, however, is a strong ink. There aren't any 30° slots left at which to angle the screen, so our choices are either to take a guess at an angle or let it share one with either magenta or cyan. Don't even think about black or yellow: black will give you the funkiest shadow you've ever seen, and yellow is at a moiré-causing angle. (In QuarkXPress, angles are set in the Edit: Edit Color dialog box; in PageMaker, it's done in File: Print>Print Color.)

Hexachrome doesn't have an angling problem because its two additional inks, orange and green, were cleverly chosen. Where there is orange ink it makes no sense to have significant amounts of cyan. Where there is lots of green ink there can't be much magenta. So green is set to the magenta angle and orange to the cyan.

But blue is not so easy. It is an opponent of yellow, not magenta or cyan. So there may be a conflict. There is a somewhat surprising way to avoid it.

When we save an image in EPS format, we can embed a ruling, as shown back in Figure 14.2. Usually, that is a terrible idea. Here, it works. Give the blue plate a 300-line screen, regardless of what screen you plan for the CMYK. Then flip a coin to decide whether to print this extremely fine screen at the magenta or the cyan angle.

It is correct that the printer won't be able to hold those minuscule blue dots on press. What a shame! No dots, no moiré. He also won't be able to hold detail in the blue plate, but that doesn't matter either: there isn't any. We are only using the blue to beef up color.

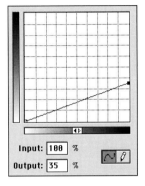

Figure 15.5 The steps in creating a fifth color plate for Figure 15.3. A: isolating the shadow areas of the image with curves. B: in a second document, using Select: Color Range to isolate the bluest areas. C: Combining A and B into a single channel, with Apply Image (Darker mode). D: C, after the application of the curve at right, which guarantees nothing higher than a 35% dot.

Problem 2, arranging for output, was a major headache until the advent of Photoshop 5, which is the first version to support fifth colors. Previously, we had to have a specialized plug-in if we did not wish to go through a lengthy kludge.

With Photoshop 5, however, we open the Channels palette, choose New Spot Channel, and define the color, as shown in Figure 15.4.

Problem 3, the lack of an adequate proof, is a poser. Some proofing systems allow us to mix up a fifth toner to simulate the ink on press, but this is risky. We may well be the very first people ever to try to make a proof with this particular blue. We won't know whether it accurately reflects how the blue ink interacts with the others.

Accordingly, we have to put our faith in the pressman to decide for us exactly how heavily to run the blue ink. If he decides to make some radical move, it had better not be to reduce the ink flow. That might wash out the blue type that the client is paying the big bucks for. If the pressman wants to step up the blue, on the other hand, it probably won't hurt the type. So we have to be conservative, and create a fifth plate that we suspect is too light.

Constructing the Extra Plate

For all the cautions and ifs and whereases that we have just gone through, making the actual fifth plate is fairly easy.

We could limit ourselves to beefing up the blue car only, but a true swashbuckler,

Figure 15.6 *In a conventional four-color image (left column) the individual channels don't have a common ancestor. In a multitone (right column) the channels are slightly different, but all are based on the same original image. This calls for extra care in generating the parent.*

realizing that blue is the second darkest of our five inks, will use it to strengthen the shadows as well. One easy way to do this is to make a copy of the CMYK image and convert it to grayscale. Then, apply a curve to it similar to that shown in Figure 15.5, resulting in the image of Figure 15.5A.

Next, we need to put some oomph into the blue areas. This is done with Photoshop's Select: Select Color Range command. With that dialog box open, we click into the area of the car that appears to us to match most closely the color of the blue ink. The Fuzziness setting will vary with the character of the image: here, I used 60.

Once this selection is made, Select: Save Selection, as a new grayscale document (Figure 15.5B).

Step 3 merely combines the two. Image: Apply Image either one on top of the other, using Darker, rather than Normal, mode (Figure 15.5C). Step 4 applies a curve to reduce the maximum dot value to 35%. If this sounds low, it isn't. Before we began, the blue in the car was at around $100^C 67^M 1^Y$. Adding 35 points of blue—a more powerful ink than either magenta or cyan—will have quite an impact.

We also have to be somewhat conservative, because we don't really know how well this blue ink will interact with the others. The CMYK inks are highly transparent, which is very desirable. If we print a magenta dot on top of a cyan one we want to see a combined color, not just magenta.

In defining the screen preview of the fifth color, Photoshop 5 uses the term *solidity*. A good ink would have a solidity of zero; something that wiped out everything underneath it, as many metallic inks do, would have a high solidity. In dealing with an unknown fifth ink, it seems pretty

dangerous to assume that it will be as transparent as it should be. I'd recommend putting in a value of 10% in this field.

Unlike Molson, the publisher of this book doesn't have the budget for five colors, so you'll just have to imagine the effect.

As long as we remember the final problem—that we should not expect monumental improvements—we won't have to imagine the improved quality in our printed images. It'll be there for all to see.

A final warning. This is highly bleeding-edge. Tell a printer that you plan to mix different screen rulings in the same image; that there is no proof; that you aren't too sure exactly what the final result will look like except that it will be better—tell a printer these things, and many a printer will make the sign of the cross and run away in panic.

Then again, some printers will cock their heads, look you carefully up and down, and say, by golly, that sounds like it has potential. Let's give it a try!

And that, why, that could be the start of a beautiful relationship.

How Strong a Duotone Effect?

The "duotone look" has become one of the most popular and powerful tools in creating effective advertising—and no wonder. Consider the advantages:

• A multitone combines the greater tonal range of a color picture with the drama of black and white.

• The choice of base hue for a multitone is able to set the mood for an overall design in a more powerful way than a full-color picture can.

• Multitones tend to look earthy, not brilliant. They are an excellent foil for full-color images: running color side-by-side with multitones will make the color images seem more vibrant.

- If a fifth ink happens to be available on press, the presence of a duotone using it will play off dramatically against any four-color images.

- Decidedly listless color originals can be made into very pleasing multitones.

Historically, multitones have been difficult and expensive—more expensive even than process color. Now, they are within everyone's reach.

What Is a Multitone?

The technical definition of a multitone is: any image where every color channel is based on the same (monochrome) information. The information can be lightened, darkened or otherwise modified in each channel, but it must derive from the same original. This can be seen in the right row of Figure 15.6. Although the cyan plate is lighter than the yellow, they are clearly related. In the full-color image at left, the cyan and yellow are different images.

Figure 15.7 Three styles of duotoning. Left, the old-fashioned way of a flat tint of color on top of a black base. Center, a default conversion to black and white and a default duotone curve applied to a color original. Right, a B/W conversion done using the methods of Chapter 13, followed by custom duotone curves.

A *true duotone* consists of two inks only. Although Photoshop permits construction of duotones using any two colors, in practice one of the colors is almost always black. The other color can be black as well. Black–black duotones, also known as *double-dot printing,* increase the dynamic range and detail in a black and white image. This method is popular in Europe, especially in art books.

In true duotones, the second ink is usually not cyan, magenta, or yellow, but a custom color that is selected specially or happens to be available on press because of the nature of the job, as in the hypothetical example of the purple logo.

To reiterate a point made earlier about fifth-color plates: if you are creating a true duotone, you have to keep the lessons of Chapter 14 in mind and step in to avoid moiré. By default in both QuarkXPress and PageMaker, an additional color is set at the black screen angle. Leave that alone, and your duotone will have both plates at the same angle and you will curse the day you ever had the idea of experimenting with fifth colors. Instead, set the fifth color either to the magenta or cyan angle, creating the 30° difference that kills moirés.

Far more common nowadays, however, is the *process duotone* — the use of CMYK inks to produce the look and feel of a true duotone, without the attendant angling and proofing problems. All of the examples in this chapter, naturally, are process duotones, since I don't have a fifth ink available. Some purists would say these are technically not duotones because they use more than two inks. When trying to simulate a green duotone, for example, we have to create what some would insist on calling a *tritone,* because it will use (at

least) cyan, yellow, and black. A sepia, or coffee-colored, look requires a *quadtone.*

Technically incorrect or not, for the sake of sanity I will henceforth refer to as a *duotone* any image that uses multiple plates but is based on a single ancestor.

Almost everyone uses one species of process duotone—the four-color black and white. Black-and-white images look richer and deeper when cyan, magenta and yellow are added in more or less equal quantities to the black, and this is standard professional practice when printing black and white and color pictures on the same form.

Where B/W and 4/c images are in close proximity, there is really no argument for doing things any other way. Newsmagazines, for example, have to use monochrome historical photographs right next to normal color images. If printed in black ink only, they would look not only colorless but lifeless. The color images would have richer blacks (since $80^C70^M70^Y0^K$ is darker

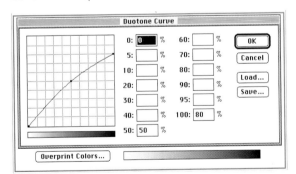

Figure 15.8 *Photoshop's multitoning dialog boxes. Once the base colors are chosen (right) preset curves can be loaded. Both the colors and the curves can be edited freely.*

than 90^K), and the screening pattern in the B/W would be more noticeable. An unwary reader might conclude from these factors that the magazine's production staff was incompetent, but a better adjective would be thoughtless.

Creating a four-color B/W image is as easy as changing from Mode: Grayscale to Mode: CMYK, but there is one small catch. Before doing it, we should go to Edit: Preferences > CMYK Setup and change the setting to Heavy GCR. The reasons for doing so are amplified in Chapter 7. Any time an image is predominantly composed of neutral grays (and this one will be *entirely* so composed) we are in danger of being torpedoed by careless presswork. The more black there is in our CMYK version, the less likely that an ink imbalance on press will cause a disastrous color cast.

In real life, of course, we do not apologize for or try to hide the use of duotones. In their classic form, we use the second ink

Specifying a Duotone: The Five Questions

1. What will the second color be?

2. Have you taken into account that the multitone will seem darker than a sample swatch of your second color?

3. Will this be a true duotone, with an additional spot color, or will it be simulated using CMYK inks?

4. Roughly how strong should the tinted effect be? In the four examples in Figure 15.9, we'd term the strength strong, moderate, light, slight.

5. Are you looking for a standard, high-contrast, reproduction, or does the design call for a softer, less-focused look?

not only for a deeper shadow, but for a better highlight as well. Purple is a dark ink, but it is lighter than black. A highlight of 0^{K}2^P is better than one of 2^{K}0^P. More range equals more contrast.

This method will, unlike my first example, give the image an overall purplish cast. We would have a purple picture with black used for depth only, more or less the same way it is in full color, not just a black and white with reinforced shadows. Clearly, one could split the difference between the two extremes in several ways. The decision would depend on how much of a purple feel we wanted.

Some writers, scientists, and other benighted individuals have actually suggested that the way to achieve the purple look is to plaster a flat tint of purple over a B/W picture. That obsolete approach dates from the days when decent duotones were difficult. Adding a tint of a second color gives the image a certain flavor, all right, but in the nostrils of the professional it also gives it a certain smell. Figure 15.7 shows the difference between such an effect and a properly constructed duotone.

As with any duotone, we are applying different curves in each channel to the same original monochrome image. Naturally, we continue to follow the rule that the steeper the curve, the more the contrast. As you might expect, the magenta and yellow use the same curve. The cyan curve has to be somewhat different, since neutral colors require more cyan than magenta and yellow. And the black curve is a law unto itself.

It is also perfectly workable to copy the original black and white into two or more plates of a blank CMYK file and then apply curves in the normal way. This is how I made the crude duotone of Figure 15.2.

Photoshop's Mode: Duotone controls are, however, one of the strongest points of the program, and the remainder of the examples in this chapter will use this method of applying curves.

Curves, Preset and Otherwise

Figure 15.8 shows Photoshop's duotone dialog box, which is accessed by changing Mode: Grayscale to Mode: Duotone. In Photoshop, one cannot convert a CMYK or RGB image directly into duotone; it must go to grayscale first. The basic two colors can be changed freely by clicking on the existing ones. They can be defined either as percentages of values from any colorspace or by their Pantone identification number.

Once we click OK, the monitor will show us what looks like a duotone. One would expect the new Photoshop document to have two channels, just as an RGB file has three channels and a CMYK file four. Frustratingly, it does not, which causes some handling problems.

Certain of these, such as producing a hybrid image duotoned in only a certain area, can only be resolved by converting the duotone file into CMYK. But if the duotone will eventually print in CMYK, we should convert the file as well, even though

Figure 15.9 Photoshop's preset duotone curves come in four levels of strength. The first always favors the colored ink more than the black; the second through fourth gradually reverse this. Below, the four default cyan duotone curves applied to the same B/W original.

page-layout programs can separate a Photoshop duotone file. Process duotones should be separated using Heavy GCR, and it won't happen unless we do it ourselves.

Each half of a Photoshop duotone is the original black and white image, modified by a curve. The curve is clearly necessary in at least the black plate, since if a significant amount of a second color were added to an unaltered black, the image would become too dark. If you have become proficient with curves, you will be able to come up with adequate duotone curves, although Photoshop's built-in ones are quite nice. What the second color is (assuming black is the first) makes a big difference. It also depends on what kind of look you are trying to achieve with the duotone, for there are many possibilities.

Assuming we are doing a duotone with black plus color X, it's a safe bet that we want the highlight to be 0^K2^X and the shadow to be 90^K90^X. Thereafter, complications set in. If X is something heavy like a purple or brown, its curve will probably have to dip in the middle. If X is light, like cyan or yellow, the curve may actually have to bulge to make the X plate heavier than the original B/W was. And if X falls somewhere in between, like red or blue, we may not need a curve at all.

If you'd like to use Adobe's preset curves and have installed Photoshop normally, they will be located in a subfolder called Goodies>Duotone Curves and can be loaded directly from the dialog box shown in Figure 15.8. In each of the colors that are included (and there are around 20), there are four variations. The first is the one that most emphasizes the second color. The fourth is mostly black with the second color added for depth in the shadows only, like

the duotone of Figure 15.2. The other two come down in the middle.

Figure 15.9 shows one image as treated by each of the four preset curves for a black-cyan duotone. Which look is best? It is purely an artistic call. One may be right for a certain project and not for another.

Aesthetically, though, there is no doubt that certain colors work better in duotones than others. Those who are successful in designing with duotones almost invariably stick with darker, subtler colors in combination with black.

As you can see, the duotones produced by Adobe's default curves are of quite respectable quality. And there is enough of a selection to let us find a curve for just about any of the infinite number of duotone colors we might be motivated to use. For example, in Figure 15.7 I used a CMYK simulation of PMS 485 as a second color because it happens to be included in the defaults. But the specific colors and curves are easily edited. The default red curve should not be used to define a cyan duotone, but it will work for just about any red. So, if we decide that the existing red is too bright and we want a dirtier-looking second color, we simply open the default duotone curve, click on the color box that specifies PMS 485, and change the value to $20^C80^M80^Y$ or whatever. Since the alteration takes seconds, we can try one color after another until we get the desired effect. Photoshop 5 introduces a big advance here: in previous versions, one couldn't preview the effect of the alteration without actually applying and cancelling the curves.

Excellent as these are, however, they are only defaults. Pictures with special characteristics need special handling. Normal rules of curvewriting have not been

Figure 15.10 Hundred-year old originals present a restoration challenge both in detail and color. To get back to the sepia look of the version at right, one has to use Photoshop's multitoning capabilities.

repealed just because we have entered a new colorspace. Whether the image is color, grayscale, or multitone, we build contrast in the same way. We find the values in the area we want to accentuate, and then arrange for the curves to be steeper there.

A Study in Sepia

The antique effect of a coffee-colored duotone is highly useful in a rapidly growing field of computer artistry: the restoration of old images.

The original of Figure 15.10 is more than a hundred years old. It's badly faded, and has damaged areas near the bottom.

Although this is a monochrome image, it pays to treat it as being in color, so that the tricks discussed in Chapter 13 can be brought to bear.

When a color image requires this much work, we ordinarily think of LAB. That makes no sense here, however. The L channel is nothing more than a grayscale rendition of the document; if we wanted that, we shouldn't have bothered to scan in color in the first place.

Instead, we should use RGB.

The normal reason CMYK is preferred over RGB, as fleshed out in Chapter 9, is that the channels are more subtle, easier to control. RGB would be better for really poor color originals, but one rarely so uses it, since LAB is better still.

In the current competition, however, LAB is disqualified. Given the two remaining choices, RGB is better. And since we aren't worried about color, we should, as a first step, set highlight and shadow in each channel just as though each were its own grayscale image.

Looking at the results in Figure 15.11, it's pretty clear why we scanned in color. Each channel now has different strengths and weaknesses. The green is the best overall. The blue has the best face of the three but the worst dress. The red has the best dress but the worst face.

The two intolerable things are the damage at the bottom of the blue channel and the featureless face of the red. I chose to take care of both of these by creating a separate blending channel, based on the green. But in this channel, instead of having a normal highlight to shadow range, I set the endpoints to be 0 and 100. I then blended 50% of this into the blue channel, killing the damage.

Next, I applied a curve to the blending channel, dropping the midpoint. This intensified detail in the dress at the expense of the face. In spite of this, the face was still better than in the red channel, so I blended 50% into the red. And having done so, I applied unsharp masking to the red and green channels, omitting the noisier blue.

As part of the sharpening process, I also trotted out the sharpening tool, running it across the eyes, the folds of the kerchief, the wrinkles in the face, and the brooch. And, because it is very easy to make a rough selection of the background, I did so, and ran the Dust & Scratches filter, to eliminate some of the more obvious noise.

The revised blending channel is shown in Figure 15.12, along with the document at this point. This burgundy dress looks strange, but who cares? It's about to go into grayscale, so the fact that the color was wrong will remain our secret.

So, Mode: Grayscale, followed by Mode: Duotone. For a default setting, I chose, under Pantone Duotones in the Photoshop Goodies folder, the first brown duotone.

Figure 15.11 *The red, green, and blue channels of the original of Figure 15.10, after setting a proper range in each, as though each were a grayscale image.*

DUOTONE AND OTHER EXTRA-INK PROBLEMS

✓One needs to be conservative in adding fifth colors to CMYK files, because there are usually not good methods of proofing, printers have little experience doing this, and the extra ink may not be as transparent as we are accustomed to.

✓Before using a fifth color in a halftone image, the screen angling issue must be addressed. By default, fifth colors use the black angle, which is usually wrong.

✓Even if there is only one other color available, and even if you do not want anyone to know you are making a duotone, you can use the second color to deepen shadows undetectably, making for a superior B/W.

✓True duotones use only two inks, one of which is almost always black and the other usually a special color. This look can be duplicated, however, by breaking the color components into CMYK.

✓The key to getting a good duotone is a good, high-contrast B/W image. If you are planning to make a *color* picture into a duotone, be sure you grasp the concepts of color-to-B/W conversion explored in Chapter 13.

✓Photoshop provides an excellent array of editable preset duotone curves. There are four curves for each color, each of which emphasizes black more than the last. The colors can be changed easily, and so can the curves.

✓True duotones using a nonprocess color are easily manufactured in Photoshop, but a lot can go wrong afterwards. There is no good way to proof them, for example. Also, screen angling problems are common.

✓As a general rule, brilliant colors are not good choices for duotone work. They can never print at their full intensity, since the darker they get, the more black appears. Earthtones and other subdued colors work better.

✓In Photoshop, a duotone is a single channel, which is not what one would expect. Certain manipulations, such as a retouch of one duotone plate but not the other, can only take place if the duotone is brought into CMYK.

✓In a process duotone or 4-color B/W image, press problems will be minimized by running a heavier black than normal. Before separating into CMYK, therefore, change Photoshop's CMYK Setup to Heavy GCR.

Figure 15.12 Left, a special channel used for blending into the red and blue channels. Right, the document just before conversion into grayscale.

This creates a second color channel based on PMS 478, or, to use its CMYK equivalent, $69^C 87^M 100^Y$. To me, this brown was too deep, so I changed the color definition to PMS 130, $0^C 27^M 100^Y$. And because I felt the image needed slightly more weight, I changed the curve for this color from one with a slight midtone dip to a straight line at a 45° angle.

This done, I changed CMYK Setup to Heavy GCR, and converted the duotone to CMYK, to get the final product on the right side of Figure 15.10.

As this image suggests, fashions change. So do possibilities: this kind of work was inconceivably difficult before the age of electronic imaging, but there is demand for it. So, in the last chapter of this book, we'll do a few more of these oldies.

Before entering that final round, a reminder: once again, the techniques we used are all closely related. Assuming a color original, you cannot produce a decent duotone without knowing how to get the most out of a black and white conversion. You can't do *that* without a good grasp of standard professional color correction. And you can't do professional-level correction without curves, blending, and sharpening—which will never go out of style.

There Are No Bad Originals

Restoring old photos is a challenge, but the techniques are often the same ones we'd use on contemporary images. Geriatric medicine is one of the growing areas of Photoshop practice. The elderly image may be damaged, it may have lost its color, but if you know your stuff, there's life in the patient yet.

udiophiles are still, a decade after the CD displaced vinyl, debating which gives the better sound. Digital sound is tinny, contrived, LP aficionados assert, while modernists say that analog recordings sound muddy, in addition to being prone to surface noise. The market has certainly chosen one method, but which should the real connoisseur prefer?

Having both a phonograph and a CD player, I'd personally be inclined to purchase the recording of the best performance, without regard to its medium or the politics of its backers. That, I think, is the best philosophy not just in the world of music, but in the digital vs. analog wars in our own industry.

There is also a fair amount of surface noise in the debates among photographers as to the merits of digital, filmless photography in comparison to the traditional chrome. Some manufacturers of digital cameras claim their products deliver quality superior to that of film; conventional photographers retort that digital shots look artificial and frequently suffer from color flare.

The debate will probably never end, as advantages and disadvantages continue to crop up unexpectedly. A few years back, digital was almost universally thought to be the way to archive images for the really long haul.

In the last chapter, we wrestled with a century-old image, upon which the ravages of age were quite evident. A digital image would have been better, right? They don't deteriorate over time, so all that retouching wouldn't have been necessary.

So, at any rate, argued many digital fanatics in the eighties, and as a result, much data was written to what was considered then to be the ultimate storage medium: a large platter with data permanently etched in. The technology rejoiced in the name of WORM, meaning Write Once, Read Many.

No doubt those WORMs from the eighties are indestructible. The only problem is, if you have one, where do you go to have it read? Probably, the same place that can read your eight-inch floppy disk, or that can play my grandfather's 78 rpm records.

Storage on CD presumably will meet the same fate. Nobody really knows how long the actual disk will last; Kodak once suggested 100 years, but this seems optimistic based on how many audio CDs have deteriorated in less than a fifth that time.

Even if the data is still viable, though, who will be able to *read* it in the year 2100, when floppies have 100 terabytes per sector? A century-old CD may be useful as a coaster for drinks, perhaps, but little else.

Accordingly, if you are hoping that your great-great grandchildren will be able to stumble on and appreciate your images a hundred years from now, use film. Unless, that is, you can rely on somebody to check the data every five years or so, and rewrite it to a more modern medium if necessary.

Knowing how to rejuvenate older images is a skill that won't lose importance in any of our lifetimes. Photo restoration is a growth area in digital imaging, and one that hasn't been written about elsewhere, as far as I know. It's an appropriate final topic for this book, because older originals can also serve as a model for handling many present-day problems.

Older originals are often absurdly flat, but many modern originals, like the bottom half of Figure 16.1, have this problem as well. Older originals often have areas of physical damage, but so do their modern counterparts. Older images are often very noisy when given a full range: almost as noisy, in fact, as the video grab that has to be upsized and printed on a full magazine page, or as the prescreened originals discussed in Chapter 14.

In short, the elderly photograph is just a variation on themes seen regularly in modern ones.

For Better or for Worse

Of the assertions I made in the first edition of this book, one of the most roundly criticized was a statement to the effect that the typical originals we work with would get worse. But scanners are getting *better,* I was assured. And people are getting more knowledgeable about Photoshop.

True enough—but four years later, we're working with worse originals nonetheless. It's become so cheap to work with color that many color projects are initiated on a shoestring budget. Professional photographers are busy, but a smaller *percentage* of the images we work with are in fact shot by professionals. Cheap stock photography is a wonderful innovation, but the technical quality of the images is, shall we say, somewhat variable. Sub-$1,000 digital cameras are improving rapidly, but are as yet well short of traditional quality standards. And then there are those prescreened originals, the images without enough resolution, and the digital restorations.

I've been teaching hands-on classes in color correction for several years. Four years ago, students would complain that the practice images were unreasonably bad, not representative of the challenges they would encounter in the real world. Nowadays, using the same images, I more frequently hear that they are unrealistically *good* in comparison to the ones the students make their money working on.

Until you've worked on really poor originals, you don't realize how much power Photoshop has. I'll plead guilty to this myself. The left half of Figure 16.1 appeared in the first edition of this book. The top version is a drum scan from a skilled operator; the bottom, a raw Kodak Photo CD scan.

Although this a professional photograph, it has a very limited tonal range, as do most other pictures of cloudy mountainsides. Such images are not the best advertisements for calibrationist systems like Photo CD, which makes no adjustment whatever for the character of the image.

For most images, I said then and still believe now, Photo CD scans can be made to match drum scans reasonably closely, provided that a Photoshop operator intervenes to do what the drum scanner operator does. For this one, however, I said that the drum scan advantage was so massive that the Photo CD version was unusable in professional contexts.

And indeed, that is what I thought at the time, because I was not only used to drum scans, but in being able to attempt to shove a can of anti-Newton spray down the throat of any operator who dared offer me a scan this bad. I looked at it, and decided it was uncorrectable, an excellent example of a self-fulfilling prophecy.

And yet, if I had tried it, instead of dismissing it out of hand, I might have gotten the result of the right-hand version. This time, since I couldn't find the original Photo CD, I started with the CMYK original at bottom left. Realizing its extreme lack of detail, I immediately converted it to LAB so as to be able to increase the steepness of the L curve in the area of the mountain. I also brought up colors by steepening the A and B curves in the manner discussed in Chapter 10. I kept both curves as straight lines, but I had to have the B cross the center line toward the blue side, because the clouds originally had a reading of 8^B or so, quite yellow.

This done, I made a copy of the image and converted the original to CMYK and the copy to RGB. I did not apply unsharp masking in LAB, as I would have done ordinarily, because there wasn't yet enough contrast in the trees to make it worthwhile.

Instead, I strengthened the magenta channel by blending in 75% of the green channel from the RGB copy, and the cyan by blending in 50% of the red.

As for the yellow, I blended 75% of the blue, not to add contrast (because yellow is such a weak ink, it doesn't contribute much detail) but because I felt that the greenery was unnaturally blue. Natural greens should have more yellow than cyan. In both the original Photo CD scan and the drum version, the inks are about equal: I downgrade the drum scan for that reason.

Next, I applied curves to the CMYK file to set highlight and shadow. The only thing out of the ordinary I did was to lower the

midpoint of the magenta curve to allow the greenery to become more saturated, without affecting the bridge, which is lighter in the magenta plate.

Finally, I sharpened the cyan, magenta, and black plates individually. The latter two got much more sharpening than the cyan, for the reasons stated in Chapter 6. As cyan is a dominant color in this image, it is home to more noise than the weaker magenta and black.

Ordinarily, of course, I'd have removed the dirt and hairs that afflict this image. I kept them in this case to demonstrate that it originates from the lower left version. Would you have known otherwise?

Birds of a Feather

Many older originals have colors that have faded badly, as in Figure 16.2, a color print from 1960. But as long as the detail has not deteriorated, the correction is easy, using LAB.

It's pretty clear we want to enhance contrast in the peacock, but also to brighten colors generally. There is also a bluish-pink cast, measurable in the foreground sand, which has a typical value of $70^L5^A–8^B$. It seems more likely to me that the sand should be yellow than blue.

The LAB correction curves, shown in Figure 16.3, are simple ones. The A and B are straight lines that cross the center

Figure 16.1 *The original for this picture was an immaculate, professionally shot chrome of this challenging subject. Above left, a professional drum scan. Below left, a raw Kodak Photo CD capture of the same film. A book about color correction asserted that the bottom image was hopeless and could not be brought to a point where it would compete with the drum scan. The image below is an attempt to prove that book wrong. Is it successful?*

vertical line above and below the center horizontal line, respectively. This brings the sand back to neutrality, while making the colors more vivid.

There are major advantages to using LAB, rather than Image: Adjust>Hue/Saturation, to bring up color in an image as lame as this one. Consider the green tailfeathers. If we were to try to saturate greens using the Hue/Saturation command, they would definitely become more brilliant, but they'd also move more toward a uniform color. A move in the B channel, on the other hand, emphasizes yellow and blue *even in areas where they are not the dominant color.* Here, the correction moves parts of the tailfeathers toward yellow and other parts toward cyan. With Hue/Saturation, we could move the feathers toward either neighboring color, but not both simultaneously.

Also, colors don't always deteriorate uniformly, as they seem to have in this image. Treating the A and B as four half-curves rather than two complete ones gives us the option to address red, green, yellow, and blue individually.

And LAB gives us the option of sharpening the L channel. While it's true that options exist for sharpening by luminosity in RGB and CMYK as well, only in LAB can we *see* the channel we're sharpening. In older images, that's usually critical. Such images are commonly full of noise. We lucked out this time: the tonality of this image isn't bad, so we can just sharpen the L, convert to CMYK, correct for highlight and shadow, and print.

Figure 16.2 *This forty-year-old print, top, has lost a good deal of color snap with age, but is easily resurrected by LAB moves, bottom.*

Whose Rays Are All Ablaze

Damaged color images are actually somewhat easier to fix than black and whites. With color, we can camouflage our retouching by working channel by channel. In black and white, we're naked. In color, we may be fortunate enough to find one channel that has detail, and build on that. With black and white, what you see is what you get.

The irritating technical challenges of the original of Figure 16.4 would be a pain in the glutei even if it were in color. We'd like to get out of this situation without doing heavy-duty retouching.

And yet this original, in addition to being solarized almost beyond recognition, is itself badly damaged. Virtually the entire lower left is a casualty. It will not be enough to just give this thing a full range. If we bring the lower left up to a reasonable darknesses the faces will die.

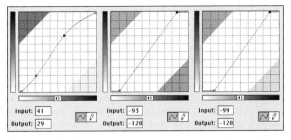

Figure 16.3 The LAB curves used to correct Figure 16.2.

Now is the time for a huddle to decide strategy. This image gives us the least to work with of any in the book, so we have to make the most of what there is.

Many of the considerations that applied to the aged original at the end of Chapter 15 also hold here. With a really poor color image, we normally think LAB. But with a monochrome original, that colorspace offers few advantages. Converting to CMYK can help, because there will then be a relatively light black channel

Figure 16.4 Solarized B/Ws like this one pose somewhat more of a challenge.

Figure 16.5 Extending the range of both colors and contrast in LAB is a good diagnostic tool in an image like this, clarifying where the damage is worst. The noise in the man's face, left, will be a major problem. Meanwhile, color variations in the boy's arm, top inset, and at the bottom of the image show where the sun has done its work.

The first stop, however, is LAB. Since there is already color variation, it must pay to exaggerate it by steepening the A and B curves. This also has the advantage of making it obvious where damage has occurred, as shown in Figure 16.5. It is clearer than ever that the lower left part of the image has lost more than the center. Accordingly, any curve we applied to deepen the lower left would, at the very least, roast the dog.

Despite our prejudice against selections and masks, we need one here, because we are going to make a move away from the art. For this, I suggest saving a copy of the L channel, zeroing out its lightest area, then imposing a 15-pixel Gaussian blur, as shown in Figure 16.6.

with which we can try some interesting contrast moves.

Here, however, the presence of the sepia color gives us a small advantage, enough for a little buccaneering. While we will eventually have to go into black and white with this image, for the time being we have color channels that each have slight differences. And because the individual channels are less subtle than in CMYK, these differences can best be exploited in RGB.

This is primitive, but it will serve as a correction mask. We load it up by returning to the original document and executing Select: Load Selection. This will enable us to apply curves that work full strength on the lower left of the image (because where the mask is white, changes are allowed) but at only partial strength on the center, because the grayness of the mask reduces the impact of the curve.

If, as seems likely, we make the center too dark nevertheless, we have the option of deselecting the mask and reinstating it with the Invert option selected. This will allow us to write curves that lighten the center without affecting the edges.

But first things first. Without touching the original L channel, we convert to RGB. The reason for not darkening the image first is that doing so would massacre the blue channel, which is going to be the darkest of the three anyway because the image starts out so yellow. Rather, we should inspect the original RGB channels to try to formulate a plan.

Figure 16.6 Since the damage is worst in the lower left, that area needs to gain weight faster than the rest of the image, but there's no sensible way of selecting it. Instead, this is a blurred version of the L channel, with curves applied to zero out the lower left. The result can be used as a mask for application of curves to the entire image. The curves will have their full effect anywhere this mask is white, but less of an impact as it gets darker.

In doing so, it can't hurt to apply straight-line curves that set the light and dark point of each to reasonable levels. The three results are shown in Figure 16.7. For a monochrome image, the three color channels are surprisingly different.

The blue channel has great contrast, but is very noisy. The red isn't as noisy, and has reasonable detail, but the area around the boy's foot is totally blown out. The green seems to have nothing to recommend it, so let's get rid of it, and create a new green that is a 50–50 blend of the red and the blue. And before working on this new RGB document, we need to save a copy of it.

When dealing with prescreened originals, as discussed in Chapter

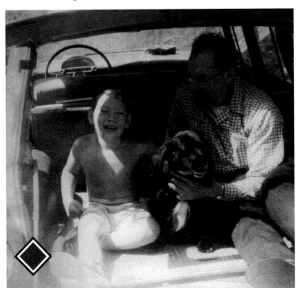

Figure 16.7 Left to right across the page, the red, green, and blue channels after contrast-enhancing curves. The red and blue each have certain strengths, but the green is mediocre and should be discarded.

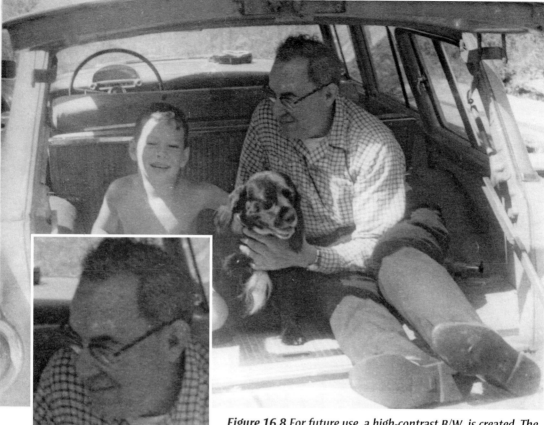

Figure 16.8 *For future use, a high-contrast B/W is created. The noise in the man's face continues to be severe (inset).*

14, it pays to have such a second, high-contrast copy that can later be used to enhance detail. So, without further ado, I use a brute-force approach, steepening all detail everywhere, converting to CMYK and steepening and sharpening the black channel, then saving a copy, converting to grayscale, and winding up with Figure 16.8. I am satisfied that this is about all the contrast that can be found in this image. I do not care that it is too noisy, or that the fleshtones and the dog are too dark.

The reason we need such a blunt instrument in reserve is that a certain amount of experimentation will be necessary with the original RGB, and experiments frequently harm contrast.

Returning, therefore, to the RGB image that existed before we made Figure 16.8, we start to play around with curves and the mask, trying to equalize the weight of the left side of the image. There is no recipe for this, of course; one must guess what the original photograph must have looked like in 1958, when it was taken. At the end, we get the image of Figure 16.9. Note the relatively light shadow. This is to make sure that the fleshtone doesn't get too dark. To get that shadow back without harming the flesh, we now convert to CMYK, using Light GCR. As the inset shows, the black

Figure 16.9 *The first conversion to CMYK. The black plate (inset) is deliberately light.*

has shadow detail, but no real weight in the fleshtone. It's simple to steepen this black until we get a properly dark shadow.

That takes care of the curving, but to create the illusion of contrast, it helps to emphasize background highlights. So, I activate the dodge tool, setting it to affect highlights, at a pressure of only 10%, and carefully lighten the circular part of the taillight, the chrome on the speedometer and steering wheel, the man's white undershirt, and the tissue in the box on the dashboard. Ordinarily, I'd look for similar opportunities in the shadows, but this time I can fall back on Figure 16.8 to enhance them.

Putting the Pieces Together

At this point, we're ready to get serious. We convert the existing CMYK document to grayscale and then to duotone, using the sepiatone settings discussed at the end of Chapter 15. Having thus eliminated the reddish tone in favor of something more appropriate, we reconvert to CMYK. We also reopen the CMYK version of Figure 16.8, not caring that it doesn't match our duotone for color.

The problem with the base image is that it simultaneously is too detailed and not detailed enough. It's too detailed—that is, too noisy—in the skintones, but not detailed enough in a number of other areas. It's

Figure 16.10 *Using layer masks to blur much, but not all, of the image. Inset above right, a blurred copy eliminates most noise. Background, it is pasted on top of the original. The holes represent where the original background is to show through, in areas where extra sharpness is needed. Inset lower right, an ultra-sharp version that will add further detail later. Bottom half of page, in orange, the actual layer mask. Do you recognize the features of the image that it is trying to protect from the blur?*

time to use of Photoshop's most powerful retouching tool: layering with the aid of layer masks.

First, using Layer: Duplicate Layer, we place a copy of the image on top of itself. On the copy, we run Filter: Noise>Dust & Scratches at a setting mild enough to eliminate most of the skintone noise. This makes the rest of the image too soft, but not to worry.

Now, with the top layer still active, choose Layer: Add Layer Mask>Reveal All. A white layer mask will appear on the Layers palette.

In areas where a layer mask is black, the lower layer is visible. Where it is white, the upper layer takes precedence. Where it is gray, we see a combination of the two layers. The darker the gray, the more it favors the bottom layer. Any Photoshop tool, filter, or curve may be used to modify a layer mask.

Commonly, however, we use the airbrush tool, set to a very low pressure. Since the layer mask starts out white, we set the foreground color to black, and start airbrushing. As we paint over the faces, we paint in the direction of the bottom, harsher, layer. There is no need to fear going too far: if we do, we simply change the foreground color to white and paint back in the direction of the top layer.

Once satisfied, we pick up the high-contrast CMYK version of Figure 16.8, copy it to the clipboard, and paste it on top of our existing sandwich, making it a third layer.

Figure 16.11 The final restoration of Figure 16.4.

We change the mode for this layer from Normal to Luminosity, so that there will be no change in color, only contrast.

Once again, we add a layer mask, choosing Hide All to make it black and so expose the center rather than the top layer. This time, we airbrush with white set as the foreground color. This paints in the direction of the high-contrast image, so we touch up the sides and posts of the car, its ornaments, the facial features, and the shadows around the legs. We also brush extra detail into the man's pants and shoes.

All these layers and masks add up to a 40-megabyte file, which should be saved just in case future editing is necessary. With a copy, we now choose Layer: Flatten Image and save the file as a TIFF or whatever other format we are looking for.

The final result of all this gallumphing around various colorspaces, masks, and layers is Figure 16.11. It proves, I think, that if our Photoshop technique is adequate, there really are no bad originals. I'll concede that the original of Figure 16.4 was not especially good, however.

Dealing with Damage in Color

Next to such B/W work, restoring even badly damaged color originals isn't daunting. The left side of Figure 16.12 is uninviting, and it doesn't help that somebody spilled orange juice on the original. But really, we have only three obstacles in the way of getting to Figure 16.13, all of which we already know how to overcome, to wit:

• The colors need to be intensified, just as in the peacock image of Figure 16.2.

• Excessive noise in the fleshtones must be avoided, exactly as in the faded monochrome we just worked on.

• A fairly large area of physical damage has to be extirpated, just as was done in Figure 10.14.

This time, there's no need to use anything but LAB, which is clearly the colorspace of choice both for waking up the sleeping colors of this image and for the retouch. The color correction should come first. The danger of retouching first is that the color correction curves may exaggerate any imperfections.

In this image, I'm the guy on the left. Inasmuch as this is a 1962 photograph, I really can't recall what the original colors were, but just by looking at the picture, I can imagine what they must have been, because the image is full of known colors. That makes it actually easier to correct than was the peacock. There is an obvious highlight in the garbage can, an obvious shadow in my hair. The garbage can itself is obviously white. The umbrella stand is certainly a neutral gray. And there's a whole gang of fleshtones. Get these colors right, and everything else will fall into place.

Measuring the neutral colors in the original reveals a mild blue-green cast, easily corrected with steep straight-line curves in the A and B channels of LAB. At the same

Figure 16.12 *This 1962 image is noisy, colorless, lacks range, and has damage in the background.*

time, range gets opened in the L channel, understanding that a further, final color correction will be needed in CMYK later. On to the retouch.

The orange blotches in the background are easily removed from the A and B channels, because there's no need to be precise. I locked off the L channel in the Channels palette so that it couldn't change, and then dropped enormous clones of the AB from elsewhere on each spot. There are lots of other ways this can be done.

Although the color is gone, the spots are still lighter than their surroundings, which means that the L channel remains to be corrected. One has to be more careful here than with the contrast-free A and B. Still, anybody who knows how to use the clone tool can take care of this. It would be a much harder retouch in either RGB or CMYK, where every channel would have to be worked on simultaneously.

Finally, we need to downplay the annoying speckling that showed up when we brought the range back to normal. As with the black and white image, this is most noticeable in the fleshtones. Unlike the black and white, this time there is also significant facial detail that we would like to enhance. These people have *eyes,* not the slits of Figure 16.14A. Noses, too.

The solution is once again layer masking, this time with three versions of the corrected file.

The bottom layer (Figure 16.14C) gets a dose of unsharp masking. The middle one (Figure 16.14D) is blurred, and the top layer is unchanged.

Figure 16.13 *After retouching the damage, correcting color, and smoothing of the fleshtones.*

This technique acknowledges that the areas that need sharp detailing are comparatively small, and that in many areas—such as faces—blurring is acceptable.

We start by adding a layer mask to the middle (blurred) layer. This time, we choose Reveal All to get a white mask. Painting with black, we let the eyes and similar detail from the sharpened version show through to the blurred layer, as shown in Figure 16.14E. This looks ridiculous, of course, but that's why there's another layer on top of it, with another white layer mask. When we paint with black on the second layer mask, we paint toward the smoother flesh and sharper features of Figure 16.14F.

Getting the Fizz Back

This book has emphasized the use of traditional methods, updated for the needs of today's images. As we have come to the end, I suggest that we honor another long-standing graphic arts tradition by celebrating with a cold beer.

Unfortunately, the beverage of Figure 16.15 resembles apple juice more than it does the kind of thing I'd like to down after a long day of Photoshop work. The color is

approximately correct, but what happened to the fizz?

Is it a bad original? It can't be, if it can be brought to the state of the pint on the right. Particularly, if it can be brought there in a minute or less, scarcely enough time for the head to settle.

The image, being a Photo CD capture, starts in LAB. Recalling similar examples with yellowish objects in Chapter 11, we save a copy, and convert the original to RGB. An examination of the channels (Figure 16.16) indicates that the bubbles in this beer exist only in the green. The head in the green is adequate but not as good as in the blue. The red channel, like certain of my relatives, occupies space without serving any useful purpose.

We now know that we will work this image at least partially in RGB, because two problems are conveniently isolated. The red channel needs to be liquidated before it contaminates every channel in CMYK, and the green channel must get special sharpening attention because in it, we have isolated the bubbles we are so interested in improving.

First, we need to make the two useful channels even better. The

Figure 16.14 The progress of a face, magnified. A: the original. B: after color correction. C: a version of B with unsharp masking in spite of the noise. D: A blurred version of B. E: Versions C and D are combined with a layer mask, leaving the features sharp and the skin blurry. F: The final version.

steeper the curve, the more the contrast, so we apply the curves of Figure 16.16, steepening the green where the body of the beer falls and the blue where the head is. As for curving the red, forget that. That channel is history.

The blue and the green are two separate sharpening problems. In the green, we are trying for the bubbles in the beer. They aren't subtle, so we need a wide Radius of 3.5, with a 400% Amount, Threshold of 5. The foam that is the blue's strength, on the other hand, has fine gradations that a

wide threshold would kill. So, we lower the Radius to 1.5.

Now it's just a question of getting the blends right. I chose to replace the red with a 65–35 blend of green and blue, feeling that the beer was more important than the head. For the same reason, I then blended 25% of the green into the blue.

The situation at this point is Figure 16.17. Happy St. Patrick's Day! But we are long since past the point where such trivialities as green beer cause us grief. We simply convert to LAB, where a copy of the

Figure 16.15 *The original beer at left looks flat in more ways than one. The correction, right, adds fizz.*

original awaits us. The old and the new L channel are compared in Figure 16.18. Replace one with the other, convert to CMYK, and we're done.

A Toast to Professional Color

And with that, we come to the end of a long journey. This image is an appropriate one to finish with, not so much because it is an effective correction but because it is an easy one—for those in the know.

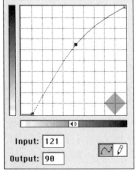 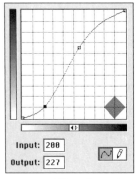

Figure 16.16 *Below, the red, green, and blue channels of Figure 16.15. Above, the curves applied to the green and blue channels (the red having been discarded).*

The battered and bleached out back of the station wagon of Figure 16.4 will take anybody a while to repair. This beer image should take about a minute. And yet (I can tell you this for a fact because I've seen many people work these two images) the typical professional gets much better results from the station wagon image than this one.

Although our field is in many ways a highly technical one, it's very different from most technical fields. It takes someone with a background in numbers to know whether a mathematician's work is credible. It takes a background in music to understand why Vladimir Horowitz played piano better than Liberace. But with us, it isn't that way. What expertise does it take to tell that the right side of Figure 16.15 looks a lot better than the left side?

Not too much—that's why we call it a *correction.* You know it's better, I know it's better, even if we can't put our finger on why. And, as we are talking *professional*

 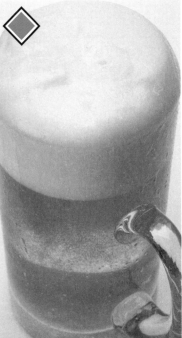 

Photoshop, this presupposes that we have clients. They will think the corrected beer is better, too; how could they not?

This image had no highlight, no shadow, no neutrals, no fleshtone, and no unwanted color. It's therefore a most atypical problem, and this may account for why professionals do so badly with it.

Throughout this book, I've tried to suggest a general way of approaching correction by the numbers. That is indeed the best way, the time-proven way, to give your images the snap they deserve. Now and then images requiring special treatment pop up, like the one we just worked on. Certainly, experience with this kind of image helps. If we've worked recently on the seltzer image of Figure 10.1, for example, we're a long way toward understanding the problems of bubble-bearing beverages.

But even without that, an intelligent artist can often work out the proper strategy. Making the following mental checklist, I find, is useful:

Figure 16.17 *After the curves and channel blending, the beer is appropriate to serve on St. Patrick's Day. But the skilled Photoshop user has no problem restoring the original color.*

- What is the object of the correction? (To make the beer look appetizing.)
- Are there obvious problems that need to be fixed? (You can't see the bubbles.)
- Is there any critical detail that an aggressive correction may damage? (The lightest area of the foam, or, in the station wagon image, the dark face of the dog.)
- Does the image have problems with color, contrast, neither, or both? (Just contrast; the original color is acceptable.)
- Is some type of local correction going to be necessary? (Not here.)
- Is the original halfway decent, or are major moves going to be needed? (The original is terrible.)

All these answers suggest both an LAB correction and that sharpening will be a critical issue.

***Figure 16.18** The L channels of the files that became Figure 16.15.*

But no matter what strategy you use, no matter what colorspace you work in, no matter what your workflow, no matter what version of Photoshop you use, certain goals are constant. Ignore them, and you condemn yourself to mediocrity. Achieve them, and you'll have professional color. They are:

• A full tonal range.

• Interest areas falling in steep parts of the correction curves, where possible.

• Strong detail in the unwanted color, if there is one.

• Accurate unsharp masking.

• The right kind of black plate.

Do these things, and you will be able to shrug off changes in Photoshop and laugh at what some call bad originals.

If you don't foresee spending a career working on images, may those you do correct be vivid, lifelike, full of detail. And if this is going to be your lifetime interest area, may it always fall in the steepest portion of fortune's curve. Let's raise our glasses to that.

NOTES & CREDITS

Most of the images in this book come from the Corel Professional Photos collection of stock photography. These images are easily accessible (in quantity, they cost about $5 per Photo CD of 100 images) and also because they are variable in quality and represent pretty well many of the problems one faces in real life.

The discs are available in packages of 10 and 200 from many mail-order outlets. Individual images can be purchased and downloaded from www.corel.com.

A couple of images from three other royalty-free vendors were so interesting that they have been repeated from the first edition. Aztech New Media, 416-449-4787, markets a 3,000-image collection, Photofile World Image Library, as a set of 24 CDs. Photodisc, Inc., 800-528-3472 or www.photodisc.com, has an extensive line of subject disks. The images shown here are from their very earliest releases and do not reflect the high quality of their current offerings. Artbeats, 800-444-9392, 541-863-4429, or www.artbeats.com, specializes in backgrounds: textured images, such as marbled paper, wood, and stone.

Two other vendors are represented with two images apiece: Digital Stock Corp., 800-545-4514 or www.digitalstock.com and CAM, Inc, the successor to low-cost vendor Hammerhead Interactive, 888-742-8871 or www.pictus.com.

CHAPTER 1

The opening shot of Grand Canyon National Park is from Corel's *Grand Canyon*

CD. The medieval church is from *Prague.* The camels image is from the Aztech New Media set. The grasshopper appears in the Corel Professional Photos Sampler CD.

The Farnsworth-Munsell color perception test, which also requires the use of a proper viewing booth, can be purchased from GretagMacbeth, 914-565-7600 or www.gretagmacbeth.com.

The assertion that people with fair complexions and blond hair see color differently from the rest of us is found in Itten, *Kunst der Farbe* (Otto Maier Verlag, 1970).

CHAPTER 2

Information about the Pantone Matching System and other color-control products can be obtained from Pantone, Inc., 201-935-5500 or www.pantone.com. Pantone swatch books may be purchased from many graphic sources.

EfiColor was a color-management XTension that used to be included as a default in QuarkXPress. The quotation concerning its efficacy comes from documentation enclosed with QXP 3.0.

Chromatic adaptation as a phenomenon of human vision was noted in 1854 in Chevreul, *The Principles of Harmony and Contrast of Colors and Their Application to the Arts,* (Reinhold, 1967 reprint).

Among the articles that have shown comparisons where some machine generated profiles are *seriously* out of whack are Adams and Ollagnier, "Scanner Profile Software for Color Management," *GATF World,* July-August 1997.

The image of schoolchildren is from Corel's *Jamaica*. The black cat is from *Cats and Kittens*, and the bride is from *Weddings*.

My definition of calibrationism appeared in *Makeready: A Prepress Resource* (MIS:Press, 1996).

Santayana, who, like Darwin, was an anticalibrationist, issued his famous epigram in his *Life of Reason*. In the very same chapter, he wrote, doubtless concerning the changing (in the name of "device independence") of the Photoshop 4 RGB standard to a plethora of choices, "Fanaticism consists in redoubling your effort when you have forgotten your aim."

Justice Stewart's comment, concerning whether a certain movie constituted "hardcore pornography" and could therefore be suppressed, came in *Jacobellis v. Ohio,* 378 U.S. 184 (1964). He wrote: "I shall not today attempt further to define the kinds of material I understand to be embraced within that shorthand description, and perhaps I could never succeed in intelligibly doing so. But I know it when I see it, and the motion picture involved in this case is not that."

CHAPTER 3

The shot of the lobsters with the wine bottle in the background is from Corel's *Grapes and Wine*. The Montréal street scene is from *Construction*. The shot with the pronounced blue cast is from *Women in Vogue*. The statue known as Christ of the Andes comes from *South America*. Both the Badlands National Park sign and the Hollywood street scene come from *Landmarks of the U.S.*

The image of the horses is from Photo-Disc 5, *World Commerce and Travel*.

CHAPTER 4

The various house cats are from Corel's *Cats and Kittens*. Their larger cousin is from *Tigers*; the people standing in the snow from *O Canada*; the bobcat from *Wildcats*; the darkened room from *Office Interiors*; and the cake from *Desserts*.

The quotation alleging that bad originals cannot be compensated for is from Bridgewater and Woods, *Halftone Effects,* (Chronicle Books, 1993).

CHAPTER 5

Complete Poems of Emily Dickinson (Johnson, editor; Little Brown & Co., 1951) is the source of the Dickinson quotes. In order of appearance, the assertion about trying to be a rose and failing is in Poem#442; about nature's use of yellow #1045; about our adjustment to lighting contitions #419; and about how to gain the good will of a flower #845.

Corel images: The rose is from *Beautiful Roses*; the woman's face from *Hairstyles II*; the forest background from *Forests & Trees*; the lime from *Food Objects*; and the woman standing in front of the door from *Women in Vogue*.

The marbled paper pattern is from Artbeats' "Marbled Paper Textures" CD. The artist is Phil Bates.

The Aruban dancer with the red feathers is from the Aztech collection.

The closing quotation is from Yule, *Principles of Color Reproduction* (John Wiley & Sons, 1967.)

CHAPTER 6

The car is from Corel's *Museum Children's Toys*. The bottle of red wine is from *Grapes & Wine* and the empty green bottles from *Still Life*. The image of the cathedral at Burgos appears in *Spain,* the woman in *Women by Jack Cutler,* and the soldier in *Army.*

El Greco's *Christ with the Cross* hangs in the Museo del Prado in Madrid.

CHAPTER 7

Copies of the full Specifications for Web Offset Publications are available for purchase from SWOP, Inc., 60 E. 42nd St. Suite 721, New York, NY 10165; 212-983-6042.

The images of the Erechtheion and the Chinese tapestry are found on PhotoDisc 5, "World Commerce and Travel."

The background image in Figure 8.1 is from Artbeats' "Marble and Granite" CD set.

The shishkebab image appears in Corel's *Cuisine* CD; the apple in *Food Objects,* and the old printed cover in *Sheet Music Cover Girls.* The bears come from CAM's *Teddy Bears.*

CHAPTER 8

A 1996 paper, "A Standard Default Color Space for the Internet" is where sRGB was originally proposed. The authors were Michael Stokes and Ricardo Motta of Hewlett-Packard, and Matthew Anderson and Srinivasan Chandrasekar of Microsoft.

The comment about sRGB being only for those who don't know any better was posted by Mr. Cox on May 29, 1998 to the newsgroup comp.apps.graphics.photoshop. Although he is an Adobe employee, Mr. Cox states that his posts do not necessarily represent the company line.

The gamut drawing of Figure 8.2 was supplied by Pantone. The complicated image of Figure 8.4 is from a set of such images used to calibrate Scitex scanners.

The blue and yellow forest scene is from

Digital Stock's *Nature & Landscapes* set of CDs. The woman wearing the dark clothing is from Corel's *Hairstyles.*

The Goya portrait of Queen Maria Luisa is in the Museo del Prado in Madrid.

CHAPTER 9

Strephon and Phyllis's love duet is from the first act of *Iolanthe.*

The beach scene is from Corel's *Jamaica;* the parrot is from *Island Vacation;* and the images of the Beverly Hilton and Las Vegas's Mirage Hotel are from *Landmarks of the U.S.*

CHAPTER 10

The parrot is the same one that appeared in Chapter 9. The sparkling water comes from Corel's *Beverages;* the cowboy from *Men of the World;* the canyon scene from *Images of the Grand Canyon;* the graffiti from *Graffiti;* and the field and lake scene from *Switzerland.*

The bighorn sheep, along with the car window, was photographed by my father.

CHAPTER 11

The image of chocolates is from Corel's *Food Textures.* Both the raspberries and the yellow pepper come from *Food Objects.* The arm holding the rose is from *Jewelry.* The model with the ghastly yellow cast is from *Women by Jack Cutler.*

CHAPTER 12

The image of the Great Wall of China is from CAM's *Around the World.*

The horse was photographed by Franklyn Higgs.

The Kodak document referred to is entitled "Optimizing Photo CD Scans for Prepress and Publishing," accessible as a

PDF file from various Web locations.

Dr. Constantine's comment to Poirot came after the great detective, in *Murder on the Orient Express,* had deliberately offered an incorrect solution to the crime.

CHAPTER 13

The allusion to the artistic uses of black and white when color was available referred to Spielberg's 1993 film *Schindler's List,* and to Michelangelo's design and construction of the New Sacristy for the Medici Chapels in Florence.

The polar bear image was shot by my father. The Chart House image is from Aztech New Media's collection.

The woman in the plaid skirt appears in Corel's *Models.* The black cat is from *Cats and Kittens,* and the image of the Cathedral of Notre Dame from *World Landmarks.*

CHAPTER 14

The image of the bareshouldered model, which is on the Corel Professional Photos Sampler disk, was scanned from *Electronic Publishing* magazine, January, 1996.

archy's plaintive question, "have you no sense" appears in Don Marquis' *archy and mehitabel.* The moth replies,

> plenty of it
> but at times we get tired of using it
> we get bored with the routine
> and crave beauty
> and excitement
> fire is beautiful
> and we know that if we get
> too close it will kill us
> but what does that matter
> it is better to be happy

> for a moment
> and be burned up with beauty
> than to live a long time
> and be bored all the while

This is, of course, an excellent philosophy for color correction.

CHAPTER 15

The crayon advertisement was part of a "Color Is Child's Play" campaign for Linotype-Hell's line of scanners.

The statement about Hexachrome raising the bar came in a 1996 press release from Richard Herbert, senior vice president of Pantone.

Pantone's plug-in that generates Hexachrome separations is called HexWrench, and is available from many sources.

The portrait is from Corel's *Oil Paintings,* the tiger from *Tigers,* the Molson race car from *Car Racing,* and the duotone series from *Steam Trains.*

Readers of the first edition of this book will recognize the bride in Figure 15.1. Also from my family archives is the image of the 19th-century woman, whom I believe to be my great-great grandmother.

CHAPTER 16

The image of the cloud-shrouded bridge in Figure 10.5 was photographed by René Suárez. The closing image of beer is from Corel's *Beverages.* All the other shots come from a box in my father's basement.

Reaching the Author

Readers are invited to send text messages to 76270.1033@compuserve.com; also DMargulis@aol.com.

BPI Bits (black or white elements) per inch in a digital file; such a file is referred to as a *bitmap.*

BPC Bits per channel in a digital image file, also called *bit depth.*

CCD Charge-coupled device, the basic image-capture technology, for the moment, of flatbed scanners and of digital cameras.

CIE Commission Internationale de l'Eclairage, an international color study and standards group.

CIELAB See LAB.

CMYK Cyan, magenta, yellow, and black, the inks universally used in color printing.

DPI Dots per inch, frequently used in very confusing ways that have nothing to do with dots; see Chapter 12.

E to E Emulsion to emulsion, describing a method by which film or plate material is duplicated.

EIAM Every image an adventure method, an overly exuberant color separation algorithm hypothesized in Chapter 8.

EPS Encapsulated PostScript, a storage format for text and graphics.

GAA Gravure Association of America, an industry group setting standards for gravure printing.

GCR Gray component replacement, the practice of using rather more black ink and rather less of the other three. Theoretically, this should have no impact on the final color. In practice there are advantages and disadvantages of doing this. See Chapter 7 for a full discussion.

HSB Hue, saturation, brightness, a colorspace not fully supported by Photoshop; see Chapter 10 for an explanation of how it works.

ICC International Color Consortium, an industry group that formulated the spec for the type of color interchange tables introduced in Photoshop 5. These are commonly referred to as *ICC profiles,* although *ICC-compatible* would be more accurate.

JPEG Joint Photographic Experts Group, now used as a synonym for a method of image compression.

KISS Keep it simple, stupid, an important principle to bear in mind before embarking on a lengthy masking foray.

LAB Also known as CIELAB, L*a*b*, or Lab color, the most prominent "device-independent" colorspace, fully supported by Photoshop. The L stands for luminance; the A and B for nothing in particular.

LCH Luminance, chroma, hue, an alternate designation for the HSB colorspace described in Chapter 10.

PCCM Politically correct calibrationist method, a separation algorithm described in Chapter 8.

PLD Pixels in the long direction.

PMS The Pantone Matching System, an almost universal method for specifying the color of non-CMYK inks, also used to describe specific colors that one wishes to achieve, whether using standard inks or ones that have been custom-mixed.

PMT Photomultiplier tube, the technology behind drum scanning, but also photomechanical transfer, a means of producing a positive black and white paper proof.

PPI Pixels per inch.

PSD Pixels in the short direction.

RGB Red, green, and blue, the additive primary colors; also, with CMYK and LAB, one of the three colorspaces fully supported in Photoshop.

RIP A raster image processor, the part of a printer or imagesetter that converts incoming data into a map of the spots that the device will print with.

RRED or **RREU** Right reading with emulsion down (up); used to specify film.

SPI Spots per inch, a measure of the resolution of an imagesetter, laser printer, or similar output device.

sRGB An implementation of RGB proposed as a standard in 1996 by Microsoft and Hewlett-Packard, severely criticized by imaging professionals ever since, and nevertheless adopted by Adobe as the default RGB in Photoshop 5. The reason for the criticism is that it restricts all monitors to colors and responses that would be characteristic of cheaper ones, and is therefore not suitable for most non-Web work. The *s* in the abbreviation was intended by its propounders to stand for *standardized;* print professionals tend to think it stands for something else, but regrettably I am not allowed to say exactly what they do think it stands for.

SSP A solution in search of a problem, descriptive of many of the ideas by those referred to herein as calibrationists.

SSPI Scanning samples per inch.

SWOP Specifications for Web Offset Publications, technical specifications for such printing propounded by an industry-supported group, SWOP, Inc.

TIFF Tagged Image File Format, the usual format in which Photoshop files are stored if one intends to print them.

TPC Total pixel count of an image.

UCA Undercolor addition, the practice of artificially adding CMY colors to deepen the shadow.

UCR Undercolor removal, the practice of only using GCR in areas where otherwise a total ink limit would be exceeded.

USM Unsharp masking; see Chapter 6.

VOT Varieties of tone in a digital file, known to many as *levels of tone.*

WORM Write once, read many times, a now-obsolete data storage format.

xyY Another colorspace variant, used in Photoshop to specify the colors of the printing inks.

YCC The native colorspace of Kodak's Photo CD, similar to LAB.

A Note on the Type

The face in use in this book is one of considerable historical interest, especially to printers. It was designed by one, Gerald Meynell of England's Westminster Press, in 1913. He prepared it especially for a new publication that focused on the printing industry. That paper, *The Imprint,* lasted only a couple of years, but the typeface, (called Imprint, naturally) has held on. It was the first successful 20th-century attempt to modernize the type forms associated with William Caslon, which typographers describe with the term *old style.* That style was not fashionable at the time, and Imprint was largely responsible for turning the tide. It is a direct ancestor of Times Roman, and presaged the interest in Garamond fonts in our own time. Its influence is still felt today in designs such as Adobe Caslon.

This letterforms of this version of Imprint are Bitstream's, but I have stripped out all width and kerning information and substituted new values.

INDEX